MOON

D1288073

ANGKOR WAT

TOM VATER

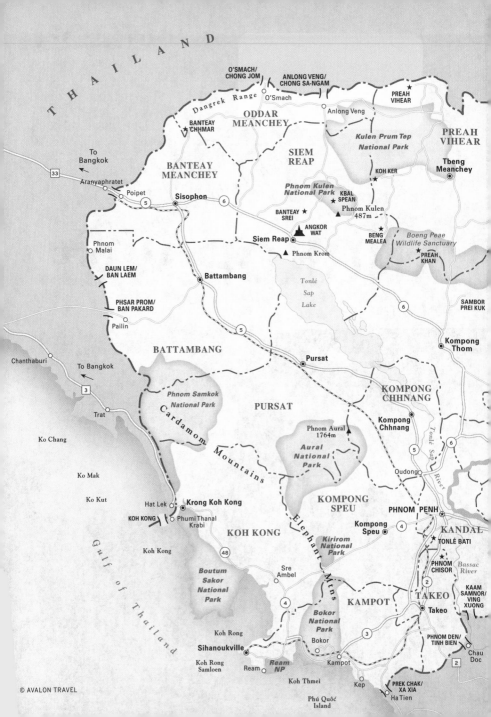

SIEM REAP
AND ANGKOR

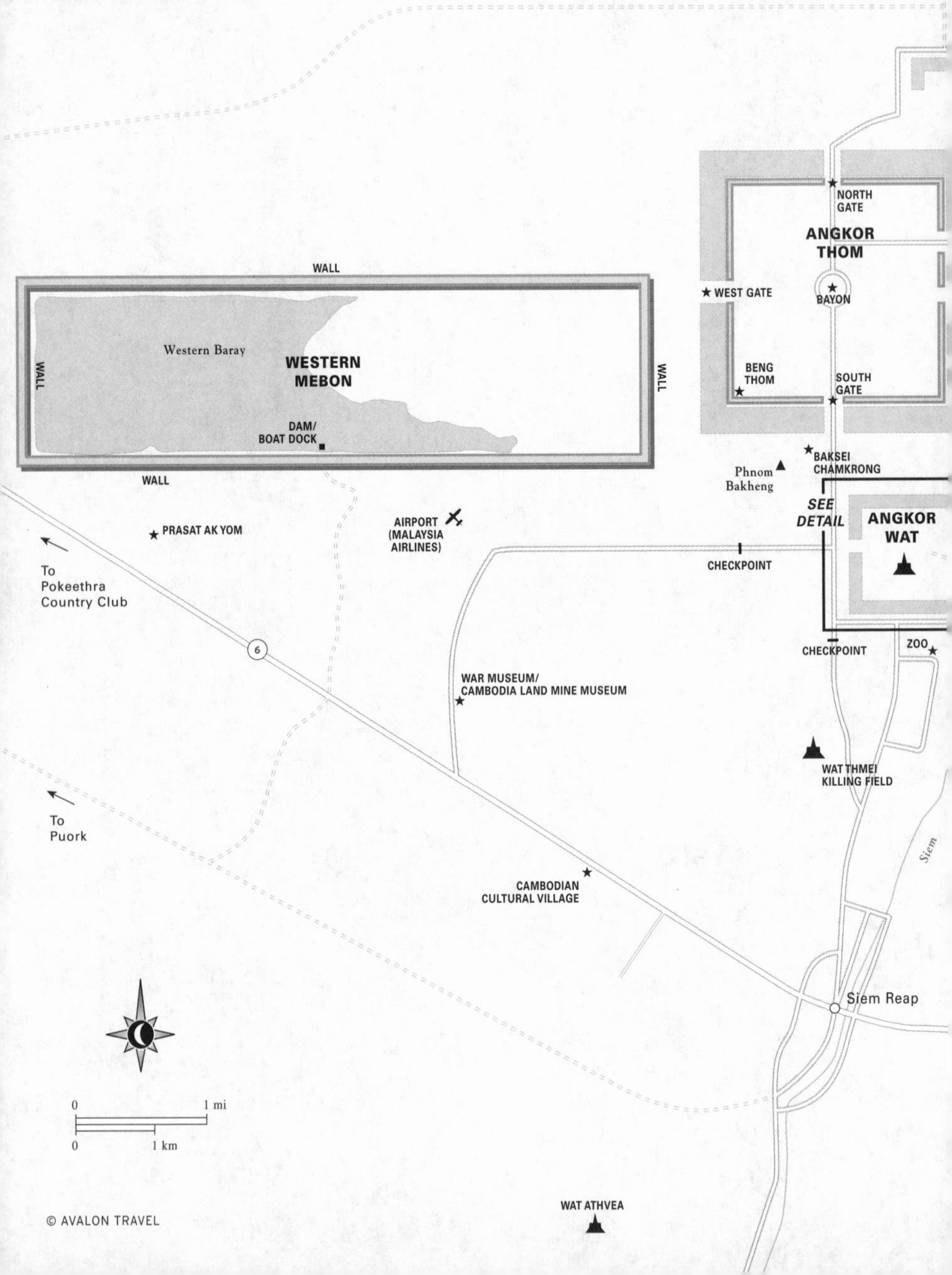

WALL

Western Baray

WESTERN MEBON

WALL

WALL

WALL

DAM/
BOAT DOCK ■

WALL

★ PRASAT AK YOM

To
Pokeethra
Country Club

6

★ AIRPORT
(MALAYSIA
AIRLINES)

To
Puork

WAR MUSEUM/
CAMBODIA LAND MINE MUSEUM
★

CAMBODIAN
CULTURAL VILLAGE
★

NORTH
GATE

**ANGKOR
THOM**

★ WEST GATE

BAYON

BENG
THOM

SOUTH
GATE

★ BAKSEI
CHAMKRONG

Phnom ▲
Bakheng

*SEE
DETAIL*

**ANGKOR
WAT**
▲

CHECKPOINT

CHECKPOINT

ZOO

▲ WAT THMEI
KILLING FIELD

Siem

Siem Reap

0   1 mi

0   1 km

WAT ATHVEA
▲

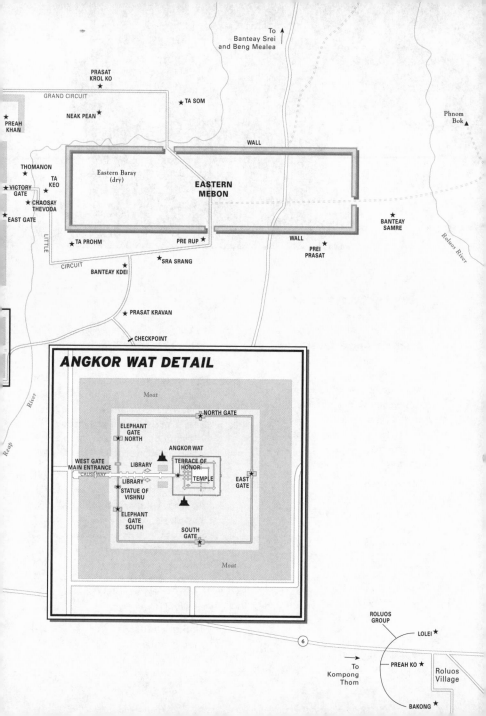

To
Banteay Srei
and Beng Mealea

PRASAT
KROL KO
★

GRAND CIRCUIT

★ TA SOM

NEAK PEAN ★

PREAH
KHAN
★

Phnom
Bok ▲

WALL

THOMANON
★

Eastern Baray
(dry)

**EASTERN
MEBON**

TA
KEO
★

★ VICTORY
GATE

★ CHAOSAY
THEVODA

EAST GATE ★

LITTLE

★ TA PROHM

PRE RUP ★

WALL

PREI
PRASAT ★

★
BANTEAY
SAMRE

Roluos River

CIRCUIT

★ SRA SRANG

BANTEAY KDEI ★

★ PRASAT KRAVAN

★ CHECKPOINT

ANGKOR WAT DETAIL

Moat

★ NORTH GATE

ELEPHANT
GATE
NORTH
★

ANGKOR WAT

WEST GATE
MAIN ENTRANCE

CAUSEWAY

LIBRARY

TERRACE OF
HONOR

TEMPLE

EAST
GATE
★

LIBRARY

STATUE OF
VISHNU
★

ELEPHANT
GATE
SOUTH
★

SOUTH
GATE
★

Moat

River

Reap

ROLUOS
GROUP

LOLEI ★

⑥

→
To
Kompong
Thom

PREAH KO ★

Roluos
Village

BAKONG ★

Contents

DISCOVER
Angkor Wat

The first rays of the sun touch the central towers of Angkor Wat. A group of young monks, their robes a luminous orange, cross the causeway to the world's largest religious building. A stone's throw away, rice paddies and golden temple roofs shimmer in the morning sun. Old women, their heads hidden under red headscarves, rest in the shade of giant banyan trees, chewing betel.

I still vividly remember my own first glimpse of Angkor Wat. I was riding a motorcycle along the wide, tree-lined road from the ticket booths toward the temples. Monkeys swung from the trees. A couple of elephants stood in the shade, waiting for passengers. I turned and followed the road running parallel to the dark green water toward the causeway. Suddenly, across the moat, I glimpsed the massive central towers rising out of the dense foliage. It was a pleasant surprise, then disbelief at the temple's form and sheer size kicked in; the forest ambience induced a personal sense of discovery.

Mass tourism has discovered Siem Reap, the boomtown nearest the temples, but the monuments will always remain a sublime experience. True marvels to behold, the temple ruins of Angkor—stone remnants of the Khmer Empire, which ruled much of Southeast Asia almost 1,000 years ago—have put

Clockwise from top left: Pub Street, Siem Reap; *devata,* Preah Khan; face of bodhisattva, Bayon temple; bas-relief of pig being cooked, Bayon temple; a strangler fig slowly crushing the walls of a shrine at Sambor Prei Kuk; Angkor Wat.

Cambodia on the map and attract more than two million foreign visitors a year. No one leaves disappointed.

And you can add to the monuments the bustling markets, the quiet streets, and the funky art galleries of Battambang; the remote forest temples away from the main highways; and the lively bars in Phnom Penh. Here, in the capital city, the smell of fried food wafts across the street, monks collect alms and policemen collect bribes, laughing children pass by on bare feet, and old men silently sit at roadside cafés, nudging glasses of thick, sweet coffee. After sunset, young lovers race their bikes through darkened, potholed streets, thousands of insects hover around flickering streetlamps, and sidewalk restaurants are crowded with foreign visitors and local families.

A journey to Angkor Wat is an adventure, an experience, a moment in time. Above and beyond the magnificent sights, visitors are rewarded by the warm welcome of Cambodia's people. Despite the country's tragic recent history, despite poverty and years of isolation, the *sourire khmer*—the Khmer smile—remains intact. Kampuchea, as the Khmer call their homeland, has a timeless, mysterious, and somewhat anarchic quality, quite unlike any land you have visited before.

Clockwise from top left: cyclists in front of Takeo temple; bas-relief of lake battle, Bayon temple; religion for sale, Central Market, Phnom Penh; temple *chedi*, Battambang.

Planning Your Trip

Where to Go

The temples around Angkor are Southeast Asia's greatest architectural gems, bar none, and the bustling capital of Phnom Penh has come a long way from a dangerous slum-scape to a chaotic but quite beautiful riverside city. Several remote temples that have lingered in deep forest, virtually forgotten for decades, have now also become accessible.

Siem Reap

In little more than a decade, Cambodia's temple town has developed from a few blocks of crumbling colonial architecture into a **bustling tourist mecca.** Siem Reap, the jumping-off point for the main monuments of the Angkor Empire, keeps on growing, and while this can be a somewhat uneven process, visitors will find everything they need here—**excellent accommodations** for all budgets, a huge **variety of food** that includes local cuisine and Asian temptations as well as Western fare, and plenty of shopping opportunities, including **attractive markets,** with a few cultural attractions thrown into the lively mix. Siem Reap remains the country's **cleanest, safest, and best organized town,** though it is the temples a few kilometers away that are the real attraction.

Angkor

Temples, temples, and more temples. Several huge imperial capitals of the Khmer Empire flourished in the northwest of Cambodia between the 10th and 15th centuries and ruled Cambodia as well as large parts of today's Thailand, Laos, and Vietnam. Today, only

wall carving, Preah Khan

© AVALON TRAVEL

laid-back atmosphere, the **best circus in Asia,** excellent accommodations, great art galleries, and fantastic trips into the surrounding countryside. Remote temples such as **Banteay Chhmar, Koh Ker, Sambor Prei Kuk,** and **Preah Vihear** have become more accessible in recent years but are **less crowded** than the main sites, although this may change in coming years.

Phnom Penh

Cambodia's **capital** has come a long way in the last decade, from a dangerous backwater to a bustling, dynamic, and somewhat chaotic boomtown, and it has rediscovered some of its **Old World charm** in the process. Yes, the streets are pretty safe—if a little clogged with traffic—and hundreds of restaurants, bars, and clubs await visitors who can **party around the clock** against a background of **colonial architecture** and Cambodia's newfound, if grossly uneven, economic regeneration. Add to that **street markets, art galleries,** and a few **museums** that are doing a good job at presenting both Cambodia's Angkor era as well as its more recent catastrophic turmoil.

temple ruins—magnificent dreams in stone—remain, and the **Angkor Archaeological Park,** a UNESCO World Heritage Site, is not only a tourist magnet attracting two million visitors each year but also the **spiritual and cultural heart** of Cambodia.

Excursions

Several temple sites and attractive towns have emerged from a long slumber and now welcome visitors. **Battambang,** to the south of Siem Reap, is Cambodia's second-largest city and offers a

When to Go

Cambodia's climate is tropical year-round, except for the highlands in the northeast where it can get cool. The best time to visit is in the **cool season,** between October and early March. But that's also the busiest time of year around the Angkor temples. During the **hot season,** from late March into June, much of the country turns into a furnace, although **Khmer New Year** in April is a special experience anywhere, especially around Angkor.

Although it also often rains in November, the **rainy season,** from June to September, is a great time to explore the temple ruins, as there are fewer visitors. Keep in mind that some of the more remote temples could be inaccessible due to the terrible road conditions. In October, head to Phnom Penh for Bonn Om Tuk, the annual water festival with three-day boat races and a city bursting at its seams with visitors from the provinces.

walkway to Neak Pean temple

Before You Go

Passports and Visas

All visitors to Cambodia must have a **passport** valid for at least six months. You can apply for a one-month **tourist visa** online or in person at any Cambodian embassy or consulate. Alternatively, visitors are issued a visa upon arrival at Phnom Penh and Siem Reap International Airports as well as at a number of border crossings.

Vaccinations

All adults should have up-to-date inoculations for **measles, mumps, rubella, diphtheria, tetanus,** and **polio.** Visitors to Cambodia should also be vaccinated against **hepatitis A.** Those intending to work in the health sector should get a **hepatitis B** vaccine. A **typhoid** shot is recommended if you plan to spend extended periods in remote rural areas, as is vaccination against **Japanese encephalitis.**

Transportation

Distances in Cambodia are short, but the roads, though improving, are bad. The main population centers are connected by paved highways, but out in the provinces, laterite dirt roads create dust storms that turn clothes red and destroy cameras. The journey from **Siem Reap to Phnom Penh** can be done by **plane, boat, bus, or taxi. The rest of the country** is mostly reachable by **bus or taxi,** although some remote sights (including Preah Khan) might, depending on weather, only be reached by pickup, 4WD vehicle, or **motorcycle.**

Driving yourself is risky, given the local driving culture, the state of the roads, and the lack of medical facilities. But it's also a great adventure, and locals welcome anyone passing by with open arms.

Visiting the Temples of Angkor

Experiencing Angkor is easy. There are no advance arrangements to be made, other than **booking a hotel room,** especially in high season.

The Temples of Angkor

The main temples of Angkor can be seen in a day, but that hardly does justice to this UNESCO World Heritage Site. Three days in Angkor gives you enough time to soak up the main structures at your leisure and get a good impression of the former might of the Khmer culture.

Visitors to the Angkor Archaeological Park use Siem Reap as a base. **Tickets** to the park—one-day, three-day, and seven-day—are available at the main entrance on the road from Siem Reap to Angkor Wat. One-day tickets are also available at a second entrance off the airport road.

There are a number of options for **getting to the temples** (and between the temples). You can get around by bicycle, in a tuk-tuk, on the back of a motorbike, or in a taxi or minivan. It takes 20 minutes to get from Siem Reap to Angkor Wat by motorbike, tuk-tuk, or taxi. On a bicycle it takes about 40 minutes. Whatever mode of transport you choose, be sure to negotiate everything in advance.

One Day in Angkor

One day is not enough to absorb the power and beauty of the Khmer Empire, but it does allow for some fleeting glimpses of its architectural highlights.

MORNING

Start very early and catch the **sunrise** at Angkor Wat, then proceed to the South Gate of **Angkor Thom** and enter the royal city to take in the recently restored **Baphuon,** the intriguing **Terrace of the Leper King** with its hidden corridor, and, of course, the **Bayon,** the most spectacular structure within the walls of Angkor Thom. The Bayon features the carved faces of the bodhisattvas, among the most iconic sights of the Khmer Empire.

AFTERNOON

Return to Siem Reap and the Old Market for lunch, or proceed to **Ta Prohm** and grab a bite there before exploring the forest temple in the

approaching the South Gate of Angkor Thom

Banteay Srei

early afternoon. Then make your way back to **Angkor Wat** for a longer visit before heading to the hilltop temple of **Phnom Bakheng** for the sunset.

Three Days in Angkor

Three days are enough for most visitors to take in all the major sites in the Angkor Archaeological Park at their leisure.

DAY 1

Start your journey at the South Gate to **Angkor Thom** and explore the royal city for the rest of the morning. There is enough time to take a close look at the Bayon (the city's most spectacular structure) as well as the Baphuon, the Terrace of the Leper King, the Terrace of the Elephants, and Phimeanakas. Have lunch at one of the food stalls near the Bayon before heading to the Victory Gate in the afternoon. Proceed to the fantastic forest temple of **Ta Prohm**, with a stop at **Ta Keo**, a simple but imposing sandstone pyramid, and explore **Angkor Wat** before catching the sunset inside the temple complex.

DAY 2

Try for an early morning start and catch the sunrise at **Angkor Wat** before proceeding to the quiet but mesmerizing temples of **Preah Khan** and **Neak Pean** as well as the temple mountain of **Pre Rup** and peaceful **Ta Som.** Head back to Siem Reap for lunch. In the afternoon, take the 30-minute ride out to the **Roluos Group** of temples, the remnants of the first major Khmer capital, and try for the **sunset at Phnom Bakheng** if you don't mind the crowds. (It's a 30-40-minute ride from Roluos to Phnom Bakheng, an hour if you are on a bicycle.)

DAY 3

No visit to the Angkor Archaeological Park would be complete without a walk around **Banteay Srei** (a 30-40-minute ride from Siem Reap), an exquisitely carved sandstone temple. Arrive before 8am to beat the crowds. During or just after the rainy season, **Kbal Spean,** a nearby riverbed full of stone carvings, is worth a side trip. Grab lunch at Banteay Srei on the way back from Kbal Spean, or, if you are skipping the riverbed, the food stalls in front of Ta Prohm are adequate for a modest meal and a chance to cool down. From Banteay Srei, take the 40-minute ride to the **Eastern Mebon**, built on an artificial island in the middle of the now-dry Eastern Baray, and the rarely visited **Banteay Samre,** almost a miniature version of Angkor Wat, then check out the smaller temples of **Banteay Kdei** and **Prasat Kravan** in the afternoon. Enjoy a last sunset at Angkor Wat before heading back to Siem Reap.

The Khmer Empire in One Week

If you have a week in Siem Reap, you can see all the main temple sites in the Angkor Archaeological Park at your own pace and also take in a couple of the more remote and far less visited Khmer monuments.

Day 1: Angkor Archaeological Park

Explore the imperial city of **Angkor Thom** in the morning. In the afternoon, head to the spectacular and gigantic **Ta Prohm,** with a stop at **Ta Keo,** and then catch the sunset at **Angkor Wat.**

Day 2: Angkor Archaeological Park

Catch the **sunrise at Angkor Wat** before

heading to **Preah Khan** and **Neak Pean,** a couple of overgrown temple compounds, as well as the temple mountain of **Pre Rup** and **Ta Som.** In the afternoon, take the 30-minute ride out to the **Roluos Group** of temples, and then try to catch the sunset at **Phnom Bakheng.** (It's a 30-40-minute ride from Roluos to Phnom Bakheng, an hour if you are on a bicycle.)

Day 3: Beng Mealea and Koh Ker

Rent a car and driver and start early in the morning for **Beng Mealea,** perhaps the most spectacular temple outside of the Angkor Archaeological Park, lying 70 kilometers to the northeast of Siem Reap. (Depending on the state of the road, it takes 1-2 hours to reach the temple by car, longer by

carved wall in Angkor Wat

Cambodia's Top 10 Temples

The god-kings of the Khmer Empire built a huge number of temples across Cambodia as well as in today's southern Laos and parts of Thailand. The most famous, Angkor Wat, now attracts up to 6,000 visitors per day. Others, almost as spectacular but more remote, attract but a handful of visitors. Any list of favorites is subjective, of course, but these 10 buildings will not disappoint.

- **Angkor Wat:** The largest religious building in the world. Awesome, stupendous; don't miss it (page 73).

- **The Bayon:** The enigmatic smiles of the bodhisattva follow visitors around this mysterious temple complex in the heart of Angkor Thom (page 80).

- **Beng Mealea:** Subsumed and enveloped by forest, this off-the-beaten-path complex has a special dark atmosphere, especially just after rain (page 97).

- **Ta Prohm:** A sprawling temple compound, preserved as the French explorers of the 19th-century Angkor saw it (page 86).

- **Banteay Srei:** Marvel at the Khmer Empire's finest carvings at this small temple just off the Angkor circuit but within easy distance of Siem Reap (page 95).

- **Koh Ker:** The remote, forest-bound former Khmer capital and temple complex with a fascinating pyramid as its main monument. More than 100 structures deep in the forest make the journey worthwhile (page 114).

- **Preah Vihear:** A politically controversial cliff-top temple on the Cambodian-Thai border with stupendous views over the Cambodian plains (page 116).

shrine, Koh Ker

- **Banteay Chhmar:** Rarely visited temple complex between Siem Reap and the Thai border—looted, overgrown, and remote enough to invoke illusions of being on an *Indiana Jones*-style mission (page 105).

- **Sambor Prei Kuk:** A pre-Angkorian temple city near Kompong Thom shows the development of architecture that would come later (page 108).

- **Neak Pean:** A minor ruin on the Grand Circuit, this small temple, constructed in a pond, comes into its own during and after the rainy season. A small, romantic gem of a building, it's a personal favorite (page 90).

tuk-tuk.) If you get there by 8am, you might well have the entire complex to yourself for an hour. Grab drinks and a modest lunch in front of Beng Mealea. Press on to **Koh Ker,** 60 kilometers from Beng Mealea. Check out the former royal capital's central pyramid temple and spend the night in a local guesthouse.

Day 4: Koh Ker, Return to Siem Reap

Spend the morning checking out the many other, smaller structures of Koh Ker and enjoy a modest lunch by **Prasat Thom** before slowly heading back to **Siem Reap** in the afternoon, passing small villages and cassava fields. In the evening,

library, Beng Mealea

consider a visit to the **Phare: The Cambodian Circus** for exceptional acrobatics.

Day 5: Day Off in Siem Reap
You might be templed out by Day 5, so relax in Siem Reap, do some shopping in the **Old Market,** or take a boat trip around the northwestern shore of **Tonlé Sap Lake.**

Day 6: Day Trip to Banteay Chhmar
Rent another car and driver and head to Cambodia's lost temple, **Banteay Chhmar,** 100 kilometers west of Siem Reap. (It takes 2-4 hours to get to the temple, depending on the state of the roads.) Hardly visited, this temple will probably be Cambodia's next big attraction in the coming years, but for now you might have it virtually to yourself. Return to Siem Reap in the evening.

Day 7: Angkor Archaeological Park
Head out to **Banteay Srei,** a true architectural gem, early in the morning to beat the crowds (it's a 30-40-minute ride from Siem Reap). During or just after the rainy season, consider a side trip to **Kbal Spean,** the nearby riverbed with carved linga. From Banteay Srei, take the 40-minute ride to the **Eastern Mebon** and **Banteay Samre,** and check out **Banteay Kdei** and **Prasat Kravan** in the afternoon. Take in a last sunset at Angkor Wat before heading back to Siem Reap.

Two Weeks of Khmer Architecture and History

This extensive and intensive schedule is for visitors with a deeper interest in Khmer architecture and history. You'll base yourself in Siem Reap (except for Day 12, when you'll be overnighting near Koh Ker).

Day 1: Angkor Archaeological Park

Visit **Angkor Wat** for an early morning sunrise and explore the bas-relief galleries at length. Have lunch in front of Angkor Wat (options range from shoestring fry-ups to an air-conditioned restaurant near the temple). In the afternoon, head to shady **Ta Prohm.** Check out **Phnom Bakheng** for the sunset if you can bear the crowds; otherwise return to Angkor Wat.

Day 2: Angkor Archaeological Park

Explore the royal city of **Angkor Thom.** Start

at the South Gate in the morning. If you are fit, climb the city wall to the right of the South Gate and walk along a narrow path on top of the wall until you get to a corner watchtower. Then follow the trail all the way to the West Gate, where your driver can pick you up and take you to the **Bayon.** Have lunch at one of the small open-air kitchens in front of the Bayon before exploring the rest of the royal city—the Baphuon, including the Phimeanakas, the Terrace of the Elephants, and the Terrace of the Leper King. In the evening, consider a visit to the **Phare: The Cambodian Circus** for exceptional acrobatics.

Day 3: Day Off in Siem Reap

Take a day off in **Siem Reap,** do some shopping, or visit the **Angkor National Museum.** Alternatively, rent a boat and take a trip along the northwestern shore of **Tonlé Sap Lake.**

fishing on the Tonlé Sap Lake

Community Tourism

"Community-based tourism" is a hot topic in Cambodia, where many worthy projects compete with more conventional—and even downright crooked—enterprises in a rapidly growing economy. The below are guaranteed ways to put your money toward a good cause. For information on **volunteering in Cambodia,** see page 229.

SIGHTS AND PERFORMANCES

- **Phare: The Cambodian Circus** is the most rewarding (and quite new) attraction in Siem Reap that contributes to the community. Performances take place in the specially constructed Big Top and are well worth a visit, especially for families. While this phenomenal circus is actually a private enterprise, its students have gone through a rigorous NGO-based training program—a great marriage of development and business (page 35).

- **The Cambodia Land Mine Museum,** located near Banteay Srei, is managed by a Canadian NGO and educates visitors about one of the terrible curses of the 20th century. The center's proceeds go to a home for destitute children (page 33).

- **Shadow Puppet Theater** shows are held weekly at the hotel **La Noria** in Siem Reap. These traditional shows are performed by kids from the Krousar Thmey NGO (page 36).

- *Apsara* **dance** performances, organized by the NGO Sangkheum Center for Children, are held at the hotel **Soria Moria** in Siem Reap (page 45).

TOURS

- **Tonlé Sap Lake Tours** are available through the **Sam Veasna Center** or **Osmose,** both of which support conservation efforts (page 58).

- **Khmer Architecture Tours** in Phnom Penh are offered by the excellent **KA Tours,** an NGO that promotes and documents modern Khmer architecture (page 162).

HOTELS AND HOMESTAYS

- **The Paul Dubrule Hotel and Tourism School,** near Siem Reap's airport, provides training in the restaurant and hotel business. Visitors are invited to stay or eat at the school (page 43).

- **Shinta Mani,** in Siem Reap, is an excellent hotel that runs a foundation to support projects in education, small business start-ups, and health care (page 45).

- **The Banteay Chhmar homestay program** provides income for local families while giving visitors a window into Khmer life (page 105).

RESTAURANTS

- **Le Café,** in Siem Reap, is associated with the Paul Dubrule Hotel and Tourism School (page 52).

- **Singing Tree Café,** in Siem Reap, supports several worthy causes (page 52).

- **Blossom Café,** in Siem Reap, is an NGO-training place that empowers Cambodian women (page 52).

- **Kinyei Café and Fresh Eats,** in Battambang, are NGO-affiliates that train local youth (page 125).

- **Jai Baan Restaurant,** in Battambang, aims for gourmet dining in an NGO setting (page 126).

SHOPS

- **Rajana,** in Siem Reap, sells products made by underprivileged Cambodians (page 39).

- **Senteurs d'Angkor,** in Siem Reap, is an outlet that works only with local people and uses only local products (page 39).

- **The Reyum Institute,** in Phnom Penh, is a Cambodian NGO that runs a free arts school for Cambodian children. Check out their interesting gallery and shop on Street 178 (page 159).

Day 4: Angkor Archaeological Park

Check out the smaller temples around the Eastern Baray, a massive (now dry) reservoir (about a 40-minute ride from Siem Reap)—these include the two small 12th-century structures by the Victory Gate, **Thomanon** and **Chaosay Tevoda;** the impressively unadorned pyramid of **Ta Keo;** the former monastery **Banteay Kdei;** and the brick and sandstone temple of **Pre Rup.** Grab lunch in front of Ta Keo, or, for more variety, head to the west gate of Ta Prohm. In the afternoon, visit **Banteay Samre,** the **Eastern Mebon,** and **Prasat Kravan** before returning to Angkor Wat for the sunset.

Day 5: Angkor Archaeological Park

Allow a whole day to meander through the sprawling **Preah Khan** temple, the smaller **Neak Pean,** and the less visited **Ta Som.** Several open-air kitchens in front of Preah Khan offer modest but adequate lunch choices.

Day 6: Angkor Archaeological Park

Start early in the morning to beat the crowds to

Banteay Srei (a 30-40-minute ride from Siem Reap), and afterward head to the forested riverbed of **Kbal Spean.** Return to Banteay Srei for lunch at one of the food stalls. On the way back to Siem Reap, stop for an hour or two at the **Cambodia Land Mine Museum.**

Day 7: Angkor Archaeological Park

In the morning, head out to the **Roluos Group** of temples (a 30-minute ride). Return to Siem Reap for lunch before visiting the **Western Baray** beyond the airport (another 30-minute ride). In the center of the gigantic reservoir stands the **Western Mebon** on a small island. In the rainy season, it's possible to reach the Western Mebon by boat. On weekends the Western Baray is a popular picnic spot for Cambodians.

Day 8: Day Off in Siem Reap

Visit the **Wat Thmei Killing Field,** take in an *apsara* dance, meander through the **Old Market,** or explore the **Angkor National Museum** if you haven't done so already.

rice harvest, Siem Reap Province

lintel, Banteay Srei temple

Day 9: Origins of Angkor

Rent a car and driver and take a day trip to **Sambor Prei Kuk,** a pre-Angkorian capital built in the 7th century, 120 kilometers east of Siem Reap (a 2-3-hour ride). Sambor Prei Kuk gives an excellent insight into how the Cambodians moved from modest brick temples to the much larger structures around Angkor.

Day 10: Banteay Chhmar

Rent a car and driver and head west for a day trip to **Banteay Chhmar,** a late-12th-century temple that is so far rarely visited. (Depending on the state of the roads and the time of year, it takes 2-4 hours to get to the temple, 100 kilometers west of Siem Reap.)

Day 11: Day Off in Siem Reap

Take a day off from the road, make a late start, and grab a tuk-tuk to reach the diminutive **Wat Athvea,** some seven kilometers to the south of Siem Reap. Head south a few more kilometers and climb the modest **Phnom Krom** hill for amazing views across Tonlé Sap. Spend the evening browsing the **Night Market.**

Day 12: Beng Mealea and Koh Ker

Rent a car and driver and head to the early-12th-century **Beng Mealea,** 70 kilometers northeast of Siem Reap. (Depending on the state of the road, it takes 1-2 hours to reach Beng Mealea by car, longer by tuk-tuk.) After exploring this incredible and overgrown temple ruin, continue to the 10th-century **Koh Ker** complex, 60 kilometers from Beng Mealea, and spend the night in a local guesthouse.

Day 13: Koh Ker, Return to Siem Reap

Explore the rest of the many **small temples** around Koh Ker before heading back to Siem Reap.

Day 14: Angkor Archaeological Park

Revisit personal highlights or take a one-day guided **cycling tour** along the Angkor Thom city walls.

One Day in Phnom Penh

Phnom Penh, despite its ever-growing volume of traffic, is still a great city to explore on foot, at least in some places. The main sites, including the two biggest markets, can be seen in a day.

Morning

A great place to start is **Sisowath Quay,** where numerous cafés offer an astounding variety of breakfasts. Explore the **Royal Palace,** including the **Silver Pagoda,** and then head across to the **National Museum,** less than a five-minute walk, to see its huge collection of Angkor relics.

Afternoon

Street 178, which runs past the National Museum, is a good place to grab lunch and wander around the local **art galleries.** After lunch, visit the nearby art deco **Central Market** (Phsar Thmey), a few minutes' walk from the riverfront.

Hitch a ride south of the city, past the Independence Monument to **S-21 Tuol Sleng Museum,** as terrible and tragic as a sight can be. From this former Khmer Rouge prison, take another short ride to the **Russian Market** (Phsar Toul Tom Poung), which offers an enormous variety of souvenirs, silks, and bootleg DVDs. It is often very hot in this crowded roofed market, so late afternoon is the best time to visit.

Evening

End the day where you started, on Sisowath Quay, to watch the sunset over the river from the **Foreign Correspondents Club,** or relax in one of the many sidewalk restaurants.

the Royal Palace in Phnom Penh

Siem Reap

Highlights

★ **The Old Market Area:** Peruse a wide variety of souvenirs in Siem Reap's sprawling market and watch the locals shop from early morning to dusk (page 29).

★ **Wat Damnak:** An active but quiet temple allows you to get away from the crowds and ruins for an idyllic afternoon stroll (page 31).

★ **Wat Athvea:** Experience local village life at this small, virtually unknown temple ruin just outside Siem Reap (page 31).

★ *Apsara Dance:* Catch a traditional Cambodian dance performance, once reserved for kings, at the Raffles Grand Hotel d'Angkor (page 35).

★ **Phare: The Cambodian Circus:** View a breathtaking acrobatic circus performance at this exceptional and internationally renowned big top (page 35).

The town nearest to the Angkor temples has grown from a tiny village 100 years ago into Cambodia's second-largest city. Some locals call it the unofficial capital, thanks to the millions of tourist dollars that have been rolling in since the late 1990s. Siem Reap translates as "Defeated Thailand," a reference to the Khmer Empire when it controlled large swaths of Siam (today's Thailand) for several centuries. Following the sacking of Angkor by the Siamese in 1431, the tables turned, and the Angkor ruins, as well as Siem Reap, were administered by Siam.

The town of Siem Reap really came into its own at the beginning of the 20th century, when the first wave of international tourists arrived. Le Grand Hotel d'Angkor opened in 1932, and tourism grew steadily until World War II. Following the war, Angkor became trendy once more and remained on the global tourist circuit until the late 1960s, when increasing turmoil in Cambodia and the neighboring war in Vietnam put an end to tourism. French archaeologists remained at the temple and tried to continue working even as the war reached Siem Reap, but in 1975 the Khmer Rouge emptied the town and drove all its inhabitants into the countryside, where many died. When the Vietnamese pushed the Khmer Rouge out of power in 1979, the new occupiers put their own troops in Siem Reap. The Khmer Rouge escaped into the forests around the town and embarked on a 15-year terror campaign on Siem Reap's citizens, the Vietnamese, and later, the United Nations Transitional Authority in Cambodia (UNTAC), which culminated in a final large-scale attack in 1993.

Today, Siem Reap is the safest city in the country and Cambodia's boomtown. In little more than a decade, this sleepy backwater has turned into a thriving, chaotic metropolis. I remember the installation of Siem Reap's first traffic lights in 2001. Three police officers stood at the chosen crossing, each armed with a megaphone, and spent the day explaining the traffic lights' function to passing traffic. At 6pm the officers went home, and the lights immediately became mere decoration. The

---

Previous: alley in the Old Market area; chiles for sale in a market. **Above:** art for sale, Old Market.

Siem Reap

To 1961

ANGKOR NATIONAL MUSEUM

THE PHARE PONLEU SILPAK CIRCUS

PHARE: THE CAMBODIAN CIRCUS

APSARA DANCE

RAFFLES GRAND HOTEL D'ANGKOR/ ELEPHANT BAR

AMANSARA

BOU SAVY GUESTHOUSE

MADAME BUTTERFLY

JASMINE FAMILY HOSTEL

VICTORY GUEST HOUSE

TAPHUL VILLAGE

TONLÉ SAP RESTAURANT

VICTORIA ANGKOR RESORT & SPA

Royal Gardens

AIRPORT RD

PANIDA RESTAURANT

THAPUL RD

STREET 02

LUCKY MALL/ BAMBOU INDOCHINE

THE HASHI RESTAURANT

SIVATHA BLVD

STREET 03

FCC ANGKOR

PRINCE D'ANGKOR HOTEL

POST OFFICE

OUM KHUN ST

THE NEST

SHINTA MANI/ ROYAL BAY INN ANGKOR RESORT

CENTRAL BOUTIQUE ANGKOR HOTEL

STREET 05

FAMILY GUESTHOUSE

SUGAR PALM RESTAURANT

CROCODILE COLLECTION

SALA BAI

THE VILLA SIEM REAP

JASMINE ANGKOR

SAMDECH TEP VONG

KANDAL MARKET

FRANGIPANI SPA

ANGKOR AIRWAYS

COMMON GROUNDS

BLOSSOM CAFÉ

THE CHANREY TREE

SEE "THE OLD MARKET AREA" MAP

THE OLD MARKET AREA

ISLAND BAR

ANGKOR NIGHT MARKET

ANGKOR TRADE CENTER

GOLDEN TEMPLE VILLA

Old Market

0   200 yds
0   200 m

THE MANDALAY KITCHEN

GOLDEN BANANA BED & BREAKFAST

To WAT ATHVEA

WAT PO

MYSTÈRES D'ANGKOR

GOLDEN ORANGE HOTEL/ GOLDEN ORANGE SPORTS BAR

BORANN, L'AUBERGE DES TEMPLES

LA NORIA

SAWASDEE FOOD GARDEN

To Lin Ratanak Angkor Hotel

BABEL SIEM REAP GUEST HOUSE

MOM'S GUESTHOUSE

CHIANG MAI THAI FOOD

STREET 20

HOME SWEET HOME

TWO DRAGONS GUESTHOUSE

WAT BO AREA

STREET 21

FRANGIPANI VILLA HOTEL

PARIS-SAIGON

STREET 22

WAT BO

LE CAFÉ

STREET 23

BOPHA ANGKOR HOTEL

SORIA MORIA

STREET 24

KARAVANSARA

APSARA THEATRE

GRASSHOPPER ADVENTURES

STREET 26

ANGKOR VILLAGE HOTEL

BARRIO

LA NICHE D'ANGKOR

TERRAZZA

PASSAGGIO

ALLIANCE ART CAFÉ

KANELL RESTAURANT

WAT DAMNAK

CUISINE WAT DAMNAK

QUAD ADVENTURE CAMBODIA

© AVALON TRAVEL

RIVER RD

CHARLES DE GUALLE

POKAMBOR BLVD

WAT BO RD

Siem Reap River

traffic on the main roads is still the biggest hazard around town, and traffic jams are not uncommon these days. In 2007 the Angkor International Hospital, Cambodia's first international-standard clinic, opened and has been treating traffic-accident victims—providing they have insurance—competently since.

Thankfully, the French town center has been tastefully restored, and it's still possible to go for a quiet walk under the trees by the Siem Reap River. Some of the villages around town have kept their simple charm and seem barely affected by the tourism circus. Touting, prostitution, and drugs are kept to a minimum, and if you are not looking for trouble, you are very unlikely to find any.

Siem Reap continues to evolve and expand, at times at a pace that is almost self-destructive: There's talk of a second international airport, and falling groundwater levels as well as pollution are becoming problems. The city center is noisy and raucous at night, with the area around Pub Street turning into a sort of club-land for young travelers. As long as Angkor is one of the world's most popular archaeological sites, Siem Reap is unlikely to stop growing.

PLANNING YOUR TIME

Few people visit Siem Reap for the city itself; it is the Angkor temples that draw visitors. But it's not an unattractive place, and by far is the most affluent town in Cambodia. The shopping is not bad, although the markets in Phnom Penh offer a greater selection of goods at slightly better prices. Several museums and a couple of attractive modern *wats* (temples), as well as cycling tours through the countryside, balloon and horse rides, swimming pools, and numerous dining options may tempt some visitors to stay a few days longer than planned. If you plan to stay for more than three days of temple visits, a day or two in town away from the ruins may make sense.

Sights

★ THE OLD MARKET AREA

A little more than a decade ago, the area around the **Old Market** (Phsar Chas), in the heart of Siem Reap and close to the river, was a rundown, dilapidated affair and a little unsavory at night. Since then, investment and restoration have taken place, and the colonial buildings around the covered market have recaptured their former grace. All this makes for a francophone ambience, a nostalgic vibe with more than a whiff of l'Indochine, and a nice space to move around in. Downtown areas in several Cambodian cities retain substantial colonial architecture, but only in Siem Reap has it been completely rehabilitated. The market itself, which is open daily, has largely become tourist-oriented—DVD documentaries on the Khmer Rouge, silk scarves, rice-paper prints of *apsaras* (nymphs cast in stone), opium pipes, and the ubiquitous *krama,* Cambodia's all-purpose head scarf. About half the market still sells products for the local community, including fruit, machine parts, and clothing. The streets around the market are lined with eateries (some budget, others upscale), shops, Internet cafés, and bars, making it a great place to stroll in the early evening. The stalls selling local products are open from the crack of dawn until early evening, while the shops selling curios open around 9am and close around 9pm.

WAT BO
វត្តបូព៌

One of the oldest temples in Siem Reap, the 18th-century **Wat Bo** (daily, free), on the eastern side of the river, has some interesting frescoes on the walls of the prayer hall, including a depiction of an opium-smoking Chinese trader.

The Old Market Area

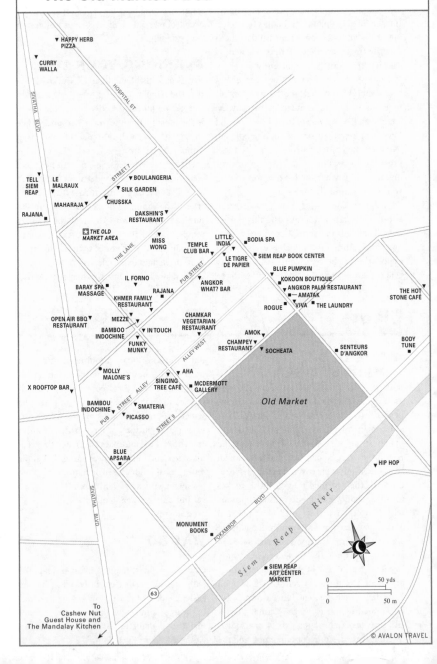

HAPPY HERB PIZZA

CURRY WALLA

HOSPITAL ST

SIVATHA BLVD

STREET 7

TELL SIEM REAP

LE MALRAUX

BOULANGERIA

SILK GARDEN

MAHARAJA

CHUSSKA

RAJANA

DAKSHIN'S RESTAURANT

THE OLD MARKET AREA

THE LANE

MISS WONG

TEMPLE CLUB BAR

LITTLE INDIA

BODIA SPA

SIEM REAP BOOK CENTER

LE TIGRE DE PAPIER

BLUE PUMPKIN

PUB STREET

IL FORNO

KOKOON BOUTIQUE

ANGKOR PALM RESTAURANT

AMATAK

BARAY SPA MASSAGE

RAJANA

ANGKOR WHAT? BAR

THE HOT STONE CAFÉ

KHMER FAMILY RESTAURANT

ROGUE

VIVA

THE LAUNDRY

OPEN AIR BBQ RESTAURANT

MEZZE

CHAMKAR VEGETARIAN RESTAURANT

AMOK

BAMBOO INDOCHINE

IN TOUCH

CHAMPEY RESTAURANT

SOCHEATA

BODY TUNE

FUNKY MUNKY

ALLEY WEST

SENTEURS D'ANGKOR

MOLLY MALONE'S

AHA

X ROOFTOP BAR

SINGING TREE CAFÉ

MCDERMOTT GALLERY

Old Market

BAMBOU INDOCHINE

STREET ALLEY

SMATERIA

PUB

PICASSO

STREET 9

BLUE APSARA

HIP HOP

SIVATHA BLVD

POKAMBOR BLVD

Siem Reap River

MONUMENT BOOKS

63

To Cashew Nut Guest House and The Mandalay Kitchen

SIEM REAP ART CENTER MARKET

0   50 yds

0   50 m

© AVALON TRAVEL

★ WAT DAMNAK

វត្តដំណាក់

Located on the eastern side of the river, the large temple compound of **Wat Damnak** (daily, free) was once a royal palace and has been beautifully restored. In the afternoon, locals come to sit by a large stone basin filled with lotus flowers and catfish. Within the temple compound, the Center of Khmer Studies is located in a handsome building dating to the early 20th century.

★ WAT ATHVEA

វត្តអធ្វា

Wat Athvea (daily, free) is a very special place. The active monastery lies in the shade of a bamboo grove next door to a small but handsome and well-preserved Angkor-era temple. The pagoda is never empty—monks, village elders, and musicians can usually be found in the prayer hall. An open reception hall and a prayer hall, along with wooden huts that serve as accommodations for the monks, make up the compound. In the prayer hall, hundreds of Buddha statues are gathered around a central shrine, and the walls are covered in frescoes depicting the life of the Buddha. Once a year, during Khmer New Year, all the statues are washed by the local people, a ceremony that entails a wild water fight. The 12th-century temple next door, surrounded by a high laterite wall, is often deserted, although local people conduct merit-making ceremonies in its single main tower.

Wat Athvea is a great place to gain an impression of what the atmosphere around the temples was like before tourism rediscovered Angkor. Just a few minutes from Cambodia's busiest shopping streets, an incredibly peaceful and relaxed ambience pervades the two buildings.

The temple buildings are off the main road between Siem Reap and Phnom Krom. The turnoff to the temple is marked by a large gate on the right about four kilometers south of Phsar Chas (the Old Market). It's not necessary to have a pass for Angkor to visit this ruin. Beyond the temple, a small village—with traditional family homes on stilts—is full of friendly teenagers keen to take visitors around the area. Some of the kids speak English fairly well and have a few facts about temple and country life ready, but don't expect a real "tour." It's the experience rather than the facts that counts here. A donation of a few dollars for the young guides is expected.

inside Wat Damnak temple complex

WAT THMEI
KILLING FIELD

 វត្តថ្មី

Although the Khmer Rouge never dared to attack the temple ruins of Angkor, many people died in the area during and after their reign, and Siem Reap Province contains numerous killing fields. **Wat Thmei** (free), an active temple on a side road between Siem Reap to Angkor, has a glass-paneled stupa in its courtyard filled with the bones of victims of the Khmer Rouge.

ANGKOR
NATIONAL MUSEUM

The **Angkor National Museum** (tel. 063/966-601, www.angkornationalmuseum. com, daily 8:30am-6pm, US$12 foreigners, US$3 Khmer, camera US$2), on the road to the temples just beyond the Le Grand Hotel d'Angkor, opened in 2007 and serves as a light introduction to the magic of the Angkor Empire. Visitors to this massive complex, a project run by a private company in conjunction with the Cambodian Ministry of Culture and Fine Arts, will be left wondering whether they are in a shopping mall or a museum, but that's not to say that a visit is a waste of time. Several exhibition galleries

on Khmer civilization, Angkor Wat, and Angkor Thom contain some fine examples of Angkorian artifacts and statues. A number of rooms equipped with comfortable seating show short informative films in nine different languages. Audio tours of the entire facility are also available. The pieces on display come from the storage of the National Museum in Phnom Penh and from Conservation d'Angkor. A highlight is the Hall of a Thousand Buddhas, which is very nicely lit and does indeed contain a thousand Buddha statues. A dome with a giant screen split into three parts almost delivers an IMAX experience. Contemporary artists also have space here, with regular exhibitions related to Angkor held in a smaller domed hall inside the museum. The museum's exit leads into a souvenir shop.

Overall, the number of artifacts is a bit light, but this is edutainment. It doesn't compare to the National Museum in Phnom Penh, but it isn't trying. The only real criticism is the high ticket price.

CAMBODIAN
CULTURAL VILLAGE

Cambodian Cultural Village (tel. 063/963-836, www.cambodianculturalvillage.com,

Wat Athvea

daily 9am-9pm, US$9 foreigners), a rather un-sophisticated theme park located on the air-port road, whisks visitors through Cambodia's turbulent history. Exhibits include replicas of temples, miniature versions of entire villages (including a so-called millionaire's house, "a place where ancient rich men stayed"), and life-size re-creations of scenes from Cambodia's past. Traditional dance perfor-mances from around the country take place at several locations in the village; check the website for times. The village made headlines when a display illustrating the presence of UNTAC in the country was limited to a for-eign soldier embracing a Khmer sex worker. That particular item has been removed, but the US$9 entrance fee is still not entirely jus-tified. A good afternoon out if you have chil-dren in tow.

WAR MUSEUM AND CAMBODIA LAND MINE MUSEUM

Two so-called museums remind visitors of the 30 years of war and its legacies that Cambodia has endured in the latter half of the 20th cen-tury. The **Siem Reap War Museum** (tel. 088/848-7351, www.warmuseumcambodia. com, daily 9am-5pm, US$5), built and man-aged by the Department of Defense, is close to town, just north of Route 6 on the way to the airport. The official ad—original spell-ing intact—reads: "The War Museum is very

unique, all kinds of old weapons used during almost 3 decades of wars in Cambodia. Tanks, Armoured Personal Carrier, Artilleries, Mortars, Land mines and small arms . . . etc. So you spend just thirty minutes or 1 hour. You'll see all these weapons."

The museum is not dedicated to any spe-cific conflict, nor, it seems, are its planners aware of any chronological relevance of re-cent warfare in Cambodia. Tanks, mortars, and antiaircraft guns rust in the sun, while the small items, a dilapidated collection of firearms, are kept in an open shed. Some of the weaponry on display was manufactured as early as the 1930s and comes from places as diverse as Vietnam, China, the Soviet Union, and East Germany. The mock minefields and a large collection of land mines remind visi-tors of the continuing scourge of these weap-ons in Cambodia.

The **Cambodia Land Mine Museum** (tel. 012/598-951, www.cambodialandmine-museum.org, daily 7:30am-5:30pm, US$3) is managed by a Canadian NGO. It's located out near Banteay Srei and is best visited during a trip to this outlying temple. There's informa-tion on land mines and a large collection of war scrap dug up from the surrounding coun-tryside, and visitors can challenge themselves by walking through a mock minefield and booby traps. Occasional photo exhibitions are held here; the proceeds go toward a home for destitute children.

Entertainment and Events

There are plenty of nighttime hangouts com-peting for those who still have some energy left at the end of the day. Bar-restaurants are in the majority, and a couple of venues offer live music. The suspicious ambience so typical of many of Phnom Penh's bars and clubs is virtually nonexistent in Siem Reap. For traditional entertainment, *apsara* dance performances are put on by several upscale hotels and numerous restaurants. And there's

always the Night Market with its bar and food court.

NIGHTLIFE
Bars

Right in the heart of old Siem Reap, **Pub Street,** the town's short but crammed night-life district, offers some appealing venues. Restaurants, bars, and clubs line this nar-row road, street vendors sell anything they can think of, and the atmosphere is safe and relaxed. Best of all, the police cordon off the area at night, so there's no motorized traffic to worry about if you stumble onto the street at 2am.

Not as old as the temples but open for business since 1998, the **Angkor What? Bar** (daily 5pm-very late) has grown from a hole-in-the-wall late-night filling station with a beer-spattered pool table into a much larger, spacious place. Every inch of wall space is covered in guests' signatures—join the club. Tables out front are a perfect vantage point to survey the action on the street. More or less directly across the road, the **Temple Club Bar** (daily 7am-very late) is a restaurant in the daytime and becomes one of the most popular nighttime hangouts in town, with pool tables, a DJ, and sports on huge TV screens. The **Laundry Bar** (daily 6pm-very late), a little northeast of Phsar Chas (the Old Market), has long been a favorite hangout for ex-pats and visitors alike. It's not as raucous as the places on Pub Street and offers a couple of pool tables, darts, big sofas, and occasional live music from around the region.

For something even more intimate and less raucous, head to the sumptuous and gay-friendly **Miss Wong** (daily 4pm-very late),

a beautifully retrofitted cocktail bar on The Lane, just north of and parallel to Pub Street. Nearby, **Silk Garden** (daily 3pm-very late) offers laid-back music, mostly reggae, in a bamboo-themed bar that also serves crepes and salads. There are occasional football (soccer) and reggae-themed parties, but it's not nearly as exciting as Pub Street—probably a good thing for those in search of a quiet evening drink.

Local expatriates often hang out at **Picasso** (daily 5pm-1am), another small but welcoming redbrick tapas bar on the southern strip of Pub Street Alley, with a long cocktail menu and snacks. It is a great place for interesting conversation, but don't expect a party. For more action, head for the long-running and popular **X Rooftop Bar** (daily 4pm-sunrise) on Sivatha Boulevard, with a pool table, a tattoo shop, food, occasional live music, DJs, and a young party-oriented clientele.

The **Island Bar** (daily 4pm-midnight), toward the back of the Angkor Night Market, is built in Balinese style and is a great place for an early evening, post-shopping cocktail or cold beer.

For an altogether different and far more upscale drinking experience, head for the **Elephant Bar** (daily 4pm-midnight), inside

Pub Street

the Raffles Grand Hotel d'Angkor. Drinks aren't cheap, but the setting and the service are perfectly postcolonial, luxurious, and laid-back in a formal kind of way. Also a little more sophisticated than your average Siem Reap filling station is the **Nest** (daily 4pm-late), a stylish and laid-back cocktail bar that also serves market international cuisine. Punters relax on stylish chaise lounges on an outside terrace that invites communication with strangers, as does the low-volume DJ-spun ambient music collection. The restaurant offers Mediterranean and Asian flavors.

Nightclubs

To party like a pharaoh, head to the **Pyramid Mega Entertainment Club** (daily 9pm-2am) on Road 6. This disco, decked out with Egyptian motifs, has room for 350 people and is a favorite for moneyed Khmer as well as visitors. There's a beer garden, a paintball course, the ubiquitous karaoke, and a Chinese restaurant attached. It is packed on the weekend. Foreign visitors are occasionally overcharged. Check your bill carefully.

Live Music

There's not a great deal of live music going on in Siem Reap. The **X Rooftop Bar** (daily 4pm-sunrise) on Sivatha Boulevard occasionally has rock or blues bands playing. **In Touch** (daily 11am-2am), a bar-restaurant serving Thai food located in the bustle of Pub Street, hosts live cover bands (mostly light jazz) upstairs from 9pm. The food isn't great, but the drinks are cheap and the music is mostly OK.

PERFORMING ARTS
★ *Apsara* Dance

Many of the upscale hotels in town put on traditional Khmer dance performances during their dinners. These usually include both classical and folk dances and tend to last about an hour. One of the most professional troupes performs the *apsara* dance on the Apsara Terrace at the **Raffles Grand Hotel d'Angkor** (tel. 063/963-888). Dinner performances (US$40, children under 12 US$25.50)

run October-May daily at 7pm (performances start at 7:45pm). Other similarly sumptuous dinner events can be attended at the **Sofitel Royal Angkor** (tel. 063/964-600), on the road to the temples, and at the **Victoria Angkor** (tel. 063/760-428).

Outside the high-end hotels, the **Apsara Theatre** (tel. 063/963-561), a massive wooden Khmer-style auditorium, is probably the best opportunity to see cultural dances in Siem Reap. Traditional *apsara* dance performances (US$25, children under 12 US$12.50) are held in the high season every day and in the low season on Tuesday, Thursday, and Saturday 7pm-9pm and include a set-menu Khmer dinner. The recently refurbished **Tonlé Sap Restaurant** on the airport road is really a package-tour venue with buffet dinners that include a traditional dance performance (US$12). Shows start daily at 7:30pm, but arrive an hour earlier for good seats.

★ Phare: The Cambodian Circus

Siem Reap now has its own big top: the **Phare Circus** (tel. 092/225-320, www.phare-cambodiancircus.org/circus, daily shows at 7:30pm, US$15-35 adults, US$8-18 children), on Comaille Road, behind Angkor National Museum, opened in 2013. The circus was founded by the art school of the same name, which first started operating in Battambang in 1998, offering theatre, music, and circus training to underprivileged children. The best students are further trained to become professional performers for the circus's highly acrobatic performances. The Phare Circus has been traveling around the world for some years—to huge international acclaim. The shows in Siem Reap change four times a week and range from interpretations of traditional folk tales to modern stories of contemporary Cambodia. They are hugely dramatic, slick, and absolutely worth seeing, for both children and adults.

Smile of Angkor

The **Smile of Angkor** (Siem Reap Exhibition

Heavenly *Apsaras:*
The Khmer National Ballet

Khmer ballet, or classical dance, is one of three categories of Cambodian dance (the others being folk and vernacular dance). Originally, the ballet was performed exclusively for the royal court. With independence from France, classical dance was introduced to the Cambodian public to celebrate Khmer culture. During the Khmer Rouge years, the art form was almost lost, but since the early 1990s the School of Fine Arts in Phnom Penh has begun to train new performers.

Dancers, all female, have to learn more than 3,500 movements, each with its own specific meaning, often symbolizing aspects of nature, such as the opening of a flower. Students train for 9-12 years to learn the intricate positions and movements the dances entail. Other dances tell the story of Cambodia's origins, a union between a hermit named Kampu and a woman called Apsara Mera. The dancing *apsaras,* who grace many temple walls, suggest that the royal ballet was most popular in the 10th-12th centuries. The School of Fine Arts shows off the results of their endurance training on special occasions such as during Khmer New Year in front of Angkor Wat.

Since mass tourism has arrived in Cambodia, many hotels and restaurants in Siem Reap and Phnom Penh offer Khmer classical dance performances as a dinner accompaniment. One of the best places to catch a high-quality performance is the Grand Hotel d'Angkor in Siem Reap.

Center Angkor COEX, tel. 097/772-977, www.asiavipa.com/smile-of-angkor-grand-epic-show.php, advance tickets US$26-43 adults, children under 130cm get in half price, walk-in $48 adults, $24 under 130cm) show is a multimedia theater spectacle recounting the glory of Angkor. The show involves hundreds of dancers, contortionists, lasers, and kitsch aesthetics in a purpose-built theater. Some of the performers are Chinese. The included buffet dinner runs daily 6pm-7:30pm, and the show runs daily 7:15pm-8:40pm. Cameras without flash are permitted.

A reviewer on TripAdvisor suggested this show is best enjoyed with hallucinogens. While I can't endorse the consumption of mind-altering substances, bear in mind that this is entertainment squarely aimed at Asian tour groups. Smile of Angkor is located to the east of town and to the north of Route 6, a 15-minute tuk-tuk ride from the Old Market.

Shadow Puppet Theater
Traditional Cambodian **shadow puppet theater** (Speik Thom and Speik Toot), performed by kids from the Krousar Thmey NGO and featuring stories from the *Reamker,* the Khmer version of the Indian *Ramayana* epic, as well as popular folk stories can be seen at the hotel **La Noria** (tel. 063/964-242,

Wed. 7:30pm-9pm), on the eastern side of the river. In low season these events may be canceled, so it's best to check ahead. Similar performances can be seen at the **Butterflies Garden Restaurant** (tel. 063/761-211, www.butterfliesofangkor.com, Tues. 7:30pm) on the road to the airport.

Beatocello
With his weekly solo cello performances and talks, **Beatocello** (www.beatocello.com), a.k.a. Dr. Beat Richner, raises much-needed funds for the Jayavarmann VII Hospital in Siem Reap and the Kantha Bopha 1 and 2 Children's Hospitals in Phnom Penh. Shows (Sat. 7:15pm) are held at the Jayavarmann VII Hospital on the road to the Angkor ruins. Admission is free, but a donation is appropriate. In the daytime, the Jayavarmann VII Hospital also welcomes blood donations. A film about Dr. Beat Richner titled *Doctor Beat and the Passive Genocide of Children* (Tues. and Thurs. 7:15pm, free) is also shown at the Jayavarmann VII Hospital.

ART GALLERIES
The **McDermott Gallery** (www.mcdermott-gallery.com), next to AHA restaurant in The Passage by the Old Market, is one of the most

attractive exhibition spaces in Cambodia and features fine-art photography from a number of well-established and emerging artists. It's well worth a visit. A second McDermott Gallery can be found at FCC Angkor, where photographer John McDermott exhibits his otherworldly and idiosyncratic infrared black-and-white photographs of the Angkor ruins. Large prints retail for US$450-3,000.

Stéphane Delaprée, a French Canadian cartoonist, paints extremely colorful naïve-style canvasses of Cambodian scenes. The artist calls his work Happy Paintings, and he has a gallery called **Happy Cambodia** in the Old Market area, as well as several other branches in the Siem Reap and Phnom Penh airports and in Phnom Penh.

The **1961** (tel. 015/378-088, www.the1961.com) is a Khmer-owned gallery, art space, artists' lab and office space, boutique, eatery, and guesthouse on the River Road near the Siem Reap River. Check out this trendy, stylish, and innovative center for exhibitions and art performances that more often than not celebrate Cambodia's post-independence golden age. Even the guest rooms are designed like gallery spaces.

Cambodian artist and designer Lim Muy Theam has opened his home to the public as a workshop cum gallery. **Theam's House** (www.theamshouse.com) is a little out of town but worth a visit for a look at Theam's paintings, lacquers, and sculptures that happily marry traditional Khmer designs with the artist's modern and highly individualistic style.

FESTIVALS AND CULTURAL EVENTS
Khmer New Year

During Choul Chnam, Khmer New Year, in April, be prepared to share Angkor with thousands of celebrating Cambodians, who travel from all over the country to picnic and celebrate among the ruins.

Angkor Photo Festival

The **Angkor Photo Festival** (www.angkor-photo.com) was created in 2005 and now draws both famous and passionate photographers from around the world to Siem Reap each year in November. Outdoor projections showcase regional and international photographers in different locations in Siem Reap.

The festival also has social goals. During their stay, well-established photographers from all over the world hold free workshops for emerging Asian photographers. The festival also has outreach programs for vulnerable people.

Happy Cambodia art gallery, Old Market

Happy New Year, Cambodia Style

For three days in mid-April, Choul Chnam, the Khmer New Year, celebrates the beginning of the Buddhist religion. The year 2016 is in fact 2559 in the Buddhist calendar. Traditionally, people gather in their local temples to make offerings. The Khmer, like the Thais, enjoy throwing copious amounts of water and talcum powder at each other and at travelers during the three-day celebrations. Thousands of Cambodians head for the Angkor temples to celebrate, picnic, and sightsee. For many of the locals, it's the first time they see the temples. Bear in mind that this is the most crowded time of year around the ruins.

During the first day of the celebrations, **Moha Songkran,** the Khmer light incense at shrines and pray. In the morning they wash their faces, at lunch their chests, and in the evening their feet with blessed water in order to attract good luck for the coming year. On the second day of the celebrations, **Wanabat,** people give to charitable causes and pray for their ancestors at the local temple. On the third and final day of the celebrations, **Tngai Laeung,** people bathe the Buddha statues in the temples, which is thought to bring good luck and longevity. They also wash the hands of their parents or grandparents, a sign of respect for the authority of elders, in the hope of being blessed by their best wishes and to receive their advice.

Angkor can be fun during the New Year, and foreign visitors have a chance to observe locals in the new pagodas around Angkor, such as at Wat Athvea, as they honor monks, bathe their Buddha statues, and even engage in water fights inside some of the prayer halls. If you happen to be in Cambodia during the New Year holidays, **Siem Reap** and **Phnom Penh** are the best places to see the festivities. In the countryside, visitors are likely to be invited to local celebrations. Prepare to get wet—and drunk.

Shopping

MARKETS

The **Old Market** (daily 9am-9pm) is located in the formerly French colonial heart of Siem Reap. Known to the locals as Phsar Chas, it has become more commercial since visitor numbers really picked up in 2003, but this most traditional of Siem Reap's markets is still divided into stalls selling curios and souvenirs and, across a central courtyard with its vegetable vendors, stalls that sell household goods and cheap electronics to local people. Along the western side, a number of well-priced Khmer restaurants cater to both foreign visitors and Cambodians. The area around the market is lined with boutiques selling handicrafts, often produced by underprivileged and marginalized people.

Kandal Market (daily 10am-7pm), known also by its English name, Center Market, is located a little to the north of the downtown area along Sivatha Boulevard. This is Siem Reap's largest market hall, squarely aimed at foreign souvenir hunters. Besides fine silks and clothing, it sells every type of trinket imaginable, much of it brought in from neighboring countries. Haggle for everything, and don't be surprised when the only other customers are tour groups. A better option with a wider variety of locally produced items is the **Siem Reap Art Center Market,** just south of the Old Market and across the river, accessible via a wooden bridge.

The **Night Market** (www.angkornightmarket.com, daily 4pm-midnight) opened in 2007 in its own little compound a few minutes' walk west of the Old Market area. A huge collection of stalls selling silks, handicrafts, luggage, and curios—many of them imported from neighboring countries—is on display. Orphans and people with disabilities get stalls at a discount, and NGOs exhibit and sell their products here, but most of what you'll see is generic souvenirs. Several films about aspects of Cambodian history are shown nightly. A food court (not always open) and a bar will keep you fueled up between browsing silks, bootleg DVDs, and jewelry.

SHOPPING MALLS

Siem Reap's first shopping mall, the **Angkor Trade Center,** located between the river and the Old Market, is a rather modest creation, with branches of Swensens and the Pizza Company along with a small supermarket on the ground floor and an inexpensive food court on the second floor. Other stalls sell bootleg DVDs and clothes. On Sivatha Boulevard, **Lucky Mall** has a toy shop, a bakery, and a supermarket.

CRAFTS AND BOOKS

A number of fashionable boutiques are located in the Old Market area. These outlets have fixed prices and are not cheap, but you will find items not available in the markets. **Senteurs d'Angkor** sells spices, tea, coffee, soaps, oils, and Khmer wine as well as silks. Very similar is **Kokoon Boutique,** which sells some pottery as well as silks and home-decor items. **Amatak** sells handprinted T-shirts, hats, and silks. The NGO-based

Rajana, on Sivatha Boulevard, sells articles made from wood as well as silks and other handmade souvenirs. **Bambou Indochine** has four branches in Siem Reap, in the Alley West, on Pub Street, in the Lucky Mall on Sivatha Boulevard, and in Siem Reap Airport, and offers high-quality, 100 percent cotton and bamboo-fiber clothing, from T-shirts to dresses in all international sizes, a great alternative to the low-quality textiles on offer in the larger markets. Also worth a visit is **Smateria,** a trendy fashion outlet in the Alley West, which creates handbags and other items from recycled materials. Items are surprisingly elegant, considering where some of this stuff originates.

More on the noisy and youthful side is the **Rogue,** also near the Old Market, where you can upload a vast range of music to your iPod or MP3 player at a fraction of its original retail price. Similar outlets exist in Phnom Penh and Sihanoukville. Besides music, trendy club wear and drinks are for sale.

The **Crocodile Collection** on Sivatha Boulevard sells reptilian belts, shoes, and wallets made not just of crocodile leather but also stingray, cobra, and ostrich leather. A little army of stuffed crocs welcomes visitors at the door. A croc wallet costs around US$100. It is

shop front, Siem Reap

reasonable to assume that the crocodile and ostrich leather is derived from animals bred specifically for this purpose, but much more likely, the cobras and stingrays are caught in the wild.

Numerous mobile book vendors, many of them maimed by land mines, move through the Old Market area and usually carry a selection of nonfiction titles about Cambodia. Inside the Old Market, several book stalls carry the same limited choice.

For a wide selection of books, some genuine and some pirated, including a whole shelf of American underground writers as well as best-sellers, classics, travel guides, and nonfiction on Cambodia, Vietnam, and Laos, head to **Blue Apsara.** Just south of the Old Market area, this is probably Siem Reap's best-stocked secondhand bookstore, run by a knowledgeable and friendly Frenchman named Thomas. A number of interesting curios are also for sale here.

Monument Books, just south of the Old Market by the river, sells new books, but they come at a high price. The selection of titles on Asia and Cambodia is not bad. There's a second branch at the airport. The **Siem Reap Book Center** near the Old Market looks like an old trader's shop in India and sells a decent selection of history and photo books, as well as stationary, office supplies, countless souvenirs of doubtful taste, and chocolate bars.

Sports and Recreation

SWIMMING

While bathing in the river that runs through Siem Reap is not recommended, a few hotel pools are open to non-guests and can offer some respite from the heat.

The largest pools in town can be found at the **Prince d'Angkor** (tel. 063/763-888, www.princedangkor.com), on Sivatha Boulevard, the **Lin Ratanak Angkor Hotel** (tel. 063/969-888, www.linratanakangkor. com), behind Phsar Samaki off Route 6, and the **Raffles Grand Hotel d'Angkor** (tel. 063/963-888, www.raffles.com), in the heart of town. For a very romantic swimming option, check out the **Kanell Restaurant** (tel. 063/966-244). The pool is located in a wonderful tropical garden, and diners are invited to take a plunge. Free towels are provided.

CYCLING

As foreigners are no longer allowed to drive their own motorized vehicles around Siem Reap or Angkor, the only alternative for visitors determined to see the area on their own terms is pedal power. Note that while the roads around the temples are pretty flat, it does get very hot on the long stretches where the tree cover has been cut. Bring sun protection and drink plenty of water. Bicycles can be rented from guesthouses for US$2-3 a day, and several companies offer cycling tours. Most notably, **Grasshopper Adventures** (Street 26, tel. 012/462-165, www.grasshopperadventures.com) conducts excellent one-day tours (US$25 adults, various discounts for kids) to the temples that get travelers off the beaten track and onto the city walls of Angkor Thom for breathtaking views that motorized tourists cannot experience.

GOLF

The closest 18-hole golf course to Siem Reap is the Nick Faldo-designed **Angkor Golf Resort** (tel. 063/392-288, www.angkorgolf.com), just six kilometers from the city along the road to the airport. A second professional-standard course, the **Phokeethra Country Club** (tel. 063/964-600, www.phokeethragolf.com/phokeethra/home.html) is 16 kilometers from Siem Reap on Route 6. This 18-hole course, complete with a driving range, restaurant, and pro shop, is managed by Sofitel. Walk-in greens fees are around US$120 for 18 holes or about US$80 for 9 holes. Cart rental is around US$30. Caddie fees may apply.

HORSEBACK RIDING

For avid riders as well as beginners, countryside horse trails can be explored from **Happy Ranch** (tel. 012/920-002, www.thehappyranch.com), located a couple of kilometers from downtown Siem Reap. Rides are US$28 per hour, or US$46 for two hours. Riders must weigh less than 90 kilograms.

ALL-TERRAIN VEHICLE TOURS

If you want to race an ATV through the Cambodian countryside, look no farther than **Quad Adventure Cambodia** (tel. 017/784-727, www.quad-adventure-cambodia.com), located on the eastern side of the river not far from Wat Damnak. Different tour packages on American-made Polaris Trail Boss ATVs are available for two-hour romps and longer full-day trips to remote corners of the province.

MASSAGES AND SPAS

Many of the upscale hotels and resorts in Siem Reap have their own spas and massage services. Outside of the hotel scene, head for **Bodia Spa** (tel. 063/761593, www.bodia-spa.com), which includes a fashionable boutique and café, located right next to U-Care Pharmacy in the Old Market area. Also recommended is the **Body and Soul Spa Massage Class** (The Passage, tel. 092/226-694, www.bodysoul-massage.com), which offers Western reflexology, Ayurvedic massage, Khmer massage, Thai massage, oil massage, and Reiki therapy. Foreigners can attend massage classes, and there are massage products for sale. **Frangipani Spa**

(Hup Guan St., tel. 063/964-391, www.frangipanisiemreap.com) offers great facilities including VIP rooms for couples and a rooftop terrace. Around the Old Market, a handful of aboveboard and cheap massage places including **Body Tune** and **Baray Spa Foot Massage** can be found. Rates are around US$8 an hour.

PHOTOGRAPHY TOURS

Several companies offer photography tours around the Angkor ruins, Siem Reap, and surroundings. Check out **Angkor Wat Photography Tours** (tel. 073/612-648, http://angkor-wat-photography.com) and **Peace of Angkor Photography** (tel. 063/760-475, www.peaceofangkorphoto.com). For Go-Pro fans, **Angkor Photography Tours** (tel. 095/633-585, www.angkorphotographytours.com/siem-reap-tour) offers one-day tours around the temples focusing on time lapse and slow motion.

COOKING CLASSES

Le Tigre de Papier (tel. 063/760-930, www.angkor-cooking-class-cambodia.com), a restaurant on Pub Street, offers half-day introductions to the Cambodian kitchen. The course (daily 10am-1pm, US$14) includes a trip to the Old Market (Phsar Chas) to purchase ingredients and two hours of supervised preparation, including both cooking and food presentation. Participants get to check out each other's creations at lunch. Courses are in English or French.

Also recommended are the two-hour cooking classes (US$12 pp) at the **Angkor Palm Restaurant** (tel. 063/761-436, www.angkorpalm.com), by the Old Market, which are held twice a day and require at least two participants.

Accommodations

UNDER US$15

One of the most reliable cheapies in town, though a bit off the beaten track, is the friendly **Bou Savy Guesthouse** (tel. 063/964-967, www.bousavyguesthouse.com, US$12, with a/c US$22), located on a garden property in a small lane just past Wat Kesararam on Route 6. The Khmer family that owns this place has a hands-on management policy, which translates into simple but clean guest rooms, personable caring service, and all the usual travel and tour programs. All rooms have en suite baths and TVs. Bou Savy has a good garden restaurant that serves a large selection of Cambodian dishes as well as backpacker fare, and it organizes its own bike and jeep tours.

Another rock-bottom place is the **Family Guesthouse** (tel. 092/648-462, www.family-siemreap.com, US$8, with a/c US$15), located on a small side street off Sivatha Boulevard, 100 meters north of Kandal Market. The small, clean guest rooms with few amenities are a steal, and there's Wi-Fi and a decent rooftop restaurant.

Located on a quiet side street in the Wat Bo area, the **Home Sweet Home** (tel. 012/824-626, www.homesweethomeangkor.com, with fan US$8, with a/c US$12) might not have any great frills, but it's a good value for your money. Guest rooms are clean and decent size, with en suite baths and TVs. Should you be bored or burned out on CNN, BBC, and HBO, or simply require more highbrow entertainment, it's possible to rent DVD players and movies (US$2). The Wi-Fi service downstairs in the restaurant is free for guests. This guesthouse, like most operations of its size, also offers a travel and visa service as well as laundry.

US$15-25

The **Victory Guest House** (Rd. 6, Taphul Village, tel. 012/516-566, www.victoryguesthouse.com, with fan US$15, with a/c US$19) has 50 clean double rooms with TVs and free Wi-Fi access, a good restaurant serving Western breakfasts (included in the room rate) and Khmer standards, and several computer terminals for guest use. Free pickup is available.

A little to the south of town by the river, the **Siem Reap Riverside Hotel** (tel. 012/517-000, www.siemreapriverside.net, US$25) offers simple, clean rooms, a small pool, a great roof terrace with views of Siem Reap, and very friendly service. Breakfast is included, and free Wi-Fi is available in the guest rooms. The Old Market is some 10 minutes away on foot.

For a good mid-range guesthouse with great service, check out the **Two Dragons Guesthouse** (tel. 063/965-107, www.twodragons-asia.com, US$15-20), near Wat Bo. Two Dragons offers 13 spotless if small guest rooms and is fronted by a restaurant that turns out good Thai dishes. There's free Wi-Fi access and a no-smoking policy in the guest rooms.

Probably one of the best almost-cheapies in town, a few minutes' walk south of the Old Market area, is the excellent ★ **Cashew Nut Guest House** (tel. 092/815-972, www.thecashewnut.com, with fan US$20, with a/c US$25). The Cashew offers just nine clean and simple double rooms. There's also a great rooftop lounge space with superb views of Siem Reap, and the management can arrange all kinds of tours, including specialized itineraries to the Angkor temples. Call ahead for free pickup anywhere in Siem Reap.

Not far away but on the noisier Wat Bo Road is **Mom's Guesthouse** (tel. 012/630-170, www.momguesthouse.com), once located in a traditional wooden building, but moved into a swankier new town house in 2007. Mom's has decent-size but slightly dark air-conditioned guest rooms (US$25) or brighter deluxe guest rooms (US$32). All room rates include breakfast, and Mom's offers all the usual travel services and has an ATM on the premises.

Off Wat Bo Road in a modern building, the Italian-owned **Babel Siem Reap Guest House** (738 Wat Bo Rd., tel. 063/965-474, www.babelsiemreap.hostel.com, US$18-25) offers simple, spotless, and recently refurbished air-conditioned guest rooms that have TVs. Guests who book in advance are picked up at the airport free of charge, and there's free Wi-Fi in the lobby as well as a pool on the premises. The restaurant serves Khmer standards, and there's a small garden bar.

A little away from the city's center on the airport road, the **Jasmine Family Hostel** (tel. 063/766-097, www.jasminefamilyhostel.com, with fan US$17, with a/c US$25) offers large, clean rooms with new furniture and a kind of backpacker boutique feel accentuated by large TVs in the rooms and a small pool downstairs. Besides the usual doubles, there's a choice of rooms sleeping three or four. Breakfast is included, and the Wi-Fi works downstairs and in some of the rooms.

Another decent budget-range option is the rather elaborately named **My Home Tropical Garden Villa** (tel. 063/760-035, www.myhomecambodia.com, US$24-30), which offers clean rooms, a saltwater swimming pool, free Wi-Fi, and complimentary bicycles (2 hours a day), just a few minutes' walk from the Old Market area.

Golden Temple Villa (tel. 012/943-459, www.goldentemplevilla.com, US$17-38), on a side street off Sivatha Boulevard south of the Old Market area, is a uniformly orange-themed building inside and out with a luscious garden overgrown with bamboo clusters. The 40 smallish guest rooms all have en suite baths with tubs and are clean and smartly kept, with silk curtains around the beds. Some rooms have air-conditioning and some have balconies, and Wi-Fi is available everywhere. Downstairs, guests can use the free Internet service, and the restaurant serves typical Khmer and Western dishes.

The **Paul Dubrule Hotel and Tourism School** (tel. 063/963-673, www.ecolepauldubrule.org, US$20-35), way out on the road to the airport, is not really a hotel at all but Siem Reap's first school training young and underprivileged Cambodians in the arts of the hotel business. The school turns out about 100 students a year, most of whom find work in the industry. Best of all, the school has four beautifully and individually designed guest rooms, each donated by a different five-star hotel and used for training purposes, hence the low rates. If you don't mind staying a little farther from the action, you can enjoy first-class international facilities at a budget price and get the chance to observe this commendable school. During the school year (Oct.-July), **Le Jardin des Délices,** an adjacent restaurant, serves the creations of the trainee cooks. The school also offers half-day upscale cooking classes; check the website for details.

US$25-50

French-owned **La Noria** (tel. 063/964-242, www.lanoriaangkor.com, US$39-59), near Wat Po Lanka, offers small but smart air-conditioned guest rooms decorated with traditional Khmer handicrafts in two-story bungalows set around a small pool in a luscious garden. The poolside bar might be just the thing after a day at the temples. Alternatively, you could get a massage treatment on the premises.

The Villa Siem Reap (tel. 063/761-036, www.thevillasiemreap.com, US$35-50), located on Thapul Road a few minutes' walk from the Old Market area, is something of a concept guesthouse that makes the most of its near-budget facilities and offers simple air-conditioned guest rooms with brilliant purple color schemes. All guest rooms have Wi-Fi, the restaurant (from US$5) downstairs has an agreeable atmosphere, and all guests can use the large swimming pool of the Princess Angkor Hotel on Route 6 free of charge. The staff is young and friendly, and the whole place exudes positive energy. And for those who need a lot of space, the Villa Bungalows (US$80)—two attractive, connected rooms in one, with breakfast included—might be just the ticket.

You can't get any more central than **Molly Malone's** (tel. 063/963-533, www.mollymalonescambodia.com, US$25-35), a small guesthouse and bar with just twelve rooms on the corner of Pub Street, right in the heart of Siem Reap's nightlife quarter. The rooms are bright and clean, even if the entrance is not, with four-poster beds, Wi-Fi, and air-conditioning. Some have bathtubs, and the rest have en suite showers. Some of the rooms are a little worn. If you are worried about noise, don't stay here—there's live music downstairs, and at night the entire area pulsates.

The smart **Ree Hotel** (tel. 063/766-888, www.reehotel.com, from US$40), also on the airport road, offers 141 nondescript but comfortable large guest rooms, impeccable service, and one of the largest pools in the vicinity. Most of the guest rooms and suites face the pool with a view of temple mountain Phnom Bakheng rising in the distance.

For a personalized stay with a Mediterranean vibe, **Central Boutique Angkor Hotel** (tel. 063/764-030, www.centralboutiqueangkorhotel.com, US$40-50), in Thapul Village a few minutes' walk from the Old Market area, offers quiet and airy bungalow-style guest rooms clustered around two pools. The best part is that the hotel is just a few minutes' walk to the town center. The staff is attentive, and the small restaurant serves a surprisingly good variety of Khmer and Western dishes. Try the fish amok, a traditional Cambodian dish using coconut milk.

A modest but smart choice is the very neat Swiss-German-managed **Passaggio** (tel. 063/964-732, www.passaggio-hotel.com, US$32-45, breakfast included), just north of Wat Damnak on the eastern side of the river. Spacious and spotless air-conditioned guest rooms with tasteful decor and furnishings, TVs, Wi-Fi, and en suite hot water are in a modern town house surrounded by a small garden. A small pool provides a chance to cool off after a long day among the ruins. The restaurant serves Khmer cuisine and international favorites with a Swiss bent—veal cordon bleu is US$8.50.

The ★ **Frangipani Villa Hotel** (tel. 063/963-030, www.frangipanihotel.com, US$40-65) offers simple, almost boutique rooms with four-poster beds, free Wi-Fi, room safes, and complimentary laundry service and bicycles at a budget price, just an eight-minute walk from the Old Market area. There's a pool and a strict no sex tourism policy. Breakfast is included. This is a great value for your money.

The **Golden Orange Hotel** (tel. 063/965-389, www.goldenorangehotel.com, US$25-30, breakfast included), located in the Wat Po Lanka area, offers nicely decorated, air-conditioned, and spotless standard international guest rooms. Some rooms have jetted bathtubs, just the thing after a long day visiting the temples. Amenities include Wi-Fi and broadband LAN Internet access, a restaurant serving Asian and Western food, a rooftop terrace with a great view across parts of Siem Reap, and all the usual services, such as tours, ticket service, and even a sports bar with a pool table.

The **Lin Ratanak Angkor Hotel** (tel. 063/969-888, www.linratanakangkor.com, US$40-104, breakfast included), behind Phsar Samaki off Route 6, is a typical Cambodian mid-range hotel offering medium-size, spotless, carpeted, and air-conditioned guest rooms with en suite baths, TVs, minibars, and Wi-Fi. One of the main advantages of this hotel is the larger-than-average swimming pool. The restaurant serves Western and Khmer standards, and children under 12 stay for free.

The gay-friendly **Golden Banana Bed & Breakfast** (tel. 063/761-259, www.goldenbanana.com, from US$32) offers simple, clean rooms and friendly service just a few minutes' drive across the river from the Old Market. There's a large pool and an adjacent, more expensive hotel option. Afternoons by the pool bar after a long day at the temples are especially recommended. Diving from the balconies is forbidden by Golden Banana Law.

US$50-100

On the east side of the river, not far from Wat Bo, the **Bopha Angkor Hotel** (tel. 063/964-928, www.bopha-angkor.com, US$50-120) offers smart and stylish guest rooms with traditional decor. Some guest rooms have private balconies, and the attractive restaurant, serving mostly Khmer dishes, is popular, even with non-guests. Try the excellent dim sum breakfast (US$3.50). A decent-size pool will help weary temple visitors relax.

Following the same concept as La Noria, the smart two-story boutique bungalows set in a lush open garden promise a pleasant stay at the friendly **Borann, l'Auberge des Temples** (tel. 063/964-740, www.borann. com, US$55, with balcony US$69), located off Wat Bo Road. Each good-size air-conditioned guest room, four per bungalow and opening onto private terraces, has an en suite bath and is carefully designed with partly antique redwood furniture and cowhide shadow puppets from the *Reamker*. The in-house restaurant (entrées around US$6) serves light Khmer and Western dishes, and there's a pool.

Located behind Wat Po Lanka, the quiet, very private, and francophone **Mystères d'Angkor** (tel. 063/963-639, www.mysteres-angkor.com, US$65-95) has handsome wood-and-stone, air-conditioned pavilions with four rooms each, set around a small swimming pool in a wonderful tropical garden complete with mango trees and coconut palms. The guest rooms are bright and beautifully furnished with traditional rosewood furniture. The main building houses the reception area, a pool table, and an excellent restaurant that serves mostly Khmer dishes; a set-menu dinner is US$8.50.

The four-story boutique hotel **Soria Moria** (tel. 063/964-768, www.thesoriamoria.com, US$50-65) is located in the Wat Bo area and offers large and bright European-style air-conditioned guest rooms with carefully selected furnishings, TVs, Wi-Fi, and minibars. The in-house fusion restaurant serves Scandinavian and Japanese cuisine. The rooftop bar, flanked by a jetted tub, is a good place to relax in the evenings. Spa treatments are also available. An *apsara* dance show, organized by the NGO Sangkheum Center for Children (www.sangkheum.org), takes place every night and is free for guests, although donations are appreciated.

La Niche d'Angkor (tel. 063/968-978, www.lanichedangkor.com, US$49-95) is a family-friendly boutique hotel with 36 large, clean rooms arranged around a large pool in a tropical garden. The smart rooms have beautifully tiled floors, Khmer furnishings, writing desks, room safes, and free Wi-Fi, and the hotel offers free pickup service. The interconnecting rooms are perfect for families. Massages are available and a spa is attached.

US$100-200

Located next to Siem Reap's Royal Residence, the **Foreign Correspondents Club Angkor (FCC Angkor)** (tel. 063/760-280, www.fcccambodia.com, garden view US$135, pool view US$150, US$270 suites) is not a media hangout, as the name suggests, but this smart boutique hotel and restaurant does follow the same philosophical and aesthetic concept as the original FCC in Phnom Penh. Guest rooms are of modest size but feature a good sense of planning and carefully arranged decor, and they have a cosmopolitan international boutique feel with attractive baths. The small saltwater pool is a welcome break from the heat, and guests may also choose to pamper themselves at the in-house spa.

The recently reopened ★ **Shinta Mani Resort** (tel. 063/761-998, www.shintamani. com, US$150-185) oozes style with 62 spacious and smart air-conditioned guest rooms that have tasteful furnishings. Guest rooms are located in cool, whitewashed galleries around a medium-size swimming pool (US$5 non-guests). A second building, the **Shinta Mani Club,** just across the road, offers the same high standards of service and design. There's Wi-fi in all the rooms, and the bathrooms are sumptuous. Stunning photographs of the Angkor monuments by John McDermott are fitted into the rooms' ceilings. The Shinta

Mani is heavily involved in the local community and runs the Shinta Mani Foundation, which supports projects in education, small business start-ups, and health care. A percentage of each room charge is passed on to the foundation.

A unique hotel experience is the **Angkor Village Hotel** (tel. 063/963-561, www.angkorvillage.com, US$155-300) in the Wat Bo area, a collection of traditional Khmer wooden stilt houses in a beautiful, spacious, jungle-like garden compound with fully grown rain trees, coconut palms, banana plants, and bamboo clusters. The wooden houses all feature en suite baths, air-conditioning, TVs, and Internet access, and there's a swimming pool.

Highly recommended is the **Karavansara** (Street 25, Wat Bo area, tel. 063/760-678, www.karavansara.com, US$65- US$110), in a quiet residential part of town just a five-minute walk from the Old Market. This boutique hotel offers spotless and comfortable guest rooms with private terraces, Wi-Fi, and TVs. The elegant suites, in a recently renovated, heritage-listed French colonial villa, are spacious and feature attractive baths. The restaurant serves great breakfasts and a good selection of Khmer dishes; it is located in a traditional wooden Khmer building, although it's also possible to have lunch or dinner by a small pool on the rooftop. What makes this resort special, though, are the large, stylish 1-3-bedroom serviced apartments (US$178-340) in a new building across the road, possibly the best of their kind in Siem Reap. Ideal for couples, families, or groups of friends who'd like to stay a little longer and don't want the bustle of a hotel, the apartments offer privacy and come with fully equipped kitchens. There's a small saltwater pool on the rooftop with great views.

If you want to get away from the city, try the ★ **Sojourn** (tel. 012/923-437, www.sojournsiemreap.com, US$165-240), not far from the tiny Angkor-era temple Wat Athvea, a few kilometers south of Siem Reap. This delightful resort offers just 10 bungalow-style villas in a beautiful garden around a large pool. Outside the gates, Cambodia's stunning countryside beckons; the property is set among paddy fields and villages. The villas are decked out in sumptuous boutique style with Khmer furnishings, and room rates include a tuk-tuk for trips into town or to the temples. The restaurant serves set meals (US$55 pp) that include wine and unlimited soft drinks and beer. The menu offers a variety of Khmer and international dishes with some vegetarian and vegan selections. The resort's cooking school, with three-hour courses (US$22), is also recommended.

If staying in town isn't your thing, and you can afford it, check out the Fiji-inspired **Navutu Dreams Resort & Spa** (tel. 092/238-914, http://navutudreams.com, US$155-220, US$315 suites), a recent arrival on the Siem Reap luxury accommodations scene. The Italian owners have transplanted their island paradise to Siem Reap and offer just 18 beautifully appointed Mediterranean-style guest rooms, decorated with objets d'art from around Southeast Asia and clustered around two pools, a restaurant, and a spa. There's also a resident yoga teacher. Rates include airport pickup, breakfast, Wi-Fi, and a free tuk-tuk to explore the temples.

OVER US$200

For the ultimate colonial-era experience in Siem Reap, look no farther than the historic **Raffles Grand Hotel d'Angkor** (tel. 063/963-888, www.raffles.com, US$345-1,900), just north of the beautifully kept Royal Independence Gardens. From the moment you approach the perfectly restored building, the Old World ambience is unbeatable. The Grand d'Angkor first opened in 1932, at the time catering to the upscale French travelers visiting the ruins of Angkor. Later, illustrious celebrities such as Charlie Chaplin and Jackie Kennedy stayed here. Today, the hotel still caters to Cambodia's most affluent guests, and the large guest rooms and suites offer all standard international amenities, always in a tasteful francophone colonial context. The swimming pool is one of the largest in town, and the Elephant Bar in the basement exudes quiet retro charm. The Grand d'Angkor is a bit formal, but that's part of the ambience. *Apsara* dance show dinners (Oct.-July, US$32) are performed on the hotel stage behind the pool. Guests can also use the hotel's tennis courts.

The Café d'Angkor offers international cuisine and breakfast, and the Restaurant Le Grand serves an exclusive selection of the best of Khmer cuisine. The Grand d'Angkor organizes exclusive tours into the surrounding countryside, including a Khmer-style ranch barbecue combined with a horseback ride, and can even provide food and beverage catering for your private jet. Finally, to get rid of your aches and pains, visit the in-house Amrita Spa, which offers massage therapies, body wraps, packs, and masks as well as specialized skin-care treatments, salt rubs, and manicures. You will be pampered.

If money is no object, the **Amansara** (tel. 063/760-333, www.amanresorts.com, from US$880 with guided tours of the temples included in the room rates) is the place to stay. Part of an exclusive resort franchise, the Amansara is nevertheless uniquely located in the former guesthouse of King Norodom Sihanouk. Built by a French architect in 1962, the property, once known as Villa Princière, oozes period style. Rooms are bright and simply luxurious, with large private courtyards, some with their own pools. There's also a larger, beautifully shaped 1960s pool, as well as a modern lap pool and a spa. The dining room is grand, and guests may enjoy private dinners on the roof, weather permitting. Guests have included Jacqueline Kennedy, Peter O'Toole, and Angelina Jolie. La classe, as the French would say.

If you can do without total authenticity but would enjoy the best possible copy of something that never really existed—namely, the colonial paradise of Indochina—then the **Victoria Angkor Resort & Spa** (tel. 063/760-428, www.victoriahotels-asia.com, US$200-220, US$435 suites), just west of the Royal Independence Gardens, will fulfill your expectations. Located in a massive colonial-style compound designed with a great eye for detail, this French-owned property is only five years old but conveys all the nostalgia you need. The airy reception area is invitingly intimate yet formal, and the guest rooms, with air-conditioning, TVs, minibars, Wi-Fi and LAN Internet access, and private balconies, are furnished

Raffles Grand Hotel d'Angkor

with perfect copies of sumptuous period furniture. The spacious suites have all been designed with individual concepts, including the Maharajah Suite and the Governor Suite, each with its own color schemes and decor. The steel-cage elevators add a nice touch, and there's a good-size swimming pool in a central courtyard. Best of all, guests can choose to be driven around the temples in genuine French 1920s and 1930s Oldsmobiles—hard to beat for a classy way to see the wonders of Angkor.

Food

ASIAN

For health-conscious Asian cuisine, the **Panida Restaurant** (tel. 015/717-575, daily 7am-10pm, entrées around US$4) offers a decent variety of vegetarian Thai food, guaranteed to be free of MSG, along with fruit shakes as well as coffees. It's located on the way to the airport, but still close enough to downtown to walk.

For an all-around Japanese dining experience, head to **The Hashi** (Sivatha Blvd., tel. 063/969-007, daily 11am-3pm and 6pm-11pm), which offers everything from nigiri sushi, sashimi, Kobi steak, robatayaki, and maki rolls. Sit at the sushi bar or at conventional tables, or enjoy zashiki seating. The beverages are Japanese too, including various wines and spirits. Sushi Moriavase, an assortment of 15 pieces, will set you back US$25.

A less pricey Japanese option, **The Hot Stone Café** (tel. 063/966-966, daily 7am-11pm) is centrally located near the Old Market. As the name suggests, some of the food is cooked on hot volcanic stones (meat and fish), but there's also sushi and sashimi on the menu. There's a great variety of teas or saki to wash it all down.

Chiang Mai Thai Food (tel. 012/980-833, daily 7am-midnight) on Wat Bo Road offers authentic and reliable Thai cuisine and is located in an air-conditioned building. Prices are modest, the food is tasty, and there's a large variety of dishes to choose from.

The **Sawasdee Food Garden** (tel. 063/964-456, daily 6:30pm-10pm) on Wat Bo Road, just north of Route 6, serves decent Thai food in a laid-back atmosphere. *Tom yum kung* (shrimp soup), served as spicy as you want, is US$5.

The **Paris-Saigon** (tel. 063/965-408, daily 11am-10pm) is a cozy, quiet restaurant in the Wat Bo area with attractive redbrick decor. The menu is predominantly French, but there are a few Vietnamese dishes as well, and a good selection of wines. Try the beef fillet (US$9.50) and *phoe bho* beef (Vietnamese beef soup, US$6). It's a great place for a quiet dinner for two.

For a less colonial evocation of the spirit of Indochina, head to **Madame Butterfly** (tel. 063/963-816, daily 10am-10pm), on the airport road a few minutes from the town center by tuk-tuk. This charming restaurant is located in a wooden house in its own tropical garden and serves a variety of Khmer and Thai as well as some French dishes; there's a good wine list.

One of the most upmarket eating options in Siem Reap, **Nest** (tel. 063/966-381, daily 4pm-midnight) on Sivatha Boulevard offers fantastic Asian and European fusion food, served under tents in a stunning garden location. After dinner, guests can while the afternoon or evening away with cocktails, ensconced in comfortable sofas—a great culinary experience that would cost a fortune in the United States.

For decent and moderately priced Vietnamese, French, and Cambodian cuisine, head to **Rega Le Toit** (tel. 012/369-102, daily 11am-2pm and 6pm-10pm), a cozy garden restaurant on the way to the temples that does a great fish amok. The house wine is not bad either.

Dishes from both north and south India can be enjoyed at ★ **Dakshin's Restaurant** (tel. 012/808-011, daily 11am-2:30pm and 5:30pm-10:30pm, entrées around US$10) in The Lane near the Old Market. The restaurant claims to own the only genuine tandoor oven in Indochina. Needless to say, the tandoor chicken is wonderful. Guests can watch their food being prepared in the open kitchen.

The cheap and cheerful **Maharaja** (tel. 063/966-221, daily 11am-10pm, entrées around US$4) manages to conjure magic at a small price in the heart of the Old Market area. Vegetarian *thalis* (US$2.50) are inexpensive and not bad; choose among five different levels of spiciness. All the usual Indian and Pakistani standards are available, from the trusty chicken tikka to creamy korma dishes. Service is prompt and friendly.

Possibly the tastiest Indian restaurant is **Curry Walla** (tel. 063/965-451, daily 10:30am-11pm, entrées around US$3), a Punjabi place on Sivatha Boulevard that does very good *dal makhni*. Both vegetarian and nonvegetarian dishes are available.

Chusska (tel. 012/212-2138, daily 11am-10pm), just north of Pub Street, is the only pure vegetarian Indian restaurant in Siem Reap. It has great chutneys and pickles, and you can choose how spicy you want your curries.

For something completely different, try the exotic within the exotic: The **Mandalay Kitchen** (tel. 063/761-662, daily 6am-10pm, entrées under US$5) is an inexpensive place a few minutes' walk south of the Old Market just off Sivatha Boulevard that serves Burmese cuisine at budget prices. Try the braised beef with pickled mustard, or diced pork with eggplant. *Mingalabar,* as the Burmese say.

INTERNATIONAL

Near the Old Market, **Happy Herb Pizza** (daily 7am-11pm) serves budget Khmer dishes and pizzas; "happy herb" means topped with marijuana. This is part of a franchise with outlets in Phnom Penh.

Tell Siem Reap (tel. 063/963-289, daily 10am-10pm, entrées from US$7) on Sivatha Boulevard, like its namesake in Phnom Penh, offers a large variety of German and Asian dishes in an air-conditioned, family-friendly environment; there's a good choice of German beers and liquors.

The **X Rooftop Bar** (daily 4pm-sunrise) on Sivatha Boulevard is one of the most popular after-dark hangouts in Siem Reap. Movies, free Wi-Fi, Western comfort food, cigars, and wines as well as a great view make this place a nice stopover on any tour through the town's nightlife area.

One of the best-value small restaurants, serving great salads, sandwiches, and pizzas, is **Boulangerie** on Street 7. The quiche lorraine is not bad either, and a variety of great bakery items is on offer. This place is popular with expatriates and is a great value for the money.

Excellent French cuisine can be found at **Barrio** (tel. 012/756-448, daily 10am-11pm) on Wat Bo Road. Sit either outside in the garden amid fountains or in air-conditioned comfort under a crystal chandelier, and enjoy French classics like escargot (snail) or a good variety of seafood dishes. The wine list is impressive. Expect to pay around US$20 a head with drinks.

Le Jardin des Délices, an excellent restaurant that is part of the Paul Dubrule Hotel and Tourism School (tel. 063/963-672, www.ecolepauldubrule.org, Tues.-Fri. lunchtime), is located way out on the road to the airport and is open only during the school year (Oct.-July); call ahead. Set lunches (US$11) are prepared by the students.

Viva (tel. 036/963-151, daily 11:30am-late, entrées around US$5) is Siem Reap's only Mexican restaurant, and it is extremely popular. Located on a corner on the north side of the Old Market, this is the place to go if you have a craving for burritos and enchiladas and want to watch the world go by from street level.

Located in a whitewashed colonial building near Wat Damnak, the stylish French **Alliance Art Café** (tel. 063/964-940, daily

10am-midnight) is a smart French restaurant run by a French chef, made especially attractive by exhibitions of Cambodian and French artists. Usually the work of 2-3 artists is on exhibit at any given time. There's also outdoor seating. The red tuna coated with sesame (US$16) is recommended, and several Khmer dishes are also on offer.

One of the best-restored and spectacular-looking colonial-style restaurants is **Le Malraux** (tel. 063/966-041, www.le-malraux-siem-reap.com, daily 10am-11pm, entrées around US$12), a modern art deco dream with a menu and wine list to suit the ambience. Located near the Old Market area on Sivatha Boulevard, Le Malraux is the kind of place you might go (scrubbed and showered, of course) after a dusty day among the Angkor ruins to enjoy a cigar and cognac and debate the legacy of the French Republic in the Kingdom of Cambodia.

For a romantic dinner, head to the **Kanell Restaurant** (tel. 063/966-244, daily 10am-10pm), run by a French couple with many years of experience in the restaurant business. French and Khmer dishes with a twist can be enjoyed in a wonderful tropical garden or in a smart air-conditioned lounge. What's more, diners who spend more than US$5 a head can also go for a dip in the restaurant's decent-size pool fringed by palm trees; free towels are provided. The salmon steak with tarragon sauce (US$13) is recommended. Kanell is located just north of Wat Damnak, a five-minute walk across the river from the Old Market.

One of the trendiest and most cosmopolitan places in town, the futuristic **Blue Pumpkin** (tel. 063/963-574, daily 6am-11pm), on the road north of the Old Market, offers not just a comfortable 2nd-floor air-conditioned lounge with Wi-Fi access but also has some of Siem Reap's best sandwiches, salads, cakes, and tarts on its menu. No wonder this place is enormously popular with the backpacker set.

If you're into Lebanese food, you can't go wrong at the sumptuous **Mezze** (tel. 097/766-343, daily 6pm-late) on Street 11 near Pub Street. Great atmosphere, Cuban cigars, and signature cocktails complete the picture. The hot and cold mezze are delicious, especially the humus and eggplant dip.

Not bad is the upscale **Terrazza** (tel. 093/565-626, daily 11:30am-10:30pm), a couple of minutes east of the Old Market. The Italian cuisine is authentic—homemade pasta, pizzas (US$6-13), and a wide variety of meat dishes. Cholesterol bombs like crème brûlée complete the picture. A deli shop selling Italian food specialties—at a price—is attached to the restaurant.

Perhaps the best Italian food in Siem Reap can be enjoyed at ★ **Il Forno** (tel. 078/278-174, daily noon-10:30pm, entrées around US$10), located in a narrow alley just off Pub Street. It offers simple but classic Italian dining, with a great variety of homemade dishes and a large selection of Italian wines. Run by an Italian family, all ingredients are imported from Italy, while the pizzas are baked in a traditional Neapolitan wood-fired oven. Try the gnocchi with four cheeses.

KHMER

Several cheap Khmer restaurants can be found tucked on the northeast side of the Old Market, all serving good-quality local dishes, most around US$3. Lots of Khmer eat here, which is as good a recommendation as any. All these eateries have English menus with photos. The best of the lot might be **Socheata,** which does an excellent fish amok (US$4). Don't be intimidated by the no-frills decor; this might be your best chance to taste genuine Khmer cuisine while visiting Seam Reap.

Another good choice for excellent street food, especially barbecue fish and meat, are the open-air eateries south of Pub Street on Street 11 and along Sivatha Boulevard, which operate from early evening late into the night. The pavement seating is excellent for people-watching along Siem Reap's busiest thoroughfare.

Young Cambodians are trained to work in the restaurant business at the nonprofit "School of Rice," **Sala Bai** (tel. 063/963-329, www.salabai.com), a small eatery on Taphul Road that opens for breakfast and lunch during the school year (Oct.-July Mon.-Fri. 7am-9am and noon-2pm). The students serve quality Asian and Western three-course set menus.

Close to the river, the elegant **Chanrey Tree** (tel. 063/767-997, daily 11am-2:30pm and 5pm-10:30pm) serves a wide variety of traditional and contemporary Khmer dishes in a modern setting. A meal with a couple of drinks will set you back about US$20, but the food is truly delicious. Check out the stew river prawn curry or, if you feel adventurous, try the braised frog leg in caramelized palm sugar and green Kampot pepper. There's a choice of air-conditioned eating inside or outside dining at a table in the garden.

The attractive **Sugar Palm Restaurant** (tel. 063/964-838, daily 11am-10pm) on Taphul Road is located on the second floor of a wooden house, a nicely furnished open balcony space, and serves superior Khmer cuisine. Grilled eggplant with minced pork (US$5) and, for the more courageous, frog legs in ginger (US$6) are typical dishes, and the wine list is extensive. Diners can also enjoy Cambodia's national dish, *prahoc* (fermented fish paste).

The **Khmer Family Restaurant** (tel. 015/999-909, daily 7am-late) is part of a colonial block reaching all the way from The Passage, a narrow alley of galleries and restaurants, to the road west of the Old Market. It serves cheap Khmer dishes in a relaxed atmosphere. Try the fried morning glory with chicken, pork, beef, fish, or tofu (US$2.50), or the fried pumpkin with a choice of the same add-ons (US$3).

Also located in The Passage, the tiny and comfortable **Chamkar Vegetarian Restaurant** (Mon.-Sat. 11am-10pm) offers a small but very attractive menu of vegetarian Khmer dishes along with some great cakes.

An altogether different dining experience in the Old Market area is the ultra-trendy **AHA** (tel. 063/965-501, daily 11:30am-late), founded by the owner of the Shinta Mani Resort. Enjoy fine wines and Cambodian and Western snack food, and marvel at the contemporary interior design, far from the rice fields of Cambodia and yet somehow sitting right near them. Start with tapas and move on to chicken spring rolls, and don't forget to try the dried snake with mango salad. The restaurant is linked to the McDermott Photo Gallery, creating an artistically inclined upmarket ambience unrivaled in Siem Reap.

selection of Khmer dishes

Check out the highly recommended ★ **Angkor Palm Restaurant** (tel. 063/761-436, www.angkorpalm.com) by the Old Market, a mid-range dining option known for its hugely popular Khmer platter of mango salad, spare-ribs, spring rolls, and stir-fried water spinach. The restaurant's charismatic owner, Bun Try, a former photographer who spent many years in France, has traveled around the world, is full of great anecdotes, and supplies the eatery with organic vegetables and fruits from his own farm near the Banteay Srei temple. The restaurant also offers twice-daily cooking classes (minimum 2 participants, US$12 pp, 2 hours).

For great upmarket Khmer food, head to the sumptuous **Cuisine Wat Damnak** (tel. 077/347-762, Tues-Sat, 6:30pm-9:30pm), located in a traditional Khmer house behind the pagoda of the same name. This restaurant uses only local seafood, herbs, and vegetables and offers guests two set menus of either five (US$24) or six (US$28) courses. The portions aren't huge, but with so many dishes on offer, even the most jaded palate should find enjoyment here. This place is very popular, so it's best to reserve tables in advance.

Facing the west side of the Old Market, the **Champey Restaurant** and the **Amok Restaurant** (daily 10am-11pm, entrées around US$5) almost flow into each other across a narrow alley. Champey has yellow decor, and Amok is kept all in blue; both eateries have the same owner, hours, and menus of great Khmer cuisine.

STREET CAFÉS AND BAKERIES

Common Grounds (tel. 063/965-687, daily 7am-10pm) is an agreeable, modern, American-style coffeehouse behind Phsar Kandal, with a great collection of coffees, cakes and tarts, free Wi-Fi, and fast Internet terminals. All profits go to NGO projects in Cambodia.

Right next to the French Cultural Center, just off Wat Bo Road, **Le Café** (tel. 092/271-392, daily 7:30am-10pm) is located in a quiet garden and offers French-style sandwiches, salads, cakes, and fruit juices, all prepared by the Paul Dubrule Hotel and Tourism School, an NGO training young Cambodians for the hotel and catering business.

The laid-back **Singing Tree Café** (tel. 092/635-500, http://singingtree.org) is in the heart of town in the Alley West, just north of the Old Market. The food is all vegetarian—and that includes the sushi and the burgers. The café is part of the NGO scene in Siem Reap, and several worthy causes are promoted here. In the upstairs lounge area, films (Thurs. 7pm) often interesting documentaries, are shown.

For cupcakes and good fair-trade coffee, head to **Blossom Café** (tel. 017/800-301, daily 10am-5pm) at the Center Market behind the hospital. This is an NGO training place empowering Cambodian women. Some of the larger cakes look spectacular.

Information and Services

VISITOR INFORMATION

The **tourist office,** next to Le Grand Hotel d'Angkor, is not terribly informed, and most visitors cull their information from local guides, hotels, and guesthouses as well as the ever-present free Canby guides (www.canbypublications.com), which list hotels and restaurants. Cambodia Pocket Guides publish a couple of booklets featuring shopping, dining, and drinking. These publications promote only the businesses that advertise.

LIBRARIES AND EXHIBITIONS

The excellent non-lending library at the **Centre of Khmer Studies** (tel. 063/964-385, www.khmerstudies.org, Mon.-Sat. 8am-noon and 2pm-5pm), located on the eastern side of the river within the Wat Damnak temple compound, promotes research, teaching, and public service in the social sciences, arts, and humanities as they relate to Cambodia. The library has a large collection of books and academic texts in English, French, Khmer, and several other languages. It's possible to have texts photocopied.

MONEY

Siem Reap is dotted with **banks** and ATMs. There are unofficial **money changers** at Phsar Kandal (Center Market) that offer a marginally better rate for riel than the banks. Banks are usually open Monday-Friday 8am-3pm or 4pm and sometimes Saturday 8am-11:30am.

All **ATMs,** including those at the airport, dispense U.S. dollars. Large-denomination ripped dollar notes will not be accepted by local businesses. **Credit cards** (especially Visa, MasterCard, and JCB) are widely accepted, but businesses usually charge a commission of a few percent for transactions. **Traveler's checks** are accepted at most banks, at some hotels, and by some money changers.

HEALTH AND EMERGENCIES

In case of a serious accident or illness, head for the **Royal Angkor International Hospital** (24-hour tel. 063/761-888, 012/235-888, 063/399-111, www.royalangkorhospital.com) on the road to the airport, which provides high-quality medical services, including an ICU and a blood bank, as well as ambulance service from anywhere in the country. The hospital can also organize medical evacuations in very serious situations. The best recommended pharmacies are U-Care in the Old Market area (tel. 063/965-396) and at the airport. Make sure you have medical insurance, which is strongly recommended in Cambodia as hospital bills can be astronomical.

INTERNET ACCESS

Siem Reap is extremely well connected to the digital global village. In fact, virtually every guesthouse and hotel provides Internet access to its guests, either on shared terminals or with Wi-Fi access in the guest rooms. Sometimes, especially in mid-range places, this service is free of charge; at other establishments, you might have to buy a card or charge the time spent online to your bill. Some bars and restaurants, including the Blue Pumpkin, Common Grounds, and the X Bar, have free Wi-Fi access, and there are plenty of Internet cafés around town, where Skype calls are usually possible. Rates average US$1 per hour.

POST OFFICE

The **post office** (daily 7:00am-5:30pm) is located on the western side of the river, a little south of the FCC, and there's no way to be certain how reliable it is. If you are shipping something valuable, **DHL** (Phsar Kandal, tel. 063/964-949) or **CPS Express** (6A Sivatha Blvd., tel. 063/963-543) might be better options.

LAUNDRY

Virtually all hotels, from budget flophouses to first-class boutiques, offer laundry service.

Getting There and Around

GETTING THERE
Air

Most of the two million international travelers who visit the Angkor ruins each year arrive at Siem Reap's modern airport. It is possible to fly into Siem Reap from the following starting points (in addition to Phnom Penh):

• **Bangkok's Don Muang Airport** (Bangkok Airways/Siem Reap Airways, Air

Asia, and Cambodia Angkor Air fly direct to Siem Reap)

- **Sihanoukville** (via Cambodia Angkor Air)
- **Singapore** (via Silk Air)
- **Kuala Lumpur** (via Malaysia Airlines and Air Asia)
- **Ho Chi Minh City** (via Cambodia Angkor Air and Vietnam Airlines)
- **Hanoi** (via Vietnam Airlines)
- **Kunming, China** (via China Eastern Airlines)
- **Cheng Du** (via Angkor Airways)
- **Inchon, South Korea** (via Korean Air and Asiana Airlines)
- **Hong Kong** (via Dragon Air and Siem Reap Airways)

The airport is six kilometers from town; a taxi costs US$9, a tuk-tuk costs US$7, and a *motodup* (motorcycle taxi) will take you for US$3. Note that airport taxes are no longer charged. Many hotels provide free pickups and drop-offs, if you make arrangements in advance.

AIRLINE OFFICES
Siem Reap has the following airline offices:

- **Air Asia:** Room T6, Phnom Penh Airport Office, tel. 023/890-035, www.airasia.com
- **Bangkok Airways/Siem Reap Airways:** Sivatha Blvd., tel. 063/965-442, www.bangkokair.com
- **Cambodia Angkor Air:** Sivatha Blvd., tel. 063/969-268, www.cambodiaangkorair.com
- **China Eastern Airlines:** 304 Steung Thmey Village, Svay Dangkum Commune, tel. 063/965-229, www.ce-air.com
- **Korean Air:** Room 120, Airlines Office Building, Siem Reap International Airport, tel. 063/964-881, www.koreanair.com
- **Lao Airlines:** 114 Sala Khanseng Village, Route 6, tel. 063/963-283, www.laoairlines.com
- **Malaysia Airlines:** Rooms 172-184, Siem Reap International Airport, tel. 063/964-761, www.malaysiaairlines.com.my
- **Silk Air:** Room 122-123, Airlines Office Building, Siem Reap International Airport, tel. 063/964-993
- **Vietnam Airlines:** Angkor Shopping Arcade, Route 6, tel. 063/964-488, www.vietnamairlines.com

Boat
The boat rides from Phnom Penh and Battambang are enjoyable in the wet and cool season, but several accidents have happened in the past, with vessels breaking down in the middle of the lake or running out of fuel, and luggage being lost. With road conditions getting better and passenger numbers on the ferry dropping off, the boat operators have raised the prices. Still, if you are itching for a bit of adventure, try the run to **Phnom Penh** (daily, 4-6 hours, US$30-35) or to **Battambang** (daily, 6-8 hours, US$18-25). The ride to Phnom Penh is only moderately scenic, but the trip to Battambang definitely has its moments, as the boat passes several traditional fishing villages on stilts before entering the Sangker River, which snakes through numerous small settlements before reaching Battambang. These ferries do not always run and are not altogether safe by Western standards, and the buses are considerably cheaper and faster.

Regional Road Transportation
Numerous bus companies do the Phnom Penh-Siem Reap run (US$8-13), with fares varying with the on-board facilities; all buses on this route are air-conditioned. **Phnom Penh Sorya Transport** (tel. 023/210-359), **Mekong Express** (tel. 063/963-662), which has deluxe air-conditioned buses, and **Capitol Guesthouse** (tel. 023/217-627) all leave frequently from the Chong Kov Sou Bus Station,

off Route 6, a few kilometers west of Siem Reap. **Giant Ibis Transport** (tel. 023/999-333) has luxury buses for US$15, including one sleeper that leaves at 11pm. **Tep Sokha Express** (tel. 023/991-414) offers a cheaper night bus alternative at US$9. The *motodups* (US$2) and tuk-tuks (US$3) can also take you there. Journey times are typically 5-6 hours, and buses depart daily 7am-2:30pm. Most guesthouses and hotels are happy to get tickets for you, and may charge an extra dollar for the service.

There are also **minibuses** running frequently between Siem Reap and Phnom Penh (4-5 hours, US$10). Companies change all the time, and some outfits seem to employ suicidal drivers. It's best to check with your guesthouse or hotel for a reliable company.

A **private taxi** to Phnom Penh is pricey, at US$60, while a ride to Battambang is US$40. Coming from Phnom Penh or Battambang might be cheaper. A ride to the border town of Poipet will also set you back about US$35-45. Coming from the Thai border, you have to deal with the Poipet taxi mafia, who might demand US$40 or more. The price will partly depend on your bargaining skills, and it is possible to negotiate down to US$35. Private taxi rates tend to fluctuate depending on gas prices.

The Siem Reap-Bangkok Run

It's possible to travel quite comfortably from Siem Reap to Bangkok overland in a day. Numerous operators offer the trip, which should take around 6-8 hours; ask your guesthouse or hotel for details.

In Bangkok, a number of operators on Khao San Road offer the trip for US$10-20, but this is fraught with scams and rip-offs. Sometimes passengers are taken through the Pailin border; at other times, the buses on the Cambodian side are so slow that travelers arrive late and tired in Siem Reap, more likely than not to accept the choice of accommodations offered by the bus touts, who collect a commission. If you make your way from Bangkok to Poipet independently, be aware that many touts and hustlers operate on the Thai side of the border. They flag down foreign pedestrians and ask them if they have visas for Cambodia. If not, they attempt to guide the hapless travelers to an agent, where they will be charged exorbitantly for a visa. In fact, visas for Cambodia are available after you have passed Thai immigration, from a clearly signposted office on the right side of the border road, before reaching most of the large casinos.

There are now direct buses from Bangkok to Siem Reap and vice versa, though travelers will still have to cross the border on foot and sort out their visas themselves. Prices are around US$25-30 (750 Thai baht). In Bangkok, buses leave from Morochit Station. Tickets can be purchased at the station. In Siem Reap, tickets can be purchased from travel agents, and passengers are usually picked up at their guesthouse. Buses leave, in both directions, 7am-9am.

Going alone from Siem Reap need not be more expensive, as there is now a bus (US$7-9) to the border in Poipet. Alternatively, take a taxi (2 hours, US$35-45). On the Thai side, you can choose a bus (150-200 baht), minibus (300-400 baht), or train (50 baht) for the trip to the Thai capital. Taxis from the clearly signposted Aranyaprathet taxi stand, right by the border, to Bangkok are just 1,900 baht (US$55) and take around 2-3 hours, depending on where you want to be dropped off in the Thai capital. If you have the money or someone to share the costs with, this is by far the most hassle-free and comfortable option. If you arrive late, find a decent hotel or guesthouse in Aranyaprathet, the town closest to the border on the Thai side. Avoid staying overnight in Poipet at all costs.

GETTING AROUND

Downtown Siem Reap is small enough to walk around, but if you are staying a bit farther out, there's a range of local transportation you can use to get around town. Besides renting a bicycle from a guesthouse for a couple of dollars a day, the cheapest options are the trusty *motodups,* motorcycle taxis that charge about 1,000 riel for a short ride, US$1 for a longer distance. Prices increase as soon as the sun goes down. A **tuk-tuk** is a safer, more comfortable, and slightly more expensive option, with rides in town around US$1-2.

Unless you are going to the airport (US$9), a **taxi** around town hardly seems worth it.

Foreigners are not allowed to drive themselves in the Siem Reap area unless they are residents. This guarantees income to the *motodups* and tuk-tuk drivers, who depend on tourist dollars.

Vicinity of Siem Reap

PHNOM KROM
ភ្នំក្រោម

For great views over Tonlé Sap Lake, head for Phnom Krom mountain, 10 kilometers south of Siem Reap on the shores of the lake. On top of the hill, an active pagoda is popular with locals, and there are also a number of towers from the 11th century. Since 2006, Phnom Krom has been considered part of the Angkor Archaeological Park and can only be visited with a valid ticket. Although there's no ticket booth here, guards sometimes demand to see a pass, and as this minor ruin is far removed from other temples, very few people make it up here nowadays.

A tuk-tuk to Phnom Krom and back will cost around US$5. It's a 20-minute walk from the base of the mountain (really a hill) to the top.

CHONG KHNEAS FLOATING VILLAGE
ជង់ឃ្នាស

Chong Khneas, populated largely by Vietnamese people, is the floating village on Tonlé Sap Lake closest to Siem Reap, and has seen a great deal of tourist traffic in recent years. As with other floating villages, expect to see schools, clinics, gas stations, and family homes as well as souvenir shops. You will also see lots of boats filled with tour groups. An interesting stopover in the village is the **Gecko Environment Center** (http://jinja.apsara.org/gecko), which informs visitors about the unique biodiversity of the area. Another regular stopover is the "Fish and Bird Exhibition,"

really just a glorified souvenir shop. If you have time and want to see more of traditional life on the Tonlé Sap, skip Chong Khneas and visit Kompong Luong near Pursat or the floating community near Kompong Chhnang.

There are several possibilities to get out to see this waterborne community. The cheapest way might be to go directly to the boat dock and get on one of the many tour boats waiting there. Two-hour trips should be about US$10, though you'll be sharing the experience with a big group. Alternatively, the most stylish way to get on the water is with the **Tara River Boat** (tel. 092/957-765, www.taraboat.com), a larger wooden vessel that offers a number of different trips on the lake. A half-day outing (daily 7am, 9am, 11am, 4 hours, US$29 pp) includes transportation from and to your hotel, a light meal, and drinks. This trip also visits a crocodile farm. A sunset trip (daily 3:30pm, 4 hours, US$36 pp) has dinner and unlimited drinks.

To get here by yourself, take the road from Siem Reap to Phnom Krom, toward the lake. As you approach the lake, you reach the departure point for the ferries to Phnom Penh and Battambang. A tuk-tuk should be US$6 for the round-trip. Many tuk-tuk drivers get a commission from agents offering boat tours; you may offend your driver if you refuse to go with the outfit suggested.

PREK TOAL BIRD SANCTUARY
ព្រែកទាល

The biosphere and bird sanctuary Prek Toal

Vicinity of Siem Reap

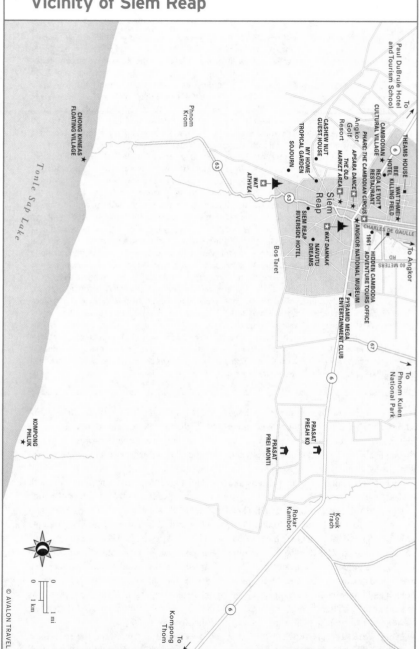

Tonle Sap Lake

CHONG KHNEAS
FLOATING VILLAGE ★

KOMPONG
PHLUK ★

Phnom
Krom

Paul DuBrule Hotel
and Tourism School

To
THEAMS HOUSE ■

BEE ■ WAT THMEI ★
HOTEL KILLING FIELD ★

CAMBODIAN ★
CULTURAL VILLAGE

Angkor
Golf
Resort

PHARE: THE CAMBODIAN CIRCUS ★

REGA LE TOY ★
RESTAURANT

APSARA DANCE ★

CASHEW NUT
GUEST HOUSE ●

MY HOME
TROPICAL GARDEN ●

SOJOURN ●

THE OLD
MARKET AREA ★

Siem
Reap

To
Angkor

CHARLES DE GAULLE

1961

60 METERS RD

HIDDEN CAMBODIA
ADVENTURE TOURS OFFICE

WAT
ATHVEA ✚

SIEM REAP
RIVERSIDE HOTEL

WAT DAMNAK ✚

NAVUTU
DREAMS

ANGKOR NATIONAL MUSEUM

PYRAMID MEGA
ENTERTAINMENT CLUB

Bos Taret

To
Phnom Kulen
National Park

PRASAT
PREAH KO

PRASAT
PREI MONTI

Kouk
Trach

Rokar
Kambot

To
Kompong
Thom

0   1 mi
0   1 km

© AVALON TRAVEL

Biodiversity and Tonlé Sap Lake

Tonlé Sap Lake is the largest natural freshwater lake in Southeast Asia. During the dry season (Nov.-May), the lake drains into the Mekong River via the Tonlé Sap River. When the rains begin in June, the Tonlé Sap River reverses its flow and feeds the lake from the Mekong, which contributes over 80 percent of the lake's water. As a consequence, the lake expands from an area of 2,500 square kilometers to 16,000 square kilometers, and water depth increases from two meters up to nine meters, providing breeding and feeding grounds for millions of migratory fish. The influx of nutrients and sediments from the Mekong contributes to the Tonlé Sap's incredible productivity.

The fisheries on and around the lake yield about 230,000 tons of fish per year, more than 50 percent of Cambodia's catch; Tonlé Sap Lake provides more than half of the country's protein intake. Some 800 fish species have been identified, making it one of the world's richest fish habitats and a biodiversity hot spot. In 1997, UNESCO designated Tonlé Sap Lake as a Biosphere Reserve in order to reduce biodiversity loss, to improve the livelihoods of people living around its shores, and to enhance social, economic, and cultural conditions for environmental sustainability.

Today, Tonlé Sap Lake faces massive environmental degradation. Overfishing, logging of the lakeshore, and construction projects such as roads, bridges, dams, and dikes around the lake all contribute to the loss of the abundance of fish as well as the reduced fertility of its floodplains. In 2000, the government passed a law to cut the fishing by half and to contain illegal fishing, but the impact of construction is changing the balance of hydrology, fauna, flora, and seasonal variation. The time, level, and duration of the annual floods affect the flora, as the water alone does not make the lake productive. Most importantly, the interplay between the biosphere and floodwaters makes Tonlé Sap the incredibly rich body of water it is. For example, tree trunks provide microorganisms such as algae to feed the fish, creating a food chain. Logging the trees kills the spawning and feeding grounds of the fish population. If the flow of the Mekong River, which brings in 87 percent of the migratory fish species, declines, a drastic change in the number of species found in the lake is likely to occur.

The consequences of upstream development, such as dam construction in China, are severe: The floods start later, their duration decreases, flooded areas decline, and less nutritious sediment is swept into the lake. As a result, the Tonlé Sap floodplain will be less fertile and fish stocks will go down, endangering the country's food supply.

is almost as overrun by commerce as Chong Khneas. It takes about two hours to get there in a boat, and you should expect to slide through tall grasses and brackish water. If you come in the dry season (Nov.-Apr.), you might be able to spot storks, ibis, pelicans, and eagles.

If you organize everything yourself, a boat to the Prek Toal Research Station will cost around US$50, where visitors have to pay an entrance fee of US$20 as well as another US$30 for a guided boat tour of the sanctuary. Sounds extortionate? It is. Many guesthouses and tour operators arrange packages at similar or just slightly higher prices. Try **Peace of Angkor Tours** (www.peaceofangkor.com). **Tara River Boat** (tel. 092/957-765, www.taraboat.com) offers a day trip (9 hours,

US$165 pp) with transfers, all fees, drinks, and an English-speaking guide that also takes in Chong Khneas and the Gecko Environment Center. All tickets, permits, and so on are included.

Serious bird-watchers might want to check the website of the **Sam Veasna Center** (tel. 063/761-597, www.samveasna.org), which specializes in bird-watching expeditions to remote sites. Costs are around US$100 a day per person. Longer trips to remote locations are also offered. Another local NGO, **Osmose** (tel. 063/765-506 www.osmosetonlesap.net) offers similar day trips from US$105 per person as well as overnight trips from US$135 to rarely visited locations.

To reach Prek Toal, take the road from Siem Reap to Phnom Krom, toward the lake.

KOMPONG PHLUK

កំពង់ភ្លុក

This group of three traditional Khmer villages rises out of the Tonlé Sap floodplain on high stilts and is less overrun by tour groups than Chong Khneas. About 3,000 people live here among mangrove forests during the wet season. In the dry season, when the lake's waters recede and leave the houses like stranded storks on their six-meter-high poles, many inhabitants move into smaller huts on stilts farther into the lake. The people of Kompong Phluk make their living from fishing and shrimp harvesting.

There are two ways to get to Kompong Phluk. In the rainy season (May-Oct.), take a boat from Chong Khneas (US$60 for 2 passengers for a half-day excursion). In the dry season, when water levels are low, it's possible to drive all the way to the community, some 16 kilometers south of Siem Reap. Alternatively, depending on water levels, you might be able to get a boat from the village near the Roluos Group of temples.

KOMPONG KLEANG

កំពង់ឃ្លាំង

With more than 10,000 inhabitants, Kompong Kleang is the largest community on the lake. Most of the community, about 35 kilometers east of Siem Reap, is built on wooden poles anchored in the lake bed. The people are Khmer and make their living from fishing. So far, visitor numbers are far fewer than at Chong Khneas, but more and more tour operators are putting this unique community on their itineraries. Around the village, flooded forest provides important spawning grounds for the Tonlé Sap's fish population. In the wet season, the houses are a couple of meters above the waterline, but once the waters have receded, the stilts can stretch up to 10 meters down to the muddy soil—quite a sight.

To get to Kompong Kleang, depending on the season and prevailing water levels, you might be able to head for Chong Khneas and catch a boat from there, or head east on Route 6 to Domdek Village, from where it's a short boat ride (US$10) in the wet season or a longer bike ride all the way to Kompong Kleang in the dry season. Some guesthouses and tour operators, including **Tara River Boat** (tel. 092/957-765, www.taraboat.com), offer half-day trips (from US$70).

Angkor

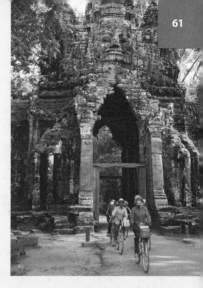

Most visitors to Cambodia come to see the temples of Angkor. Located in forests to the northwest of Tonlé Sap Lake, the sprawling ruins of the Angkor Empire are simply without equal in Southeast Asia. The interplay of forest and ruins gives the former Khmer capital its otherworldly, fantastical atmosphere. Even widely traveled and jaded culture hounds cannot help but be moved by the scale and sensuousness of these buildings.

More than two million visitors entered the Angkor Archaeological Park in 2013. For Cambodians, Angkor lies at the heart of national identity, as much an ancient success story and an object of immense pride as a psychological burden for a country with such a tragic recent history.

For more than 500 years, Angkor dominated the political and cultural affairs of much of Southeast Asia, and the Khmer Empire spread into large parts of Thailand as well as Laos and Vietnam—restored temples in Thailand and Laos attest to this—before falling victim to its own grandeur and the forest in the 15th century. In the late 13th century, the imperial city of Angkor Thom had around one million inhabitants, and the temple of Ta Prohm alone had more than 80,000 servants and staff, while in Europe, Paris had a population of just 25,000.

Angkor Wat is the largest religious building in the world, and its surroundings play host to the highest concentration of temples in the world. The temples were declared a UNESCO World Heritage Site in 1992. Around the temples, life goes on as it has for hundreds of years. Siem Reap Province is one of the poorest in Cambodia, and rice fields continue to be tilled by oxen and plow, just as they were during the Khmer Empire's heyday. In fact, many aspects of Cambodian life have not changed much in the past 1,000 years. Since the fall of Angkor in 1431 at the hands of the Siamese, the country has been sliding from one tragedy into another, and many Cambodians dream of one day recapturing some of the country's former glory.

What is considered Angkor today, part of the Angkor Archaeological Park, spreads over some 230 square kilometers, and besides

---

Previous: inner courtyard of Angkor Wat; faces of the bodhisattva, South Gate, Angkor Thom. **Above:** South Gate, Angkor Thom.

Highlights

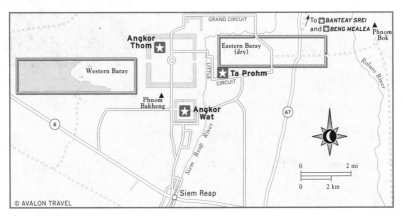

★ **Angkor Wat:** The greatest of great temples, Angkor Wat is a monumental dream in stone (page 73).

★ **Angkor Thom:** Cambodia's last imperial city is surrounded by a three-kilometer wall and moat. At its center, the Bayon is a spectacular temple dominated by towers adorned with the enigmatic smiling faces of the bodhisattva (page 78).

★ **Ta Prohm:** The forest-covered temple of

Tomb Raider fame is the most romantic ruin in the Angkor Archaeological Park (page 86).

★ **Banteay Srei:** This small 10th-century temple features some of the most exquisite carvings of the Khmer Empire (page 95).

★ **Beng Mealea:** Away from the crowds and subsumed by forest, this remote temple offers visitors one of the most atmospheric experiences of any Khmer temple (page 97).

Angkor

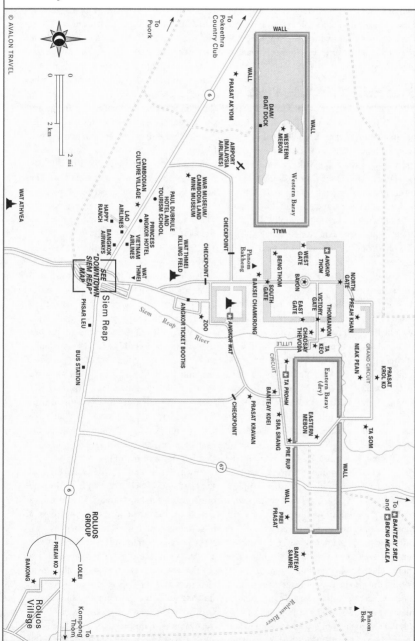

© AVALON TRAVEL

To Pokeethra Country Club

To Puork

0   2 km
0   2 mi

WAT ATHVEA

WALL

DAM/ BOAT DOCK

WESTERN MEBON

Western Baray

WALL

WALL

WALL

PRASAT AK YOM

AIRPORT (MALAYSIA AIRLINES)

WAR MUSEUM/ CAMBODIA LAND MINE MUSEUM

CAMBODIAN CULTURE VILLAGE

PAUL DUBRULE HOTEL AND TOURISM SCHOOL

PRINCESS ANGKOR HOTEL

HAPPY RANCH

LAO AIRLINES

BANGKOK AIRWAYS

VIETNAM AIRLINES

WAT THMEI KILLING FIELD

WAT THMEI

CHECKPOINT

CHECKPOINT

"DOWNTOWN SIEM REAP" MAP

SEE

Siem Reap

PHSAR LEU

BUS STATION

Siem Reap River

ANGKOR TICKET BOOTHS

ZOO

Phnom Bakheng

BAKSEI CHAMKRONG

ANGKOR WAT

ANGKOR THOM

WEST GATE

BENG THOM

SOUTH GATE

BAYON

EAST GATE

VICTORY GATE

NORTH GATE

PREAH KHAN

THOMANON

CHAOSAY THEVODA

TA KEO

GRAND CIRCUIT

NEAK PEAN

PRASAT KROL KO

LITTLE CIRCUIT

TA PROHM

Eastern Baray (dry)

BANTEAY KDEI

SRA SRANG

EASTERN MEBON

TA SOM

PRASAT KRAVAN

CHECKPOINT

PRE RUP

WALL

WALL

PREI PRASAT

BANTEAY SAMRE

To BANTEAY SREI and BENG MEALEA

67

6

ROLUOS GROUP

PREAH KO

LOLEI

BAKONG

Roluos Village

Roluos River

To Kompong Thom

Phnom Bok

Angkor Wat and Angkor Thom, includes all the other temples in the region. Most temples lie a few kilometers to the north of Siem Reap, while the structures known as the Roluos Group, which slightly predates Angkor, can be found 15 kilometers east of Siem Reap.

PLANNING YOUR TIME

The temples of Angkor can be visited in many ways. If you are incredibly pressed for time, a quick one-day trip through Angkor Wat, Angkor Thom (including the Bayon), Ta Prohm, and Banteay Srei will give you a superficial impression of the Khmer Empire. Three days are a must to soak up the architectural majesty of the area, and a week allows you to visit outlying and remote temples. Farther-afield sights such as the temples Beng Mealea or Koh Ker, or the biosphere and floating village on Tonlé Sap Lake, can be reached on day trips, so even two weeks around Angkor need not be boring.

Most visitors follow the most logical routes, created by French archaeologists 100 years ago: the **Petit Circuit,** the 17-kilometer short route, which leads past all the main temples; or alternatively, the **Grand Circuit,** the 26-kilometer long route, which offers countryside vistas but does not include some of the temple highlights, such as Ta Prohm. The temples of the Roluos Group are not part of either route and can be visited on a separate half-day excursion.

As one day is enough time to complete the Petit Circuit, you might think that this is sufficient time to marvel at the temples. Indeed, it could be argued that visitors who spend just a single day among the ruins will have far less impact than three-day visitors. But perhaps too brief a glance at the Angkor temples, seen in passing as a series of monuments stuck in the dry soil of a poor country, does not do justice to Khmer culture and your own sense of discovery. To be sure, the majority of travelers who visit Angkor nowadays arrive as part of a package tour. They travel in air-conditioned buses, isolated from the environment, and inside the temples they are firmly tied to their guides and camcorders. In this sense, Angkor—like the pyramids of Giza, the Coliseum in Rome, and the Acropolis in Athens—has become part of the global archaeological tourist path, traversed in the same manner by millions every year. Individual travelers can be more flexible and can take their time, giving the temples space to breathe and to fit into the country as a whole. Rather than checking off temple after temple, it might be worth lingering here and there. The atmosphere of each set of ruins changes significantly depending on the time of day, the light, and the numbers of visitors and local people present.

HISTORY OF THE ANGKOR EMPIRE

The history of Angkor begins at the dawn of the 9th century. In the preceding centuries, smaller empires and fiefdoms had fallen and risen in the region we now recognize as Cambodia. Most of them had fallen under the control of the court of Java in Indonesia, although some recent studies suggest that Java could in fact be Chenla, an earlier Khmer kingdom. Whatever the case, the first great Khmer king, **Jayavarman II** (AD 802-850) declared himself *devaraja* (divine ruler) of the kingdom of Kambujadesa; he established several capitals, including one at Phnom Kulen, northeast of Siem Reap, and later another at Hariharalaya, near Roluos.

Toward the end of the 9th century, **Indravarman I** (AD 877-889) built the first of the great Angkor temples, **Preah Ko,** as well as the **Bakong,** and began work on a huge *baray* (water reservoir) at Hariharalaya. His son, **Yasovarman I** (AD 889-900) expanded on his father's achievements, finishing the *baray* and creating yet another royal city, Yasodharapura, located around **Phnom Bakheng,** today's most popular sunset spot within the Angkor Archaeological Park. Yasovarman I might also have been the Khmer king who began construction of the mountain temple of **Preah Vihear.** Other kings came and went, power struggles among different royal families and with the neighboring Cham continued, and the capital briefly moved out to Koh Ker before returning to the Angkor area.

Suryavarman II, who ascended the throne in 1113, extended the Khmer Empire to its largest territory. He also built **Angkor Wat,** yet following his death in 1150, the empire fell apart once more. Only his cousin, **Jayavarman VII,** managed to reunite the kingdom under the crown in 1181, fight off the Cham, and commence the Khmer Empire's last great renaissance. Jayavarman VII converted from Hinduism to Mahayana Buddhism, founded the last great Khmer city, **Angkor Thom,** and oversaw Angkor's most prolific period of monument building. In less than 40 years, hundreds of temples—as well as libraries, *dharamshalas* (rest houses), and hospitals—were hastily constructed along new roads that now connected large parts of the kingdom. Many of the monuments built under Jayavarman VII are artistically inferior and stylistically impure because the speed of construction was so frenetic. It seemed like the last god-king knew that time was running out. Jayavarman VII had some of Angkor's most enduring iconic buildings constructed, including **Ta Prohm** and the **Bayon.** In 1203, the king annexed Champa and effectively extended his empire to southern Vietnam. But with the death of Jayavarman VII in 1218, the moment had passed, and Angkor slowly went into decline.

Hinduism was briefly reintroduced by **Jayavarman VIII** in the late 13th century, resulting in a concerted and presumably costly act of vandalism that saw the defacing of many Buddhist monuments, including Ta Prohm and Preah Khan. Buddhism soon returned, but in a different form, Theravada Buddhism, which puts less emphasis on the divinity of the king; it has survived in Cambodia to this day. Perhaps this loss of spiritual authority affected later kings. Perhaps, as new research suggests,

the Angkor Empire had overreached, ruined the environment around Siem Reap, and was ready to give way to something else.

Repeated incursions by the Siamese culminated in a seven-month siege of Angkor Thom in 1431, after which **King Ponhea Yat** moved the capital southwest to Phnom Penh. Other reasons for the demise of this great empire are also plausible. The Khmer Empire had been built on the back of an agrarian society, and trade was becoming more important in Southeast Asia. Angkor Thom was too isolated, too far from the coast, and too far from the Mekong River to be able to keep up with new challenges. Following the move to Phnom Penh, the temples remained active, yet were slowly taken over by the forest.

"REDISCOVERY" OF ANGKOR

Angkor is unlikely ever to have been completely abandoned, although precise information on the activities around the ruins between the 15th and 18th centuries is sketchy. Following the last onslaught by the Thais in 1431 and the gradual shift of the capital toward Phnom Penh, monks continued to live around Angkor Wat until the 16th century. The Cambodian court apparently returned to Angkor for brief periods during the 16th and 17th centuries.

Around the same time, an early report by the Portuguese writer Diego De Couto apparently referred to a Capuchin friar visiting the region in 1585 and finding the temples in ruins, overgrown by vegetation. So impressed were early visitors from Europe, the Middle East, and other parts of Asia that some wildly speculated that the Romans or Alexander the Great had built the temples.

A trickle of these adventurers and traders, many of whom had settled at the court in Phnom Penh in the 16th century, began to take note of the ruins, either by hearing other people's accounts or traveling there themselves, a 10-day journey at the time. A group of Spanish missionaries even hoped to rehabilitate the ruins and turn them into a

Chou Ta-Kuan: Angkor's Chronicler

Chou Ta-Kuan, a Chinese diplomat in the service of Emperor Chengzong of Yuan, grandson of Kublai Khan, traveled from Wenzhou, on the East China Sea coast, past Guangzhou and Hainan, along Vietnam's coast, and up the Mekong River as far as Kompong Cham, from where he took a smaller vessel across Tonlé Sap Lake to arrive at the imperial city of Angkor Thom in August 1296. Chou Ta-Kuan was neither the first nor the last Chinese diplomat to visit the seat of the Angkor Empire, but he stayed for 11 months and took notes. *The Customs of Cambodia,* the only surviving first-person account of life in the Khmer Empire, is one of the most important sources available to scholars and laypeople to understand Angkor. Not only did the diplomat describe the city of Angkor Thom, but he also shed some light on the daily lives of ordinary Cambodians. With his report, Chou Ta-Kuan gives today's visitors an opportunity to imagine how the ruined splendor of the temples must once have been a busy metropolis and how, at its height, a million people could have lived and worked here.

center of Christian teaching. A Japanese interpreter, Kenryo Shimano, drew the first accurate ground plan of Angkor Wat in the early 17th century. Japanese writing on a pillar inside Angkor Wat is said to have been carved by his son, who later visited the site in honor of his adventurous father. Other foreigners—including an American, a Brit, and several French explorers—published their accounts of visiting the temples, but no one really took note.

In 1858, Henri Mouhot, a French naturalist who lived on the island of Jersey, set off on an expedition sponsored by the British Royal Geographical Society and reached Angkor in early 1860. Mouhot spent three weeks at Angkor, surveyed the temples, and continued up the Mekong River into Laos, where he eventually died of a fever (possibly malaria). His notes were published in 1864, a year after Cambodia had become a French protectorate.

RESTORATION OF ANGKOR

In 1863, a year before Mouhot's report was published, Vice Admiral Louis-Adolphe Bonard, the governor of the French colony of Cochin China (South Vietnam), visited Angkor and decided that it had not been the Romans or any other foreign power who had built the magnificent temples, but rather the now-impoverished Cambodians.

The idea of restoring Cambodia (and its people) to its former grandeur encouraged the population back home in France to support the republic's quickly expanding and unpopular colonial efforts in Southeast Asia. Angkor became a symbol of this drive, and as a consequence, it was soon very much a focus of attention at the highest levels of the French administration. Thailand was already under the influence of the British (a British photographer, John Thomson, published the first images of Angkor Wat in the 1860s), and the race was on to find a trade route into China, which was just beginning to open up to foreign commerce. Cambodia and the Mekong River were to play a key role in this race.

In 1866, the **Mekong Exploration Commission,** led by Ernest Doudart de Lagrée, France's representative in Cambodia, and accompanied by Francis Garnier, Louis Delaporte, a photographer named Gsell, and several others, set off to find out whether the Mekong was navigable. On the way, they made a planned detour to Angkor and took detailed scientific notes. Louis Delaporte's watercolors and drawings, fanciful though they were, and Gsell's photographs of the temples, along with route maps and extensive descriptions of temples and the lives of Cambodians, were published in two volumes in 1873 as *Voyage d'exploration en Indo-Chine.* As the French public was not aware of Henri Mouhot's British-funded efforts, Garnier and Delaporte (Doudart de Lagrée had died by this time) got all the credit for the "discovery" of Angkor. Their findings were well presented and included, for the first time, outlying temples such as Beng Mealea, Preah Khan, and Wat Nokor, east of Angkor, as well as Khmer temples in southern Laos. Of course, in the eyes of superior-minded Europeans, the temples could not compete in grandeur with efforts back home, and the early explorers claimed that "Cambodian art ought to perhaps rank its productions behind the greatest masterpieces in the West."

But slowly, in the minds of these early archaeologists and consequently the French public, the true dimensions of the Khmer Empire began to emerge. In 1867, at the Universal Exposition in Paris, visitors were presented with giant plaster-cast reproductions of the temples. In the following years, Delaporte returned to Cambodia and began to systematically remove statues, sculptures, and stonework to Europe. Soon after, he became the director of the Indochinese Museum in Paris, which began to amass a collection of Angkorian artifacts. Around the same time, the first tourists began to arrive. They also took souvenirs with them, many of which disappeared into private homes in France. In 1887, the French architect Lucien Fournereau made extensive and detailed drawings of Angkor Wat and other temples that, for the first time, presented Europeans with accurate scientific representations of Khmer architecture. Hendrick Kern, a Dutchman, managed to decipher the Sanskrit inscriptions on temple walls in 1879, and the French epigraphist Étienne Aymonier undertook a first inventory of the temples around Angkor, listing 910 monuments in all.

In 1898, the École Française d'Extrême-Orient (EFEO), founded by the colonial masters to study various aspects of their Far East possessions, began to work in Cambodia, and soon efforts were made to start clearing the forest from some of the ruins. The EFEO created a road network around the ruins, the Petit Circuit and the Grand Circuit, which are still used by many visitors. To this day, the EFEO has been the body most consistently involved in the study and restoration of Angkor.

The Cambodians were never consulted about any of France's activities around Angkor. The French writer Pierre Loti remarked in 1912 that France "was idiotically desperate to rule over Asia, which has existed since time immemorial, and to disrupt the course of things there." He felt that the French presence was disrupting the continuity of Cambodia, where the royal dancers appeared to step out of the past into the present, unchanged by time. Loti said, "Times we thought were forever past are revived here before our eyes; nothing has changed here, either in the spirit of the people or in the heart of their palaces." The French artist Auguste Rodin was so taken with the dancers that he followed them around France on their visit in 1906.

At the time, Angkor, in Siem Reap Province, still belonged to Siam. It was only in 1907 that France forced Siam to hand over three provinces that had been under Siamese control, including Siem Reap. From then on, France, the colonial masters of Indochina, were in control of the temple—until the beginning of World War II, when the area briefly returned to Siamese control because Siam had aligned itself with the Japanese, who had wrested control of the colonies from the French (although officers from the collaborating Vichy France government continued to administer the rest of Cambodia).

Following World War II, France regained control of Cambodia and the Angkor temples until independence in 1953. This long-term continuity meant that the EFEO had a total monopoly on the research conducted on Angkor, which enabled the scientists involved to develop a coherent body of work over the years. In 1908, Conservation d'Angkor, the archaeological directorate of the Cambodian government, was established in Siem Reap and became responsible for the maintenance of the ruins. The office's first curator, Jean Commaille, originally a painter who had arrived with the Foreign Legion, lived in a straw hut by the causeway to Angkor Wat, and wrote the first guidebook to Angkor before being killed by bandits in 1916.

Commaille's successors further cleared the forest, and, in 1925, Angkor was officially opened as a park, designed to attract tourists. Soon the **first batches of foreign visitors** arrived by car or by boat from Phnom Penh or Bangkok, and guided tours on elephant back were conducted around the temples. Many of these early tourists, for the most part rich globe-trotters, stole priceless items from among the ruins or carved their names into the ancient stones. Little could be done about the thefts except to search a few posh hotel rooms. Tourism continued to increase, and in 1936 even Charlie Chaplin did a round of the temples.

In the meantime, the EFEO's research techniques continued to evolve, and became more integrated. Initially, different specialists had worked on different aspects of reconstruction and research; it was only in the late 1920s that several disciplines were combined— with spectacular results. Now the Bayon and Banteay Srei could properly be dated, and Angkor's chronology finally took shape. Influenced by the Archaeological Service of the Dutch East Indies, the EFEO, under curator Henri Marchal, began to undertake **complete reconstructions of temples** in the 1930s, most notably of Banteay Srei. Following World War II, as Cambodia moved toward independence, the EFEO moved its headquarters to France, and Conservation d'Angkor now ran the largest archaeological dig in the world, with the French staff slowly being complemented by French-educated students from Phnom Penh. Excavations could now be undertaken farther afield at locations like Sambor Prei Kuk, the pre-Angkorian ruins near Kompong Thom.

In the 1960s, Angkor began to be used as a backdrop for movies, most notably *Lord Jim*

and some of King Sihanouk's feature films. The ever-growing popularity of the temples meant increased looting, and many statues had to be removed and replaced with plaster copies.

Soon there were new challenges to the continuing restoration efforts—war was coming. Following Sihanouk's fall from power in 1970, the French staff of the EFEO carried on working on the temples for another two years, until they were forced to leave as the **Khmer Rouge** was closing in. Local workers continued with their efforts until 1975, when the revolutionary communists forced them into the fields to work or executed them. Angkor was once again abandoned. Through the long years of communist revolution and the subsequent civil war, the temples remained off-limits both to researchers and casual visitors, and the forest grew back over the monuments. The Khmer Rouge was too superstitious to destroy the temples, even though they destroyed virtually every modern temple in the country, but many research documents went up in flames. Luckily, much of the work the EFEO had done since its inception, some 70 years of solid systematic research, had been copied and taken to Paris.

Following the invasion of Cambodia by Vietnam, work slowly resumed in the 1980s. First, the **Archaeological Survey of India** sent a team to restore Angkor Wat. The efforts of this enterprise have been widely criticized, but it should be kept in mind how very dangerous a country Cambodia was at the time, and that the Indian scientists had few materials and few local experts to work with. At the same time, a Polish scientific delegation engaged in excavations around the Bayon. In 1989, the **Royal University of Fine Arts** was reopened in Phnom Penh in order to train a new generation of archaeologists.

In 1991, after 20 years of neglect and devastation, not just of the ruins of Angkor but of Cambodia as a whole, the **United Nations Educational, Scientific, and Cultural Organization (UNESCO)** established an office in Cambodia. Soon after, the **World Monuments Fund** became the first NGO to establish a branch at Angkor, followed shortly by the return of the EFEO. France and Japan soon pledged large funds for safeguarding the ruins, which by now were once again being looted at a frightening rate. Through the 1990s, new information garnered with technologies not available prior to 1972, including aerial photographs and even space-based radar images obtained by NASA's space shuttle *Endeavour,* began to be systematically assimilated into the larger body of research.

In 1992, Angkor Wat, along with 400 other monuments in the area, was listed as a **UNESCO World Heritage Site.** This officially made Angkor one of the world's most important cultural sites, a move designed to protect the remnants of the Khmer Empire from further looting or indiscriminate development.

Cambodia now has an article in its constitution that calls on the state to preserve the country's ancient monuments. UNESCO is the international coordinator for overseas contributions to the upkeep of the temples. While restoration efforts have continued, and while UNESCO has been pushing for sustainable development, in 1995 the Cambodian government created the **Authority for the Protection and Management of Angkor and the Region of Siem Reap (APSARA),** an NGO in charge of research, protection, and conservation of cultural heritage as well as urban and tourist development.

THE FUTURE OF ANGKOR

In the Angkor Archaeological Park, the sheer number of visitors now poses the gravest threat to the ruins. Wooden walkways and stairs such as those at Angkor Wat, Ta Prohm, and Beng Mealea reduce some of the damage caused by large numbers of visitors, but with current figures at more than **two million visitors per year,** questions of sustainability continue to arise. For this reason, APSARA has been a mixed blessing. Placed under the double supervision of the Presidency of the Council of Ministers (technical supervision) and the Ministry of Economy and Finance (financial supervision), the organization's responsibilities are split into two distinct and sometimes contradictory areas—protection and exploitation. In 1999, the Cambodian government awarded a 10-year lease to manage the income generated by the temples to a private company called Sokimex. This setup, parliamentarians claimed in 2014, lacks transparency. Attempts by UNESCO to stem the worst commercial exploitation, such as the elevator and footwear projects that followed, have had some success.

But Siem Reap's urban infrastructure has not been able to keep pace with tourism development, leading to a **breakdown in water distribution** and a **lack of drainage.** This is turn is affecting the temples, which are slowly subsiding along with the falling water table. The Bayon is sinking into the sandy ground, and cracks are widening between its carefully assembled stones. In high season, some 6,000 visitors a day clamber across the temples, traffic jams within the park have become commonplace, and the once-romantic sunset spot at Phnom Bakheng is now so crowded with thousands of visitors every evening that tourists have to book advance tickets in high season just to catch the sunset here.

Recent debates about sustainability have centered on **diversifying tourism** in Cambodia. But even if some of the two million or so visitors could be persuaded to look at temples farther afield, most first-time visitors will most likely still want to see Angkor. Projections show that by 2020, the kingdom is likely to welcome seven to eight million visitors a year—and most of them will head for Angkor.

Incidentally, a French-Australian-Cambodian research project called the **Greater Angkor Project** indicates that, at its height, Angkor Thom was surrounded by an urban sprawl the size of modern-day Los Angeles, and therefore it was probably the **world's largest preindustrial urban** settlement. According to scientists from Sidney University, the Khmer capital was in an urbanized wasteland, stripped bare of its forests, its rivers diverted, and dependent on a sophisticated irrigation system that proved to be unsustainable. This, scientists suggest, was the reason for the collapse of one of the world's great empires. And, according to the Greater Angkor Project, the same mistakes are being made again. The planned new airport, which is meant to vastly increase arrival capacity at Siem Reap, is a case in point.

Exploring the Temples

INFORMATION
Entry Tickets and Hours of Operation

All visitors to the Angkor Archaeological Park must have valid tickets. Visitors are checked at virtually all temples. If you lose your ticket, there's no replacement, and you will have to buy another one.

Tickets are available at the main entrance on the road from Siem Reap to Angkor Wat. **One-day** (US$20), **three-day** (US$40, valid for 7 days), and **seven-day** (US$60, valid for 1 month) tickets are available and no longer have to be used on consecutive days. Note that if you purchase a ticket for the Angkor temples around 5pm, it is possible to squeeze in a quick free visit before the park closes at sunset. (Park employees won't count this first evening visit as one of your allotted days, meaning that you'll still have your full number of days to spend at the park.) Some visitors use the afternoon prior to their passes becoming valid to visit Phnom Bakheng for the sunset views.

One-day tickets are also available at a second entrance off the airport road. Three-day and seven-day tickets need to have a photograph of the ticket holder attached. There's no need to bring your own picture. Visitors are photographed while purchasing their tickets.

The ticket booths on the main road open at 5am, and entry to the temples is possible 5:30am-sunset. **Banteay Srei** closes at 5pm while **Kbal Spean** closes at 3pm. Don't buy tickets anywhere else, as they are likely to be fakes.

Several of the more remote temples are not covered by the tickets. Entrance to **Phnom Kulen** costs an unreasonable US$20, while visitors to **Beng Mealea** have to shell out a reasonable US$5. The even more remote **Koh Ker** costs US$10. Always carry your tickets; they are checked at every major monument.

Security

The Angkor Archaeological Park has been de-mined, and robberies are virtually unheard of, making the area around the temples one of the safest places in Southeast Asia.

GETTING THERE AND AROUND

There are numerous ways to explore the temples of Angkor. The distance between the temples is too far to walk, not least because it is hot almost year-round, so it's best to have some form of wheels.

For years, having a local *motodup* (motorcycle taxi) take visitors around was the most common way to tour the Angkor Archaeological Park, and this is still possible, though few visitors choose this rather uncomfortable transport option. Daily rates are around US$10, and a tip is expected. **Tuk-tuks** (around US$15 per day) are far more popular and comfortably seat two people (or up to four, if necessary). Note that for temples farther away from Siem Reap, such as Banteay Srei, higher rates apply. A **taxi** will set you back around US$20-30 per day, a **minibus** around US$40-50 per day, more to the outlying temples. For more remote temples such as Preah Vihear, consider renting a **Jeep** or other 4WD vehicle (around US$80). To reach Beng Mealea

Cycling Angkor

Since many visitors have had motorcycle accidents on the roads around the temples, the local authorities have banned tourists from driving their own vehicles around Siem Reap or Angkor. Bicycles are the exception to the rule.

The temple park is ideal for cyclists, although tour buses, taxis, and tuk-tuks cause traffic jams in the mornings and late afternoons on some of the roads among the main temples. Generally, though, a bicycle is the perfect alternative to motorized transportation, and the cycling experience is much more in tune with the magnificence of the temples and the forest. All the roads among the temples are paved, and there are no notable hills to climb. While many of the roads are shaded by the forest, it does get infernally hot in the summer, so make sure to drink plenty of water (available from stalls near virtually every temple) and use sunscreen. Make sure you lock your bike anywhere you plan to leave it.

The ideal route is the 17-kilometer **Petit Circuit,** which starts at Angkor Wat, leads past Phnom Bakheng into Angkor Thom and past the Bayon, then leaves Angkor Thom toward Ta Keo and Ta Prohm before returning to Angkor Wat.

Bicycles can be rented from guesthouses for US$2-3 a day. You can also join an organized cycling tour around the temples. **Grasshopper Adventures** (Street 26, Siem Reap, tel. 012/462-165, www.grasshopperadventures.com) offers excellent itineraries around the temples or through the adjoining countryside. **Cambodia Cycling** (382 Monul 1, Group 8, Savay Dangkum, Siem Reap, tel. 063/963-440, www.cambodiacycling.com) offers similar trips. A typical tour with both companies costs just under US$40 (not including admission to the temples) and starts at 7:30am, although routes vary. The back roads to the temples lead along the picturesque Siem Reap River and rows of traditional stilt houses. Once in the Angkor Archaeological Park, cyclists ride along the massive city wall surrounding Angkor Thom, the last capital of the Khmer Empire. They follow the course of the city's broad moat, stopping at crumbling guard towers that even intrepid motorized visitors to the temples have never seen. Emerging from dense forest to see the Bayon, the multiple-faced temple in the heart of Angkor Thom, is a breathtaking experience—the temples and the forest seem to conspire to create a more intimate experience that you'd never get from a tour bus or taxi. Bike tours are also an excellent way to meet fellow travelers.

and Koh Ker from Siem Reap, a normal taxi is sufficient. Your hotel or guesthouse will be able to arrange any of these options.

However you choose to get around, be sure to negotiate everything in advance. Local drivers can get very contrary if they feel that they have been taken advantage of. Make sure both parties agree on pickup and drop-off times, itineraries, availability during lunch breaks and in the evenings, and the exact price. Pay only when the day is done and you are back where you started. If the driver did a good job, feel free to tip above the agreed-on rates.

TOURING THE TEMPLES

Exploring the temples with a guide can definitely enhance the experience and deepen your understanding of the magnificent civilization that once ruled these buildings. The **Khmer Angkor Tour Guides Association** (KATGA, tel. 063/964-347, www.khmerangkortourguide.com) is the organization for official tour guides based in Siem Reap. The guides are trained by the Ministry of Tourism and the APSARA Authority. English- and French-speaking guides cost US$20-30 per day. Guides fluent in other languages, including Spanish, German, and Japanese, are likely to cost more.

Your hotel or guesthouse will be able to arrange an English-speaking guide for around US$30 a day. Note that tuk-tuk drivers and *motodups* are not allowed to guide tourists through the temples.

Numerous travel agents offer guided day

tours (around US$60). This includes the US$20 temple entrance fee as well as a guide, transportation, and lunch. Sometimes a visit to the Angkor National Museum is also included. Three-day, two-night hotel and temple packages with pickup from the airport, transportation, accommodations, temple admission, and an English-speaking guide cost US$170-250 or more, depending on the cost of accommodations and the number of people in the group; this can also be booked through a local agent. If you book a tour as a group with a local travel agent, significant discounts are likely. Four-six-day packages to the temples are also offered, and some tour operators make sure they benefit the local communities through their involvement with various aid projects.

Tour Operators

The following travel agents in Siem Reap offer standard tour packages for Angkor, from one day to one week, with longer itineraries for locations farther afield.

- **Angkor T.K. Travel & Tours** (tel. 063/963-320, www.angkortk.com) offers competent single- and multiday tours around the temples at competitive prices.

- **The World of Cambodia** (tel. 063/963-637, www.angkor-cambodia.org) organizes small-group tours of the temples for mid- and high-budget travelers, including hotels and guides.

- **AboutAsia** (tel. 092/121-059, U.S. tel. 914/595-6949, www.aboutasiatravel.com) runs tour packages around the temples and the rest of the country that involve the local community.

- **Khmer Detours** (tel. 088/8969-093, www.khmerdetours.com) offers standard tours to the temples and other nearby attractions, mostly on or around Tonlé Sap Lake.

SOUVENIRS

In the unlikely event that you are offered anything that looks like an antique or a genuine artifact from the Angkor era, refuse to purchase it; otherwise, you will become part of the international illegal trade in cultural artifacts. If you get caught at the airport with ancient carvings or even Buddha statues from the 19th century, you will certainly be arrested and charged.

Replicas of virtually every major structure or sculpture seen around the Angkor temples can be bought in Siem Reap and around some of the temples, made from virtually every material imaginable, including wood, bone, marble, and metal, and to suit all budgets. Groups of children sell drinks, wooden cowbells, T-shirts, and other small items in front of some of the ruins. They can be persistent, but bear in mind that the money they earn goes to the villages, rather than into the pockets of businesspeople and the government. A number of musical instruments, including drums, an ingenious mouth harp made from bamboo, and a fiddle with the sound body usually covered in snakeskin, are also offered in front of some of the temples.

APSARA, the nongovernmental organization in charge of the temples, has been making efforts to get rid of unregistered vendors and has even banned some older local monks from entering Angkor Wat, arguing that they might scare visitors.

Angkor Wat and Angkor Thom

The massive temple complex of Angkor Wat and the walled royal city of Angkor Thom are the centerpieces of what is left of the Khmer Empire today. They are also the main attractions for the millions of tourists that flock to Cambodia each year. The Angkor Archaeological Park contains other outstanding gems, but the sheer bombast of Angkor Wat and the vast dimensions of the greatest of the Cambodian royal capitals are hard to beat for grandeur and projection of absolute power. Consequently, Angkor Wat can be extremely busy in season; the same goes for the Bayon, the heart of Angkor Thom. It may be best to visit these sites very early in the morning or at sunset to avoid the large tour groups.

★ ANGKOR WAT

អង្គរវត្ត

Angkor Wat, a Hindu temple or mausoleum, is the **largest religious building in the world,** and with the pyramids and the Taj Mahal is one of the most beautifully impressive structures ever built. Thousands of people labored for three decades to create this magnificent dream in stone. But this 12th-century temple is much more than its sublime architecture can convey: It is the heart and soul of Cambodia.

Many Cambodians have never had an opportunity to visit Angkor Wat, yet the temple represents the country's heritage and culture for every Khmer. Angkor Wat has been on every national flag in one shape or another since 1863. Since the mid-1990s, it has also become one of the world's best-known and most visited tourist sites. Angkor Wat means "royal monastery city," which is probably a variation on the Sanskrit word *nagara,* which means capital. The word *wat* is Thai for temple, and the term was probably added when the building became Buddhist.

The sheer size of Angkor Wat, more than anything else, throws the first-time visitor.

The **moat** is 1.5 by 1.3 kilometers long and 200 meters wide, and it still carries water today. Simply walking around the complex takes a couple of hours. The vastness of Angkor Wat makes it difficult to guess its exact shape, even as you stand on the **causeway** in front of the entry towers (take a few steps to the left, off the terrace that marks the start of the causeway, and you will be able to see all five towers). The causeway is 250 meters long and 12 meters wide. Without the benefit of elevation, though, it's hard to fathom just how far—and in which directions—the building spreads out. The view from Phnom Bakheng gives visitors a pretty good idea as to its size. The rectangular shape of the temple is spread across 210 hectares.

Angkor Wat was built during and perhaps beyond the reign of Suryavarman II (1113-1150) and is thought to have served as a temple or a mausoleum. The latter is more likely, as Khmer temple gates usually face east; at Angkor, the main gate faces west.

Angkor Wat is a classic temple-mountain, a replica of the Hindu universe. The five towers represent the different peaks of Mount Meru, home to the Hindu pantheon, which sits in the center of the universe. The walls surrounding the sanctuary stand for the mountain ranges at the edge of the world. The moat symbolizes the cosmic ocean. Angkor Wat was dedicated to Shiva, and many of the temple's proportions and architectural elements correspond to aspects of Hindu cosmology. Like many other classic-era Khmer temples, Angkor Wat was built from sandstone blocks and laterite.

After crossing the causeway, visitors reach the outer enclosure running along the western side of the compound in the shape of a gallery, pierced by five entrances. Three towers, partially collapsed, sit on top of the enclosure. Underneath the central tower, a *gopura* (entrance hall) serves as an antechamber to the inner courtyard of the enclosure. Immediately

Angkor Wat

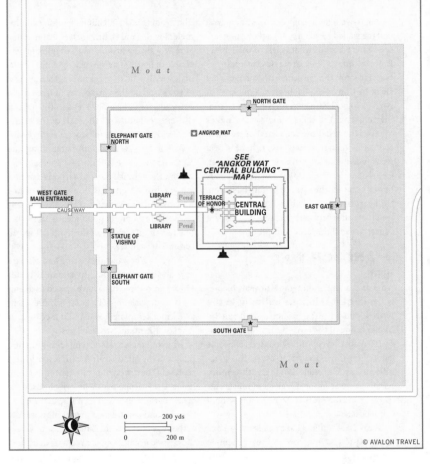

Moat

NORTH GATE

ANGKOR WAT

ELEPHANT GATE
NORTH

SEE
"ANGKOR WAT
CENTRAL BULDING"
MAP

WEST GATE
MAIN ENTRANCE   LIBRARY   Pond
CAUSEWAY   TERRACE   CENTRAL   EAST GATE
                                 OF HONOR   BUILDING

                       LIBRARY   Pond

STATUE OF
VISHNU

ELEPHANT GATE
SOUTH

SOUTH GATE

Moat

0   200 yds
0   200 m

© AVALON TRAVEL

to the right, inside the enclosure, rests a large **statue of the Buddha,** usually with a couple of old women in attendance lighting incense. As you step through the *gopura,* Angkor Wat rises straight ahead, at the end of another raised promenade, 350 meters long and 9 meters wide, that leads across open ground past two small **libraries** and a couple of **lotus ponds.** The magnitude of the building really becomes obvious as you approach the sanctuary along this promenade. The pond on the right usually contains more water than

the one on the left and is a great place to get atmospheric shots of Angkor in the late afternoon. Locals offer visitors the chance to sit on a horse and have their picture taken. Surprisingly, they get quite a few customers.

Angkor Wat is built on three levels, each one smaller and higher than the last, culminating in the 65-meter-tall central tower.

First Level

The **Terrace of Honor** connects the promenade to the first level, which is framed by galleries on all sides facing outward. The galleries contain incredible bas-reliefs that cover almost all of the inner wall space. Ignoring those for the moment and approaching from the promenade and walking straight on toward the central tower, visitors pass by two inner galleries, both in the shape of a cross.

To the left, the **Hall of Echoes** has great acoustics, if you manage to get a moment alone inside. To the right, the **Gallery of a Thousand Buddhas** did once contain many Buddha statues from the 14th century, a time when the Khmer Empire had permanently converted to Buddhism.

Beyond these two galleries, four courtyards with basins for ritual bathing feature windows with stone balusters made to look as if they'd been carved from wood, as well as a frieze of *apsaras.* The pillars around the pools feature Khmer and Sanskrit inscriptions.

BAS-RELIEFS

One of the highlights of visiting Angkor Wat, if not Cambodia, are the bas-reliefs all around the galleries. Two meters high, this narrative in stone covers 1,200 square meters with kings and battles, gods and demons, heaven and hell, and the greatest stories from Hindu mythology.

Like a graphic novel for giants, drawn with incredible grace and an amazing eye for detail and atmosphere, the bas-reliefs are like a window into another world. The pillars that support the gallery roofs at regular intervals throw shadow patterns across the images that only enhance their energy. The bas-reliefs of Angkor Wat are truly a repository of sublime art, a testament to human creativity. Some of the bas-reliefs look like they have been polished. This could be due to them having been painted or because many people have run their hands over them.

Moving counterclockwise from the Terrace of Honor:

The Battle of Kurukshetra: The southern part of the western gallery depicts the battle of Kurukshetra, part of the *Mahabharata,* a Hindu epic, in which the clans of Kaurava and Pandava annihilate each other. The two armies march toward one another from opposite ends of the bas-relief and clash in its center among elephants and chariots ridden by officers. Arrows fly in all directions, and troops are engaged in bloody close-quarters combat.

Scenes from the *Ramayana* (southwest): The pavilion on the southwestern corner contains a bas-relief depicting scenes from

Angkor Wat

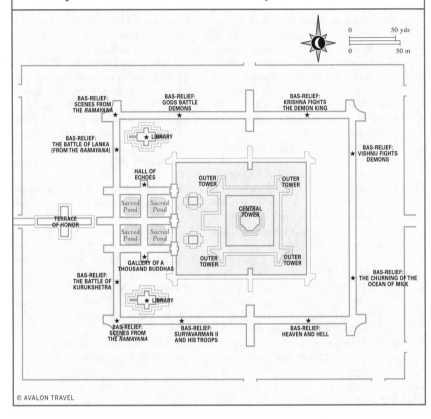

Angkor Wat Central Building

0   50 yds

0   50 m

BAS-RELIEF:
SCENES FROM
THE *RAMAYANA*

BAS-RELIEF:
GODS BATTLE
DEMONS

BAS-RELIEF:
KRISHNA FIGHTS
THE DEMON KING

BAS-RELIEF:
THE BATTLE OF LANKA
(FROM THE *RAMAYANA*)

LIBRARY

BAS-RELIEF:
VISHNU FIGHTS
DEMONS

HALL OF
ECHOES

OUTER
TOWER

OUTER
TOWER

Sacred Pond   *Sacred Pond*

CENTRAL
TOWER

TERRACE
OF HONOR

Sacred Pond   *Sacred Pond*

GALLERY OF A
THOUSAND BUDDHAS

OUTER
TOWER

OUTER
TOWER

BAS-RELIEF:
THE BATTLE OF
KURUKSHETRA

LIBRARY

BAS-RELIEF:
THE CHURNING OF THE
OCEAN OF MILK

BAS-RELIEF:
SCENES FROM
THE *RAMAYANA*

BAS-RELIEF:
SURYAVARMAN II
AND HIS TROOPS

BAS-RELIEF:
HEAVEN AND HELL

© AVALON TRAVEL

the *Ramayana,* another famous Hindu epic (the Khmer version is the *Reamker*), including Krishna lifting Mount Govardhana in order to defeat Indra. Some of the bas-reliefs in this pavilion were damaged by leaks.

Suryavarman II and His Troops: The western part of the southern gallery features a historical scene, with Suryavarman II, the Khmer king who built Angkor Wat, sitting under royal parasols, inspecting his army and getting ready for battle.

Heaven and Hell: The eastern part of the southern gallery is nothing short of brutal. Yama, the god of hell, judges and divides mankind into those who move upward to heaven or downward, through a trap door,

into hell, where they are tortured, maimed, and killed over and over. The scenes of men with whips pushing endless lines of the condemned ahead of them seem like macabre visions of Cambodia's more recent past.

The Churning of the Ocean of Milk: On the southern side of the eastern gallery, the greatest of all the bas-reliefs depicts one of the most important Hindu myths: the churning of the ocean of milk. Ninety-two *asuras* (demons) on the left and eighty-eight *devas* (gods) on the right grab the serpent Vasuki at opposite ends and pull back and forth for 1,000 years as they try to produce *amrita,* the nectar of immortality. The serpent coils around Mount Meru, which serves as the implement to churn the ocean. Gods and demons stretch across the entire panel. Above them, *apsaras* dance in the heavens. A four-armed Vishnu dances in the center of the panel. A demon king holds the head of the serpent while the god of monkeys, Hanuman, holds its tail high over the *devas'* heads. Below the temple mount and the dancing Vishnu, Kurma, a reincarnation of Vishnu in the shape of a tortoise, provides a solid base in the churning ocean for Mount Meru to rest on. Mythical sea creatures swim around the bottom of the panel.

Vishnu Fights Demons: The northern part of the eastern gallery depicts Vishnu doing battle with innumerable demons. This bas-relief is most likely from a later date, probably produced in the 16th century, and is somewhat less sublime than the main panels in this gallery, but still captivating.

Krishna Fights the Demon King: The eastern part of the northern gallery shows Krishna riding a *garuda,* a mythical half-man, half-bird figure. Bana, the demon king, arrives from the opposite side. Krishna is stopped short by a burning city, Bana's home, but finally overcomes the demon with the help of the *garuda,* who manages to extinguish the flame.

Gods Battle Demons: On the western side of the northern gallery, a battle between gods and demons rages. The 21 Brahman gods all ride their traditional mounts—such as Brahma riding a goose and Vishnu mounted on a *garuda.*

Scenes from the *Ramayana* (northwest): In the northwestern pavilion, as in the southwestern pavilion, scenes from the *Ramayana* are played out, including a depiction of Vishnu with his wife Lakshmi by his feet and numerous *apsaras* floating above his head.

The Battle of Lanka: The northern part of the western gallery displays a key scene from the *Ramayana,* the battle of Lanka, in which Rama fights with the demon king Ravana in order to claim his wife, who has been abducted to Lanka. In order to win the fierce battle, Rama calls upon the services of Hanuman, god of the monkeys, who attacks Ravana as the demon god rides a huge chariot and commands an army of brutal warriors. Once past this amazing tableau, the Terrace of Honor is just ahead.

Second Level

Moving east from the galleries on the first level, steps lead to the second level. Its outside

detail of battle scene on bas-relief, Angkor Wat

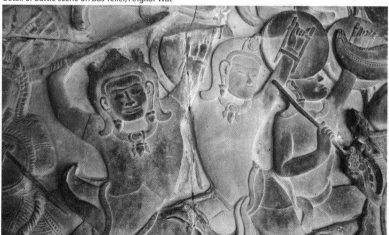

wall is undecorated, but on the inside, more than 1,500 *apsaras* vie for the attention of everyone passing. Alone or in small groups, each of the celestial dancers is slightly different from the next; it is hard to imagine a space more intent on celebrating the sensuousness of female beauty.

Third Level

The third level was off-limits to all but the king and his high priest. It forms the base that the five towers, which represent the peaks of Mount Meru, stand on, with four of the towers on the corners and the fifth right in the center.

The views from the very top reveal the symmetrical nature of the temple complex and reinforce what a wonder this building is. The third level is framed by an open gallery, which affords great views across the surrounding forest. Libraries, courtyards, and stairways surround the central tower, which rises 42 meters above the third level, and 65 meters above the ground. Originally, the small sanctuary underneath the tower housed a statue of Vishnu. Today, locals light incense in front of a contemporary Buddha statue here.

The stairs up the **central tower,** which ascend at an awe-inspiring 40-degree angle, were closed for many years after several accidents, but have recently been reopened. It is now once more possible to get to the very top of Cambodia's greatest monument, via a wooden stairway. Visiting time at the top is limited to 15 minutes, and it is likely that you'll have to wait in line. But the views are worth the effort and the wait.

★ ANGKOR THOM

អង្គរធំ

The crowning achievement of Jayavarman VII, the greatest of all the Khmer kings, was the construction of Angkor Thom, his "Great City," in the late 12th and early 13th centuries. Spread over an area of 10 square kilometers, surrounded by an 8-meter-high laterite wall, 3 kilometers long on each side, as well as a 100-meter-wide moat, this massive settlement is likely to have once supported a population of some one million people. Incidentally, the city walls can be walked. There are well-worn **trails on top of the walls,** and while some cycling tour companies use these shady forested trails, there's hardly anyone else around. At the corners of the city walls, small **watchtowers** make for great and very quiet resting places. Tour groups never come this way. The easiest way to get up onto the city wall is to head for the

devatas, inner courtyard, Angkor Wat

Angkor Thom

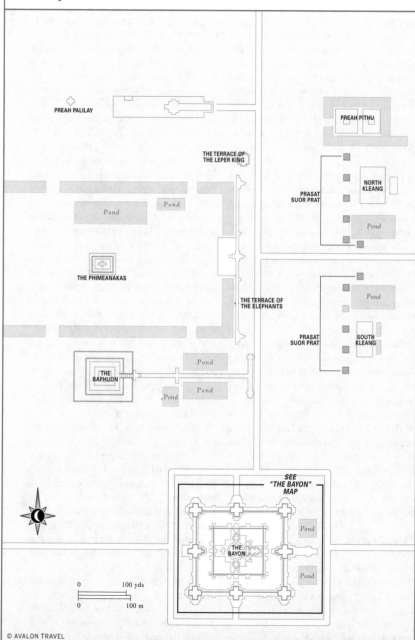

PREAH PALILAY

PREAH PITHU

THE TERRACE OF
THE LEPER KING

PRASAT
SUOR PRAT

NORTH
KLEANG

Pond

Pond

Pond

THE PHIMEANAKAS

THE TERRACE OF
THE ELEPHANTS

PRASAT
SUOR PRAT

Pond

SOUTH
KLEANG

Pond

Pond

THE
BAPHUON

Pond

Pond

SEE
"THE BAYON"
MAP

Pond

THE
BAYON

Pond

0   100 yds

0   100 m

© AVALON TRAVEL

South Gate. To the left of the gate, a small trail leads up onto the wall and then along it, with the moat on the left and forest on the right.

Visitors enter Angkor Thom via wide causeways that lead through five giant gates, crowned by *gopuras,* facing the cardinal directions (the eastern wall has two gates, the East Gate and the Gate of Victory, which connects the temple of Ta Prohm to the Terrace of the Leper King and the Terrace of the Elephants), with four impassive faces of the bodhisattva, the enlightened one, staring at everyone arriving and departing.

The causeways are lined by two balustrades formed by 54 gods on the left and 54 demons on the right, with each group holding a *naga* snake, a reference to the Churning of the Ocean of Milk, the Hindu myth at the heart of Khmer culture. The roads running through the main gates all lead toward the Bayon, at the very center of Angkor Thom. The entire city is a representation of the Hindu universe, with the walls and moat symbolizing the mountain ranges and cosmic ocean surrounding Mount Meru.

The royal entourage, from the king down to the priests and generals, lived within the city walls, while the commoners lived in wooden houses, probably much like traditional Khmer houses today, beyond the outer enclosure.

In the heart of Angkor Thom, the **Terrace of the Elephants** and the **Terrace of the Leper King** are most likely the foundations of a palace complex. The royal buildings were built of wood, and no one is sure what they looked like. Nevertheless, the structures that are left hint at the grandeur of Angkor Thom, the last great capital of the Khmer Empire.

The Bayon

 បាយ័ន

More than 200 faces on 54 towers stare down at the world with what the French termed the *sourire khmer* (Khmer smile). Ambivalent, compassionate, and cruel at the same time, enigmatic for its mystery, the smile follows every visitor around the temple building, which is second in popularity only to Angkor Wat.

Some researchers believe the faces belong to the bodhisattva Avalokitshvara. Others think they represent the king himself: powerful, terrible, and compassionate, his eyes set on even the most remote parts of a vast kingdom at any given time. Perhaps both interpretations are true. What's certain is that visitors can feel the stares of the impassive faces wherever they are inside the Bayon. Jayavarman VII was truly a Big Brother of antiquity.

The history of the Bayon is shrouded in as much mystery as the famous smiles on its towers. The temple was built on top of an older structure and was initially dated to the 9th century. It was discovered to be a Buddhist structure in 1925, and the fact that the Bayon is at the exact center of the great city also eluded visitors for a long time. After the death of Jayavarman VII, who followed Mahayana Buddhism, the temple served as a Hindu and later Theravada Buddhist institution.

The Bayon is built on three levels. Incredible bas-reliefs cover some of the walls of the first and second levels, while the third level is dominated by the 54 towers and the central sanctuary. On the **first level,** an outer gallery is marked by eight *gopuras,* four of them at each corner and another four constructed at the middle point of each gallery. Inside the gallery of the first level, a couple of libraries can be found in the eastern courtyards.

The **second level** is bordered by another gallery, marked by four towers on the corners and four *gopuras,* again at the middle point of each gallery. Quite a bit of the second level has collapsed, and as you scramble across boulders and take small detours, it's easy to lose your orientation. Restoration work may also make access to some areas of the second level a little difficult.

The **third level** is circular in shape, unusual in Khmer temple architecture, and contains the **faces of the bodhisattva Avalokitshvara** arranged around the temple's central sanctuary.

The Bayon

TOWER

TOWER

TOWER

BAS-RELIEF: ★
WAR WITH SIEM AND
ROYAL PROCESSION

BAS-RELIEF:
MILITARY PROCESSION
AND HERMIT WITH TIGER ★

BAS-RELIEF:
MILITARY PROCESSION ★

TOWER

TOWER

TOWER

TOWER

TOWER

TOWER

TOWER

TOWER

BAS-RELIEF: ★
CHURNING OF THE
OCEAN OF MILK

BAS-RELIEF:
SHIVA ON LOTUS ★

SANCTUARY

BAS-RELIEF: ★
CIRCUS AND ANIMALS

BAS-RELIEF:
SCENES FROM THE
MAHABHARATA ★

STORY OF THE
LEPER KING ★

BAS-RELIEF:
NAVAL BATTLE ★
AND DAILY LIFE

LIBRARY

LIBRARY

TOWER/BAS-RELIEF:
WOODEN PALACE ★

BAS-RELIEF:
WAR WITH THE CHAM ★

TOWER/EAST GATE

BAS-RELIEF: ★
BATTLE WITH
THE CHAM

TOWER/BAS-RELIEF:
PROCESSION OF WARRIORS ★

STEPS

Pond

Pond

© AVALON TRAVEL

0   20 yds
0   20 m

BAS-RELIEFS

The incredible bas-reliefs of the Bayon stretch for some 1.2 kilometers. The Bayon's main entrance faces east, and the main bas-reliefs are briefly described starting from here, moving clockwise, with the bas-reliefs on the right.

First Level

The bas-reliefs on the first level were accessible to ordinary people and offer visitors a rare glimpse of what daily life for Cambodians must have been like during the Angkor era. Perhaps they served educational purposes: to inform the people of the merits of Buddhism. Some bas-reliefs were never finished.

War with the Cham: The southern part of the eastern gallery is divided into three tiers and shows the Cambodian army on its way home, victorious after fighting the Cham. On the lowest tier, the army, moving on elephants and oxcarts and accompanied by musicians, returns to Angkor. On the far right, Chinese traders can be seen. In the middle tier, fallen soldiers are returned home, and on the top tier, Jayavarman VII, protected by a parasol, heads a procession, along with his commanders, on the back of an elephant.

Wooden Palace: The southeast corner pavilion contains unfinished bas-reliefs of a wooden palace and a boat.

Naval Battle and Daily Life: The eastern part of the southern gallery is dedicated to the naval battle between the Khmer and the Cham that took place on Tonlé Sap Lake in 1177. On the right, most easterly panel, hunters, men playing chess, women searching for head lice, and musicians are depicted on a lower tier. On the left panel, the battle is fierce, and some soldiers are eaten by crocodiles after they have fallen into the water. On a lower tier, a woman gives birth, food is prepared, and another game of chess is in progress.

Military Procession: The western part of the southern gallery was never completed, although it does show a military procession, complete with crossbow-wielding soldiers mounted on elephants, as well as a sophisticated catapult on wheels.

Military Procession and Hermit with Tiger: The southern part of the western gallery is unfinished and shows a military procession passing through mountainous countryside as well as a hermit climbing a tree to escape an attacking tiger. Farther on, a standoff between two crowds is about to spill over into violence.

War with Siem and Royal Procession:

faces of the bodhisattva, Bayon temple

The northern part of the western gallery contains scenes of close-up fighting between the Khmer and the Siamese, as well as a procession of the king on his way to meditate in the forest.

Circus and Animals: The northern gallery features a circus in its far-right corner, including jugglers and acrobats, while the royal court looks on. A procession of animals includes the now-extinct rhinoceros as well as a pig, a rabbit, a deer, a fish, and a lobster. There's also a scene of meditating holy men in the forest and a group of women by a river receiving gifts.

Procession of Warriors: The northeast corner pavilion features yet another procession of warriors and their pachyderm rides.

Khmer Battle with the Cham: In the northern section of the eastern gallery, the Khmer appear to be gaining on the Cham in battle, and even the elephants rip into each other.

Second Level

The bas-reliefs on the second inner level were accessible only to the king and his priests and feature scenes from Hindu mythology as well as a few depictions of battle and everyday life. Given that Jayavarman VII introduced Mahayana Buddhism to the Khmer Empire, this seems somewhat incongruous. But many things about the Bayon are not fully understood yet. The bas-reliefs on the second level appear either to predate the rest of the temple by several hundred years—and were from the time of Yasovarman I, a Hindu king who ruled at the end of the 9th century—or they postdate Jayavarman VII's reign and were placed in the Bayon by Jayavarman VIII, a Hindu king, during the late 13th century. The panels of the inner galleries, separated by doors and towers, are smaller, are not in as good condition, and are more fragmented than those on the outside.

Starting from the eastern entrance again, some of the highlights include several depictions of **Shiva** in the southern gallery; the **Churning of the Ocean of Milk** in the northern part of the western gallery; Shiva in

several **scenes from the *Mahabharata*** on the eastern side of the northern gallery; and the **story of the leper king,** which depicts a king being bitten while fighting a snake, then being observed and treated by a holy man and surrounded by women who examine his hands—just to the right of the main entrance in the eastern gallery.

The Baphuon

ប្រាសាទបាពួន

A classic temple-mountain representing Mount Neru, the Baphuon was built in the 11th century, and therefore precedes Angkor Thom. Originally a Hindu temple dedicated to Shiva, the Baphuon adjoins the royal palace enclosure. Its base measures 120 meters by 100 meters, and it is about 35 meters tall, minus its tower, which has collapsed. On its western side's second level, a reclining Buddha, 9 meters tall and 70 meters long, was constructed in the 16th century.

In the 1960s, the EFEO began the huge reconstruction process, using the method of anastylosis, a technique that calls for the total dismantling and subsequent rebuilding of a structure. Unfortunately, by the time the Khmer Rouge made work on the temple impossible in 1972, this immense undertaking was unfinished, and the plans were lost in the chaos that ensued. What was left was a sea of stones lying around in a loosely organized fashion.

The challenge of rebuilding the temple was taken up again in 1995, and the Baphuon reopened fully restored in 2011.

The Phimeanakas

ភិមានអាកាស

The Phimeanakas is a 10th-century temple-mountain close to the royal palace area of Angkor Thom. The central tower has collapsed, and the three original levels were long ago looted of their architectural subtleties. The royal enclosure is also largely in ruins. The royal palace would have been built of wood, and there's no consensus on what it might have looked like.

The Terrace of the Elephants

This 350-meter-long terrace was once covered in wooden pavilions. From here, Jayavarman VII could inspect his troops as they marched into Angkor Thom from the Victory Gate. The terrace takes its name from the carved elephants on its eastern side, and it faces a central square where the troops would have marched in procession.

Carvings of lions and *garudas* can be found on the middle section of the terrace's retaining wall.

The Terrace of the Leper King

The jury is still out as to whether the 15th-century statue found on top of this platform to the north of the Terrace of the Elephants is a Khmer king with leprosy or Yama, the Hindu god of death. The outer walls of the terrace are covered in bas-reliefs of mythical beings and *apsaras*. The structure might have served as the royal crematorium. Most interestingly, there is a hidden inner wall on the terrace's south side. Visitors can walk along a narrow corridor crammed with several tiers of carved scenes in pristine condition, including *apsaras, nagas,* kings and demonic dancers, elephants, and a river with fish.

Other Structures

Many other ruins are dotted around the enormous enclosure of Angkor Thom. **Preah Palilay,** erected during the reign of Jayavarman VII, is a small, atmospheric Buddhist temple with a chimney-like tower located north of the royal enclosure. Facing the Terrace of the Elephants across the central square, two so-called **kleangs** (the somewhat misleading Khmer word for storeroom) may have once served as royal guesthouses. The *kleangs* are older than Angkor Thom and were probably built in the 10th century. They are fronted by **Prasat Suor Prat,** a series of 12 laterite towers. Also built by Jayavarman VII, the towers once housed sacred statues or linga.

To the north of the *kleangs,* **Preah Pithu** is a group of five small temples, most of them Buddhist. Not too many visitors bother to come here, and the atmosphere is very peaceful and relaxed.

The Temples of Angkor

While most visitors are understandably drawn to Angkor Wat and Angkor Thom, those monuments only tell part of the story. There are countless other important and spectacular structures within the Angkor Archaeological Park that give insight to the power and architectural eloquence of the Khmer Empire. Must-sees include the *Tomb Raider* temple Ta Prohm, which once had some 80,000 employees; the red sandstone citadel of women, Banteay Srei, which sports some of the most sublime carvings of the Angkor era; and the rather less visited but no less impressive, sprawling Preah Khan, with its countless corridors. Many smaller structures are also worth exploring, not least because they are free of large tour groups.

PHNOM BAKHENG

វត្តភ្នំបាខែង

Wat Bakheng was the very first temple-mountain constructed in the Angkor area. Dating back to the late 9th century, this Hindu temple marked the move from the smaller capitals around Roluos and sat at the heart of the royal capital of Yasodharapura. The temple's base is carved from the mountain itself, and the climb up the front stairway is steep. Nevertheless, Wat Bakheng is the **most popular sunset spot** in the Angkor Archaeological Park and attracts thousands of visitors every night because of its fine views of Tonlé Sap Lake and Angkor Wat peeking out of the surrounding forest. Since 2013, authorities restrict visitor numbers to the temple at sunset, and in high season travelers sometimes have to book access in advance. Skip the evening rush hour and come here first thing in the morning instead.

Elephant rides to the top (US$20) are available. Rumors of an escalator to be constructed have persisted for years; let's hope it will never happen.

BAKSEI CHAMKRONG
បក្សីចាំក្រុង

Located north of Phnom Bakheng, Baksei Chamkrong is a small but attractive pyramid-shaped temple built in the mid-10th century, just after the Khmer capital returned from Koh Ker to the Angkor area. The structure was originally dedicated to Shiva. Built from bricks and laterite, it has some sandstone decorations and is 12 meters tall.

Baksei Chamkrong means "the bird who shelters under its wings," a reference to a story about a Khmer king trying to flee Angkor as his city was besieged by a foreign army. A giant bird suddenly swooped from the sky and took the king under its wings, protecting him from the onslaught.

THOMANON
ធម្មនន្ទ

A contemporary of Angkor Wat, the small but graciously designed Thomanon was built in the early 12th century during the reign of Suryavarman II, and similarities are especially apparent in the design of the towers. Extensive restoration work in the 1960s did wonders for this Hindu temple, located on the left side of the road, just outside the Victory Gate on the way to Ta Keo.

CHAOSAY TEVODA
ចៅសាយទេវតា

Just across the road from the Thomanon, this small temple has a similar floor plan and looks like it was built in conjunction with it. In fact, Chaosay Tevoda was built some years later. It features additional *gopuras* and a library, and it is slowly being restored.

TA KEO
តាកែវ

A few hundred meters east of the Victory Gate, Ta Keo is a towering, unadorned temple pyramid that rises above the canopy of the surrounding forest. Built in the early 11th century during the reign of Jayavarman V from massive sandstone blocks, Ta Keo, facing east and dedicated to Shiva, was never completed, for reasons unknown. The total lack of decoration, bas-relief or otherwise, gives

Phnom Bakheng at sunset

Angkor from the Air

For a totally different view of the temples, try Angkor from above. There are three different possibilities to see Angkor from the air, each with their own merits. The most straightforward way is to search for the **yellow balloon** (tel. 012/520-810) that is tethered near Angkor Wat, on the road to the airport, and jump board. The balloon (US$15 pp) rises to a height of 200 meters, and the views of Angkor Wat, Phnom Bakheng, and the surrounding countryside are impressive.

More impressive still are the 40-minute balloon rides around the temples offered by **Angkor Hot Air Ballooning** (tel. 069/558-888, www.angkorballooning.com). Flights (US$125 pp) are offered daily around 6:10am and 5pm, weather permitting. Operators pick customers up at their hotels or guesthouses and drop them off again following the flight.

Far more exclusive but even more breathtaking is a ride in a helicopter. Two outfits currently offer scenic flights (from US$90 pp). **Helistar Cambodia** (tel. 063/966-072, www.helistarcambodia.com) and **Helicopters Cambodia** (tel. 012/814-500, www.helicopterscambodia.com), a New Zealand outfit with an excellent safety record, are both based at the airport. They are not cheap, but it is quite an experience.

Finally, if you have high-altitude vertigo, a ride on an **elephant** (US$10-20 for 30 minutes) may suffice. You still get better views than on foot, but the height is more manageable. During the day, elephants can be hired around the Bayon and the South Gate of Angkor Thom. In the afternoon, they tend to move to Phnom Bakheng in order to take visitors to this hilltop temple for the sunset.

---

this temple a unique and singularly powerful appearance—it seems built like a fortress. Nevertheless, the steep climb to the top, via any of the four stairways at the cardinal points, is worth the effort. The views across the trees are great, and the ambience among the five towers up top is somehow quietly dignified, perhaps because not very many people come up here.

★ TA PROHM

តាព្រហ្ម

More than any other major monument in the Angkor Archaeological Park, Ta Prohm is a trip back in time. When the French began to push the forest back from the ruins at the beginning of the 20th century, the EFEO decided, for aesthetic reasons, that one temple should be left in its forest context, just the way French explorers had stumbled upon the ruins some 50 years earlier. That's the reason some scenes of the movie *Tomb Raider* were shot inside the temple.

Of course, much work has been done on this huge, sprawling temple complex, and the forest around the site has long been well managed—though several large silk cottonwood and strangler fig trees have enormous roots sprouting across boulders and galleries, giving the site its unique *Lost World* feel.

Ta Prohm is a very handsome temple, built in the late 12th and early 13th centuries by the greatest of the Khmer kings, Jayavarman VII, to serve as a Mahayana Buddhism monastery and university. The rectangular temple complex is not a temple-mountain like Angkor Wat and is therefore not built in ascending levels. The temple sanctuary is surrounded by five walls and a series of long, low buildings. The outermost laterite wall is 1,000 by 700 meters long, and the entire complex covers 650,000 square meters.

In the 13th century, Ta Prohm was home to more than 12,000 people, including 18 high priests, 2,700 officials, and more than 600 dancers—with another 80,000 people living in 3,000 villages outside its walls to provide services. But the temple's possessions extended well beyond serfdom: Ta Prohm's vaults were said to hold more than 500 kilograms of golden dishes, 35 diamonds, 40,000 pearls, and 500 silk beds.

The monastic study center was a powerful concern indeed. Four *gopuras*, with heads

Ta Prohm

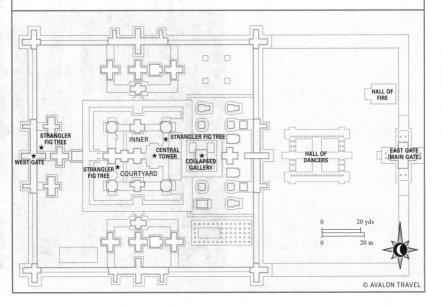

similar to those on top of the towers at the Bayon, provided access through the outermost wall into the complex, although today only the east and west entrances are open. Access is generally from the west, so most visitors get in via the back door. Have your driver drop you off at the **eastern** *gopura* and enter the temple the way it was designed to be entered.

Much of the ground between the fifth and fourth wall is overgrown by brush and large trees, but in its time, it must have been a small city, with wooden homes for the many staff. Two moats, on both sides of the fourth wall, have long been dry.

There are few bas-reliefs on the walls of Ta Prohm. Scholars speculate that these might have been destroyed following Jayavarman VII's death and Angkor's reconversion to Hinduism, although there are some carvings of Buddhist iconography. Some of the *apsaras* had their heads cut off by looters many years ago. Several independent buildings stand freely within the complex. In the outermost enclosure, a **Hall of Fire,** a rest house or the

home of a sacred flame, stands alone to the east of the sanctuary. In the eastern part of the fourth enclosure, a **Hall of Dancers,** a structure Jayavarman VII had built in several of his temple complexes, features carvings of dancing *apsaras*. The central sanctuary is entirely unadorned. Its walls may have once been covered in silver.

But it's not so much the temple itself, although it is vast and gracious, as the interplay between stone and forest that impresses visitors so much. And as many walls, corridors, and galleries have collapsed because of the forest's intrusion, the temple's layout does not become apparent because of the circuitous route visitors must take. Several stretches of ground within the three central enclosures are so strewn with boulders that wooden walkways have been erected to make progress easier, and visitors are strongly discouraged from climbing across collapsed walls. As Ta Prohm is afforded more shade by the forest than the other major monuments, the temple is not a bad place to visit when the sun is high.

In October 2011, international media reported that Indian archaeologists had found a massive Buddha statue, 2.4 meters in height, with its head missing, that had been entwined with the roots of a tree and become unearthed in heavy rains. It is the largest such find in the Angkor Archaeological Park in some 80 years. The statue, which could also have been modeled on Angkor god-king and builder of Ta Prohm, Jayavarman VII, rests on a base of *naga* snakes, dates from the 12th century, and was originally about four meters in height.

The scholar Claude Jacques remarked that Ta Prohm, more than any other Khmer temple, tempted writers into descriptive excess. Enough said.

BANTEAY KDEI

បន្ទាយក្តី

Just southeast of Ta Prohm, Banteay Kdei, built during the reign of Jayavarman VII, is yet another temple complex that served as a monastery. Due to inferior building materials, large parts of this temple have collapsed, and much of the Buddhist imagery was vandalized in the 13th century following the death of Jayavarman VII and the brief return of Angkor to Hinduism.

Banteay Kdei lies directly opposite Sra Srang, a reservoir that holds water year-round. In the dry season, a small island temple can be seen poking through the water's surface.

PRASAT KRAVAN

ប្រាសាទក្រវាន់

This 10th-century Hindu temple was reconstructed by the French in the 19th century and sports its five original towers. Located to the south of Ta Prohm on the road back to Angkor Wat, Prasat Kravan was built from brick. Its interiors feature the only brick bas-reliefs in the Angkor area—notably depictions of Vishnu riding a *garuda* in the central tower and Lakshmi holding the trident of Shiva and the discus of Vishnu in the northernmost tower. Few visitors stop here, and while it's not the most atmospheric location, the bas-reliefs are worth checking out.

Ta Prohm

PRE RUP

ប្រែរូប

Situated south of the Eastern Baray, Pre Rup, along with the Eastern Mebon, was one of the first temples built by King Rajendravarman II after the capital moved back to Angkor from Koh Ker in the late 10th century. Pre Rup, Rajendravarman II's state temple, is a classic temple-mountain, dedicated to Shiva, with five towers on a raised platform.

Built from red brick, laterite, and sandstone, the temple sits amid two enclosure walls. Within the walls, the temple rests on a main platform built on three levels. Right in front of the temple within the outer wall and facing east, six **towers** flank the entrance. One tower, on the immediate right as you enter the complex, might never have been built or has been demolished. The second enclosure is entered via four small *gopuras* at the cardinal points and contains several **long houses,** perhaps resting places for pilgrims. Two **libraries** with large towers are located just inside the

Pre Rup

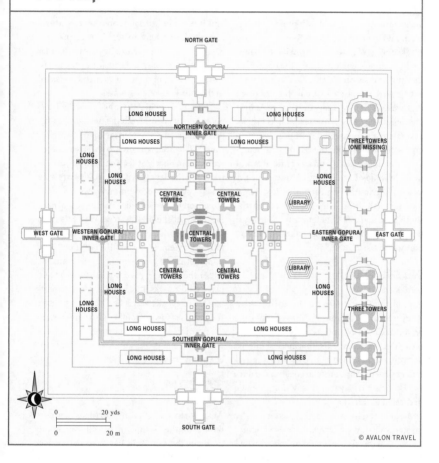

courtyard entered through the **eastern gopura.**

The central platform of Pre Rup, split into three levels, is accessed via four stairways leading up from the *gopuras.* Next to the stairways, stone lions stand guard. The first two levels are built from laterite, while the third, top-most level is constructed from sandstone. On the first level, numerous small shrines containing linga stand facing east. The five central towers on the third level, one in each corner and one in the center of the top platform, contain some interesting bas-reliefs,

notably Vishnu and his avatar, as well as flying *apsaras.*

EASTERN MEBON
មេបុណ្យខាងកើត

The construction of the Eastern Mebon precedes that of Pre Rup by a decade, and the similarity in building style is obvious. The Eastern Mebon was the very first temple constructed by Rajendravarman II after the Khmer capital moved back from Koh Ker to Angkor, and it was dedicated to his parents. It follows the same design as Pre Rup: It is a temple-mountain dedicated to Shiva, surrounded by two walls, constructed on three levels, and crowned by five towers. The temple is built from a combination of brick, laterite, and sandstone, much like other early Angkorian structures. Impressive two-meter-high stone elephants guard the corners of the first and second levels. The towers were once covered in stucco. Today, the red brick that was originally underneath, and is best photographed in the late afternoon, is visible. Several lintels are covered in impressive carvings with themes from the Hindu pantheon.

The temple was built on an artificial island in the middle of the Eastern Baray, which is now dry. The Eastern Mebon is just 1,200 meters north of Pre Rup on a direct north-south axis, and 6,800 meters east of the royal temple-mountain of Phimeanakas on a direct east-west axis.

NEAK PEAN
 នាគព័ន្ធ

Part of the Grand Circuit, beautiful Neak Pean is small, a bit out of the way, and otherworldly. Located to the east of Preah Khan on a direct east-west axis, this modest **island temple** was designed as an oasis of peace and reflection—part of a hospital constructed during the reign of Jayavarman VII and hence dedicated to Buddha.

Neak Pean stands in the center of the Jayatataka Baray, which measured 3.5 kilometers by 900 meters and could only be reached by boat in its day. Today, the reservoir is once again flooded part of the year, and Neak Pean stands on an island within a pond reached via a long wooden walkway that leads through a stretch of flooded, sublimely beautiful forest. The pond is surrounded by four more smaller ponds. Four pavilions stand between the central pond and these smaller ponds, once used by pilgrims to absolve themselves of their sins. In each pavilion, a waterspout in the shape of a head conveyed water from the main pool into the smaller pools. There's an **elephant's head** in the northern pavilion, a **human head** in the eastern one, a **lion's head** in

the southern one, and a **horse's head** in the western one. These smaller ponds represent the elements of water, earth, wind, and fire, and it is thought that people with illnesses came to bathe here to regain their natural balance with nature. Neak Pean was a Khmer spa. The entire complex sits in a walled enclosure, which in turn is located on an island in the *baray*.

Neak Pean, which means "entwined serpents," got its name from the two *naga* snakes that coil around the central island, which is round. The heads of the two snakes are separated, facing each other and forming an entrance to the sanctuary. The **sculpture of a horse** appears to be swimming away from the temple on its eastern side. The horse is a manifestation of the bodhisattva Avalokitshvara and was rebuilt from fragments by the EFEO during the temple's restoration in the 1920s.

Sometimes a group of blind musicians sits under the bushes by the side of the pond and plays, lending this little location even more atmosphere. Neak Pean is best visited just after the rainy season in October-November when the *baray* contains a lot of water, lending the temple and its surroundings an eerie and otherworldly ambience.

TA SOM
តាសោម

Also worth a visit is the northeasternmost temple on the Grand Circuit, the small and peaceful Ta Som. Built like a miniature version of Ta Prohm and dedicated to the father of Jayavarman VII, this late-12th-century Buddhist shrine has several *gopuras* with four smiling faces on top. The eastern *gopura* is being split and crushed simultaneously by a ficus tree and makes for a great photo. Surrounded by three laterite walls, the temple is built on a single level and contains some fine carvings.

PREAH KHAN
ព្រះខ័ន

Located on the Grand Circuit and, much like Ta Prohm, left largely unrestored, Preah

Khan is a huge, sprawling temple complex of rectangular enclosures around a typically small Buddhist sanctuary. Also like Ta Prohm, the temple was built during the reign of Jayavarman VII in the late 12th and early 13th centuries and served as a center of learning and meditation. It also had an equally impressive retinue. More than 100,000 people were connected to Preah Khan, a royal city in its heyday, supporting more than 1,000 teachers as well as 1,000 dancers.

Preah Khan means "sacred sword," a reference to a sacred sword that Jayavarman II, the first Angkorian king, handed to his successor—and that was subsequently handed down from generation to generation. The words *preah khan* are Siamese, though, so the story of the sword could have originated there.

Consecrated in 1191, Preah Khan stands on two older palace complexes. The process of anastylosis, the dismantling and rebuilding of a structure, has been utilized here. In the 1930s the forest (except for the large trees) was removed, making the site much more accessible. Nevertheless, the trees around the site remain impressive, and with fewer visitors than Ta Prohm, Preah Khan is a good place to witness the interplay between stone and nature in peace.

Preah Khan was a temple of the Mahayana Buddhist sect, and many of its carvings were disfigured and destroyed following the death of Jayavarman VII and Angkor's brief return to Hinduism. Within its enclosure, Preah Khan contains many smaller, independent **Hindu shrines and temples.** The temple complex was built right to the shore of the Jayatataka Baray, to the east. It's best to enter from this side.

Preah Khan has four enclosure walls, the longest of which runs 700 by 800 meters. The complex was once surrounded by a moat and spreads across an area of some 140 hectares. This outer wall, constructed of laterite, contains sandstone sculptures of *garudas,* formerly topped by Buddhist images, destroyed long ago, at 50-meter intervals all the way around the complex. Four gates, at the cardinal points, offer access. Each entrance features a causeway crossing the moat, lined by gods and demons carrying *naga* snakes, similar to the causeways at the gates of Angkor Thom.

Visitors first come upon the **Hall of Dancers.** The lintels above the eight doorways all feature exquisite carvings of dancing *apsaras.* Just north of this building, a structure of unknown purpose has baffled scientists for decades: a **two-story**

Hall of Dancers, Preah Khan

building with no discernible stairway and round columns, similar to Greek designs and unique to Angkor. The inner enclosures around the sanctuary can appear labyrinthine, due to the many galleries, low corridors, and walls with false windows. The walls used to be covered with huge bronze plates. The inner sanctuary today is a stone stupa, which was added many years after the temple's inception.

THE WESTERN BARAY AND WESTERN MEBON
បារាយខាងលិច និង មេបុណ្យខាងលិច

The Western Baray, located a few kilometers north of Siem Reap International Airport, is an incredible 8 kilometers long by 2.3 kilometers wide and continues to carry water year-round. On weekends, it's a favorite **picnic spot.** Snacks and drinks are sold at stalls along the dam on the southern side of the reservoir. In the center of the *baray,* the Western Mebon, a small temple in poor condition built in the 11th century during the reign of Udayadityavarman, can be visited by boat and features remarkable carvings of animals. The Western Baray is off the usual temple circuits, but it's worth a visit for its local life and the lack of crowds.

THE ROLUOS GROUP
ប្រាសាទរលួស

The Roluos Group of temples, named for its proximity to the modern village of Roluos, was part of the city of Hariharalaya, the first great Khmer capital. Located some 13 kilometers southeast of Siem Reap and founded by Jayavarman II in the early 9th century, Hariharalaya was the template for the later building frenzies of the Khmer kings. It was the first royal city established in the Angkor area and remained the capital of the Khmer for 70 years. Its last ruler, Yasovarman I, was the first king to build a temple at Angkor, at Phnom Bakheng, where he moved the capital in 905. The temples of this era were built of brick and feature high and square towers on low bases. Structures such as *gopura* and libraries were first introduced during this time.

The detour to the Roluos temples is well worth the effort, and entrance fees are covered by the pass to the Angkor Archaeological Park. There are three major temples at Roluos: Preah Ko, Bakong, and Lolei, all of them dedicated to Hindu deities.

Preah Ko was one of the very first temples built at Hariharalaya, and hence one of the first temples built in the Angkor area. Its outer walls have almost gone, so the temple

approaching the Bakong

The Roluos Group

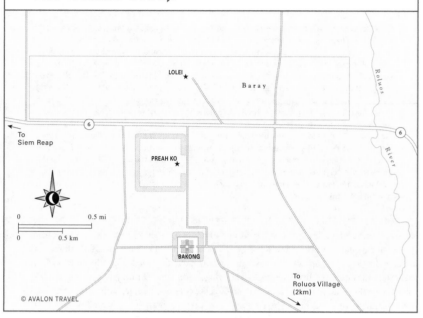

LOLEI ★

Baray

Roluos

To
Siem Reap

6

6

PREAH KO ★

River

0   0.5 mi

0   0.5 km

BAKONG

To
Roluos Village
(2km)

© AVALON TRAVEL

complex seems quite small today, but it's well worth a visit, not least for its exquisite carvings. Preah Ko means "temple of the bull," named after stone *nandis* (sacred bulls), remnants of which stand on the eastern side of the temple. Originally, the building was surrounded by a moat and traversed by causeways. Beyond the *nandis,* a brick wall, pierced by two *gopuras* to the east and west, contains the sanctuary: a low platform with six brick towers. Unlike other temples, Preah Ko does not seem to be too concerned with symmetry. The six towers are not evenly spaced, and those on the east are larger than the ones on the west. Preah Ko was dedicated to the king's ancestors, and each tower contained a Hindu deity. The carved decorations on the towers' false doors, columns, and lintels are worth checking out. The three towers on the east feature male guardians and are thought to have been dedicated to paternal ancestors, while the towers on the west have female goddesses flanking the doorways

and were most likely dedicated to maternal ancestors.

The **Bakong** was built after the death of Jayavarman II, and it became the state temple of the Khmer Empire during the reign of Indravarman I. It stood at the heart of the city of Hariharalaya. The Bakong was the first temple-mountain built by a Khmer king, and, as a temple dedicated to Shiva, its sanctuary probably contained a linga. The site is surrounded by a rectangular wall 900 meters by 700 meters long, which in turn was surrounded by a moat. Causeways lead through the outer wall, lined with *naga* balustrades. An inner wall can be passed through at four *gopuras* located at the cardinal points. The temple faces east, so it's best to enter from that side.

As at Preah Khan, there's a processional space, lined with stone serpents to pass before reaching the inner compound. Numerous well-preserved buildings stand to the left and right: libraries, *dharamshalas*, and what are

The Story of Banteay Samre

Once upon a time, a farmer named Pou, a member of the Samre community, an indigenous minority living near the Kulen mountain, got hold of seeds with supernatural powers. He planted the seeds and soon harvested the most delicious sweet cucumbers anyone had ever tasted. As a sign of respect, he took his harvest before the king, who found them so tasty that he ordered Pou to kill anyone who might enter his field. During the rainy season, the royal household ran out of cucumbers, and the king himself decided to visit Pou to get a resupply. But the king arrived at Pou's field after dark, and the farmer, thinking the monarch an intruder, killed him with a spear. Pou buried the king in the center of his field. As the king had no descendants, his advisors sought the wisdom of a Victory Elephant as to who should be the successor. The elephant promptly marched to Pou's field and identified the farmer as the rightful ruler. Pou had himself crowned, but the court dignitaries refused to show him respect: after all, he was just a Samre. Frustrated, Pou left the capital and moved to Banteay Samre. He called all the court's dignitaries, and all those who showed respect to the royal regalia of his predecessor were decapitated. Overcome by Pou's compassion, the remaining dignitaries accepted his authority, and the kingdom was ruled in harmony ever after.

assumed to be crematoriums. Set around the platform that the sanctuary stands on are eight brick towers, open to the east only, their stairways guarded by stone lions. The towers have false doors in the other directions, featuring fine carvings. The platform the sanctuary sits on is built in five levels. On the first three levels, stone elephants—they get smaller as you ascend—stand on the corners. The fourth level is dominated by 12 sandstone towers, each of which contains a linga. The sanctuary itself, a square tower with a lotus spire, was built later than the rest of the temple, probably in the 12th century.

The temple of **Lolei**, built a little later than the other two monuments at Roluos, was erected during the reign of Yasovarman I and was dedicated to Shiva. Originally, Lolei stood on an island in the middle of a huge *baray*, which helped to irrigate the area around Hariharalaya and was the first reservoir built by a Khmer king. Lolei features just four brick towers, all of them in poor and overgrown condition, but some incredible carvings and inscriptions remain. An active modern pagoda operates within the temple compound.

BANTEAY SAMRE

បន្ទាយសំរែ

Banteay Samre is a little bit out of the way

and is best visited while on the way to or from Banteay Srei. It's worth the effort, though, as the road to the temple leads through local villages and open countryside. The mid-12th-century Hindu temple, built during the reign of Suryavarman II, is located on the eastern side of the Eastern Baray and resembles Angkor Wat in style, though not in dimensions. The temple's name refers to a group or tribe of people, possibly an indigenous minority related to the Khmer, who used to live around Phnom Kulen and are mentioned in a folk story.

Banteay Samre has been reconstructed utilizing the anastylosis technique (the complete disassembling and rebuilding of a structure), and by all accounts it was just a pile of rubble prior to the restoration work. The Banteay Samre complex is square in shape and features a moat, now dry, within its outermost enclosure wall, which in turn is pierced by four *gopuras* at the cardinal points. The wall around the inner temple complex is raised above floor level and features pavilions on its four corners. It's best to enter through the eastern *gopura* into the inner part of the temple. This route leads to a platform and a long hall that in turn leads to the central sanctuary. Two libraries can be seen north and south of the hall. Banteay Samre sees relatively few visitors.

Banteay Srei

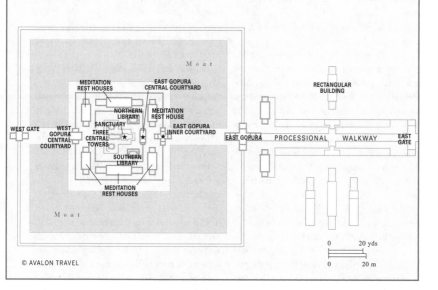

Curiously, the upper bas-reliefs of the sanctuary feature Buddhist scenes.

★ BANTEAY SREI
បន្ទាយស្រី

Banteay Srei, the "Citadel of Women," lies 38 kilometers (30-40 minutes in a tuk-tuk) from Siem Reap and is a little off the usual temple circuit. But this late-10th-century temple complex, though modest in size, is one of the highlights of the Angkor Archaeological Park and should not be missed. It features some of the **finest carvings** in the world and has been extremely well restored.

Small by the usual bombastic dimensions of Khmer monuments, Banteay Srei was built during the reign of Rajendravarman. It's the only temple known to have been built not under the authority of a king but by Yajnyavaraha, a Brahmin advisor to the king, who dedicated the complex to Shiva. Originally the site was called Tribhuvanamahesvara or Isvarapura. Banteay Srei was once enclosed by three walls and a moat, though only two walls remain today. It is best to enter through a *gopura* on the temple's east side. Before reaching the central temple compound, visitors pass along a **processional walkway** flanked by galleries, walls, and more *gopuras*. North of the walkway, a single building features a brilliant carving of **Vishnu as a man-lion.** Step into the inner compound through another *gopura* and you are facing the central part with the best carvings. All around the compound, six annex buildings may have served as **meditation rest houses.** Inside the temple compound, virtually every bit of wall space is covered in exquisite carvings. The soft red sandstone can be carved almost like wood and therefore allows for incredible detail and texture. The central shrines, three in all, were dedicated to Shiva and Vishnu and are guarded by mythical figures with human bodies and animal heads. These are replicas; the originals have been stolen or removed for safekeeping. The walls are covered with carved foliage as well as geometric patterns. The **central towers** are covered with male and female divinities. The females wear such heavy earrings that their ear lobes are elongated. The lintels above the doorways to the central sanctuary are embellished with scenes from the *Ramayana*, including the abduction of Sita.

Two **libraries** east of the central sanctuary, made of brick, laterite, and sandstone, also feature outstanding carvings. The eastern side of the northern library (on the right as you approach from the east) is decorated by depictions of Indra, god of the sky, as he scatters celestial rain across the building's eastern side, while a *naga* snake rises from the deluge. The western side depicts Krishna killing his cruel uncle, King Kamsa, as shocked women look on.

The southern library's western side is covered in carvings telling the story of Parvati trying to attract Shiva, who is in deep meditation. Parvati gets Kama, god of love, to shoot an arrow into Shiva's heart. Shiva promptly gets angry and burns Kama to ashes. He does notice Parvati, however, marries her, and brings Kama back to life. If only things were as simple in real life.

On the eastern side of the southern library, a scene from the *Ramayana* unfolds. Ravana, king of the demons of Lanka, tries to gain access to Mount Kailash, home of Shiva and Parvati. As he is barred from entering, he lifts the entire mountain and shakes it. Shiva in turn brings down the mountain on top of Ravana, who acknowledges Shiva's might and sings his name in praise for 1,000 years.

Banteay Srei was further expanded in the 11th century and was probably in use until the 14th century. The temple complex was not "discovered" by the French until 1914 and became famous only when celebrated French writer André Malraux tried to steal four *devatas* (goddesses) in 1923. During the 1930s, Banteay Srei was the first Angkor monument to benefit from the process of anastylosis, and it was only in 1936 that the true age of the temple was established. Sadly, the temple has been looted several times since Malraux's early efforts to deplete Cambodia's heritage, and even concrete replicas of sculptures that have been moved to Angkor Conservation have been attacked.

Banteay Srei is best seen in the early morning or late afternoon, when the red sandstone really comes to life. Because of its modest size, the site tends to be overcrowded, but by late afternoon (the temple closes at 5pm) the big groups have left.

stone guardian, Banteay Srei

Phallic or Not? The Cult of the Linga

The linga, or lingam, according to Merriam-Webster's dictionary, is "a stylized phallic symbol that is worshipped in Hinduism as a sign of generative power that represents the god Shiva." In fact, there is no agreement among scholars, mystics, and academics as to what the linga actually represents. It's thought that perhaps the linga was initially understood simply as a cylindrical shape that represented the formlessness of creation, and later became associated with Shiva. Later still, the linga came to be seen as the divine phallus of Shiva and was worshipped as a representation of the creator and destroyer of the universe. Usually the linga rests on a square pedestal, called *uma*, or yoni, that represents the vagina. Some scholars and mystics, such as Swami Vivekananda and Christopher Isherwood, disagree with this latter interpretation. Everyone agrees, though, that the linga has been worshipped for a very long time. It precedes Hinduism and has its origins either in early Buddhism or animism. It goes back at least to the Indus Valley civilization. In Cambodia, linga are found everywhere around Angkor and pre-Angkorian temple sites, perhaps first introduced by Jayavarman II. Linga are usually in temple sanctuaries, where worshippers have been pouring water over them for centuries. As a result, the water is said to become sacred. One of the most spectacular linga sites around Angkor is Kbal Spean, where hundreds of linga have been carved into the rocky riverbed. The water rushes across the carved stones and then feeds the rice fields below, perhaps symbolizing fertility. It is best to visit during or just after the rainy season, when the river carries enough water to give the site some ambience.

KBAL SPEAN

ក្បាលស្ពាន

Some 12 kilometers beyond Banteay Srei, the riverbed of Kbal Spean makes an interesting detour during and after the rainy season (May-Oct.). This **River of a Thousand Linga** lies at the foot of Phnom Kulen and features impressive carvings of linga and several figures in its rocky riverbed. It's a 40-minute walk to get to the river section with the carvings. Note that this site closes at 3pm, so it's probably best visited in the morning or around noon; because you'll be walking through forest, it shouldn't be too hot. The area around the carvings can be quite polluted by plastic left by picnickers. Even here, some carvings have been hacked out of the river by looters in recent years. There's also a **waterfall,** with some carvings on top. Do not stroll off the well-trodden paths into the forest, as the area may still be mined.

Vicinity of Angkor

★ BENG MEALEA

បឹងមាលា

No doubt one of the most stunning temples in Cambodia, **Beng Mealea** (US$5) is still somewhat off the beaten track, but this atmospheric forest ruin is bound to see a lot more visitors in the near future as roads improve. Built in the early 11th century during the reign of Suryavarman II, this temple compound is about one square kilometer in size, roughly predates the design of Angkor Wat (although there are no bas-reliefs here and it is much smaller), and stands on an ancient Khmer crossroads among Angkor, Koh Ker, and Preah Vihear.

More than any temple in the Angkor Archaeological Park, Beng Mealea is an experience. Overgrown by forest and collapsed on itself, the compound is a huge jumble of broken towers, underground galleries, unidentifiable piles of rubble, massive walls, and corridors, adorned with false doors and

Beng Mealea

NORTHERN CAUSEWAY

OUTER WALL (FIRST WALL)

LIBRARY

SECOND WALL

THIRD WALL

WESTERN CAUSEWAY

INNER SANCTUM

CRUCIFORM TERRACE

EAST GATE (MAIN GATE)

EASTERN CAUSEWAY

GATE INTO SECOND ENCLOSURE

DHARAMSHALA

DHARAMSHALA

LIBRARY

SOUTH GATE (TODAY'S ENTRANCE)

SOUTHERN CAUSEWAY

SCALE NOT AVAILABLE

© AVALON TRAVEL

windows and split open by roots that have been pushing apart the brickwork for centuries. Temples don't come any more *Lost World* than this.

Have a local guide show you incredible corners and pathways where the first rays of the sun break in long thin strips of bright light through the tall trees that grow out of the temple walls and play over the smiling faces of *apsaras,* the temple's celestial dancers. To make access a little easier, a wooden walkway was constructed during the shooting of the French movie *Two Brothers* by Jean-Jacques Annaud in 2002, a tale of two tiger cubs in colonial Cambodia.

The main temple is surrounded by a moat and several outbuildings, possibly **libraries**

and *dharamshalas* (rest houses) and is reached via a broad causeway lined with *naga* snakes. Until recently, Beng Mealea was heavily mined. On my first visit in 2001, warning signs still surrounded the entire compound, and demining continued into 2007. Stick to the well-trodden paths.

In front of the temple, several small restaurants, which serve cheap Cambodian standards and cold drinks, are lined up by the roadside. Tickets to the temple must be purchased from the guards on the causeway approaching the main (thoroughly collapsed) gate. The ticket for the Angkor Archaeological Park is not valid to visit this temple.

Beng Mealea is 70 kilometers to the northeast of Siem Reap and can easily be reached on

Beyond the Tourist Trail: Cambodia's Best Remote Temple Sites

While the temples around Siem Reap now see literally millions of visitors, it requires only a little extra effort to escape the crowds and check out some more remote locations where you might even find yourself almost alone among splendid Khmer ruins. And if you want to take a trip deep into the Cambodian rainforest, more gigantic temple complexes await. Don't stray off the beaten tracks, though: Some remote temples could still be mined.

- **Wat Athvea:** A small Angkor-era temple in good condition, located just six kilometers south of Siem Reap on the road to Tonlé Sap Lake, is flanked by an active pagoda and a friendly village (page 31).

- **Beng Mealea:** A spectacular 12th-century forest temple, 70 kilometers northeast of Siem Reap, far enough away to avoid the crowds. Large parts of this huge compound have collapsed, and high walls, underground passages, and huge creeper trees create an eerie atmosphere (page 97).

- **Banteay Chhmar:** An overgrown and remote 12th-century temple site featuring towers with the faces carrying the *sourire khmer,* the famous Khmer smile. Despite heavy looting in recent times, this temple site, 61 kilometers north of Sisophon, is worth visiting for its ruined grandeur and sheer remoteness (page 105).

- **Preah Khan:** Truly a lost site in Preah Vihear Province, the roads to this remote temple complex north of Kompong Thom are so bad that the site is only accessible by motorcycle or, if you have the funds, by helicopter from Siem Reap. A road will no doubt be built soon, but for the moment, Preah Khan remains the most remote temple complex in Cambodia (page 112).

- **Koh Ker:** Almost an archaeological park in its own right, the 10th-century Koh Ker complex, a former Khmer capital 70 kilometers northeast of Siem Reap, contains almost 100 monuments, including the impressive Prasat Thom, a seven-tiered pyramid in a forest clearing. The area is still being demined, and despite good road connections, relatively few visitors make it out here (page 114).

- **Preah Vihear:** Breathtaking views reward adventurous travelers who brave dust and potholes to reach this cliff-top border temple, in recent times the center of political and military tensions between Cambodia and Thailand (page 116).

a one-day round-trip in a car or on a motorcycle. Follow Route 6 from Siem Reap toward Phnom Penh and turn left at the small town of Dam Dek. From here it's another 35 kilometers. Alternatively, head for Banteay Srei and then Phnom Kulen and follow the base of the mountain for 25 kilometers until you reach a crossing, where you turn left onto a mostly paved road, which takes you to the temple after another 10 kilometers. Note that this road is private; bikes have to pay US$1 and taxis are charged US$2.50 each way. The road can get flooded and turn into a mud bath during the rainy season. Unfortunately, there are no accommodations around the temple yet. A taxi from Siem Reap should cost around US$60, a *motodup* at least US$25; journey time is 1-2 hours. Many hotels organize tours to the temple for around US$25 per person. There is now a small shop by the roadside in front of the causeway to the temple, where it's possible to buy drinks.

PHNOM KULEN
ភ្នំគូលែន

Phnom Kulen (US$20) is a mountain and something of a private national park. Inside the park, a **waterfall** is quite impressive in the rainy season. A **River of a Thousand Linga,** on the other hand, is best seen in the dry season, when stone carvings (similar to those at Kbal Spean, a site that is included in the Angkor ticket) in the riverbed are clearly visible. Cambodians consider Phnom Kulen the cradle of the Khmer Empire—it was here that Jayavarman II declared a unified nation under a single ruler in AD 802. The spot gets very crowded with picnickers on weekends, and there can be quite a lot of garbage lying around.

What's more, entry to the site is US$20. (Entry to national parks in Cambodia is usually US$5, but Phnom Kulen is under the authority of a Cambodian businessman with good political connections.) The fee is as much as you would spend in a day around Angkor Wat, even before your transportation costs are factored in. Considering that there are no remarkable ruins to see here, for many it's not worth it—unless you are a waterfall fanatic.

It's possible to hire a *motodup* (around US$15) for the 100-kilometer round-trip, or a taxi (around US$30). From the ticket booth at the park entrance, it's 10 kilometers to the waterfall. If you are prepared to walk from here, the entrance fee is reduced to US$10.

Excursions

Look for ★ to find recommended
sights, activities, dining, and lodging.

Highlights

★ **Banteay Chhmar:** One of the barely discovered gems of Angkor, this remote temple to the west of Siem Reap sees relatively few visitors (page 105).

★ **Sambor Prei Kuk:** This collection of small temples, built in the 7th century, offers visitors a look at the architectural legacy of local Cambodian rulers who preceded the Angkor god-kings (page 108).

★ **Koh Ker:** This royal capital features an impressive temple pyramid from the 10th century, surrounded by almost 100 smaller structures. It makes for a great combined trip with Beng Mealea (page 114).

★ **Bamboo Trains:** Powered by water pump engines, these homemade wooden platform

handcars race up and down dilapidated railway tracks to get local produce and people from their homes to the markets in Battambang (page 121).

★ **Phare Ponleu Selpak:** Battambang's circus, the best in the region, is the bedrock of Cambodia's creative talent and has turned out countless students in the last decade (page 122).

★ **Wat Banan and Wat Phnom Sampeau:** Two hilltop temples and the villages and rice paddies between make for a fantastic day trip through Cambodia's rural communities, whether on the back of a motorcycle, in a tuk-tuk, by bicycle, or on the Bamboo Train (pages 128 and 129).

To delve deeper into Cambodia's architectural heritage, explore wonderful stretches of the Cambodian countryside, or just get away from the tourist crowds around the main temples, it's worth considering a number of rewarding excursions around Siem Reap—most of them within a day's travel of the temple town.

To learn more about Cambodia's rise to Asian superpower, the temple complexes of Sambor Prei Kuk, which predates Angkor by several hundred years, along with Koh Ker and Banteay Chhmar should be of interest. The laid-back city of Battambang offers quiet colonial-era boulevards, possibly the best circus and arts center in Southeast Asia, a couple of spectacular hilltop temples, and trips through local villages where visitors can experience rural life in Southeast Asia that has mostly already disappeared from neighboring Thailand and Vietnam. Getting here from Siem Reap is no longer problematic, the road is in good condition, and during and after the rainy season, the boat journey across Tonlé Sap Lake and along the Sangker River is highly recommended, as is a short ride on the Bamboo Train, a local means of transportation that has recently been gentrified for foreign visitors.

For the more adventurous, the cliff-top temple of Preah Vihear, on the Cambodian-Thai border, or the extremely remote and hardly visited Preah Khan temple complex (not to be confused with the Preah Khan temple inside Angkor) are beckoning.

PLANNING YOUR TIME

The destinations in this chapter are rather spread out, and each one is worth a visit in its own right. Battambang is at least an overnight trip from Siem Reap, though in order to fully appreciate the town's flair and its surrounding attractions, 3-4 days should be planned. Banteay Chhmar, Sambor Prei Kuk, and Koh Ker can all be done as long day trips from Siem Reap but are far more rewarding destinations if you stay overnight nearby to experience a sunrise or a sunset, or at the very least, see the monuments before or after the brutal midday glare of the sun.

Previous: Prasat Thom, Koh Ker; Wat Samrong. **Above:** shrine, Sambor Prei Kuk.

Excursions

THAILAND

LAOS

Dangrek Range

Ta Phraya

Aranyaphratet

Poipet

33

5

Phnom Malai

Phnthrad

Ban Phankrad

Pailin

57

BATTAMBANG

WAT PHNOM SAMPEAU

59

Sisophon

BANTEAY TOP

BANTEAY CHHMAR

BANTEAY MEANCHEY

36

ODDAR MEANCHEY

Anlong Veng

Phnom Samkok National Park

Stung

Sangker

Battambang

WAT BANAN

PHARE PONLEU SELPAK

BAMBOO TRAINS

5

6

Phnom Krom

ANGKOR WAT

BANTEAY SREI

68

Phnom Kulen National Park

KBAL SPEAN

Phnom Kulen 487m

Siem Reap

KOH KER

Kulen Prum Tep National Park

PREAH VIHEAR

PREAH VIHEAR

Trat

Phnom Sat Lake

Tonlé

Pursat

146

148

PURSAT

Dam Dek

SIEM REAP

67

Stung Chikreng

BENG MEALEA

Sroyong

Stung Sen

64

Tbeng Meanchey

KOMPONG LUONG

5

KOMPONG CHHNANG

Tonlé Sap River

6

Kompong Thom

Baray

6

Phnom Santuk

71

To Skuon and Phnom Penh

30B

Mekong River

KOMPONG THOM

64

PREAH KHAN

Boeng Peae Wildlife Sanctuary

Phnom Daik

SAMBOR PREI KUK

Kompong Trabek

Stung Sap

N

0   20 km
0   20 mi

Banteay Chhmar and Around

A latecomer on the Cambodia temple trail, Banteay Chhmar is one of the last large and remote Angkor-era monuments yet to experience mass tourism. As the roads to the temple have improved, it is possible to visit on a long day trip from Siem Reap, but nearby homestay projects and several hotels in the otherwise unremarkable town of Sisophon, a couple of hours south, make an overnight stay perfectly feasible.

★ BANTEAY CHHMAR

បន្ទាយឆ្មារ

Not many visitors make it to the temple of **Banteay Chhmar** (US$5). This is not only because access is difficult but also because this Angkor-era temple, built during the reign of the great god-king Jayavarman VII, has been looted heavily in recent years. Nevertheless, the trip, especially just after the rainy season, is rewarding.

The temple complex, surrounded by a moat, has many similarities to the royal city of Angkor Thom, including a causeway lined by stone guards (only two remain) holding *naga* snakes. Beyond the causeway and past a *dharamshala* (rest house for pilgrims), which is in reasonably good condition, an arched gate opens into the inner courtyard containing Bayon-style towers complete with the smiling faces of the bodhisattvas and huge trees, which creates a remote forest ambience reminiscent of Beng Mealea or Ta Prohm.

Despite the looting, some impressive carvings remain, including lintels and *apsaras,* although most of these heavenly dancers have had their heads cut off. On the temple's western wall, a 32-armed carving of Vishnu and another deity with 22 arms were once part of a group of eight such carvings. The other six were chiseled off, loaded onto trucks, and driven to Thailand in 1998. Luckily, the trucks were intercepted at the border. Several temple walls are covered with vivid scenes of warfare, both on land and on the water, between the Khmer and the Cham. Local kids will point out all the highlights to you. Numerous smaller temples lie strewn around the vicinity of the main complex. The admission fee is collected by local military. The Global Heritage Fund has been involved in conservation efforts for some years.

Accommodations and Food

At the time of writing, several simple guesthouses were being built near the temple. More intriguing, there is also a **homestay program** (tel. 097/516-5533, www.visitbanteaychhmar.org/homestays, US$7 per night) with rooms offered in private homes near the temple.

There's a small restaurant next to the Banteay Chhmar temple that serves simple Khmer food.

Getting There

Banteay Chhmar is 60 kilometers from Sisophon on Route 69, which continues to the small, dusty town of Samroeng and O'Smach on the Thai border. There is no public transportation from Sisophon to the temples other than a couple of early morning shared taxis (1 hour, US$4-5), but a *motodup* (motorcycle taxi) (US$15 round-trip) will take you. From Siem Reap, the journey can be done in about four hours on a motorcycle, three hours in a car.

BANTEAY TOP

បន្ទាយទ័ព

On a signposted bumpy trail that forks off the road some 15 kilometers south of Banteay Chhmar, the small temple of **Banteay Top** (free), also called the Army Citadel, is a ruined site among rice paddies. Dating from the same era as the much larger Banteay Chhmar

The Theft of Ancient Artifacts

When the Siamese sacked Angkor in 1431, they took whatever they could chisel off the walls with them. Ever since, the temples of the Angkor Empire have been looted, and Cambodia's cultural heritage continues to be plundered to this day. After the Siamese, the Burmese looted Angkor in the 16th century and took more statues with them. In the 1870s, some years after Cambodia had become a French protectorate and Henri Mouhot had rediscovered the ruins, another Frenchman, Louis Delaporte, on an exploratory mission to the temples, took a wealth of statues and lintels back to France, where they can be seen at the Guimet Museum in Paris to this day. While this was sanctioned by the French government, the plan by the French writer André Malraux, who later became Minister of Culture in France, to steal several important pieces from Banteay Srei backfired when he was arrested for trafficking antiquities and thrown in jail. Malraux's connections soon got him out of his predicament, though.

In 1925, the area around the temples was declared a national park, and looting subsided for a few years until the chaos of World War II brought new opportunities for thieves; priceless objects disappeared in large numbers until Cambodia's independence in 1953. As the country slid into the Vietnam conflict in the late 1960s, a trickle of artifacts continued to move across its borders, and following the Vietnamese liberation in 1979, the Khmer Rouge, who had retreated to the Cambodian-Thai border, not far from the temples, engaged in smuggling statues.

But the worst was yet to come. As the United Nations Transitional Authority in Cambodia (UNTAC) moved into Cambodia in the early 1990s and the country's borders opened once more, the temples became accessible to an unprecedented wave of professional looters, some of them Cambodian police or military, who stole specific items for wealthy overseas collectors, destroying many significant structures that had survived 800 years since being abandoned. The audacious removal of an entire temple wall from Banteay Chhmar near Sisophon in 1998 is one of the best-known examples of these widespread activities. Members of the Cambodian military spent four weeks carving the desired stones out of the temple with circular saws; luckily, in this event, the priceless carvings were intercepted at the Thai border and returned to Cambodia. Several American and European museums have also returned statues, and the United States and other countries have banned the import of Cambodian antiquities.

Looting also takes place on a smaller, less professional scale. Villagers or road builders sometimes come across temple structures and burial sites. In 2001, I passed through the village of Phum Snay, near Poipet. Within days of the discovery of a number of pre-Angkorian graves, local people had dug up their entire village, under the guidance of a foreigner who photographed and bagged each item found. The smuggler disappeared with the best pieces, and for weeks after, locals stood by the road side selling beads, precious stones, and pottery until the site was entirely depleted. In 2007, Cambodian villagers even looted a Khmer Rouge-era killing field for a few earrings of gold. As long as poverty is widespread in Cambodia, no amount of public campaigning or education will stop people from digging up and selling their national heritage for a song. And the looting continues.

In 2003, Michel Trenet, the undersecretary of state at Cambodia's Culture and Fine Arts Ministry stated that almost all sites of antiquity and temples far from towns are being destroyed. Since then, looting and the sale of looted items abroad has continued. A 2011 study from the U.S. Lawyers' Committee for Cultural Heritage Preservation stated that the U.S.-based auction house Sotheby's sold hundreds of ancient Khmer artifacts in the 1990s without proper documentation. As long as the art market in the West is open to stolen goods from Angkor, and as long as countries like Thailand and Singapore facilitate the illegal transfer of antiques, the looting is unlikely to stop until there's nothing left worth stealing. At least museums in the West seem to be changing tack. In 2013, the New York Metropolitan Museum of Art returned several Angkor-era items to Cambodia, and other museums are discussing similar moves.

complex, Banteay Top is worth a visit if you are in the area, not least for its isolated ambience. No extra fees are levied at this quite abandoned location. Note that the province of Banteay Meanchey, in which the temples lie, is still heavily mined in places; never leave the well-traveled paths.

SISOPHON

ស៊ីសុផុន

The provincial town of Sisophon has no attractions but can serve as a decent place to stay for the night if you'd like to catch Banteay Chhmar in the early morning.

Accommodations

Sisophon, the town nearest to the temples, does not have great accommodations options. Right in the heart of town, the only place worth trying is the **Golden Crown Hotel** (tel. 054/958-444, with fan US$7, with a/c and hot water US$15).

The **Phnom Sway Hotel** (tel. 012/656-565, US$7-15), in the northwest part of Sisophon, appears to be going for delusions of grandeur with its rather expansive facade, although it offers similar facilities as the Golden Crown.

Food

The best place to eat in Sisophon may be the **Phkay Preuk Restaurant** (from US$2), in the west part of town, which serves Cambodian standards as well as some Thai dishes. Otherwise, try your luck in the market area, where a number of cheap Khmer eateries cook up Cambodian dishes (from US$1).

Information and Services

There are a couple of **banks** in Sisophon that offer to cash traveler's checks as well as cash advances and currency exchange. ACLEDA Bank has a 24-hour **ATM** machine that accepts Visa cards.

There are a few **Internet** places around Sisophon; two of them are on the opposite side of the street that the Golden Crown Hotel is on.

Getting There

Sisophon is served by buses from Phnom Penh (US$10-12), including **Capitol Tours** (tel. 053/953-040) and **Neak Krorhorm** (tel. 023/219-496). From Siem Reap, some 100 kilometers east, it's possible to catch a morning bus (US$5). Moving west to Poipet and the Thai border (US$3), some 50 kilometers away, is an hour by bus. Buses to Battambang (US$3) also take an hour. More frequent are the shared taxis and pickups that congregate at the bus station and go in either direction when they are full. A taxi from Siem Reap to Sisophon is US$25. Buses, pickups, and shared taxis leave from the new bus station a few minutes to the east of the market.

Getting Around

Sisophon is quite spread out and not nearly attractive enough to invite a stroll. *Motodups* charge around 1,000 riel to get around town.

Sambor Prei Kuk and Around

For anyone interested in the origins of the Angkor Empire, Sambor Prei Kuk is worth a visit, as the monuments at this former capital predate the temples around Angkor by at least 300 years and offer insights into how Cambodian architecture developed up to its zenith in the 12th century. The nearby town of Kompong Thom has no particular sights to offer, although the local market is worth a visit, and there's a decent selection of hotels if you want to postpone a long return trip to Siem Reap.

★ SAMBOR PREI KUK
សម្បូរព្រៃគុហ៍

The large **Sambor Prei Kuk temple complex** (US$3), 35 kilometers north of Kompong Thom town and about 125 kilometers east of Siem Reap, was built in the 7th century and was part of the pre-Angkorian capital of the Chenla Empire, Isanapura. Isanapura was Hindu and spread over several square kilometers; its heyday was 500 years before Angkor, and the site remained active for hundreds of years.

Three groups of temples are in light forest, each with a central tower amid smaller structures, ponds, and broken walls. It is a short stroll among the groupings. The temples were bombed by the United States in the early 1970s and later vandalized by the Khmer Rouge. Despite the damage, a visit is well worth it, especially if you have not been to Angkor Wat yet—not least because you will have the temples largely to yourself. Well, almost: Small groups of persistent young girls follow visitors from temple to temple, selling colorful scarves. Several drink and food stalls have set up shop around the temples. Local guides, most of them teenage boys with a surprising amount of knowledge on the area, charge US$3 to take visitors around all three temple groups.

Beyond the three main groups of temples,

many more ruins lie half buried in the undergrowth—all together there are said to be 280 structures. Archaeologists continue to work around the site. Although Sambor Prei Kuk has been demined, visitors should not leave well-trodden paths when exploring smaller structures. The entrance fee is collected at a toll bridge one kilometer before the temples. Allow at least a couple of hours to explore the complex.

Prasat Sambor

This structure, closest to the road, was dedicated to a reincarnation of Shiva. Some brick carvings on the crumbling outer walls remain. Across the road from Prasat Sambor, a small shrine is slowly exploding as the roots of an old banyan tree work their way into the brickwork. One tower in this group contains a headless statue of Durga, while another houses a statue of Harihara, an amalgamation of Shiva and Vishnu. Both figures are replicas; the originals are housed in the National Museum in Phnom Penh.

Prasat Yeai Poen

The Prasat Yeai Poen group lies in denser forest and features an interesting wall with four circular carvings—so-called medallions—one of which depicts Shiva surrounded by monkeys.

Prasat Tao

Prasat Tao, the temple of the lion, does have two original stone lions guarding its main structure. The lions were smashed by the Khmer Rouge but have been well restored. Aside from the main tower, the smaller shrines around this complex have been badly damaged.

Getting There

A good dirt road leads from Kompong Thom all the way to Sambor Prei Kuk. It takes just

Sambor Prei Kuk

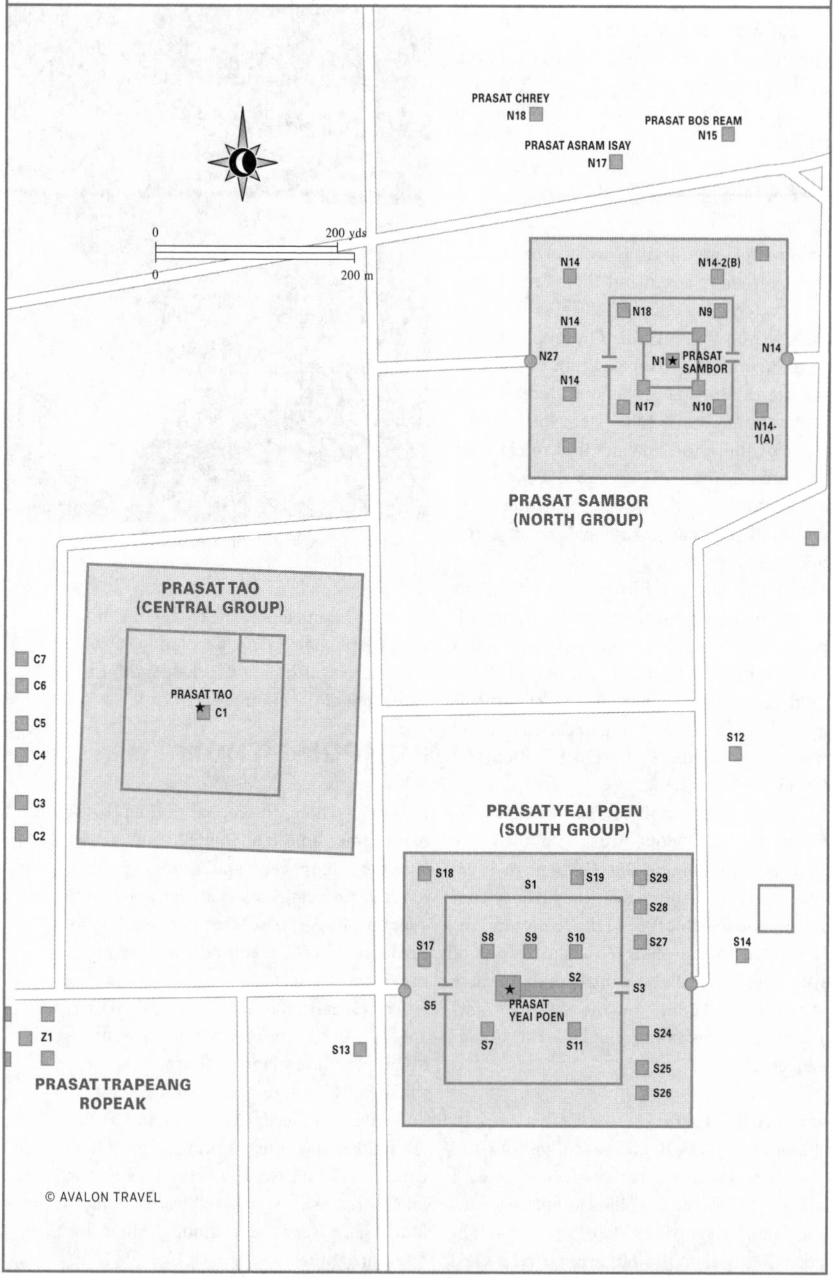

PRASAT CHREY
N18

PRASAT BOS REAM
N15

PRASAT ASRAM ISAY
N17

0   200 yds

0   200 m

N14   N14-2(B)

N18   N9

N14

N27   N1 ★ PRASAT SAMBOR   N14

N14

N17   N10

N14-1(A)

**PRASAT SAMBOR
(NORTH GROUP)**

**PRASAT TAO
(CENTRAL GROUP)**

C7
C6
C5   PRASAT TAO
C4   ★ C1

C3
C2

S12

**PRASAT YEAI POEN
(SOUTH GROUP)**

S18   S1   S19   S29

S28

S17   S8   S9   S10   S27   S14

S2

S5   ★ PRASAT YEAI POEN   S3

S7   S11   S24

Z1   S13   S25

S26

**PRASAT TRAPEANG
ROPEAK**

© AVALON TRAVEL

under an hour on the back of a motorcycle, a little faster in a taxi. Fare for a *motodup* (US$15 round-trip) includes waiting at the temple. A taxi should be around US$25.

Sambor Prei Kuk is reachable from Phnom Penh or Siem Reap on a long day trip. Expect to pay US$60 for the one-day round-trip journey.

PHNOM SANTUK
ភ្នំសន្ទុក

This temple mountain is worth the trip for the great views alone, but there are a number of interesting temples as well as reclining Buddhas on this hillside. On top, an active pagoda welcomes visitors. From the base of the mountain, a stairway guarded by *naga* snakes with almost 1,000 steps leads to the top. For those too lazy or tired to clamber up (and pay the US$2 entrance fee), there's a trail to the left of the steps around the mountain that can easily be done on a dirt motorcycle.

On the way to Phnom Santuk from Kompong Thom, the small village of Samnak produces stone carvings, many of which stand by the side of the road. All sorts of traditional items are produced here, from elephants to god-kings, including huge replicas of the famous Jayavarman VII statue, which was found at Preah Khan.

Also worth a visit is the **Santuk Silk Farm** (tel. 012/906604, free), established by Vietnam War veteran Bud Gibbons in 2006. The farm can be found near the turnoff from the main road (Route 6) to the temple mountain. Visitors can observe the cultivation of silkworms and silk weaving Monday-Friday 7am-11am and 1pm-5pm and Saturday 7am-11am. Silk items can be purchased at reasonable prices.

Getting There

Phnom Santuk is 20 kilometers southeast of Kompong Thom and can easily be visited on a day trip from town. Follow Route 6 back toward Phnom Penh for 15 kilometers to a sign-posted turnoff on the left. From here, it's less

a draftsman sketching a shrine at Sambor Prei Kuk

than five kilometers to the base of the mountain. It's possible to hire a *motodup* (US$6-8) for the trip, which should include waiting time at the foot of the mountain.

KOMPONG THOM
កំពង់ធំ

Kompong Thom, the capital of the province of the same name, is on Route 6 about halfway between Phnom Penh and Siem Reap. Due to its strategic location as a halfway point on the country's busiest road, the town is quite prosperous and lively, in contrast to some smaller provincial capitals.

The town itself is not particularly remarkable as a destination, but it is the jumping-off point to several interesting temple sites in the area. Roads are paved, so it's not dusty, and there are decent facilities and accommodations for those planning a trip into the countryside. It's worth visiting the market, and there are a few colonial traces along the Stung Sen River as well, although these don't warrant a visit.

Kompong Thom

STREET 105

WAT KOMPONG

SCALE NOT AVAILABLE

STREET 103

ACLEDA BANK   MITTAPHEAP HOTEL

STREET 101

Stung   Sen

STUNG SEN

STUNG SEN ROYAL HOTEL

NEARY KLAHAN   INTERNET

PRUM BAYON I   PRUM BAYON II

DECHAUVAT

DAMBEYCHANKLA

Market   6

DEKCHOMEAS

AMERICAN RESTAURANT   ARUNAS HOTEL   TOURIST OFFICE

VIMEAN SOUR GUESTHOUSE   PRACHEATHEPATAY

POST

STREET 1   STREET 2

STREET 3   STREET 4

© AVALON TRAVEL   STREET 6

Sights

THE MARKET

Phsar Thmey, in the center of town, is a good place to hunt for local fruit, or, for those with more eclectic tastes, fried grasshoppers.

WAT KOMPONG

វត្តកំពង

The town's main temple, with a pagoda that was reportedly built in the 17th century, is west of the bridge. Some of the younger monks speak a little English. The main prayer hall

was closed when I visited, but it is said that there's a bizarre mural in the hall that depicts the funeral of the Buddha, with King Sihanouk and some 1960s world leaders in attendance.

Accommodations

UNDER US$15

The towering **Arunas Hotel** (tel. 062/961-294, US$8, with a/c US$15) has the strategic advantage of standing right by the bus stop and a stone's throw from the central market; hence it attracts many of the visitors staying overnight. Many bus companies break here for lunch, so the hotel's restaurant is periodically flooded by hordes of passengers before returning to its usual quiet. The hotel is not a bad value, offering clean guest rooms with TVs and bathtubs. Guest rooms with air-conditioning have bathtubs and fridges. Avoid the 4th floor, which has karaoke rooms and is noisy at night. The adjacent guesthouse of the same name has simpler guest rooms (from US$4).

The **Mittapheap Hotel** (tel. 062/961-213, with fan US$7, with a/c US$15), at the bridge on the west side of the Stung Sen River, is another mid-range hotel with clean and comfortable guest rooms.

US$50-100

A little out of town by the river, the friendly and upscale **Sambor Village Hotel** (tel. 062/961-391, with a/c US$50, suite US$80) is made up of a collection of smart bungalows in a well-kept garden by a small pool. The restaurant serves comfort food. The hotel organizes sunset boat tours for US$10 a head, a nice way to wind down after a day at the temples. This is as close as you will get to luxury in Kompong Thom.

Food

The restaurant in the Arunas Hotel serves Khmer and Chinese dishes, and it isn't bad. For a few items of comfort food, head around the corner to the **American Restaurant** (tel. 092/579-410, daily until 9pm), an ice cream parlor and hamburger restaurant run by an American-Khmer couple. The ice cream is homemade, and it's really great. There is Internet access and mountain bikes for rent.

Information and Services

The **tourism office** in Kompong Thom is in a wooden building on a lane across the road from the Arunas Hotel and has a brochure with information about the province. A little English is spoken.

Kompong Thom has a provincial **hospital,** but in case of accident or serious illness, return as quickly as possible to Phnom Penh or Siem Reap.

Kompong Thom has an **ACLEDA Bank** and a **Canadia Bank,** both of which cash traveler's checks and have ATMs that accept Visa cards. Numerous money changers are located around the market.

There's an **Internet** place in a lane opposite the Stung Sen Hotel.

Getting There

The temples are just 35 kilometers north of Kompong Thom town. You can take a *motodup* (about US$10 round-trip), and if you are

driving, the journey, on unsurfaced but clearly signposted roads, should not take more than an hour. Head east of town for about five kilometers until the turnoff for Tbeng Meanchey on Route 64. Follow this potholed stretch of road, which leads through rice paddies and small villages, for 10 kilometers to the turnoff to the temples, on the right; the temples are about another 12 kilometers.

Kompong Thom is about halfway between Phnom Penh and Siem Reap on Route 6. Frequent buses make this journey, and all of them stop in Kompong Thom. The journey from Phnom Penh (US$5) takes just three hours. To Siem Reap (US$4) is also three hours. By shared taxi or minibus (US$6), the journey is a bit faster. A private taxi will cost US$20-25 to Phnom Penh or Siem Reap.

Mr. Hem John (tel. 012/185-7385) is an excellent local driver who speaks English well and knows the province like the back of his hand.

Getting Around

Plenty of *motodups* hang around the hotels and the market and will take you anywhere in town for 1,000-2,000 riel.

Preah Khan, Koh Ker, and Preah Vihear

The biggest and remotest temple in Cambodia, Preah Khan, has been heavily looted since the end of the civil war and is in poor condition. Bad roads to the temple make this a dry season-only trip for the very adventurous. Preah Vihear, a Hindu cliff-top ruin straddling the volatile Cambodian-Thai border and offering spectacular views, is a better option, if the political situation allows. Both monuments can be reached from the dusty and unremarkable provincial town of Tbeng Meanchey. The 10th-century Koh Ker temple complex is best reached from Siem Reap, although an overnight stop near

the ruins is highly recommended—visitors might have the impressive central pyramid, Prasat Thom, all to themselves for sunset or sunrise.

PREAH KHAN
ព្រះខ័ន

Preah Khan (US$5), called Prasat Bakan by locals, is the largest temple complex in Cambodia, and in fact is the largest temple area constructed during the Angkor Empire. The entire complex stretches over five square kilometers and includes a *baray* (reservoir) that is three kilometers long. The island temple of Prasat Preah Thkol stands in the middle of the reservoir.

At the western end of the *baray,* **Prasat Preah Stung** is the most impressive temple and sports the enigmatic faces of Jayavarman VII (similar to those on the Bayon), who is said to have lived here. The famous head of Jayavarman VII that graces thousands of images and statues in souvenir shops in Cambodia was found here, followed a few years later by its body. Both are now on display, reunited, of course, at the National Museum in Phnom Penh.

At the eastern end of the *baray,* **Prasat Damrei,** the temple of the elephants, has lost its outer walls, but its central and quite small pyramid structure is still standing. It is uncertain when exactly construction of temples began in this area, but some structures are said to date back to the 9th century.

The main structure of **Preah Khan** was probably built by Suryavarman I (1010-1050) and was originally a Hindu temple, like Preah Vihear to the north, even though Suryavarman I was a Buddhist. He made Buddhism the state religion, but did not force people to convert from Hinduism. Suryavarman II, the god-king who built Angkor Wat, also lived here, which suggests that the site was a significant second imperial city in its time. Jayavarman VII undertook large-scale additions and reconstruction in the late 12th-early 13th century, during a time when Angkor was occupied by the Cham.

The temple of Preah Khan itself was once surrounded by a giant moat, similar to the one around Angkor Wat, although little of that is visible today, and the *naga* snakes on the bridges are long gone. Inside the moat, a *dharamshala* (guesthouse), built by Jayavarman VII, survives. Many of the temple towers in this central enclosure have collapsed, and the entire compound looks a bit like a battlefield. For now, Preah Khan is rarely visited, partly because it's a long way away from the Angkor Archaeological Park, partly because the roads to the temple are not in great shape, and partly perhaps because it

has been looted so many times. The history of looting Preah Khan is almost as complex as that of the temple itself. The Frenchman Louis Delaporte, in charge of the first expedition exploring the temples, stole significant parts, which are now on display at the Guimet Museum in Paris. Despite this, the central area was still intact in the mid-1990s. But as Cambodia's civil war was drawing to a close, gangs with drills and diggers moved in and took everything they could pry from the walls. It's thought that many of the towers collapsed for this reason. In its heyday, tens of thousands of people lived around the temples in order to support the royal elite. A 100-kilometer highway used to connect Preah Khan with Angkor Thom via the forest temple of Beng Mealea. Remnants of this road can be found in the forests west of Preah Khan, including some bridges with *naga* heads. The temple area has been cleared of land mines, but as always in Cambodia, it's safest to stick to well-trodden paths.

Getting There

There is no need to travel all the way up to the provincial capital of Tbeng Meanchey to access Preah Khan. The best way to get here is from Kompong Thom, first along Route 6 toward Siem Reap to the turnoff of Route 64, a few kilometers west of town. Route 64 snakes north for about 65 kilometers and is currently in such appallingly bad condition that it is likely to be impassable in the rainy season. Turn left off Route 64 after the village of Phnom Daik; the temple is clearly signposted. Follow a narrow unsurfaced road, also very bad and sandy in places, for another 60 kilometers until you reach Prasat Preah Stung, the first of the temples. There's a village on the way, where water and gas can be purchased. It's also possible to stay with a local family (bed and dinner US$5) here, easy to arrange if you are traveling with a *motodup.*

No regular transportation comes up here, so renting a motorcycle or car (a 4WD vehicle is preferable) is unavoidable. An overnight round-trip with a *motodup* from Kompong

Koh Ker

PRASAT TRAPANG ROSEI
PRASAT DEI CHNANG
PRASAT DAR TONG
PRASAT LEUNG (I)
PRASAT THNENG (H)
PRASAT THOM GROUP
PRASAT G
SOUTHERN GROUP
LINGA SHRINE
PRASAT ANDONG (F)
PRASAT THOM
PRASAT KRACHAP (E)
PRASAT D
RAHAL (BARAY)
PRASAT BANTEAY PICHEAN
ANDONG PRENG
PRASAT CHAMRES
PRASAT CHRAP
PRASAT KOH SOKUM
PRASAT CHHIN
PRASAT DAMREI
PRASAT KHNA
PRASAT ANG KHNA
PRASAT BA (PRASAT B)
PRASAT KRAHOM
PRASAT NEAN KHMAU
SOUTHERN GROUP
0   500 yds
0   500 m
PRASAT PRAM
© AVALON TRAVEL

Thom costs US$50. Taxis cannot make this journey because the road is too rough. Some *motodups* also offer a three-night, four-day round-trip to Kompong Thom via Preah Khan, Koh Ker, and Preah Vihear. Be sure you have the stamina to sit on a bike without suspension on the worst roads in the world for days on end before embarking on this circuit.

Forget about visiting this temple in the rainy season.

★ KOH KER

កោះកេរ្ដិ៍

Koh Ker (US$10) is an experience. As recently as 15 years ago, the only way to get to this vast temple complex, which served as Angkor's capital AD 928-944, was by helicopter. Even today, the area around the temples remains heavily mined, and it is imperative that visitors not stroll more than 100 meters from the buildings and stay on well-trodden paths. I witnessed the search for and destruction of land mines near the road between the various structures in December 2008. But this should not deter visitors, because Koh Ker more than compensates for the trouble of getting here and the small risk of being here.

Almost 100 structures, about 40 of them noteworthy, are spread across a forested area of 35 square kilometers. The main temples are so spread out that you need a car or bike to travel among them.

Truly impressive is **Prasat Thom,** the largest temple. Reached via a number of gates and corridors lined with large, partially collapsed pillars, the main temple structure is some 40 meters high, overgrown with weeds, and reminiscent of an ancient Central American pyramid, made all the more impressive by the wide-open area around it that is in turn surrounded by an impressive but crumbling wall. The stairway to the top is precarious and currently closed to visitors, but if you do make it to the top, the views over the surrounding forest are fantastic.

Prasat Pram, near the entrance to the complex, is made up of five towers, all heavily overgrown with vegetation, with two buildings slowly being strangled by the roots of a ficus tree. **Prasat Krahom,** the second-largest temple group, has a somewhat eerie and forlorn atmosphere—a jumble of broken towers, doorways subsumed in the undergrowth, huge pillars, and the finely carved window columns so familiar at Angkor.

Huge stone linga can be found inside several smaller towers, including **Prasat Thneng** and **Prasat Leung.** South of the *baray,* a broken stone elephant can be found by **Prasat Damrei.** At **Prasat Nean Khmau,** just one impressive tower remains standing.

Many smaller temples lie on a circuitous road through the forest. Tickets for the Koh Ker complex must be purchased at the tollbooth entrance to the area. If no one is in the tollbooth, employees of APSARA, the ministry in charge of the temple, will catch up with you in one of temples.

Accommodations and Food

The best place to stay is the **Mom Morokod Guesthouse** (tel. 012/865-900, US$9) near the toll gate, which offers huge guest rooms with attached baths in a concrete building,

Prasat Thom, Koh Ker

with nothing in them but comfortable double beds. There's electricity in the evenings.

Alternatively, a number of cheap guesthouses have opened in the nearby village of Srayong. Try the **Ponloeu Preah Chan Guesthouse** (tel. 012/498-058, US$5), which has tiny, fan-cooled guest rooms in a wooden house with baths downstairs.

A number of decent food stalls with basic menus in English in front of Prasat Thom are open until about 7pm. In Srayong, several small food stalls and restaurants can be found around the market.

Getting There

There are two ways to get to Koh Ker. The most comfortable journey is by taxi (US$80) or *motodup* (US$20) from Siem Reap, some 120 kilometers southwest, via the temple of Beng Mealea. By car, follow Route 6 toward Phnom Penh and take a left in the village of Dam Dek, 35 kilometers south of Beng Mealea. From Beng Mealea, it's another 60 kilometers to Koh Ker. The road is not bad, but because it's private there is a toll (cars US$2.50 one-way, motorcycles US$1 one-way).

The other, more adventurous, but far more arduous way to get to Koh Ker is from Kompong Thom via Tbeng Meanchey. The first part of the trip, some 160 kilometers, is mostly awful. Round-trip from Kompong Thom by taxi (US$150) or *motodup* (US$100) involves an overnight stay to allow enough time to see the temple complex. Count on six hours for the entire journey. The 70-odd kilometers of unsurfaced road from Tbeng Meanchey to the toll gate of the temple complex are not too bad, at least in the dry season. A taxi (around US$60 round-trip) or *motodup* (US$15 round-trip) take around two hours each way for this stretch. Some *motodups* also offer a three-night, four-day round-trip (US$150) from Kompong Thom via Preah Khan, Koh Ker, and Preah Vihear. Being fearless helps on this journey.

PREAH VIHEAR

ព្រះវិហារ

Above all, the Hindu temple of **Preah Vihear**

(free) offers some of the most breathtaking views in Cambodia. This large complex sits on top of a 700-meter-high cliff that drops sharply to the Cambodian plains to the south. Climbing up from the base of the hill and the border via an ancient stairway will leave you out of breath but allow you to appreciate the amazing location all the more.

Preah Vihear was probably built during the reign of Suryavarman I (1010-1050) and dedicated to Shiva, creator and destroyer of the universe. Successive kings added to the complex, including Suryavarman II (1113-1150).

Inside the temple, several stone pavilions, so-called *gopuras,* in varying states of collapse and decorated with detailed and beautiful carvings, are arranged around several courtyards. The *gopuras* are linked by causeways, some lined with *naga* snakes. This makes the temple complex almost 800 meters long. The third *gopura* contains a carving of the churning of the ocean around Mount Meru. A more sophisticated and famous rendition of this story is a highlight of the bas-relief galleries around Angkor Wat. The main sanctuary of the temple is the best-preserved structure and sits right at the edge of the cliff.

For years, virtually all visitors to the temple came from Thailand and paid 400 baht to the Thais to enter the area (a so-called national park) and another US$10 to the Cambodians to enter the temple. There is no official border crossing at Preah Vihear, and visitors from Thailand have to be back across the border by 5pm. Due to the military and political deadlock between the two countries over the temple, access from Thailand has been impossible since mid-2008. From the Cambodian side, access is free for the time being. Other, smaller Khmer temples line the border all the way back to Anlong Veng, but these can only be visited from Thailand.

Safety Concerns

The temple's recent history is as dramatic as the views across the plains below, and at the time of writing, both Cambodia and

Whose Temple Is It Anyway?

The magnificent temple of Preah Vihear, which straddles the Cambodian-Thai border, has been a bone of contention as well as a political tool hampering relations between the two countries for half a century. Listed as a UNESCO World Heritage Site in 2008, the remote site has become a symbol not of peace but of small-minded nationalism and petty internal and foreign politics. The conflict surrounding the site continues to contribute significantly to the prejudices and misconceptions that have existed among the populations of both nations for decades, if not centuries.

The border between Thailand and Cambodia was first drawn up by the French in 1907, who put the temple in Cambodian territory. The Thais did not protest, but shortly after France's exit from Indochina, invaded the temple with a military force in 1954 and claimed it as their own. In 1959, Cambodia went to the International Court of Justice to protest Thailand's occupation. The court focused on the legality of the earlier French demarcation and Thailand's reaction to it and decided in favor of Cambodia. Mass demonstrations against Cambodia and the International Court followed in Thailand. In a gesture of generosity, Prince Sihanouk, then Cambodia's leader, offered Thais free access to the temple and assured his neighbors that they could keep any artifacts they had already carted away from the monument. In 1975, the temple was the last site in Cambodia to fall to the Khmer Rouge, and in 1998, Preah Vihear was the last site to be given up by the Khmer Rouge fighters. Since then, it has been accessible from the Thai side only, until the Cambodians built a road in 2003.

But the squabbling between the two Buddhist kingdoms over this ancient sacred site was far from over. Cambodia applied for UNESCO World Heritage status for the temple, and inclusion of the site was debated, and, following renewed Thai protests, deferred in 2007. Soon after, Thailand changed its mind and supported Cambodia proposing the site for formal inclusion on the World Heritage List. Yet a few months later, Thailand withdrew that support again, because of protests playing on patriotic sentiment launched by a nonparliamentary ultranationalist movement in Thailand. At the same time, Cambodian Prime Minister Hun Sen used the territorial squabble over the temple to win more votes in his country's general election in 2008. Thailand promptly massed troops around the temple. Despite official Thai protests, Preah Vihear finally became a World Heritage Site in July 2008, and the Cambodians swiftly introduced their own troops into the area, making for a highly volatile standoff between the two countries. Several skirmishes ensued, and both sides suffered casualties. Some parts of the temple were damaged in the fighting, and access from Thailand has been closed ever since. In the months following the military encounters, the conflict widened to other smaller temples along the two kingdoms' border. A joint commission has been set up to defuse the situation and to finally demarcate the border. Following a general election in 2011, a government more to Hun Sen's liking took control in Thailand. Also in 2011, the International Court of Justice ruled that both sides in the conflict should withdraw their troops, and the conflict soon ended, prompting observers to remark that the loss of life around the temple was the result of political maneuvering and little else. Nevertheless, a heavy troop presence remains.

Thailand still had hundreds of troops stationed in the area. Some travel agents discourage tourists from visiting. Nevertheless, plenty of hardy travelers make it to Preah Vihear every year. Note that the area around the temple is still heavily mined—never step off the well-trodden paths. Several soldiers sustained horrific injuries from land mines in the recent 2008-2011 spat between Thailand and Cambodia.

Accommodations and Food

Sre Am, the village at the foot of the mountain, 27 kilometers from the temple, has a few guesthouses. The best of the lot is the **Sok San Guesthouse** (tel. 097/715-3838, US$9-16). As the road is likely to be improved, some tourism infrastructure around the temple is expected to be established soon. Some drink and snack stalls have sprung up around the temple, and you will be able to find basic food in the village.

Getting There

The easiest way to get to Preah Vihear is from Thailand, if the border is open. The nearest town with accommodations in Thailand is Kantharalak, also the best place to access the temple from the Thai side, though this access point remains closed. There has even been talk of having a cable car constructed to make access from the base of the Dangrek Mountains easier.

For now, there are two routes to get to the temple from the Cambodian side. Most straightforward is access from the provincial capital of Tbeng Meanchey, 110 kilometers south of the temple. This road was severely damaged in 2008 because of the heavy military hardware that was dragged up to the temple during the conflict with Thailand. But due to its strategic as well as economic importance, this is likely to change very soon, and perhaps significant improvements will be made. A shared taxi (US$8) or private taxi (US$80 round-trip) from Tbeng Meanchey takes two hours in the dry season. There are direct buses from Phnom Penh and Siem Reap to Sre Am, the nearest village to the temple, operated by **GST** (tel. 077/881-193, daily at 7am from either location). It's also possible to find a shared taxi to Preah Vihear in Siem Reap (3 hours, US$10), or a private taxi (US$70 one-way).

Alternatively, there is a gravel road to Preah Vihear east from Anlong Veng, just 90 minutes by shared taxi (US$7) or private taxi (US$60). Some *motodups* offer a three-night, four-day round-trip (US$150) to Kompong Thom via Preah Khan, Koh Ker, and Preah Vihear. In a taxi, the round-trip (US$150-200), minus Preah Khan, which can only be accessed by motorcycle, takes two nights and three days. Make sure to arrange in advance

who pays for the driver's bed and food as well as parking fees and road tolls. Always check for the latest security updates before embarking to the temple.

TBENG MEANCHEY
ត្បែងមានជ័យ

Tbeng Meanchey is the provincial capital of Preah Vihear Province, but aside from being the jumping-off point for trips to the temples of Koh Ker and Preah Vihear, there is absolutely no reason to come here. A dusty town with a couple of main roads and a handful of hotels, Tbeng Meanchey has no sights or attractions and sees few foreign visitors.

With the publicity and controversy surrounding the 2008 announcement that Preah Vihear is now a UNESCO World Heritage Site, the town may well develop in the coming years, as better roads have been built to make the temples in the province more accessible to visitors. On the other hand, if the main road to Preah Vihear is further improved from Anlong Veng, to the west, Tbeng Meanchey is likely to retain its current status as an insignificant backwater. Preah Vihear Province is very poor, and infrastructure is limited. Much of the area is home to magnificent tropical forests, although these are quickly being logged. Note that parts of Preah Vihear Province are still mined; never leave the well-trodden paths.

Accommodations

The **Happiness Guesthouse** (tel. 017/409-822, US$5-7 d, with a/c US$17), called Sopheak Meangkol in Khmer, at the far end of town, is one of the best cheapies, with simple and passably clean guest rooms. The Sabay Sabay Drink Shop is next door.

A much better option is the **Home Vattanak Guesthouse** (tel. 064/636-3000, US$16), the only accommodation in town of international standard. With large, smart rooms with nice bathrooms, and free Wi-Fi in the lobby, this is a great place to wash off the dust of the Cambodian roads and take a breather.

Food

The **Mlop Dong Restaurant,** next to the Monyroit Guesthouse, serves Khmer standards (daily until 9pm, from US$2). The more swanky **Dara Reah** (daily until 9pm, from US$3) is near the pagoda on the main road and serves better versions of the same food.

Information and Services

Tbeng Meanchey has a provincial **hospital,** but in case of accident or serious illness, return as quickly as possible to Phnom Penh. If you are somewhere in the province near the Thai border, your best bet is to cross into Thailand and seek medical attention there.

There's a rarely occupied **tourist office** in town that's supposed to be open Monday-Friday 7:30am-11:30am and 2pm-5pm.

Tbeng Meanchey has an **ACLEDA Bank**

that cashes traveler's checks and has an **ATM** that accepts Visa cards. Numerous money changers can be found around the market.

MSN Computers offers **Internet** access 7am-6pm.

Getting There

A daily bus leaves Phnom Penh for Tbeng Meanchey at 7am (US$8), taking around seven hours and passing through Kompong Thom around 10am. A taxi from Kompong Thom costs around US$45, from Siem Reap about US$50, and from Preah Vihear US$50. Much cheaper shared taxis can be picked up in Siem Reap and Sre Am. A new road is currently being built between Tbeng Meanchey to Thala Bovit, on the banks of the Mekong, which should soon provide a direct route all the way from Siem Reap to the highlands of Ratanakiri and the Lao border.

Battambang

បាត់ដំបង

Colonial vistas, great hotels and decent restaurants, a thriving arts scene, and some of the most interesting, accessible, and beautiful countryside anywhere in Cambodia—Battambang is really coming into its own as a quiet tourist destination in Cambodia. With better roads, it's possible to make the run from Siem Reap in less than three hours by taxi, but this northwestern town is worth at least a couple of nights' stay if you'd like to explore all of its attractions.

Battambang is Cambodia's second-largest city and lies on the southern side of Tonlé Sap Lake, 290 kilometers from Phnom Penh. This attractive and laid-back population center is actually 50 kilometers from the lake, connected by the year-round navigable Sangker River. Colonial as well as splendid modern Khmer architecture from the 1960s, numerous lively pagodas, and above all, fantastic trips into the stunningly beautiful surrounding countryside make Battambang a great stopover between Phnom Penh and the

temples of Angkor. There are some wonderful accommodation options for all budgets, several great restaurants, and a lively local arts scene. Battambang is also the home of the Phare Circus, a circus and theater school supporting disadvantaged kids. The Cambodian government is making some efforts to safeguard architecture of historical value. As a consequence, this welcoming city is fast becoming a popular destination.

HISTORY

The region around Battambang was part of Siam (now Thailand) from the 15th century until the early 20th century, when it was returned to Cambodia under the French colonial authority. The Thais returned in the 1940s, with the help of the Japanese, and held on until after World War II, when the Allied Forces pressured Thailand to return the region to Cambodia. Battambang Province was Cambodia's economic powerhouse, producing much of the country's rice, until

Battambang

VISHNU STATUE

To
PHARE PONLEU
SELPAK

TAXI STAND

FRENCH CULTURAL
CENTER

BANAN
HOTEL

VIETNAMESE
CONSULATE

SIEM REAP
FERRY DOCK

CAPITOL
TOURS

SEE
GREATER
MAP

BAMBU

PHKA
VILLA

STAR HOTEL

SORYA
TRANSPORT

WAT
DAMREY SAW

BATTAMBANG
MUSEUM

WAT
SANGKER

WAT
PACHHAA

WAT
PIPPITHARAM

TEO
HOTEL

SKY
DISCO

SENGHOUT
HOTEL

AU CABARET
VERT

TOURIST
INFORMATION

BAMBOO
TRAIN
CAFÉ

PARK
HOTEL

GOVERNOR'S
OFFICE

TA DAMBONG
STATUE

SUNRISE
COFFEE HOUSE

CANADIA
BANK

RIVERSIDE

ROYAL HOTEL

PHSAR
NATH

WAT BOVIL

COMFORT
INN

JAAN BAI
RESTAURANT

UCB BANK

RIVERSIDE BALCONY

LUX
GUESTHOUSE

FRESH EATS
MAKE ART
SPACE

KINYEI CAFÉ

ANZ ROYAL BANK

CHHAYA
HOTEL

JEWEL
IN THE
LOTUS

POMME
D'AMOUR

SOKSA
BIKE

STUDIO ART
BATTAMBANG

LOTUS BAR
AND GALLERY

GECKO CAFÉ

ONE MORE SMOKIN POT

FLAVOURS OF INDIA

MADISON CORNER

WHITE
ROSE

CHINESE NOODLE
RESTAURANT

THE
COLONIAL

SMOKIN' POT
RESTAURANT

LA VILLA

BAMBOO TRAINS

TRAIN STATION

0   200 yds
0   200 m

POST OFFICE

© AVALON TRAVEL

Sangker

Stung Sangker

the Khmer Rouge takeover in 1975. With the Vietnamese invasion in 1979, Pol Pot's troops fled northwest toward the Thai border, and for the next 18 years the province was engulfed in a vicious civil war that has left the area dotted with thousands of land mines that are still being cleared today. During the civil war, Battambang served as the government army's headquarters. As recently as 1996, the Khmer Rouge operated close to the city, around Wat Banan. Nearly two decades later, Battambang is again becoming a center of local commerce.

ORIENTATION

Battambang stretches north-south along both sides of the Sangker River. The main town center is on the west side of the river, which can be traversed on three bridges in the downtown area. Many of the most attractive colonial buildings flank both sides of the river, including the spectacular Governor's Mansion

Bamboo Train, Battambang

Nath is busy from early morning, and there are several banks with ATMs attached, as well as money changers, located in the streets around the building.

Battambang is a regional center for rubies and sapphires, which are mined in nearby Pailin and cut and polished in the city. Numerous gem dealers are located around Phsar Nath. If you don't know anything about gemstones, beware: There's a good chance that you could end up with a fake.

Wats

Numerous Buddhist temples are dotted around town, many of them built in the early 20th century during the French occupation.

Battambang Museum

សារមន្ទីរបាត់ដំបង

Worth visiting is the **Battambang Provincial Museum** (Street 1, tel. 092/914-688, daily 8am-11am and 2pm-5pm, US$1), located in a handsome ocher Cambodian building on the riverfront. The museum contains a small collection of Angkorian and pre-Angkorian statues, lintels, and other artifacts. Many of the items on display appear to have been partly looted; statues are more often than not missing their heads. The official operating hours can be flexible. Photography is not allowed inside the building.

★ Bamboo Trains

ឡូរី

The Bamboo Trains, also called Funny Trains, are a unique way to travel in the region. As Cambodia's railroad system is barely functioning (although a major restoration program financed by Japan is in progress), people around Pursat and Battambang have set up their own train system—running little bamboo platforms up and down the tracks, powered by engines meant for water pumps. It's well worth hitching a ride for a few kilometers just for the experience.

The Bamboo Trains, called *norry* by the locals, zip along shaky rails at 30-60

on Street 1, which is unfortunately closed to the public. Visitors coming from Phnom Penh along Route 5 will encounter a giant statue of Dambong, a giant guard holding the Bat Dambong, the "Disappearing Stick," from which the city takes its name.

In spite of its turbulent history, Battambang is now perfectly safe. Well-trodden paths have long been cleared of land mines and unexploded ordnance. It's wise to err on the side of caution in the countryside, however, and it's advisable to hire local guides to destinations outside the city, especially to rarely visited places.

SIGHTS
The Market

Phsar Nath is located in a great-looking art deco structure right in the heart of town. Long narrow aisles run the length of the building, crowded with stalls offering mostly clothing and household goods. Around the outside of the market, countless stalls sell foodstuffs from dragon fruit to smoked river fish. Phsar kilometers per hour. They occasionally almost derail when there's a gap in the tracks, and they frequently stop to disassemble when there's oncoming traffic—most likely another Bamboo Train. These very basic modes of transportation carry up to 20 passengers at a time as well as cows, pigs, and motorcycles. The Bamboo Trains have been around since 1980, when locals first built them with wooden wheels and powered them by hand. Later, tank or tractor wheels were added. A 35-kilometer ride is likely to cost US$5-8, but for those with sensitive behinds, shorter journeys of just a few stops are recommended.

The *motodup* guides in Battambang take travelers to Ou Dambang, a small village five kilometers from town that serves as the main departure point for the Bamboo Trains. Partly assembled Bamboo Trains linger in the shade of a bombed-out station building here, while the drivers, who have formed a kind of union of *norry* operators to ensure equal earnings, sit in the shade, play cards, and wait for customers.

Because the road network between outlying villages are slowly improving and the railroad tracks are due to be rehabilitated, the Bamboo Trains will one day disappear. A ride on one of these contraptions is a truly amazing experience and gives great insight into the daily toil of ordinary Cambodians.

★ Phare Ponleu Selpak

ស្ថិរពន្លឺសិល្បៈ

Phare Ponleu Selpak (tel. 053/952-424, http://phareps.org) is one of Battambang's and perhaps Cambodia's greatest attractions. This association is so much more than a circus. Thought up in a refugee camp on the Thai-Cambodian border and brought to life by eight young students and their French teacher, this project has turned into an excellent educational center for disadvantaged Cambodian youngsters. Besides a real circus with a big top whose performers have been touring in Europe, Africa, Australia, and Asia since 2002, this institution also creates theater

performances and has a music school as well as an art school.

Performances (adults US$14, under 14 US$7) are held almost daily at 6:45pm, and there's also a good after-show restaurant. Needless to say, PPS, as it is also known, is deeply involved in local community life, and by 2011 thousands of students had passed through its doors, received an education, and gone on either to teach new students or into employment elsewhere. Phare Ponleu Selpak is definitely worth a visit, as it is highly entertaining and one of the best educational institutions in the country. It is located on Route 5 a few kilometers out of Battambang; visitors get a free ride back to their hotels. A second Phare big top opened in Siem Reap in 2013.

ENTERTAINMENT
Nightlife
BARS

The bar of choice in Battambang is currently the **Madison Corner** (daily 6am-midnight), which started off as a French crepe and ice cream parlor but is now a happening little bar serving cold beer and a wide range of spirits (as well as ice cream). Run by the gregarious Patrice and his wife, Nary—they also own the nearby Pomme d'Amour Restaurant—this is a popular gathering place, a few minutes south of Phsar Nath, once it gets dark in Battambang.

The very agreeable **Riverside Balcony** (Tues.-Sun. 4pm-midnight), on the west bank of the Sangker River in the far south of the city, is the smartest place in town. This bar-restaurant is located on the upper-floor terrace of an old Khmer building. It has a pool table, a limited menu of French and Mexican dishes, and a large choice of drinks, including draft beer. Pizzas are around US$6, and the pork fillet is great. In the evenings, foreign NGO staffers congregate here.

For insomniacs, the gay-friendly **Comfort Inn** (daily until 2am), also a small guesthouse located opposite the Royal Hotel, serves cold beer and spirits late into the night.

NIGHTCLUBS

A few years ago, you could observe drunken policemen draw their guns on the dance floor of the local Khmer nightclubs. These days, tempers ignite less frequently, and a visit to the **Sky Disco** can be a great cultural experience. Expect Khmer renderings of popular Thai and European club numbers, plenty of beer, and, for the local VIPs, bottles of whisky and dancing girls.

Art Galleries

Prior to the Khmer Rouge years, Battambang was a thriving arts center. Many of the country's most important musicians, actors, and visual artists of the 1960s and early 1970s hailed from the city. Most of them were killed by the communists. In recent years, a small but vibrant arts scene has sprung up in Battambang. The **Make Art Space** (Street 2.5, tel. 017/946-108), founded by Khmer-American artist Kat Eng and local artists Mao Soviet and Phin Sophorn, concentrates on collaborations between international and Khmer artists. "Rising above the shadows of Cambodia's dark history, a contemporary art scene MAKES it all from scratch" is the center's slogan. Check out exhibitions of paintings by local and international artists.

Also worth a visit is the **Lotus Bar and Gallery** (Street 2.5, tel. 092/260-158). Set up by British curator Darren Swallow with a little help from local artist Chov Theanly and British artist Nicolas C. Grey, Lotus marries a beautiful arts space with a trendy bar that is often the venue for music, art, and poetry performances.

The artist-ran **Sammaki Gallery** (Street 2.5) is a community arts space supported by the Cambodian's Children Trust that puts on regular shows and workshops. It's also a meeting place for local artists, who can use a computer here and brainstorm on their projects.

Studio Art Battambang (Street 1.5, tel. 010/743-074), located in an old shop house and opened in 2012 by Sokhom Roeun and Bo Rithy, both graduates of Phare Ponleu Selpak, is a space where local artists meet and work.

SHOPPING

The art deco **Phsar Nath** in the heart of town is where Battambang shops. Plenty of fresh food and produce, clothes, and household goods are on offer. For a good selection of locally produced souvenirs and handicrafts, head to the **BTB Souvenir Shop** (Street 2.5, south of the market). The **Smiling Sky Bookshop** (Street 3) offers a decent selection

colonial-era buildings in downtown Battambang

of secondhand titles. **Jewel in the Lotus** (Street 2.5) sells clothes, bags made by minorities, hill tribe bags, retro movie posters and postcards, and other vintage items, as well as Cambodian rock and roll music from the Golden Age, some on vinyl.

SPORTS AND RECREATION
Cycling Tours

Soksabike (corner of Street 1.5, near Phsar Nath, tel. 012/542-019, www.soksabike.com) offer tours through the delightful countryside around Battambang. Besides riding through picturesque villages, participants experience the manufacture of rice paper, get to taste local rice wine and seasonal fruits, and get a chance to contribute to the livelihoods of the people they visit through the fees paid for the tour. Half-day local industry tours (daily 7:30am, US$27) are available; full-day tours (US$40) include lunch. Half-day tours finish in time for lunch, while full-day tours are back in town by 4pm.

Meditation

It's possible to embark on a Buddhist meditation retreat at the **Battambang Vipassana Center** (tel. 012/689-732, www.latthika. dhamma.org) at a temple 15 kilometers south of the city. Visit the website to apply. The 10-day retreats are free, but a donation is expected as all the teachers are volunteers.

Cooking Classes

For cooking classes, head to the **One More Smoking Pot Restaurant** (Street 2.5). Half-day courses (daily 9am, US$10) include a trip to the local market to buy ingredients and a chance to cook three different local dishes. And, of course, participants get to eat each other's concoctions.

ACCOMMODATIONS

Since 2005, a whole range of hotels has opened around the city. In fact, there's an oversupply of rooms in Battambang. That said, some of the long-established budget places are a bit

rundown, so the new kids on the block are more in tune with the boom and bustle of Cambodia's second-largest city.

Under US$15

The **Royal Hotel** (tel. 016/912-034, www.asrhotel.com.kh/, with fan US$5, with a/c and hot water US$10), located on a side street off Phsar Nath, is one of Battambang's longest-running and most reliable budget guesthouses. It offers clean, no-frills guest rooms. A rooftop restaurant serves international backpacker favorites as well as a selection of Khmer dishes. A small army of *motodups* hangs around outside, ready to take guests to the sights surrounding Battambang.

Centrally located near Phsar Nath, brand-new, clean, and topped by one of the best rooftop terraces in town, the friendly ★ **Senghout Hotel** (tel. 012/530-327, www. senghouthotel.com, from US$13) offers great little guest rooms with TVs, fridges, and Wi-Fi included.

The **Chhaya Hotel** (Street 3, tel. 053/952-170, www.chhayahotel.com, with fan US$5, with a/c US$10) is one of those worn-down budget places, with clean but dingy guest rooms. The hotel has long offered trips through the countryside with one of the *motodups* working here. It also sells boat, train, and bus tickets; arranges for taxis; and has a free pickup service from the ferry dock or the bus stop.

The **Park Hotel** (tel. 053/953-773, with fan US$6, with a/c US$12), on the east side of the river, is a better option, a kind of almost-three-star modern hotel that's really a budget place. Guest rooms are spacious; some have hot water, TVs, and fridges.

The **Lux Guesthouse** (on a side street parallel to Street 3, tel. 092/335-767) offers large and clean rooms, with hot water, air-conditioning, fans, TVs, free Wi-Fi, fridges, and minibars. Not bad for US$9-23, less in the low season.

A long-running favorite with visiting NGO staffers, the reliable **Teo Hotel** (tel. 012/857-048, US$11-44), built in the 1960s, is located in the southern part of town and offers clean, air-conditioned rooms with hot water and TVs.

US$15-25

The **Star Hotel** (tel. 053/953-523, www.asrhotel.com, US$15), owned by the same people as the Royal, opened in 2008 in the northern part of town. Large, spotless guest rooms have air-conditioning and TVs, and are well worth the rates. The rooftop restaurant offers cold beer, good views, and a limited but decent menu. Fast Internet service (US$1 per hour) is available in the lobby.

A new kid on the block, the modern and garishly painted **Banan Hotel** (tel. 012/739-572, www.bananhotel.com, US$15-25) is clean and comfortable, with rooms tastefully kitted out in heavy Khmer chintz. There's a rooftop pool but no restaurant.

US$50-100

★ **La Villa** (tel. 053/730-151, www.lavilla-battambang.com, US$75) is as French an experience as you are likely to have in Battambang. Located on the east bank of the Sangker River, this colonial mansion, under French management, offers seven incredibly well-restored air-conditioned guest rooms furnished with wonderful art deco items. The small suites upstairs are especially romantic, but the two guest rooms on the top floor, with low-slanting roofs, are also great. The restaurant offers French cuisine, and there's a small garden with a pool out the back. Guest rooms are a little cheaper for single occupants.

Also French but of contemporary design, **Au Cabaret Vert** (tel. 053/656-2000, www.aucabaretvert.com, US$85) has just six large bungalows (one with facilities for disabled guests) in an attractive garden. The yellow huts aren't much to look at from the outside, but the guest rooms are actually very comfortable with attractive baths attached. The water in the natural pool is fed through a wall of plants, and the restaurant (US$5-19) offers a good selection of French dishes as well as Khmer standards.

The newcomer in town is the British-owned **Bambu** (KO St., tel. 053/953-900, www.bambuhotel.com), located on a quiet side street on the east side of the river. Opened in 2010, this boutique-style resort has just 16 guest rooms clustered around a saltwater pool. All guest rooms are elegantly furnished and spacious, have a private terrace or balcony, and offer air-conditioning, TVs and DVD players, safes, iPod docks, and free Wi-Fi. The restaurant offers Asian fusion fare. Ground-floor doubles are US$90, upstairs rooms are US$95, and suites are US$120.

Also delightful, though not quite as upscale, is the **Phka Villa** (KO St., tel. 053/953-255, www.phkavilla.com), a few doors down from the Bambu Hotel on the same lane. Located in a walled compound, smart and spotless bungalows (US$55) with attached baths stand around a reasonable-size swimming pool flanked by a bar and restaurant (entrées US$6-10). The food is mostly Asian with some European standards and breakfast.

FOOD

Numerous food and drink stalls set up along the western riverfront in the afternoon and evening. Several large garden-style restaurants around town are crammed with beer waitresses and serve as the main entertainment venues for the male half of Battambang's population.

The **Sunrise Coffee House** (Mon.-Sat. 6:30am-8pm), in a side street off Phsar Nath, on the same street as the Royal Hotel, has a Christian vibe and offers cakes, sandwiches, breakfasts, a book exchange, and a chance to scrawl your name onto a wall or ceiling to join the hundreds of others who have passed through. On the menu, an entire page is dedicated to coffee.

The neat NGO-affiliated **Kinyei Café** (Street 1.5, daily 7am-7pm), located in a French colonial-era townhouse, trains local youngsters in the arts of cake and fresh coffee. Occasional arts and music performances complete the picture.

Also good for breakfast is **Fresh Eats**

(Street 2.5). This small café is part of an NGO that trains young Cambodians in the art of catering, serves all-day Western breakfasts, and offers free Wi-Fi.

The **White Rose** (Street 2), set back from the river near the iron bridge, is a no-frills corner restaurant that offers reasonably priced Khmer and Thai standards. It's possible to sit by the roadside and watch life go by. Beef Lok Lak is US$2.

Next door to the White Rose, the simple **Chinese Noodle Restaurant** (Street 2, daily 6am-7:30pm) is unfortunately not signposted in English, but it does have an English menu. A bowl of beef soup with freshly made noodles is 5,000 riel.

Battambang's only Indian eatery, the pretty good **Flavours of India** (Street 2.5, tel. 053/731-553, US$5-8) offers a wide selection of Indian standards, including many vegetarian dishes. You can also have your subcontinental favorites delivered directly to your hotel room.

For Vietnamese and Western dishes, head to the **Riverside** (daily 6:30am-8:30pm), facing the river just north of Phsar Nath, which has an English-language menu with color photos so you know exactly what you are ordering. Excellent Vietnamese coffee is 3,000 riel, while a beefsteak will set you back US$4.

Right in the heart of town, the attractive **Gecko Café** (Street 3, daily 8am-10pm) is located upstairs in an old colonial corner building overlooking a busy intersection on Road 3 just south of the market. The balcony seating is great, and there's a modest menu of good Western and Khmer dishes. Fish *amok*, a mild fish curry, is US$3.50. The café, owned by a friendly American, also offers a massage service and rents out motorcycles, and there's a cheap Internet shop right underneath.

The **Smokin' Pot Restaurant** (tel. 012/821-400, daily 7am-11pm, from US$2) is a small hole-in-the-wall restaurant with a phenomenally large menu of Khmer and Thai dishes as well as a page of Western comfort food. The restaurant also has another branch, **One More Smokin' Pot Restaurant** (Road 2.5), that offers similar fare and is the site of daily cooking courses (US$10).

One of the best places in town to eat is the ★ **Pomme d'Amour** (Street 2.5, daily 11am-10pm), also known as Apple of Love, which serves excellent French cuisine. Try the chicken in black panther sauce (US$8) or the duck fillet in onion jam (US$12). Needless to say, the wine list is excellent.

★ **Jai Baan Restaurant** (Street 2, Tues.-Sun. 11am-10:30pm) is an extremely popular, NGO-managed restaurant with a contemporary fusion vibe otherwise unheard of in Battambang. Expect great food, including Khmer dishes, tapas, and excellent tofu burgers, alongside a good selection of cocktails and possibly the best coffee in town. Portions are small but quality is high throughout.

Across the river down by the iron bridge in the south part of town, the **Bamboo Train Café** (US$1-6) offers a large selection of Khmer and Western dishes and has a pool table. It is a great place for lunch or an early dinner, with very friendly service. The Bamboo Train Café Special Salad (US$5), the restaurant's signature dish, is fantastic—green salad with couscous, fried eggplant, tomatoes, and chicken.

INFORMATION AND SERVICES
Visitor Information

Battambang's **visitor information center,** located in a small kiosk next to a French-era house on the west side of the Sangker River, is staffed by a large number of young and enthusiastic trainees. The friendly youngsters hand out maps of the province with some of the major sites. For comprehensive online information on Battambang, check out www.visitbattambang.com.

Longtime Cambodia traveler and academic Ray Zepp has written a book called *Around Battambang* (US$10 in shops and hotels around town), which contains incredibly detailed cultural information on the entire province. All profits from the book go toward funding the German Christian NGO

Evangelischer Entwicklungsdienst, which supports HIV-positive orphans and monks in raising AIDS awareness.

You can apply for visas at the **Vietnamese Consulate** (Street 3, tel. 053/688-8867, Mon.-Fri. 8am-11am and 2pm-4pm), in the north part of Battambang. Apparently, it's less of a hassle here than in Phnom Penh.

Money

There are numerous banks and quite a few 24-hour **ATMs** in town. **Canadia Bank, ANZ Royal Bank,** and **UCB Bank** are located near Pshar Nath. All change money and traveler's checks and have ATMs. The **ACLEDA Bank/Western Union** is located on the east side of the river. Money changers can be found around the market and are easily recognized by the glass counters filled with bundles of different currencies.

Health and Emergencies

The **Battambang Provincial Hospital** cannot be recommended for anything but the most minor wounds. If you have a serious injury or disease, cross the border to Thailand as quickly as possible and seek medical attention there.

Internet Access

Numerous cheap Internet cafés can be found around town, and many hotels also have Internet facilities. Expect to pay US$0.50-1. Almost every guesthouse and hotel now has Wi-Fi.

Post Office

The newly restored post office is on the east side of the river, but don't send anything from here unless you have to; if you do, don't expect it to arrive.

GETTING THERE
Air

There are currently no commercial flights to Battambang, and the airfield is in pitiful condition, but this is likely to change in the future.

Train

At the time of writing, the railroad line between Phnom Penh and Battambang, originally built by the French in the 1920s, was being restored with money from the Asian Development Bank and Australia Aid; it is planned to reopen in 2015. Eventually, the tracks will go all the way to the Thai border via Sisophon.

Boat

Boats for Siem Reap leave every morning at 7am from the ferry dock on the west side of the river, just north of the stone bridge. The journey takes 6-8 hours, depending on the water level. En route, the ferry passes numerous small villages along the river before joining Tonlé Sap Lake. Passengers disembark in Phnom Krom, some 11 kilometers from Siem Reap, where they are accosted by hordes of touts. The tickets are a whopping US$18-25, and the boats do not meet international safety standards, although it is one of the most scenic river journeys you can take in Cambodia. At the height of the dry season, the journey can take much longer. There are no regular boats running from Battambang to Phnom Penh.

Regional Road Transportation

Three bus companies—**Neak Krorhorm** (tel. 023/219-496), **Phnom Penh Surya,** and **Rith Mony**—run several air-conditioned buses to Siem Reap (3 hours, US$4-5) daily from 6:30am.

Since Route 5 has been upgraded, numerous bus companies make the run from Phnom Penh (US$5-7) to Battambang in 5-7 hours. Early buses leave both cities daily from around 6:30am. The last buses depart around 2:30pm. Buses of Phnom Penh's **Sorya Transport** (tel. 023/210-359) leave from Route 5 on the east side of the river near Wat Bo Knong.

Capitol Tours (tel. 053/953-040), **Paramount Angkor** (tel. 023/427-567), and **Neak Krorhorm** (tel. 023/219-496) have offices near the Star Hotel. Most hotels and guesthouses can arrange tickets.

Shared taxis to Phnom Penh are around 30,000 riel. Shared taxis leave from the taxi stand on Route 5, on the way to Sisophon. Private taxis can be taken from Battambang to Phnom Penh (4 hours, US$70). A private taxi can be taken to Siem Reap (3 hours, US$40) and to the border at Poipet (2 hours, US$30).

GETTING AROUND

The easiest way to get around town if you don't want to walk is with a trusty *motodup*, which sits waiting for customers on virtually every street corner. Some hotels, especially the backpacker places, have a small army of drivers attached to their businesses. Rates around

town should be 1,000-2,000 riel. If you want to hire a *motodup* for the day to see some of the sights outside town, expect to pay US$6-10, depending on how far you are planning to go. Alternatively, hire a tuk-tuk, which will set you back US$20-25 a day to the standard tourist sites and back.

Most hotels also offer taxi services. Around town, it's US$25 a day; day trips around the area should be no more than US$40. Mr. Odom (tel. 012/912-744 or 016/862-664, leangodom@yahoo.com) is a competent driver who speaks fluent English, French, and Thai. He is based at the Chhaya Hotel but is happy to drive clients not staying there.

Vicinity of Battambang

WAT EK PHNOM

វត្តឯកភ្នំ

The 11th-century Wat Ek Phnom (US$2) is not particularly spectacular in itself, as it has been looted, but it makes a nice excursion through the villages to the north of Battambang. There's a modern temple nearby.

The temple is situated among rice fields about 10 kilometers north of the city. Follow the river road (Street 1) pretty much all the way to the temple. A round-trip with a *motodup* should cost US$6-8.

WAT SAMRONG

វត្តសំរោង

Wat Samrong (free) is located in a beautifully atmospheric compound to the north of Battambang. An old crumbling *chedi* as well as a prayer hall built during the French occupation, several stupas, and a new temple building stand among tall coconut palms. During the Khmer Rouge years, more than 10,000 people were killed here and left to rot in ditches around the temple compound. A stupa containing some of the bones of the victims was erected behind the temple in 2008. Frescoes on the walls of the building

graphically relate the suffering of the people of Battambang during this time and are captioned in English.

Behind the stupa, rice fields and palm trees make a beautiful backdrop, but the many ponds among the fields still contain the bones of thousands of victims. The people living around the temple make sweet sticky rice, a popular and tasty local snack sold by the roadside in bamboo tubes.

Wat Samrong is eight kilometers north of downtown Battambang. It's best to hitch a ride with a local *motodup* (US$5 round-trip).

★ WAT BANAN

វត្តបាណន់

The *motodups* in Battambang usually offer rides to the Angkor-era hilltop temple of Wat Banan and the modern temple of Wat Phnom Sampeau as a combined day trip through the countryside around Battambang. Wat Banan, constructed in the 11th century, sits on top of a hill surrounded by a vast expanse of paddy fields. Near the food stalls at the bottom of the hill, you will be accosted by tourist police who demand US$2 to enter the temple grounds. Keep the receipt, as this payment entitles you to visit Wat Phnom Sampeau as well. A broad and well-restored stairway takes about 10 minutes to climb.

There are five intact towers on the hilltop, and the views across the plains are spectacular. Many of the carvings have been destroyed by looters. The figures of elegant *apsaras* are still here, but their heads are missing. Make sure you stay on the paths; there may still be plenty of rusty small-caliber ammunition lying around, and parts of the steep forested ravines of the hill may still be mined. Drink sellers have assembled their stalls at the foot of the hill as well as up by the temple.

The temple mountain is about 20 kilometers south of Battambang. Follow the road on the west bank of the Sangker River (Route 154) until you see Wat Banan on the right side of the road. A dirt road leads directly to the mountain. There's a shortcut through beautiful paddy fields and villages to Phnom Sampeau, but it's difficult for a motorcycle in the rainy season and a struggle in a car any time of year. A round-trip by *motodup* that also takes in Phnom Sampeau should cost around US$15.

The road to Wat Banan passes through **Wat Kor Village,** a collection of hundred-year-old traditional Khmer houses surrounded by luscious gardens.

★ WAT PHNOM SAMPEAU

វត្តភ្នំសំពៅ

This temple sits on a forbidding, forest-covered limestone rock protected by steep cliffs. The more than 700 steps to the top are a strenuous affair, but there is a new road that takes about 20 minutes on foot.

A local legend tells of a crocodile that loved the beautiful Rumsay Sok. The crocodile's love went unanswered, so it smashed the ship that Rumsay Sok and her fiancé, a local prince, were traveling on and killed the couple. In revenge, the local villagers drained the sea, and the crocodile perished. Phnom Sampeau is thought to be the sunken sailing boat, while another nearby hillock represents the crocodile.

Fighting between government forces entrenched in Phnom Sampeau and the Khmer Rouge on Crocodile Mountain continued until 1997. Wat Phnom Sampeau, like so many temples, was used as a killing site during the Khmer Rouge years. Prisoners were led to the mouth of a deep cave shaft, pushed down, and then machine-gunned. It's possible to climb down into two caves where small shrines with bones remind visitors of the atrocities committed here. Old women try to encourage

a tower of the hilltop temple of Wat Banan

visitors to buy candles, and the atmosphere is appropriately somber. A metal cage, which is locked for fear of theft, contains human remains. A man sitting at the top of the stairs might charge you US$1 to enter.

The modern temple contains some garish murals. The views from the top of the rock across the perfectly flat plain toward Thailand are impressive. Just below the main buildings, a couple of old artillery pieces (one is a 1944 Soviet cannon) linger in the forest. On the side of the mountain, a giant face of the Buddha has been carved into the rock face. Drink sellers can be found at the foot of the hill as well as up by the temple. A brand-new temple of the same name was constructed at the foot of the hill in 2008.

Phnom Sampeau (US$2) is about 15 kilometers south of Battambang along Route 57 to Pailin. A round-trip by *motodup* that also takes in Wat Banan should cost around US$15.

KAMPING POY RESERVOIR
កំពីងពួយ

This large reservoir, flanked by an eight-kilometer-long dam, was one of the Khmer Rouge's many engineering disasters. Thousands are said to have died during the dam's construction despite Pol Pot's declaration that under his watch the Khmer people would build like the great master builders of Angkor, something of a delusion, as the Khmer Rouge had killed all the engineers. Today, the area is a popular picnic place and swimming hole for locals, who arrive in great numbers on weekends. Vendors selling drinks and fruit ply their trade along the water's edge.

The reservoir is signposted on the left on Route 57 about 15 kilometers south of Battambang. From this turnoff, it's another 15 kilometers along a road flanking a canal. A *motodup* ride from Battambang costs around US$15.

PAILIN
ប៉ៃលិន

With much of the area still saturated with land mines (never leave the well-trodden paths), only people really interested in Cambodia's recent and dark past are likely to get any mileage out of this town. There's a dusty market where it's possible to buy flip-flops made from car tires, a nod to the Khmer Rouge's glorious past (the movement made much of their cheap and effective rubber footwear). The only truly interesting sight is **Phnom Yat,** a temple mountain, which affords great panoramic views over the town and the denuded hills beyond. This temple is amazingly gaudy and features a representation of hell, in which life-size human figures are tortured in various terrible ways.

The Chrork Prum border crossing to Thailand (daily 7am-8pm) is 22 kilometers beyond Pailin. On the Thai side, public transportation is available.

History

Famous Cambodian singer Sinn Sisamouth wrote several songs about Pailin, and the region south of Battambang is rich in folklore, but Cambodia's long wars have seen to the gradual and almost total decline of Pailin's fortunes. It was in this area, in nearby Samlot, where peasants first rose against the Sihanouk government in the 1960s. And it was to Pailin, among other places, where the Khmer Rouge fled following Vietnamese liberation and from where they conducted the vicious guerilla war of attrition that was to last another 18 years—until 1996, when Hun Sen, leading the government forces, cut a deal with Khmer Rouge leader Ieng Sary to absorb his fighters into the Cambodian army. In exchange, Ieng Sary and his comrades crawled under the rock called Pailin and struck it rich with gems and logging. The plundered resources were sold in Thailand, for the most part, and Khmer Rouge generals soon owned sumptuous villas in Thai provinces bordering Cambodia. Following the death of Pol Pot in 1998, many of the other Khmer Rouge leaders retired to Pailin, and the town became a semiautonomous zone within Cambodia with de facto rule by the Khmer Rouge. Until 2001 there was even a border crossing into this absurd free state.

In the late 1990s, Pailin was a boomtown, and people from all over Cambodia moved here, having heard that they could become rich overnight. Few did, and the gemstones ran out. Most of the trees in the area were logged and sent west. The town was left with brothels and destitute inhabitants, some of them Khmer Rouge, others perhaps their victims. In 2002, I saw Khieu Samphan, the Khmer Rouge's Brother Number 2, strolling around the streets of Pailin with impunity. But with the gemstones gone, the locals forced into working on monoculture plantations controlled by Thais, and the Khmer Rouge leaders finally in jail, Pailin has turned from a fiefdom of mass murderers into a dusty urban slum.

What is perhaps most amazing is that the Khmer Rouge were so concerned about destroying all aspects of decadent Western influence in Cambodian society, yet under their watch, Pailin became as perfect an expression of debauched decadence and rot as one might never wish to see. For a while, even boxing matches between people with disabilities were organized around town.

Accommodations

Since Pailin's glory days are a thing of the past, the choice of accommodations in town is limited. A number of fleabag hotels, where rooms can be rented by the night or the hour, can be found around the market. Better to stay a little outside. The best option is **Memoria Palace** (tel. 015/430-014, http://memoriapalace.com, US$45), a sprawling and luxurious property out of town. Located in a huge garden area, the smart, simple rooms are huge (the suites are 95 square meters) and come with all the usual amenities, including free in-room Wi-Fi. There's also a large pool, a good restaurant offering Khmer standards, and super friendly service. This is a great romantic getaway in a location as unlikely as Pailin.

A little farther from town, the **Bamboo Guesthouse** (tel. 053/405-818, US$10-15) is on the road to the border and offers smart bungalows with air-conditioning. In the evenings, local military and police sometimes congregate at the restaurant for drinking binges. On the Cambodian side of the nearby border, several casino hotels have been carved out of the tired, dusty soil and offer decent air-conditioned guest rooms for around 500 baht.

Food

Pailin is no culinary paradise, and your best bets in town are a number of cheap eateries around the market. For decent Thai food, try the little **Heineken Beer Garden** (dishes around 100 baht) in the parking lot in front of Caesar's Palace by the border.

Getting There

Route 57 used to be one of the worst roads in the country, all the way from the outskirts of Battambang to downtown Pailin, and the drive to Pailin was a bone-jarring experience. In the 2008 rainy season it took 13 hours by taxi. Since then, things have improved, and potholes have been filled in. Two regular buses run from Battambang to Pailin (daily 7:30am and noon), and you can take a shared taxi (about 25,000 riel) or a private taxi (about US$50-60). Depending on your mode of transportation, the journey takes 2-5 hours. The road from Pailin to the border is now also in decent condition.

Phnom Penh

J ust 15 years ago, Phnom Penh, located in the south-central region of Cambodia at the confluence of the Tonlé Sap, Mekong, and Bassac Rivers, was one of the most dangerous and dilapidated capitals in the world. Gun crime

was common, people slept on broken sidewalks, and hardly any streets were surfaced. But relative political stability in recent years has had a miraculous effect: For the time being at least, Phnom Penh is once more becoming the "Pearl of Asia," a vaguely charming backwater capital on the banks of the Tonlé Sap River.

With the war truly over, some of the French colonial architecture intact, fascinating and sometimes grim traces of Cambodia's recent past lingering among quickly accelerating urban development, and more than 200 bars and restaurants catering to visitors, Phnom Penh is one of the most enigmatic of Southeast Asia's capitals, a dynamic blend of old and new, the traditionally cultured and brash modernity. There's a great deal to be discovered. What's more, with a quickly rising population and relatively few high-rises, and a 20th-century urban feel, the city has seen little of the kind of futuristic development seen in Bangkok and Kuala Lumpur.

This is changing, however, and the time to visit the Cambodian capital to soak up its past is now. Soon traffic and chaotic urban development will rob the city of its old-world charm.

Today, old men still pedal their cyclos slowly along the Sisowath Quay looking for a fare in the afternoons, just as they did in the 1960s. Around them, thousands of motorcycles swirl with mad abandon. Young lovers cavort on the manicured lawns around the riverfront and in the shadow of Independence Monument, while the newly rich show off their imported cars around the NagaWorld Casino. Long-tail fishing boats ride the choppy waters of the Tonlé Sap River, making catches right in front of the Royal Palace, while half-naked kids use a makeshift platform to jump into the brown water.

Phnom Penh's population today is around 2.2 million, 90 percent Khmer and 90 percent Buddhist. The largest minorities are the Vietnamese and the Chinese, but there's also a sizable community of Westerners living here.

Previous: the Chanchhaya Pavilion, which fronts the Royal Palace; coconut vendor. **Above:** colonial architecture, Post Office Square.

Look for ★ to find recommended
sights, activities, dining, and lodging.

Highlights

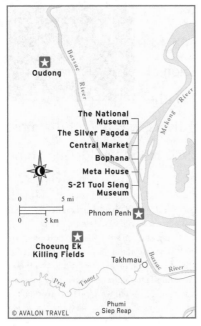

Cambodia would be complete without taking a look at the country's recent tragic past. The Tuol Sleng Museum, a former Khmer Rouge interrogation center, is a memorial to the genocide that swept the kingdom from 1975 to 1979 (page 148).

★ **Bophana:** At Cambodia's Audiovisual Resource Center, visitors can watch hundreds of hours of digitized film footage from Cambodia, from 100-year-old French reels to the movies of King Sihanouk (page 152).

★ **Meta House:** Phnom Penh's most vibrant cultural center, aligned to Germany's Goethe Institute, holds almost daily events, mostly in English, including lectures, films, panel discussions, exhibitions, and live music (page 156).

★ **Central Market:** Actually called Phsar Thmey (New Market) in Khmer, this imposing art deco building, constructed in 1935, is one of the city's best-known landmarks and most-visited markets, offering everything from produce to pirated clothes and books (page 157).

★ **Choeung Ek Killing Fields:** This site, just 15 kilometers from Phnom Penh, was the final destination for most of the prisoners held at S-21. It is just one of thousands of similar sites in Cambodia, a grim reminder of the reign of terror of the Khmer Rouge (page 179).

★ **Oudong:** Several stupas cover three low hills west of Phnom Penh, all that's left of a former royal city that served as Cambodia's capital from the 17th century until 1866. The views from the top are spectacular (page 179).

★ **The Silver Pagoda:** Located inside the Royal Palace complex, the Silver Pagoda contains priceless historical objects that survived the Khmer Rouge reign (page 144).

★ **The National Museum:** Set in a luscious garden, this impressive 1920s building houses the country's largest collection of antiquities and hosts traveling exhibitions (page 144).

★ **S-21 Tuol Sleng Museum:** No visit to

PLANNING YOUR TIME

While virtually all visitors to Cambodia head for the magnificent temples of Angkor, the country's capital is worth a visit as well. It's possible to see the most important sights around town in a single long day. In three days, you can take it all in at a more leisurely pace. Above all, it's the atmosphere of Phnom Penh that makes visitors stay longer than expected. Unlike neighboring metropolises Bangkok or Ho Chi Minh City, Phnom Penh remains, despite the urban squalor, very much a manageable and sometimes beautiful city. Wander the markets or the narrow streets off the riverfront, or lose yourself after sundown in some of the hundreds of bars and restaurants around town, and you may easily get stuck for a week, especially if you get sucked into the nightlife the city offers after midnight.

ORIENTATION

Phnom Penh is an easy city to navigate. The French created their colonial capital on a drawing board, and hence all the roads in central Phnom Penh run roughly parallel. Even more convenient is the fact that all streets except for a few main thoroughfares were numbered in 1979, after street names had been changed countless times by different regimes in previous decades. Uneven street numbers run parallel to the Tonlé Sap River, roughly from north to south, and the numbers increase the farther you travel south. Even street numbers run perpendicular to the river and increase toward the west. The city's busiest road is **Monivong Boulevard,** which runs parallel to the river from north to south and is home to the largest number of businesses as well as many mid-range hotels. **Norodom Boulevard** runs parallel to Monivong, but farther east and closer to the river. This major thoroughfare, which starts at Wat Phnom and crosses Independence Monument, is lined by colonial villas and several embassies. **Sisowath Quay,** also called "Riverside," runs directly along the Tonlé Sap River and is lined with hotels, restaurants, and small shops. Locals and travelers congregate along the landscaped river promenade in the afternoon.

HISTORY

After Angkor was attacked by the Siamese in 1422, the Cambodian king Ponhea Yat moved the capital to Phnom Penh. Today, some historians argue that the Khmer king's main reason for shifting his capital was not just Siamese aggression but a regional economic shift from agriculture to trade. In a changing world, Angkor, far from the Mekong, was no longer a location central and accessible enough to sustain a nation. Phnom Penh, on the other hand, made an ideal trade location from where it was possible to control river traffic from Laos, including the flow of fish products and pottery from the Tonlé Sap basin, and the Chinese goods coming up from the Mekong Delta to the south.

Initially, though, Phnom Penh remained the capital for only a few decades, and by 1494 the city had moved to Basan, later Lovek, and finally Oudong. By the 17th century, both the Vietnamese to the east and the Siamese to the west had begun to reassert themselves, and caught between two stronger neighbors, Phnom Penh was sacked by the Siamese in 1772.

Due to shifting political alliances, Phnom Penh did not become the permanent capital until the French arrived in 1862 during the reign of King Norodom I. The new colonial masters occupied a city of some 25,000 people, introduced town planning, and quickly constructed canals and a port.

By the 1920s, Phnom Penh was known as the "Pearl of Asia," and the city continued to grow for the next 40 years. While the French left many important landmarks, the city really came into its own in the 1960s under the reign of King Sihanouk, until the Vietnam War spilled over into the kingdom in the early 1970s and Phnom Penh became a refugee center for millions of Cambodians. When the victorious communists, the Khmer Rouge, eventually entered Phnom Penh on April 17,

Phnom Penh

© AVALON TRAVEL

0 ___ 1 mi
0 ___ 1 km

To ★ CHOEUNG EK
KILLING FIELDS

DRAGONAIR ■ THAI AIRWAYS
INTER-
CONTINENTAL ● ■ EVA AIR

MONIRETH

BLVD

LEGEND
CINEMA ■

OLYMPIC
STADIUM ■

Olympia
Market

Markets

SEE
"SOUTH OF
SIHANOUK BOULEVARD"
MAP

WAT MOHA
MONTREI ▲

S-21 TUOL SLENG
MUSEUM ★

Russian
Market

MAO TSE TUNG BLVD

THE ROCK
ENTERTAINMENT
CENTRE ▼

MONIVONG BLVD

NORODOM BLVD

MAO TSE TUNG BLVD

MONIVONG
BRIDGE

PREAH SIHANOUK BLVD

WAT LANKA ▲

INDEPENDENCE
MONUMENT ★

META HOUSE ■

WAT
BOTUM ▲

Bassac River

205
404
199
348
238
298
286
336
163
143
288
320
105
432
96
302
310
63
57
436
466
308
240
141
115
111
271
414
155
163

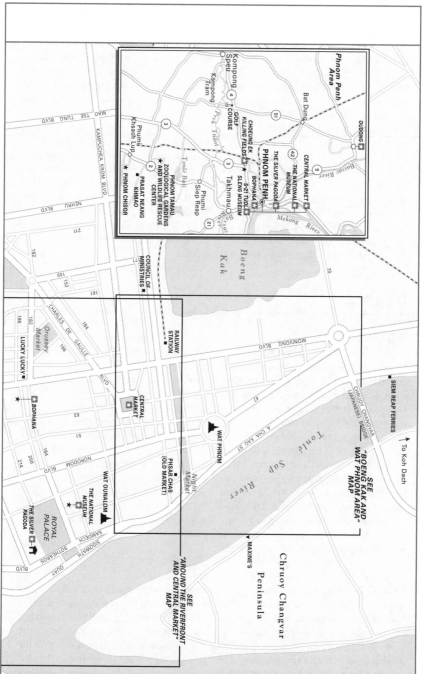

Phnom Penh Area

Kompong Speu
Kompong Tram
GOLF COURSE
Prek Thnot
Phumi Khsach Lup
Tonlé Bati
Phumi Siep Reap
Takhmau
★ PRASAT NEANG KHMAO
■ ZOOLOGICAL GARDENS AND WILDLIFE RESCUE CENTER
★ PHNOM TAMAU
■ PHNOM CHISOR
Bat Dung
★ CHOEUNG EK KILLING FIELDS
★ S-21 TUOL SLENG MUSEUM
BOPHANA
THE SILVER PAGODA
THE NATIONAL MUSEUM
CENTRAL MARKET
PHNOM PENH
OUDONG
Bassac River
Mekong River

MAO TSE TUNG BLVD
KAMPUCHEA KROM BLVD
NEHRU BLVD
182
211
169
152
161
171
Boeng Kak

RAILWAY STATION
Orussey Market
CHARLES DE GAULLE
182
198
166
LUCKY LUCKY ■
194
BOPHANA
CENTRAL MARKET
COUNCIL OF MINISTRIES ■
MONIVONG BLVD
WAT PHNOM
PHSAR CHAS (OLD MARKET)
Night Market
63
51
NORODOM BLVD
184
200
214
WAT OUNALOM
THE NATIONAL MUSEUM
ROYAL PALACE
THE SILVER PAGODA
SAMDECH SOTHEAROS
SISOWATH QUAY
BLVD

Tonlé Sap River

A CHA XAO ST

SIEM REAP FERRIES ■
CHRUOY CHANGVAR (JAPANESE) BRIDGE
MAXINE'S ▼
Chruoy Changvar Peninsula
→ To Koh Dach

SEE "BOENG KAK AND WAT PHNOM AREA" MAP

SEE "AROUND THE RIVERFRONT AND CENTRAL MARKET" MAP

1975, they immediately drove the city's entire population into the countryside. The Cambodian capital became a virtual ghost town, serving only as administrative center. People began to drift back into Phnom Penh after the Vietnamese invasion and liberation in 1979. But, as many of the city's original inhabitants had been killed, Phnom Penh was now largely populated by displaced refugees from the countryside.

When the United Nations Transitional Authority in Cambodia (UNTAC) showed up in 1992 with 22,000 soldiers and millions of dollars, the capital immediately turned to a two-tier economy—one for foreigners, powered with U.S. dollars, the other for locals, with Cambodian riel. This has not changed since the end of the U.N. mission a year later;

the U.S. dollar is the currency dispensed by all ATMs around town.

Since 2003 roads have been paved, public areas have been rehabilitated from rubbish dumps to green spaces, and the guns have disappeared from the streets—even if the disenfranchised poor remain just that. Some of the historical French buildings have been restored, but a fair number have also been knocked down and replaced by chrome and glass monstrosities, which points to a blander future. In 2009 the first skyscraper was constructed along the riverfront, not far from the Royal Palace, despite a law stipulating that buildings not be higher than Wat Phnom. Since then, other ambitious and sometimes disastrous urban development projects have followed.

Sights

BOENG KAK AND WAT PHNOM AREA

In a city emerging from decades of conflict, development can be swift and brutal. Until a few years ago, the area around Boeng Kak Lake was one of Phnom Penh's most notorious red-light districts. More recently, the alleys that stretched to the eastern shore of the lake served as the city's backpacker district, but the cheap guesthouses and restaurants were closed in 2011, and most residents in the area have been evicted by police. Footage of these violent expressions of state power have circled the world, but despite internationally supported campaigns, the state-private investor nexus in Phnom Penh pushed ahead with demolitions, beatings, and arrests. The reason: Boeng Kak Lake, which serves as a reservoir for monsoon runoff from the Mekong River, was being filled in. The disappearance of this body of water contributed to flooding in the city center in 2010 and 2011. The hard-gained land was to be used for new luxury property developments, but in 2013 the investors pulled out, abandoning the city's most controversial

and fought-over land development project. While original residents continue to be arrested and locked up, the area's future remains uncertain—an unmitigated disaster for the city and a blemish on the country's already checkered human rights reputation.

The area around Wat Phnom symbolizes the city's history and continuity. It is the founding spot of Phnom Penh, and during the French occupation, the streets around this small hill were the heart of the capital. Today, with many foreign embassies (including the new U.S. Embassy) located in the neighborhood, it is once more a prosperous part of town.

Wat Phnom
វត្តភ្នំ

Every great city starts with a legend, and Phnom Penh is no exception. It is said that in the 14th century, a wealthy widow called Daun Penh discovered five Buddha statues that had been washed up on the shore of the Mekong River in several tree trunks. To commemorate this miraculous event, Daun Penh

Boeng Kak and Wat Phnom Area

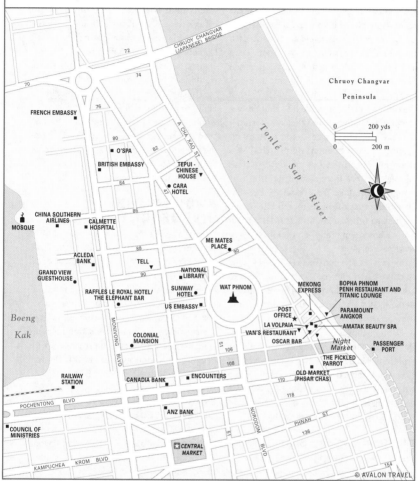

had a small hill built, crowned by a temple to house the Buddha statues, which she named after herself and which is said to be today's Wat Phnom, the city's highest hill. The name of Cambodia's capital is a combination of the Khmer word for hill, *phnom,* and the name of the wealthy widow, Penh.

Today, it costs US$1 to climb the wide staircase flanked by *naga* snakes to the temple at the top, which is usually busy with local visitors making offerings. The original structure disappeared long ago; the current building dates from 1926. Behind the temple, a small shrine dedicated to Daun Penh, who is today considered to be a powerful spirit, also draws a lot of visitors. A large white *chedi* contains the ashes of Ponhea Yat, the Khmer king who moved the capital from Angkor to Phnom Penh in 1422.

In 2008, the **Wat Phnom Fine Arts and Culture Museum** (daily 9am-5pm, US$2) opened in a building just below the temple.

There's nothing much in the museum yet except several glass tanks upstairs that are filled with miniature figures and cardboard cutouts reenacting moments in Cambodian history. By far the most remarkable are the scenes of the Khmer Rouge's entry into Phnom Penh and the city's subsequent evacuation. Apart from that, it's barely worth the entrance fee.

There's plenty of activity around the base of the hill. Especially on weekends, Wat Phnom is a popular hangout, and there are fortunetellers, gamblers, vendors, and even an elephant on hand to entertain people. Those who want to ensure good luck for the future can get vendors to release birds from tiny wooden cages (for a fee, of course). The vendors claim that the birds return after being set free. At times, a small stage is set up, and noisy Khmer pop groups do their best not to scare people away.

Nearby is the **National Library and Archives,** also housed in a restored French building in a small, well-maintained garden. Between Wat Phnom and the enormous and heavily fortified U.S. Embassy, a bronze statue of Daun Penh was erected in 2008. Be aware that if you attempt to photograph the embassy building, even from a passing tuk-tuk, you are likely to be stopped by security personnel who will insist you hand over your film or delete your images. Phnom Penh's only McDonald's is housed within the embassy walls.

The Post Office Square

Phnom Penh's central post office is housed in a beautiful ocher colonial building, which was restored in 2001. A few hundred meters east of Wat Phnom, the building faces a square lined with French colonial buildings. It's easy to imagine the idyllic pre-Khmer Rouge atmosphere while strolling around the area.

The French Embassy

Located on Monivong Boulevard, the French Embassy is surrounded by a high wall and is not an attraction. Nonetheless, some of the most dramatic scenes during the fall of Phnom Penh in 1975 took place here. As the communists entered the city, most of the foreigners still in Phnom Penh, along with their Cambodian friends and families, sought refuge here. The Khmer Rouge ordered the French Embassy staff to hand over all Cambodians, except women married to foreigners. Refusal, the communists threatened, would lead to the death of everyone inside the embassy. The French had no choice but to hand over almost 600 Cambodians, most of whom were never seen again. Some 10 days later, the embassy was closed and the remaining foreigners were taken to the Thai border. Scenes in Roland Joffe's movie *The Killing Fields* recount this tragedy.

AROUND THE RIVERFRONT

For many visitors, the heart and soul of Phnom Penh is around the banks of the Tonlé Sap River. Some of Phnom Penh's major sights jostle for attention with an astounding number of restaurants, cafés, and bars. In the evening, thousands of Khmer cruise up and down Sisowath Quay, socializing from the back of their motorcycles, as travelers and the occasional Western film star rub shoulders with begging mine victims, and brightly lit river cruises slowly pass by on the river.

The Royal Palace and Silver Pagoda Complex

ព្រះបរមរាជវាំង វាំង និង វត្តព្រះកែវមរកត

Both the Royal Palace and the Silver Pagoda are located in the same riverfront complex, surrounded by high walls 500 by 800 meters long and fronted by a large square. The palace complex was built in the 1850s. Its full Khmer name is Preah Barom Reachea Vaeng Chaktomuk, and it currently serves as the home of King Norodom Sihamoni, who was crowned in the palace in 2004, as well as his father, former King Norodom Sihanouk. Most of the **palace grounds** (daily 7:30am-11am and 2pm-5pm, US$6.50/25,000 riel, still camera US$2, video camera US$5) are open to the public.

The construction of the palace complex

Around the Riverfront and Central Market

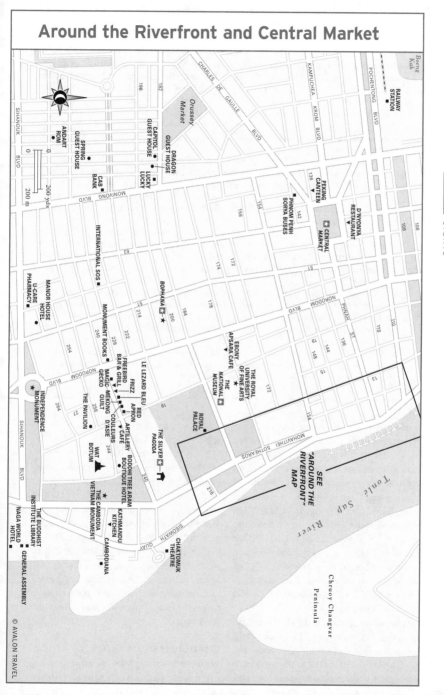

RAILWAY STATION

Boeng Kak

CHARLES DE GAULLE BLVD

KAMPUCHEA KROM BLVD

POCHENTONG BLVD

108
106

Orussey Market

198
182

CAPITOL GUEST HOUSE
DRAGON GUEST HOUSE

PEKING CANTEEN
136

D'NYONYA RESTAURANT

SIHANOUK BLVD

ANDART ROM
SPRING GUEST HOUSE

CAB BANK
LUCKY LUCKY

MONIVONG BLVD

142
PHNOM PENH SORYA BUSES
154

CENTRAL MARKET

0   0
0   200 yds
0   200 m

158
172
174
57

NORODOM BLVD
PHNAR ST

118
110

INTERNATIONAL SOS
63

U-CARE PHARMACY
MANOR HOUSE HOTEL

MONUMENT BOOKS
254
240
228
222

214
200
BOPHANA
184
178

EBONY APSARA CAFÉ
THE NATIONAL MUSEUM

THE ROYAL UNIVERSITY OF FINE ARTS

144
136
148
19
15
13

172

LE LEZARD BLEU
FRIZZ
FREEBIRD BAR & GRILL
MAGIC MEKONG GECKO QUILT
COULEURS D'ASIE
RED APRON
ARTILLERY CAFÉ
BOODHITREE ARAM BOUTIQUE HOTEL

154

NORODOM BLVD
INDEPENDENCE MONUMENT

264
256
27
THE PAVILION
WAT BOTUM
244
THE SILVER PAGODA
61

ROYAL PALACE

MOHAVITHEI SOTHEAROS

216

SEE "AROUND THE RIVERFRONT" MAP

SIHANOUK BLVD

THE CAMBODIA VIETNAM MONUMENT
CAMBODIANA
240

SISOWATH QUAY
KATHMANDU KITCHEN
CHAKTOMUK THEATRE

Tonle Sap River

THE BUDDHIST INSTITUTE LIBRARY
NAGA WORLD HOTEL
GENERAL ASSEMBLY

Chruoy Changvar Peninsula

© AVALON TRAVEL

Ghost Town 1975-1979

During the civil war, in the months leading up to the collapse of the U.S.-backed military government of General Lon Nol, thousands of refugees fleeing the fighting among the factions came to Phnom Penh, which quickly grew from a population of 500,000 to more than two million people. On April 17, 1975, the Khmer Rouge entered Phnom Penh. Initially there was some rejoicing as Pol Pot's revolutionary communists conquered the capital, but this soon turned to terror as the Khmer Rouge, many of them battle-hardened teenagers, immediately drove virtually all of Phnom Penh's inhabitants into the countryside, telling people that the Americans were about to bomb the city, which was not true.

The Khmer Rouge believed cities represented capitalism and the root of all evil. Cambodia's urban centers were simply abandoned. Homes, schools, and hospitals were emptied in a matter of days, and those who could not walk were killed or left to die. Wealthy and educated urbanites were branded as "New People" or "April 17 People" and treated especially harshly. Anyone connected to the old regime or the United States was killed. Forced into rural communes, many "New People" perished in the following years.

Phnom Penh turned into a ghost town; money was abolished, and banks, post offices, and schools closed. A few government ministries and factories stayed open, and the Tuol Svay Prey High School was turned into the infamous Tuol Sleng Prison, where alleged enemies of the state were interrogated and tortured before being executed at the Choeung Ek Killing Fields 15 kilometers from town.

As Cambodia shut down for genocide, most foreigners left. Several embassies did stay open throughout the Khmer Rouge's rule of terror, however, among them Yugoslavia, Albania, Romania, North Korea, Vietnam, Laos, Cuba, and, of course, China. Pochentong Airport was closed to international flights, except to welcome occasional supply planes from Beijing, which continued to bankroll the Khmer Rouge revolution. By the end of 1975, Phnom Penh had ceased to exist as an urban community. Some 20,000 communist party members and factory workers were said to be living within the city limits for the next four years. On January 7, 1979, the Vietnamese army invaded, conquering and liberating a virtually deserted Phnom Penh.

started after King Norodom abandoned the temporary capital of Oudong and moved back to Phnom Penh. It was built over more than a decade on the grounds of the old citadel Banteay Kev, which had been constructed by King Ang Chan in 1813 and was later destroyed by Siamese troops in 1834. Within the palace walls, numerous royal buildings stand in a well-maintained tropical garden that seems light-years away from the urban commotion beyond the palace walls. The layout of the complex changed numerous times between 1866 and 1970, and many of the older buildings have been replaced.

The palace complex is divided into three compounds: the Throne Hall compound; the walled enclosure of the Silver Pagoda; and the Khemarin Palace area, today's royal residence, which is separated from the rest of the buildings by a wall and is not accessible to the public.

There's a souvenir shop near the ticket booth at the main entrance on Sothearos Boulevard, which sells CDs, postcards, books, videos, and kitsch objects. Cameras are not allowed to be used inside the Throne Hall or the Silver Pagoda, and flash photography is prohibited altogether. English-speaking guides wait near the ticket booth, and it is worth hiring one if you are interested in Khmer culture and architecture. Their rates are negotiable, but US$5-10 is appropriate. A tour of the royal compound should take about two hours.

CHANCHHAYA PAVILION

While the complex's main entrance is located near the Silver Pagoda, visitors

The Royal Palace and Silver Pagoda Complex

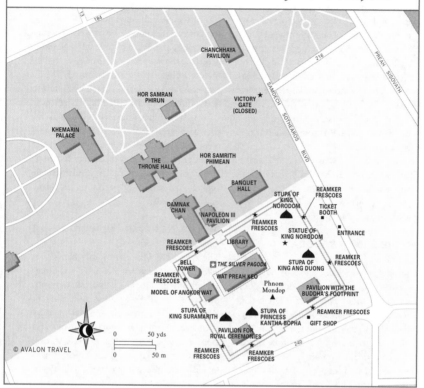

generally first head for the Chanchhaya Pavilion, north of the Throne Hall area. The front of the palace complex faces the Tonlé Sap River across a wide square and is dominated by the Preah Thineang Chan Chhaya, a rectangular building complete with golden spires; usually a giant image of the king is looking out over the wide square directly in front of the palace walls. The open-air pavilion is the only building clearly visible from outside the palace walls. It is occasionally used for dance performances and is also a perfect platform for members of the royal family to watch processions marching past on Sothearos Boulevard. The current pavilion was constructed in 1913, replacing an earlier wooden structure.

THE THRONE HALL

The Throne Hall does indeed contain two thrones, along with busts of Cambodia's former kings. In Khmer, it is called Preah Thineang Dheva Vinnichay, which means "Sacred Seat of Judgment." It was built in 1915 and inaugurated by King Sisowath in 1919, replacing an older wooden hall. From here, the royal household once carried out its duties and directed policy. The ceiling frescoes depict scenes from the *Reamker,* the Cambodian retelling of the *Ramayana.* Its central spire is 59 meters tall.

OTHER BUILDINGS IN THE THRONE HALL COMPOUND

Several smaller buildings are of note, especially the **Napoleon III Pavilion,** the first structure to be erected within the palace compound. The pavilion was originally built in 1869 for Empress Eugenie of France, wife of Napoleon III. Fortunately, Napoleon's royal N on the doors of the building did not have to be removed when the pavilion was gifted to King Norodom in 1876. The building is made entirely of iron and houses a small museum presenting royal memorabilia. **Hor Samran Phirun** is a small former royal guesthouse that now houses gifts from foreign heads of state. **Hor Samrith Phimean** contains royal regalia and dress.

Two other larger structures, the **Damnak Chan,** which houses the administration of the royal palace, and the **Villa Kantha Bopha,** a 1950s Western-style villa built for foreign guests, are closed to the public.

★ THE SILVER PAGODA
វត្តព្រះកែវមរកត

The impressive Silver Pagoda is named for the silver tiles that cover its floor, laid during King Sihanouk's pre-Khmer Rouge reign. There are more than 5,000 tiles, each weighing more than one kilogram.

The Khmer name for the temple is Preah Vihear Preah Keo Morakot, the "Temple of the Emerald Buddha." The original temple was constructed 1892-1902 and was made of wood and stone; the current building, built of concrete and Italian marble, dates from 1962 and uses the same design as the original.

Wat Preah Keo houses a great collection of national treasures, including Cambodia's Emerald Buddha, a 17th-century crystal Buddha. Even more impressive is a nearly life-size golden Buddha, dressed up in royal regalia and encrusted with more than 9,500 diamonds, commissioned by King Sisowath. Most of the other more than 1,500 objects are Buddha statues made from gold, silver, and bronze, some inlaid with diamonds, as well as objects used in Buddhist ceremonies. These were donated to the temple by the king, his family, and various dignitaries. The Silver Pagoda also contains what are said to be ashes of the Buddha, brought from Sri Lanka in the 1950s. No monks live here, but Wat Preah Keo is used by the king to listen to monks' sermons as well as for some royal ceremonies.

The temple building and several smaller structures—including a library, several stupas, *chedis,* and galleries covered in frescoes depicting the *Reamker*—were constructed in the late 19th and early 20th centuries. The library contains a collection of sacred Buddhist texts and a collection of Buddha statues. During the Khmer Rouge rule, many of the treasures were looted; King Sihanouk and members of his family were kept within the palace grounds as virtual prisoners, forced to grow their own vegetables. There's also a small concrete model of Angkor Wat on the Silver Pagoda grounds.

★ The National Museum
សារមន្ទីរជាតិ

The **National Museum** (daily 8am-5pm, US$3), on the corner of Street 178 and Street 13 behind the Royal Cremation Ground, houses the world's greatest collection of Khmer art. The museum was designed by French archaeologist George Groslier and constructed between 1917 and 1920. During the Khmer Rouge years, the museum was looted and its director murdered. In the 1990s, this stunning Khmer-style terra-cotta structure of several open galleries, all linked via a picturesque central courtyard, was threatened by bats in the roof, but these pests were contained by the installation of a second roof during extensive renovations in 2002.

Today, more than 5,000 objects are exhibited, and many more remain in storage. The museum primarily houses artifacts from the Angkor period, but there are also large collections of pre-Angkorian objects as well more recent items on display.

As you come in, the **East Gallery** contains a giant 10th-century sandstone statue of a *garuda* (mythical half-man, half-bird figure). On display here are also numerous Buddha statues, made from sandstone, copper, and bronze, dating as far back as the 6th century, as well as practical items such as bowls, candleholders, and elephant bells. Another highlight in this section is the Reclining Vishnu, a huge 10th-century bronze of which only the head, arms, and torso survive. This statue, which was found in Western Mebon, is most likely the same one that was described by Chinese traveler Chou Ta-Kuan, who visited Angkor in the 13th century, as having been inlaid with countless precious stones, gold, and silver. The far right corner of the East Gallery contains a small collection of prehistoric objects.

More impressive is the **South Gallery,** with its pre-Angkorian Buddha statues, as well as statues of celestial dancers with narrow waists, full breasts, and wide hips. The highlight is an image of Vishnu, standing three meters tall, from the 7th century. The rest of the South Gallery is given over to stunning examples of Angkor-era artworks up to the 11th century, including part of a wall from Banteay Srei.

The **West Gallery** houses artifacts from the late Angkor period, including a famous statue of god-king Jayavarman VII from the 12th century. There's also a sculpture of his head, with the faint and infamous *sourire khmer,* the Khmer smile, as the French called it, both cruel and compassionate, on its lips.

Finally, the **North Gallery** presents more recent objects. Besides collections of old firearms and cannons, the wooden cabin of a royal barge, dating back to the 19th century, bedecked with fine carvings, is a highlight. King Norodom's funerary urn, made of wood and precious metals, is equally impressive at three meters in height.

In the museum's courtyard, the giant statue of the Leper King, taken from the terrace of the same name in Angkor Thom, is another highlight of this fantastic museum.

Apart from being a great exhibition space, the National Museum is also the last safe refuge for many Angkor-era artifacts. Looting continues unabated at many temples, and no doubt many of the objects on display here would have long ago disappeared into private collectors' vaults had they been left in their original locations. Perfect examples of this are two magnificent wall panels showing a multiarmed Lokesvara that were stolen from Banteay Chhmar in 1998. The panels were pried from the temple structure and smuggled into Thailand, where the smugglers were caught by police, who eventually returned the panels to Cambodia.

Photography is allowed only on the grounds and around the central courtyard. A

the National Museum

souvenir stall inside the museum sells books and postcards, including a guide to the artifacts on display. Competent English-speaking guides can be found around the ticket booth; expect to pay US$5-10, and be sure to negotiate a price prior to embarking on a tour.

There's such an overwhelming number of artifacts on display that it's easy to lose yourself for a couple of hours. If you can't make it to Angkor, the National Museum is the best place to get at least a small insight into Cambodia's magnificent past. If you do intend to visit Angkor or have already been there, the collection will deepen your understanding of the incredible cultural creativity of the Angkor period.

Wat Botum

វត្តបុទម

The **Temple of the Lotus Blossoms** (daily 7am-5pm, donation) is a large pagoda complex located at Street 7, near Sihanouk Boulevard, and was founded in 1422 by Ponhea Yat, the Khmer king who moved the capital from Angkor to Phnom Penh. Wat Botum got its name from its original location: It once stood on an island in the center of a pond. The temple only received its current name during the French period, and it has been rebuilt numerous times, most recently in 1937. As the temple is the seat of the Thammayut sect of Buddhism, which was introduced by the Siamese and is said to be close to the aristocratic establishment and the monarchy, the ashes of numerous dignitaries and royals have been interred in stupas here. The walls of the pagoda are covered in frescoes depicting the life of the Buddha.

Wat Ounalom

វត្តឧណ្ណាលោម

The seat of Cambodian Buddhism and the most important active temple in Cambodia, **Wat Ounalom** (daily 7am-5pm, donation) is situated along Sisowath Quay on the riverfront, 300 meters north of the Royal Palace. Founded in 1443, the temple compound is massive and contains more than 40 buildings.

In 1975 the Khmer Rouge killed the abbot and many of the monks. Some of the buildings were vandalized, but restoration started as soon as the Vietnamese invaded in 1979, and the temple has since been rebuilt to its former glory. Cambodia's supreme patriarch lives here, and there's a stupa containing an eyebrow of the Buddha, along with schools and a library.

The Cambodia Vietnam Monument

ស្តូបមិត្តភាពកម្ពុជាវៀតណាម

Remembering the liberation of Cambodia from the Khmer Rouge by the Vietnamese, this rather austere communist-style monument, dominated by a stone carving of gun-toting troops, was constructed in 1979. Today, it's a popular meeting point for locals in the evenings. The park around the monument, located on Sothearos Boulevard a few hundred meters south of the Royal Palace, features a fountain light show that attracts hundreds of people in the early evening.

AROUND CENTRAL MARKET

The Olympic Stadium

ពហុកីឡដ្ឋានជាតិ

You're right in thinking that the Olympic Games never took place in Cambodia. Yet there's an Olympic stadium of Olympic proportions, nowadays called the **National Sports Complex** (daily 7am-early evening, depending on events), located in the west part of the city, a little north of Sihanouk Boulevard. Based on designs by renowned Cambodian architect Vann Molyvann, the complex was built in the early 1960s to host the Games of the New Emerging Forces (GANEFO), a sports initiative thought up by the Chinese. The games took place just once, in Cambodia, in 1966. Eighteen countries participated, and Cambodia won 13 gold medals.

During the Khmer Rouge years, the lawn in the stadium was turned into a cabbage field. Buildings include the stadium, which seats 84,000; a hall for boxing, which seats

10,000; and an Olympic-size swimming pool. Following years of neglect, the complex has now been restored. The halls and courtyards are used for political events and concerts. **KA Tours** (www.ka-tours.org), which offers architectural tours around the city to highlight Cambodia's recent architectural heritage, organizes regular trips to the stadium. Of course, it's easy just to drop in on your own and watch Cambodian sports enthusiasts train.

SOUTH OF SIHANOUK BOULEVARD

Largely residential, the area called **Boeung Keng Kang**—located south of Sihanouk Boulevard, east of Monivong Boulevard, and west of Norodom Boulevard—has always been considered the foreigners' district. It forms the heart of today's wealthy expatriate community, with many NGOs, embassies, and international companies based here. Plenty of middle-class and wealthy Khmer live here, too. There are some excellent mid-range hotels and restaurants in the area, especially on Street 278.

Independence Monument
វិមានឯករាជ្យ

The Vimean Ekareach, or Independence Monument, is located at the intersection of Norodom and Sihanouk Boulevards. Built in the late 1950s, the structure, designed by renowned Cambodian architect Vann Molyvann, takes the form of a lotus-shaped stupa reminiscent of similar building elements used at Angkor Wat.

Today, the monument commemorates Cambodia's independence from foreign rule and the country's war dead. During important national holidays, a flame is lit on the interior pedestal by a royal or high-ranking government official, and the steps are covered in floral tributes. The green space stretching down toward the river used to be a notorious red-light district but has been rehabilitated. These days, food vendors set up their carts in the evenings, when the monument is lit in red, blue, and white, the colors of Cambodia's flag. In 2013, a statue of King Norodom Sihanouk was erected a little to the west of Independence Monument.

the Olympic Stadium

Vann Molyvann's New Khmer Architecture

Phnom Penh was built by the French, but its modern character is attributable mostly to one man. Vann Molyvann, born in 1926 in Kampot, studied first law and then architecture in Paris in the 1940s. He was taught by Le Corbusier and returned to Cambodia in 1955 to be appointed by King Sihanouk as the country's chief national architect.

The post-independence years were heady times for Cambodia. The country was at peace; the king was a dynamic man and had dynamic plans for his people. His far-reaching cultural vision is perfectly represented by Molyvann's building style, called **New Khmer Architecture,** which sought to marry traditional Khmer and modern aesthetics and succeeded in creating a unique architectural style. Molyvann's monuments for an independent Cambodia integrated well with the older colonial cityscape. His most prominent structures include **Independence Monument,** the **Olympic Stadium** (now the National Sports Complex), the **Institute of Foreign Languages at Phnom Penh University,** and the **Capitol Cinema.**

Molyvann left Cambodia in 1972 but returned in 1993 and became Minister of Culture, Fine Arts, Urban and Country Planning. Sadly, many of his buildings, including the National Theater and the Council of Ministers, have recently been demolished to make space for more modern buildings. Molyvann published a book called *Modern Khmer Cities.*

Wat Moha Montrei

វត្តមហាមន្ត្រី

One of the most visited of the more than 20 pagodas in Phnom Penh is **Wat Moha Montrei** (daily 7am-5pm, free). King Monivong bestowed the temple's name, which means "The Great Minister," after one of his ministers had taken the initiative to start its construction in the 1930s. The pagoda walls are covered in frescoes depicting the life of the Buddha. The murals inside the main hall date from the 1970s; they also show the life of the Buddha and are known for their modern touches, such as *apsara* dancers in place of angels and depictions of men in modern uniforms. During the Khmer Rouge years, Wat Moha Montrei was used as a granary. The temple lies just south of the Olympic Stadium at the turnoff for Street 123 from Sihanouk Boulevard.

★ S-21 Tuol Sleng Museum

ស-២១ សារមន្ទីរតុកស្លែង

In August 1975, four months after the Khmer Rouge had taken control of Phnom Penh, the Tuol Svay Prey High School, south of Sihanouk Boulevard on Street 350, was converted into **Security Prison 21,** an interrogation and torture center, also called Tuol Sleng. Between 1975 and 1979, an estimated 17,000 people—men, women, and children—were imprisoned here. Many of them, especially in later years, were themselves members of the Khmer Rouge who had been accused of betraying the party in an ever-expanding cycle of internal purges. Even high-ranking members of the Cambodian communists were incarcerated and tortured. A few foreigners, mostly caught at sea, were also sent to S-21.

All prisoners were photographed and forced to tell their life stories, from childhood memories to the moment of their arrest. They were then assigned to their cells and systematically tortured in order to force a confession that suited the interrogators. Food was virtually nonexistent, and any challenge to the guards or failure to obey the myriad rules of S-21 resulted in severe, often deadly beatings. Prisoners were hung, electrocuted, and suffocated with plastic bags, and water-boarding was routinely applied to inmates. The confessions extracted usually contained the names of all the people prisoners knew. Often, those named were then also arrested and tortured. Most importantly, interrogators pried confessions of spy conspiracies out of the prisoners, a reflection of the regime's paranoia. Inmates confessed to either working for the CIA or the KGB. Few if

South of Sihanouk Boulevard

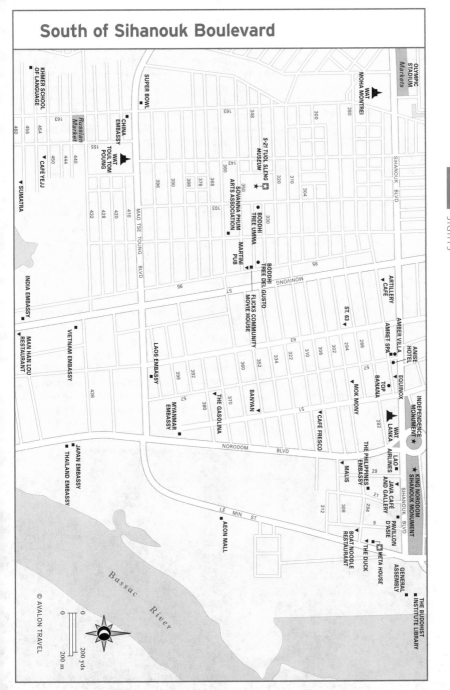

© AVALON TRAVEL

any of the inmates were likely to have done any such thing.

Initially, prisoners who had been killed were buried in the school yard, but as more space was needed, those inmates who had been "processed" were taken to Choeung Ek, executed, and buried in mass graves. More than 1,700 people worked at the prison, many of them teenagers. They were led by Comrade Duch, whose real name was Kang Kek Iew, a former schoolteacher who had been imprisoned and tortured in 1967 by King Sihanouk's security services for his affiliation with Cambodia's fledging communist movement. Prior to the Khmer Rouge takeover in 1975, Duch established torture centers in the communist-controlled provinces and developed his interrogation techniques. When Phnom Penh fell, he set up several prisons in the capital, which were amalgamated into one large center, S-21, in 1976.

When the Vietnamese liberated Phnom Penh in 1979, Duch fled with other Khmer Rouge cadres, too hurried to destroy the meticulous files kept on inmates. Nevertheless, he did take the time to execute the few remaining prisoners. Duch, who became a schoolteacher once more in refugee camps in Thailand, distanced himself from the Khmer Rouge after the movement's collapse in 1997. He became a Christian and worked for World Vision, an NGO. He was eventually recognized by photojournalist Nic Dunlop and arrested in 1999. In 2007, Duch was indicted on charges of crimes against humanity by the Cambodia Tribunal. His trial began in February 2009, and in 2010 he was convicted and sentenced to 35 years in prison. He claims that he just followed orders. Duch lost his appeal in 2012, and his sentence was extended to life.

Very few people survived S-21. Among them, Vann Nath, a Cambodian artist, was spared because he painted portraits and created busts of Khmer Rouge leader Pol Pot. Since 1979, Vann Nath has painted the crimes of the Khmer Rouge. Many of his paintings, depicting life at S-21, are on exhibition at the museum. Vann Nath wrote a memoir of his time at Tuol Sleng, titled *A Cambodian Prison Portrait: One Year in the Khmer Rouge's S-21 Prison,* which is widely available in Phnom Penh. He died in 2011.

The torture center was discovered by Vietnamese war photographer Ho Van Thay and has been partly preserved the way the Vietnamese found it, initially as a propaganda tool to show the world why it had been necessary to invade Cambodia. Some cells have

S-21 Tuol Sleng Museum

The Khmer Rouge United Nations Trial

The trial of the former senior Khmer Rouge leaders has been under way since 1997, when the Cambodian government requested the United Nations assistance in setting up what's commonly known as the Cambodia Tribunal. In 2001, the Extraordinary Chambers in the Courts of Cambodia for the Prosecution of Crimes Committed during the Period of Democratic Kampuchea (Extraordinary Chambers or ECCC) was created through laws passed by the National Assembly.

From the outset, the international dimension of the crimes committed by the Khmer Rouge has been excluded from the tribunal's responsibilities. Neither China, who bankrolled the genocide, nor the United States, who conducted massive bombing campaigns that killed hundreds of thousands of Khmer civilians and drove thousands more into the hands of the radical communists, have any interest in having their policies and actions relating to the rise of the Khmer Rouge examined. The Cambodian government is also keen to limit the scope of the trial—many of today's leading politicians are tainted by the country's past.

In 2003, after years of wrangling, mostly over influence and money, and despite reports of massive pre-trial corruption, the Cambodian government reached an agreement with the U.N. about how the trial is to be conducted, with both Cambodian and international judges. Throughout its creation, the court has been beset by funding problems, but finally, in 2006, then-Secretary General of the U.N. Kofi Annan appointed seven judges. Shortly after, the Cambodian justice minister announced the appointment of 30 Cambodian and U.N. judges to preside over the tribunal.

Between July and December 2007, five suspects, all of them elderly and frail, were indicted. Khieu Samphan, Nuon Chea, Ieng Sary, Ieng Thirit, and Kang Kek Iew, also known as Comrade Duch, were arrested on charges of crimes against humanity, including genocide. It is unlikely that further indictments will follow, as the Cambodian judges are keen to limit the case to the top Khmer Rouge echelon. Hearings started in February 2008, while the tribunal was still looking for millions of dollars in funding. In February 2009 the actual trial started, with Duch as the first defendant. He was convicted in July 2010 and received a 35-year sentence, from which 16 years was immediately shaved off for the time he had already spent behind bars. Duch appealed the verdict and lost his appeal in 2012; his sentence was changed to life in prison. In late 2011, the court ordered Ieng Thirit released as she was allegedly suffering from Alzheimer's, but this decision was overturned a month later. Ieng Sary died in March 2013 and escaped conviction. Khieu Samphan and Nuon Chea were finally convicted in 2014 and received life sentences for crimes against humanity.

Controversy and widely published allegations of corruption dogged the court for years, not least due to the refusal of the judges, under pressure from Prime Minister Hun Sen, himself a former Khmer Rouge, to look at further indictments of prominent Khmer Rouge (cases 003 and 004), some of whom live openly in Cambodia today and have become wealthy business tycoons or holders of local administrative offices. There is a real danger that the U.N.-sponsored court is reinforcing the Cambodian culture of impunity in which the powerful dictate the law. It remains uncertain whether more alleged war criminals will be indicted.

The tribunal has had a mixed response among ordinary Cambodians, who lived through decades of hardship and terror. Young Khmer have little knowledge of the horrors their parents lived through; up to now school textbooks have omitted the Khmer Rouge years and, incredibly, some young Khmer do not believe the genocide ever took place. But the survivors of Cambodia's darkest period may find some kind of closure if convictions continue. The international media, however, has painted the trial as a farce that does little to address Cambodia's troubled, dark past.

been left undisturbed, while others are now lined with thousands of photographs of inmates. It also contains a large collection of photographs of the damage the Khmer Rouge wrought on Cambodia, the paintings by Vann Nath, as well as shelves of the skulls of some of the victims of S-21. A new exhibition in some of the upstairs rooms throws new light on some of the inmates, including the foreigners killed in S-21, as well the main perpetrators.

A visit to the **S-21 Tuol Sleng Museum** (daily 7am-11:30am and 2pm-5:30pm, US$3, camera US$5) is a heart-wrenching experience, and visitors may ask themselves why they should confront so much horror. Yet in order to understand Cambodia's recent tragic history and the way it is today, a visit to a site of Khmer Rouge atrocities is extremely helpful. Many of the English-speaking guides waiting in the reception area lost family members in S-21, and a tour is highly recommended. Rates are negotiable, but expect to pay US$5-10. It's hard to put a price on an experience like this.

A souvenir stall on the premises sells photocopied books on Cambodian history. *S-21: The Khmer Rouge Killing Machine,* a 2003 feature documentary by renowned Cambodian director Rithy Panh, follows artist Vann Nath and another survivor back to S-21, where they confront some of the prison's former guards.

Wat Lanka

វត្តលង្កា

In the 13th century, Buddhist monks from Sri Lanka, who had come to Cambodia as teachers and quasi-missionaries, introduced monastic education and became advisors to the Cambodian monarchy. Located southwest of Independence Monument, **Wat Lanka** (daily 7am-5pm, free), Cambodia's first center for the study of Theravada Buddhism, was established in 1422 by King Ponhea Yat. Since its founding, the temple has served as a meeting place for Sri Lankan and Cambodian monks, who gave it the name Wat Lanka. The temple was used as a warehouse by the Khmer Rouge, and hence it escaped total destruction.

Wat Lanka has been restored under the supervision of Queen Mother Norodom Monineath, King Sihanouk's wife. Colorful wall frescoes recount the life of the Buddha on the ground level and upper floor of the pagoda.

★ Bophana

បុប្ផាណា

Bophana (64 Street 200, tel. 023/992-174, www.bophana.org, Mon.-Fri. 8am-6pm, Sat. 2pm-6pm, free) is an audiovisual resource center founded by renowned Cambodian film director Rithy Phan and open to the public. It is set up to archive images and sounds of the Cambodian memory and to make them widely available. It also trains Cambodians in the audiovisual professions by welcoming foreign film productions, and through its own artistic projects. The center offers visitors the opportunity to view many hours of digitized film footage, from 100-year-old French reels to the movies of King Sihanouk. To get a glimpse of what life before the Khmer Rouge was like in Cambodia, the center's growing collection of footage is the best and most easily accessible starting point.

Bophana hosts exhibitions and concerts in its downstairs reception area. Movies and documentaries are usually shown at the center on Saturday; check the website for details. Films can be searched and watched at individual screens upstairs; the archive is continually expanding, and archive consultation is available (Mon.-Fri. 8am-noon and 2pm-6pm, Sat. 2pm-6pm).

Entertainment and Events

NIGHTLIFE

Take care in any of the city's upscale Khmer nightclubs—a few rich kids like to exploit the fact that they are above the law and sometimes direct their aggression toward foreigners.

Boeng Kak and Wat Phnom Area
BARS

Well worth a visit is **The Elephant Bar** inside the Raffles Le Royal Hotel (Street 92, tel. 023/981-888), if only to check out the history of this fantastic luxury hotel. It's a great place to watch Cambodia's high society relax to the tunes of a lounge pianist below a ceiling covered in murals depicting, yes, elephants. Cocktails are not cheap, but if you drop by during happy hour (daily 4pm-8pm), it's not too painful. Forget about your budget for a second, close your eyes, and just think of all the celebrities, from Jackie Kennedy to Angelina Jolie, who have pulled into this history-laden watering hole over the past decades.

In recent years, a number of nightspots have opened on tiny Street 104, and the choice of venues, from sleazy hostess bars to upmarket bistros, is somewhat eclectic. Some visitors might find this road a little too sordid after nightfall. Of all the hostess bars in the area, **Oscar's Pub** (Street 104, daily 3pm-late) is perhaps the most interesting. Just as dark and dingy as the rest, it offers a live band, with the proprietor on drums, churning out rock and funk hits. Guests are welcome to hit the stage. **The Pickled Parrot** (4-6 Street 104, tel. 023/986-722, www.tonlesapguesthouse.com), another bar-hotel, is somewhat more lowbrow but offers an international menu with Australian steaks (around US$10). Most importantly, the Pickled Parrot is open daily 24-7 and has a pool table and Wi-Fi for guests.

KHMER NIGHTCLUBS
One of Phnom Penh's longest-running discos, the **Casa Nightclub** (5 Street 47, daily 7pm-2am) has a reputation for raucousness and is rarely visited by foreigners, but it makes for an interesting night out. Expect live music and questionable Chinese techno.

Around the Riverfront
BARS
The **Cadillac Bar** (219 Sisowath Quay, tel. 011/713-567, daily 8pm-1am) is a great slice of Americana right on Phnom Penh's riverfront. The bar's motto is "Just Rollin' on the River," and besides ice-cold beer and cocktails, there's a fine selection of food, including burgers, salads, and pasta dishes (US$3-10). Expect loud classic rock and very friendly, hassle-free service.

A few minutes' walk from the river, **Sharky Bar** (126 Street 130, tel. 023/211-825, www.sharkysofcambodia.com, daily 4pm-2am), Phnom Penh's oldest rock-and-roll bar, appears to have it all—great hamburgers and Tex-Mex dishes, pool tables, scores of hostesses, big-screen TVs for sports events, and draft beer. The atmosphere is somewhere between raucous and desperate, a kind of Hooters with loud music, and it's probably not for everyone. In recent years, Sharky's, as the locals call it, has become a decent live-music venue that organizes a mini rock festival, aptly named Penh-Stock.

Street 136 is another strip of garish hostess bars, hotels, and restaurants—a mini Las Vegas in the tropics. The standout venue here is **The Red Fox** (daily 10am-2am), a dark and dingy bar that has no hostesses and is a favorite meeting place of many of the city's expatriates.

Altogether unique is the **Space Hair Salon and Bar** (Street 136, www.spacehairpp.com, daily 9am-1am), both hair salon and gay bar offering cheap beer and impromptu drag shows.

Visit **Alley Cat** (in an alley of Street 19 behind the National Museum, daily

10am-10pm), a little hard to find but worth the effort, for an early evening drink. You'll find beer, Mexican food, and occasional live music in a grungy informal atmosphere.

More salubrious and downright classy, **The Mansion** (3 Sothearos Blvd., daily 5pm-late) calls itself a Heritage Bar and is located in one of the city's most attractive—and most dilapidated—colonial buildings, a stone's throw from the Royal Palace. A good selection of cocktails and wines and occasional dance and music performances in the courtyard make this an attractive early evening venue.

LIVE MUSIC

The Memphis Bar (3 Street 118, tel. 012/871-263, daily 5pm-4am), probably Phnom Penh's longest-running live-music venue, is close to the riverfront. The cover bands (Tues.-Sat.) that rock the house or play blues are pretty good.

CASINOS

Yes, Phnom Penh has long been a gambler's paradise. The only official casino is the **Naga World Hotel** (tel. 023/228-822), right on the banks of the Tonlé Sap River, south of Sihanouk Boulevard and next to Samdech Hun Sen Park. Casual dress is OK, but you shouldn't turn up in shorts or flip-flops. The hotel has more than 500 rooms. The roulette tables are separated by small water channels running through the casino hall at the foot of an *Indiana Jones*-reject fiberglass mountain. There's a wine-and-cigar bar as well as a karaoke bar called Club 88, open until 5am. In all there are 1,000 gaming machines and almost 180 table games. "Be a star tonight," their ads read.

Around Central Market
BARS

Howie's Bar (32 Street 51, daily 7pm-6am) is a small hole-in-the-wall bar, next to the Heart of Darkness, run by a friendly Khmer who returned from the United States a decade ago. This is a no-frills filling station offering loud rock music, ice-cold air-conditioning, a pool

Phnom Penh for Gay Travelers

A number of bars and hotels in the capital openly welcome gays and lesbians but tend not to be exclusively gay. Among them are the **Manor House Hotel** (21 Street 262, tel. 023/992-566, www.manorhousecambodia.com); **2 Colours** (225 Street 13), opposite the National Museum, a gay- and lesbian-friendly bar; the **Blue Chili** (36 Street 178), which puts on cabaret shows on weekends; and the incredible **Space Hair Salon and Bar** (Street 136, www.spacehairpp.com), both hair salon and bar. The infamous **Heart of Darkness Bar** (26 Street 51) is a gay-friendly place, too.

table, friendly service, cold beer, and sports on the TV. It's not a bad place to finish off the night.

The **Zeppelin Café** (109 Street 51, tel. 012/881-181, daily 5pm-4am) is run by Mr. Jun, who surely has the largest collection of vinyl records in Cambodia. His musical tastes are firmly anchored in the 1970s: Expect progressive rock, heavy metal, punk, and, of course, Led Zeppelin. There's occasional live music, cold beer, and Chinese snacks. The place keeps moving, so check for its current location.

Right around the corner, **Slur Bar** (28 Street 172, daily 11am-2am), near Pontoon, is a bit of an enigma. The ambience is strictly sports bar, but there's good live music most nights, including the city's best jazz improv shows, punk rock bands, and your usual cover acts.

KHMER NIGHTCLUBS

The **Heart of Darkness Bar** (26 Street 51, daily 7pm-late) is Phnom Penh's most legendary nightspot. The venue borrows its name from a Joseph Conrad novel set in Africa, but the bar actually started off as a kind of shrine to Tony Poe, a CIA operative in Laos who served as the template for Colonel Kurtz in Francis Ford Coppola's 1979 movie

Apocalypse Now. The Heart, as locals call it, opened in the late 1990s and has evolved from Phnom Penh's dingiest foreigner hangout to one of the trendiest nightspots in Southeast Asia. While marijuana-laden bowls no longer line the bar and most expatriates now go elsewhere, the atmosphere remains raucous, if not edgy—besides backpackers and taxi girls and boys (sex workers), patrons include young, rich, and spoiled Khmer who occasionally like to prove their immunity from the law, and, as a consequence, several shootings have occurred on the premises in recent years. It's the Wild East, all right—you have been warned. The best time to drop by is after 11pm. The place stays open until the last patron goes home.

These days, **Pontoon** (Street 51 and Street 172, daily 4pm-4am) is giving the Heart a run for its money. This trendy bar-nightclub, which regularly features local DJs, used to be located on a boat moored on the banks of the Tonlé Sap River, but the partying got so wild that it sunk in 2008. Briefly relocated to another stretch of river, it is now in the heart of town and features a dark Kubrickian interior and an extensive cocktail menu. This is one of the best late-night hangouts in Phnom Penh. Pontoon is gay-friendly, special parties happen on weekends, and it is frequented by taxi girls later in the evening.

South of Sihanouk Boulevard
BARS

Not far from Independence Monument, quite a few bars and restaurants have opened on Street 278. One of the most relaxed is **Equinox** (3A Street 278, near Street 51, daily 11am-very late), which also doubles as an art gallery for photo exhibitions. Food can be ordered from Setsara, a Thai and French restaurant next door. Besides friendly service, there's Wi-Fi, table soccer (possibly the only one in Phnom Penh), a pool table, a long cocktail list, and even some trendy clothes for sale.

The Gasolina (56-58 Street 57, Tues.-Sun. 10am-4am) is a great garden bar, popular with the NGO crowd on weekends. It hosts occasional live events and parties. It's best in the afternoons and is child-friendly, too.

KHMER NIGHTCLUBS AND DISCOS

"Bored . . . , lonely . . . , hungry . . . ?" reads the advertisement for **Martini Pub** (45 Street 95, www.martini-cambodia.com, daily 7pm-3am), a kind of multipurpose club left over from the UNTAC days. Martini can be pretty rough, or entertaining, depending on your point of view, with scores of hostesses vying for customers. There's a bar, an open-air food court, a pool table, and an ice-cold indoor disco.

The Rock Entertainment Centre (468 Monivong Blvd., daily 6pm-4am) is the city's largest disco, a huge cavernous place that features live DJs, bands, and canned techno and attracts the city's young and wealthy. Entry is free, but the drinks are a bit pricey (beer around US$3).

THE ARTS
Art Galleries

The smart and relaxed **Java Café and Gallery** (56 Sihanouk Blvd., tel. 023/987-420, www.javaarts.org, daily 7am-10pm), close to Independence Monument, puts on regular exhibitions of Khmer and foreign artists; openings are often packed. Its upstairs balcony location, with views across the park; a great menu of coffees, teas, and sumptuous snacks (from US$4), including great sandwiches and vegetarian dishes; and free Wi-Fi and a regular expatriate crowd have also made the Java Café a popular breakfast and lunch spot. Check the website for events.

The eclectic **XEM Design: La Galerie** (13D Street 178, tel. 023/722-252) is run by Cambodian artist and designer Em Riem, who works with paint, ceramics, and sculpture.

Sa Sa Art (Street 360, sasaart.info) is run by a group called Stiev Selapak—the art rebels—and is the city's only not-for-profit, artist-run space dedicated to experimental art practices. It is located in a historical and vibrant apartment complex called The White

Building. Check the website for current projects and exhibitions.

Theater and Performance

Located right on the river, **Chaktomuk Theatre** (tel. 023/982-210) hosts occasional culture performances; call for details. The **Sovanna Phum Arts Association** (166 Street 99, tel. 023/221-932, Fri.-Sat. 7:30pm) puts on weekly traditional performances that include dance and shadow puppetry.

Cinemas

There are numerous cinemas scattered around the city, usually showing homegrown horror flicks or badly dubbed Thai and Hollywood movies. The **Flicks Community Movie House** (39B Street 95, 90, Street 136 and 8, Street 258, tel. 078/809-429, www.theflicks-cambodia.com, US$3.50 per day adults, US$2 under age 18) is a community cinema for local expatriates; travelers, of course, are welcome. It shows a wide variety of movies and documentaries on a six-meter-wide screen, and ice cream and snacks are available. Early morning yoga classes (US$5) are also held here.

The grandly named **Legend Cinema** (City Mall, 3rd Fl., Street Monireth, tel. 088/954-9857, www.legend-cinemas.com, US$3, 3-D movies US$5) is the city's first real international-standard screen and shows first-run English-language movies. Showtimes start daily at 10am, and the last shows are at 10pm.

Brand new is the **Major Cineplex** on the 2nd floor of the monstrous Aeon Mall (Sothearos Blvd., www.majorcineplex.com.kh/cinema/theatre), which shows international blockbusters.

Cultural Centers
★ META HOUSE

Meta House (37 Sothearos Blvd., tel. 023/224-140, www.meta-house.com, Tues.-Sun., opening times depend on events) is Phnom Penh's first art, media, and communication center, offering a forum for artists from around the world. The center hosts exhibitions and workshops and stages regular events, including film showings, poetry readings, concerts, and excellent political talks and workshops. Meta House is supported by the German Goethe Institute. It's a great place to hang out and connect with local and expatriate artists. There's a smart bar-restaurant in the building. The spacious gallery downstairs showcases excellent photography and art exhibits by contemporary Cambodian and international artists. Check the website for events; film showings generally start at 7pm.

FRENCH CULTURAL CENTER

The **French Cultural Center** (218 Street 184, tel. 023/721-383, www.institutfrancais-cambodge.com), now known as l'Institut français du Cambodge, organizes regular film events, often showing vintage French movies. The center's movie schedule is published in the *Phnom Penh Post*. The center has recently been refurbished, and the smart French restaurant that's attached is recommended.

Shopping

MARKETS
★ Central Market

ផ្សារធំថ្មី

The attractive art deco structure of **Central Market** (daily 7am-5pm) is locally known as Phsar Thmey, which actually means New Market. This ocher-colored dome-like structure is one of the city's most prominent landmarks. The market stands on a former swamp area, which was drained by the French in 1935; the building was completed in 1937. Around the main entrance you are likely to be accosted by mine victims selling photocopied books. They can be persistent, but keep in mind that this is the only way they can make a living. Also around the entrance, numerous vendors sell T-shirts with slogans such as "I survived Cambodia" alongside a bewildering variety of cheapish souvenirs and curios. The bootleg bookstalls sell decent maps of Cambodia as well as beautifully simple hand-drawn greeting cards, produced with watercolors and featuring traditional Cambodian themes.

All around the market building, a little city of covered stalls sells mostly fresh food. Simple food stalls offer noodles and fresh coffee. Inside the cavernous building, hundreds of small shops sell fake watches and sunglasses, cheap electronics, brand-name clothes and DVDs, also fake, as well as fresh meat, which is definitely real. Numerous money changers ply their trade here; if you are after riel, they offer roughly the same rates as the banks and it's quicker. Sometimes, blind musicians, guided by street children, pass through the market area, singing somber tunes while playing the *tro,* a two-stringed fiddle-like instrument, whose sound box is covered in snakeskin.

Phsar Thmey is at the eastern end of Kampuchea Krom Boulevard, about a five-minute walk along Street 130 from the riverside. In 2010, the main building was renovated and received a new coat of paint.

The Russian Market

ផ្សារទួលទំពូង

During the Vietnamese presence in the 1980s, Russians often came shopping at

inside Central Market

the **Russian Market** (daily 7am-5pm) for Western goods they could not get elsewhere, hence the name. In the late 1990s, it was also possible to purchase large quantities of marijuana as well as AK-47s here, but the bad old times are long gone. Known as Phsar Toul Tom Poung in Khmer, the Russian Market has no architectural finesse—and, in the summer, the narrow aisles between the stalls crammed with products can seem like the inside of an oven—but the market does retain a very special atmosphere. The choice of curios and souvenirs is much more varied here than at Central Market. Decent-quality silk as well as silver, gold, precious stones, large wooden carvings, and opium pipes are also on display. The Russian Market has the largest selection of bootleg CDs and bootleg DVD movies in the country. Most shops let customers test the discs prior to purchase. Other sections of the market specialize in machine tools and other local products, and there are numerous food vendors and coffee stalls both inside the area and in the surrounding streets. Located in the far south of the city, off Mao Tse Tung Boulevard, the Russian Market is best visited after a trip to nearby Tuol Sleng.

Old Market

ផ្សារចាស់

Phsar Chas, also known as Old Market, though not a tourist market, used to be worth a visit. Located near the riverfront between Streets 108 and 106, the various stalls sold mostly fruits and vegetables, which made for a rather fermented atmosphere on hot days. Unfortunately, parts of the market burned down in November 2014, and it remains to be seen whether it will be reconstructed or whether the land will be used for other purposes.

Orussey Market

ផ្សារអូរុស្សី

Orussey Market (daily 7am-5pm) is a general market that used to be located in the middle of the road on the northern side of the Olympic Stadium, but has since been moved into a concrete building on Street 182. Orussey is worth a visit for the sheer variety of products on offer, although none of it is geared toward visitors. Expect food, clothes, and household goods.

The Night Market

A night market, selling curios, clothes, and souvenirs, is held Friday-Sunday between

stalls full of crafts and souvenirs in the Russian Market

Streets 106 and 108, just off Sisowath Quay. Popular with locals and visitors, more than 100 stalls offer clothes, souvenirs (not all of them made in Cambodia), and a huge selection of food. Be sure to haggle.

SHOPPING MALLS
The Sorya Mall

Phnom Penh's first shopping mall, complete with an escalator, which is ridden with fascination and respect by out-of-towners, **Sorya Mall** (Street 63, near the Central Market) is filled with the usual bootleg products—video games, computer software, DVDs, and handbags. Somewhat more genuine are branches of BB Burgers and the Pizza Company, which offer familiar-looking fast food, prepared for Asian palates. On the roof, a cinema, a roller-skating rink, and a games arcade are very popular with the city's teenagers. Views across the city are spectacular.

The Paragon Mall

Some Cambodians can afford to buy sofas for US$3,000 a pop. The **Paragon Mall** (Street 214, near Independence Monument) is proud to be the most ostentatious shopping space in the capital and in the country—until the day a larger mall opens, of course. The rapidly growing number of middle-class Cambodians makes this mall profitable, while one-third of the population continues to survive on US$0.50 a day. But the Paragon is more than a place full of stuff for people who already have everything: There's a large supermarket on the ground floor as well as a good food court.

The Aeon Mall

The latest addition to Phnom Penh's shopping opportunities is a U.S.-style über-mall called **Aeon** (Sothearos Blvd., http://aeonphnompenh.com, daily 9am-10pm), crammed with fast-food joints, department stores, and a multiplex cinema. For all those travelers who come to Cambodia to feel like they are back home, this is the place to be. Expect Western products at high prices. Copies of most of the stuff on sale here can be bought for a fraction of the price at most of the city's markets.

CRAFTS AND BOOKS

Street 178 has been dubbed Gallery Street. Running alongside the National Museum, the road was initially home to family workshops churning out garish paintings of Angkor Wat. Many of these shops are still operating, and some of the colors on the huge canvasses are positively psychedelic. In recent years, a number of galleries and boutiques selling contemporary art and crafts have joined the more traditional artists and created a small but vibrant scene that hosts regular exhibitions and has begun to publish books on modern Khmer art and architecture. A number of NGO craft shops are also found in the area.

Reyum (47 Street 178, tel. 023/217-149, www.reyum.org) is the most notable gallery. It regularly shows the work of Cambodia's most cutting-edge artists, runs its own publishing house, and sells a wide variety of books on Asian art. Books published include nonfiction works on art, but the company also puts out Khmer-language books for children. Profits are reinvested in publishing additional titles. Besides exhibitions, Reyum presents lectures and music performances. The Reyum Institute, a Cambodian NGO, runs a free arts school for Cambodian children. Visiting artists from the United States, Canada, France, Japan, and other Asian countries introduce students to new artistic techniques.

Visitors with deep pockets might want to take a look at what's exhibited at **Mekong Art** (33 Street 178), which offers a wide selection of high-end contemporary and traditional Cambodian art objects including statues, silk products, furniture, and home wares.

Pavillon d'Asie (24/26 Sihanouk Blvd., tel. 023/221-909) is part art gallery, part boutique and also offers contemporary and traditional Cambodian art with a particular emphasis on sculptures in wood, bronze, and stone as well as antiques.

Asasax Art Gallery (192 Street 178, tel. 023/217-795, www.asasaxart.com.kh) is another exhibition space worth a visit. Mr. Asasax is a well-established Cambodian artist who sells his original work (paintings from around US$25), which often feature traditional motifs executed with contemporary techniques.

Stéphane Delaprée, a French Canadian cartoonist, paints extremely colorful canvasses with Cambodian scenes. The artist calls his work Happy Paintings, and even former King Sihanouk has praised Delaprée for his contribution to contemporary Cambodian art. Stef's paintings can be viewed at his **Happy Painting Gallery** (Sisowath Quay, www.happypainting.net), underneath the FCC and next to Café Fresco.

Virtually next door, **Orange River** (367 Sisowath Quay, tel. 023/214-594) sells a wide variety of silk products including clothes, pillow cases, and handbags, all produced by local people.

Street 240 also has a fair number of resident art and crafts shops (as well as great bars and restaurants). Drop by the **Magic Gecko** (87 Street 240) for silk products, some of them with geckos; the upmarket **Le Lezard Bleu** (61 Street 240) for high-quality Khmer art, both traditional and contemporary; or **Mekong Quilts** (49 Street 240, www.mekongquilts.org), which, as the name suggests, sells quilts and bedspreads. Profits go to projects in the Cambodian countryside. **Couleurs D'Asie** (33 Street 240), which sells funky home decorations such as fusion furniture and silk products, is also worth checking out.

One of Phnom Penh's largest wine and spirits retailers, **Red Apron** (15-17 Street 240) is also located in the area. This place has a huge selection of bottles from around the world and supplies many of the hotels and restaurants in town.

Monument Books (111 Norodom Blvd., tel. 023/217-617) is Phnom Penh's largest (and, unfortunately, only) outlet for new and genuine books. Having no competition, Monument's prices are high. Nevertheless, there is a wide selection of regional and international titles. Travel guides and run-of-the-mill thrillers are especially well stocked, as is a great deal of academic background on the region. The shop now also houses a quiet and relaxed café. There's also a small branch at the airport. For a great selection of used books, visit **Bohr's Books** (5 Sothearos Blvd., tel. 012/929-148), near the National Museum. Unlike in many shops in the city, books are clearly organized and easy to find, and the owner, Chea Sopheap, is a genuine bookseller: He knows what people read. Bohr's Books buys or exchanges secondhand titles, and prices are very reasonable. In 2011, a second shop (47 Street 172) with an equally wide selection of secondhand titles opened in Phnom Penh's new backpacker area.

Sports and Recreation

SWIMMING

Numerous hotels have swimming pools, and the larger ones are at the **InterContinental** and **Le Royal.** For a cheaper alternative, check out the pool at the Olympic Stadium, the only Olympic-size pool in town.

The **Phnom Penh Water Park** (Airport Rd., tel. 023/881-008, daily 9:30am-6pm, Mon.-Fri. US$2, Sat.-Sun. US$3) is extremely popular with Cambodians, who flock here on weekends to enjoy water slides and a wave pool. It's pretty quiet on weekdays, when the large slides are closed, and is least crowded in the morning.

BOWLING

Phnom Penh's best bowling alley is **Super Bowl** (113 Mao Tse Tung Blvd., daily 10am-very late). Sessions cost US$6-9 per hour, depending on the time of day.

CYCLING

Highly recommended tour operator **Grasshopper Adventures** (29 Street 130, tel. 012/462-165, www.grasshopperadventures.com) offers fantastic cycling trips around Phnom Penh. Safety conscious, with great guides and good mountain bikes that have been imported from Thailand, the company offers a variety of tours, including the half-day Islands of the Mekong Tour (US$39), which takes quiet back roads through local communities and farmland to witness village life in the Cambodian countryside close to the capital, and the full-day Oudong Tour (US$75), which leads along abandoned railroad lines to Oudong Mountain to see classic friendly Cambodia village life. Longer trips from Phnom Penh to the coast and into Vietnam are also available. There's another branch of Grasshopper Adventures in Siem Reap that organizes cycling trips around the Angkor temples.

Many of the cheaper guesthouses in Phnom Penh rent bicycles for around US$3 a day. Ride carefully; the Cambodian capital's traffic is unforgiving.

GOLF

There are several golf courses around the Cambodian capital. The closest one is the **Royal Cambodia Phnom Penh Golf Club** (023/366-689), just 5 miles from the city, set among rice fields with lots of palm trees, sand traps, and water hazards. Here you will have a chance to rub shoulders with Cambodia's kleptocratic politicians and business tycoons. For a more sedate game, try the **Cambodia Golf and Country Club** (Office 56, Street 222, tel. 023/363-666, www.golfincambodia. com), 35 kilometers south of the city along Route 4. Greens fees in Phnom Penh are cheaper than in Siem Reap. During the week, it's possible to pay US$40 to play 18 holes. It's US$70 over the weekend.

GO-KARTS

Kambol Go-Karting (Route 4, tel. 012/804-620, daily 9am-6pm) has a one-kilometer-long track off Route 4, seven kilometers past the airport. It's US$10 for a 10-minute race. Some visitors report that the carts are badly maintained and the brakes don't work.

SHOOTING RANGE

In the same area as Kambol Go-Karting, Phnom Penh's **Shooting Range** (Route 4, past the airport) offers visitors the opportunity to shoot an AK-47 (US$30 for 30 rounds) or throw a hand grenade. The range has been threatened with closure by a government keen to avoid promoting violence.

TABLE TENNIS

Yes, Phnom Penh now has its very own table tennis club, the **54 Langeach Sros Club** (Street 172), on a small street opposite Wat Sarawan. Nonmembers are welcome to play. Renting a racket and table is just 6,000 riel per hour. Many locals also come here to play chess; boards are provided.

HORSEBACK RIDING

If you want to learn to ride in Cambodia, contact the **Cambodia Equestrian Centre** (tel. 012/231-755), an international-standard riding school located at Northbridge School on Northbridge Road.

MOTORCYCLE RENTAL

One of the cheapest places to rent a motorcycle in Phnom Penh is **Lucky Lucky** (413 Monivong Blvd., tel. 023/220-988). A 150-cc bike starts at US$4 per day, and a 250-cc dirt bike costs around US$15 per day. A better option with more reliable and slightly more expensive bikes for rent is **Angkor Dirt Bikes** (1319 Street 349, www.toursintheextreme.com).

TRADITIONAL MASSAGE AND SPA

Cambodia has its own traditional massage technique. There are plenty of massage places in Phnom Penh, some more traditional than others. Recently, several boutique spas have opened around town. One of the swankiest is the **Amara Spa** (Sisowath Quay and

Street 110, tel. 023/998-730, www.amaraspa. hotelcara.com). Also popular is the **Amatak Beauty Spa** (101 Sisowath Quay, tel. 070/212-345). For Thai and Balinese-style massage, head to **O'Spa** (4B Street 75, tel. 012/852-308, http://ospa-cambodia.com).

GYMS

Most of the gyms in Phnom Penh are located in international hotels. Head for the **Amrita Spa** at Le Royal (Street 92, tel. 023/981-888, daily 6am-10pm) or the **Clark Hatch Fitness Center** at the InterContinental (296 Mao Tse Tung Blvd., tel. 023/424-888, ext. 5000, Mon.-Fri. 6am-10pm, Sat.-Sun. and holidays 8am-8pm). Early in the morning, locals exercise on the square in front of the Royal Palace or en masse at the Olympic Stadium. It's worth the spectacle even if you don't want to participate.

ARCHITECTURAL TOURS

KA Tours (www.ka-tours.org), an NGO promoting and documenting modern Khmer architecture, offer tours around the city that take in Phnom Penh's architectural landmarks from the 1960s, including the Olympic Stadium. Group tours are US$15-48 per person. Private tours can also be organized (US$60 for 2 people, US$75 for 4 people).

RIVER CRUISES

Numerous boat operators offer short and long river journeys. Short hops along the Tonlé Sap River are best at sunrise for views of Phnom Penh's skyline, though sunset cruises can also be sublime. Bring your own food and drinks and chill out on the water. Boats can be found along the riverfront between Street 130 and Street 178 as well as near the pier at Street 104, just north of the Night Market. Outings should be around US$10 per hour. Day trips and longer excursions are offered by **Satra Boat** (Street 94, corner of Street 13, tel. 012/432-456).

KHMER LANGUAGE COURSES

If you are going to spend some time in the country, you might want to learn some Khmer. There are several language schools in town; call **Khmer School of Language** (52 Street 454, tel. 023/213-047, www.cambcomm. org.uk/ksl) or check around guesthouses and hotels for private tutors. One-on-one lessons usually cost around US$70-100 for a month's worth of daily lessons (five days a week).

aboard a river cruise ship

Accommodations

Phnom Penh offers accommodations for every budget, from cheap flophouses where a double room costs a few dollars to exquisite boutique and luxury hotels that will set you back hundreds of dollars per night. The best area to stay is near the river and main sights, around the riverfront or around Central Market. All room rates quoted are for double occupancy in high season, but given Cambodia's currently booming economy, expect prices to rise, especially at the lower end.

WAT PHNOM AREA
US$15-25

Among the cheapest sleeping options in Phnom Penh, **Encounters** (89-91 Street 108, tel. 089/530-185, dorm US$5, room US$12) offers clean dorm rooms with bunk beds and mattresses on the floor, both mixed and single sex with fan or air-conditioning, as well as safety lockers and a free laundry service. Some travelers have reported that the lockers aren't safe, so take care of your stuff here.

The **Grand View Guesthouse** (Boeung Kak Lake, off Street 93, tel. 099/723-136) no longer has grand views as the lake's been filled in with sand, but it's cheap and cheerful enough with rooms around US$10. The rooftop restaurant still offers good sunsets even if the swamp below is not particularly attractive. This is one of the last survivors of Phnom Penh's erstwhile backpacker area.

Me Mates Place (5 Street 90, tel. 023/500-2497, www.mematesplace.com, US$25, dorm beds US$10) is all white minimalist chic with a restaurant doing breakfasts, a small bar, a pool table, and free Wi-Fi downstairs. The small but neat guest rooms have flat-screen TVs and attractive baths.

US$25-50

The very decent and recently refurbished **Cara Hotel** (18 Street 47, at Street 84, tel. 023/430-066, www.hotelcara.com, US$45-60)

offers large, spotless, and slightly boutiquey guest rooms furnished in Ratanakiri wood; a decent breakfast is included.

US$50-100

Right next to Wat Phnom and the U.S. Embassy, the **Sunway Hotel** (1 Street 92, tel. 023/430-333, http://phnompenh.sunwayhotels.com, from US$99) is something of a business place, but it's well located away from the city bustle and therefore a good spot to retreat to after a hot day in the city. The rooms are large if a little anonymous.

Excellent fully furnished and serviced guest rooms, especially suitable for business travelers and expatriates, can be rented, either per night or long term, at the swish **Central Mansion** (1A Street 102, tel. 012/958-619, http://centralmansions.com). Located close to Wat Phnom, this residential building offers studio and 1-3-bedroom apartment packages, which include the use of a large pool, Wi-Fi, a gym, laundry service, drinking water, and parking. Small units cost US$80 per night, US$900 per month; larger units are US$100-350 per night, US$1,600-6,500 per month.

Over US$200

The foremost address for colonial style and international luxury is the ★ **Le Royal** (Street 92, tel. 023/981-888, www.raffles.com, US$270), located in its own well-kept tropical gardens off Monivong Boulevard. In the late 1960s and 1970s, this handsome building served as a base for foreign media and featured heavily in Roland Joffe's movie *The Killing Fields* (though the Railway Hotel in Hua Hin in Thailand served as a stand-in for Le Royal in the film). This Raffles hotel has now been restored to its former glory. Expect first-class service along with plenty of Old World charm and history. A large swimming pool and a gym are available for guests. For those who can afford it (suites up to US$2,000), it's a great place to be based to experience the capital. Even if you don't stay here, it's worth dropping by for a drink to marvel at the splendor.

AROUND THE RIVERFRONT
Under US$15

Since the backpacker hotels by Boeng Kak Lake were closed and demolished, a row of cheapies, as well as several restaurants, shops, and bars, have sprung up on Street 172, within easy walking distance of the National Museum.

★ **The Last Home Guest House** (21 Street 172, tel. 016/307-134, last_home_gh@ yahoo.com) is a budget hotel in the heart of Phnom Penh. Less than a stone's throw from the National Museum and just a few minutes' walk from Sisowath Quay and the Royal Palace, the Last Home has long been a favorite with travelers and expatriates. Owner Sakit promises "real food" and "real people," and she means it. The Last Home, besides offering clean, decent-size guest rooms (from US$7) with TVs and showers, as well as larger guest rooms (US$20) with air-conditioning and big windows to the street, serves excellent home cooking, both Western dishes and a selection of Asian favorites. The guesthouse also arranges visas for China, Vietnam, and Thailand, and is a reliable place to book onward tickets or arrange for local transportation. The Last Home has good security, a definite bonus in the city center.

Almost next door, the similar **Longlin 2 House** (Street 172, US$10, with a/c US$13) has clean guest rooms with Wi-Fi included. The in-house restaurant serves breakfast and Khmer dishes, burgers, and pasta. The older **Longlin House** (159 Street 19, tel. 023/992-412, US$10, with a/c US$13) is right around the corner and offers a similar deal.

US$15-25

Mama Veary's (26 Street 172, tel. 011/399-123, from US$20), formerly called Super Star, offers clean guest rooms with Wi-Fi and

air-conditioning, TVs, fridges, and seating areas. This is a great value for the price.

The Indochine 2 Hotel (28-30 Street 130, tel. 023/211-525, www.indochine2hotel. com) is a relatively characterless but reliable and clean hotel in an excellent location close to the riverfront. Popular with tour groups, the hotel also has a restaurant and bar that never seems to close, but with so many attractive nightspots in walking distance, it's hardly noteworthy. Double rooms (US$25) have attached baths and air-conditioning; larger rooms (US$30-40) also come with a window.

The **Velkommen Inn** (23 Street 144, tel. 077/757-701, US$18-36), under Norwegian management, offers very clean double and triple guest rooms. The larger balcony rooms have great river views as well as air conditioning, fans, in-room safes, minibars, cable TV with 70 channels, hot water, sofas, and dining tables.

The reliable **Bright Lotus Guest House 1** (22 Street 178, tel. 023/990-446, US$16, with balcony US$30) offers simple midsize and clean guest rooms with high ceilings. All guest rooms feature TVs, air-conditioning, and hot water. Free Wi-Fi for two hours a day is included in the room rates.

Also on Phnom Penh's new budget street is the user-friendly **Hometown Hotel** (35 Street 172, tel. 023/986-296, www.hometown-hotel.com, US$15-18). Large, bright guest rooms, accessed via a rather grand stairway, have Wi-Fi, air-conditioning, and TVs. Service is friendly, and bus and plane tickets can be arranged.

A little up the road, the recently opened **Sundance** (61 Street 172, tel. 016/802-090, www.sundancecambodia.com, US$20-50) is almost a boutique property and offers small but very smart guest rooms with large beds and their own computer terminals. There's a small swimming pool out back and a lively bar with a pool table imported from Canada.

US$25-50

Comfortable air-conditioned guest rooms can be found at the large, clean, and basic

Dara Reang Sey Hotel (45 Street 118, tel. 023/428-181, www.darareangsey.com, US$28-50). Some guest rooms have balconies, and guests who stay more than seven days get free Internet access; otherwise it's US$1 per hour. The in-house restaurant (around US$3) serves decent Khmer dishes. The hotel can arrange visas, transportation, and city tours.

The **Silver River Hotel** (37 Street 172, tel. 023/210-077, www.silverriverhotel.com) is a rather grand glass-and-concrete edifice in the heart of backpacker land on Street 172. Small, smart international-standard guest rooms with Wi-Fi, air-conditioning, and TVs are US$47, larger deluxe guest rooms are US$40. Breakfast is included.

The very well located **Diamond Palace II Hotel** (29 Street 178, tel. 023/224-169, www.diamondpalace-hotel.com, US$20-50) offers clean bright rooms, all with air-conditionin, opposite the National Museum. Breakfast and Wi-Fi are included.

US$50-100

A great place to stay is the very green **Boddhi Tree Aram Boutique Hotel** (70 Street 244, tel. 012/565-509, www.boddhitree.com, US$76). Submerged in potted palm trees and situated next to the residence of the British ambassador, this delightful small hotel has a restaurant terrace; guest rooms are well designed, clean, and bright and include breakfast and Wi-Fi access. Note that the same owners have opened two more Boddhi Trees around town.

Located in a stunning colonial villa, surrounded by high protective walls and just around the corner from the Royal Palace, ★ **The Pavilion** (227 Street 19, tel. 023/222-280, www.thepavilion.asia, US$80-95) is one of the nicest mid-range places in town. The main building has smart and bright guest rooms with hardwood floors, some with a balcony looking out on the swimming pool and garden. A 1960s villa next door serves as an adjunct with equally fine guest rooms, and there are some glass bungalows (US$45). The staff is friendly and efficient; there's free

Internet for guests and a poolside bar. The only drawback: This place appears to have a discriminatory attitude toward mixed-race couples.

The smart ★ **Bougainvillier Hotel** (277 Sisowath Quay, tel. 023/220-528, www.bougainvillierhotel.com) offers large, beautifully decorated guest rooms filled with lovely wooden furniture in a careful blend of modern boutique and Old World styles. Guest rooms with a riverside view and a balcony are US$100; those with windows on the back are US$75. The hotel restaurant serves very good Khmer cuisine as well as great steaks.

The **Frangipani Royal Palace Hotel** (27 Street 278, tel. 023/223-320, www.frangipani-palacehotel.com, US$70) offers spacious and bright boutique rooms a stone's throw from the Royal Palace and close to the National Museum. There's a rooftop pool and a great rooftop bar and restaurant with excellent views of the palace and across the river. There are three other Frangipani hotels in Phnom Penh, but this one's got the best location.

US$100-200

One of the most luxurious addresses in Phnom Penh is the **Amanjaya Pancam** (1 Street 154, 023/219-579, www.amanjaya-pancam-hotel.com, US$135-175), an exquisite boutique hotel with ultra-modern suites that have subtle lighting, hardwood floors, and contemporary interiors influenced by Cambodian designs. All suites have air-conditioning, safes, TVs, Wi-Fi, and minibars. The equally well-designed ground-floor restaurant, K-West, is also recommended and serves a wide variety of Asian and European dishes.

One of Phnom Penh's modern-style upmarket hotels, the **Cambodiana** (313 Sisowath Quay, tel. 023/426-288, www.hotelcambodiana.com.kh, US$100-360), right by the river and a short tuk-tuk ride from the Royal Palace, offers all the usual international-standard amenities, including a swimming pool, a gym, shops, and several restaurants. The huge in-house Q-Ba nightclub and casino is one of the city's trendiest nightspots, with live music, a huge selection of drinks, and regular party events. A breakfast buffet is included in the room rates.

Right on the riverfront, **The Quay** (277 Sisowath Quay, tel. 023/224-894, www.thequayhotel.com) is one of Phnom Penh's finest boutique hotels. Opened by the people behind the FCC, The Quay is a futuristic experience. Everything is white, with decor reminiscent of the film *A Clockwork Orange,* and the guest rooms are simple but luxurious. The windowless doubles (US$70) at the back are a bit claustrophobic, especially for the cost, but the front suites (US$105), with hardwood floors, spacious baths, and balcony views of the Tonlé Sap, are fantastic.

AROUND CENTRAL MARKET
Under US$15

The somewhat rundown **Capitol Guest House** (154A Street 182, tel. 023/217-627, US$5, with a/c US$15) is one of Phnom Penh's longest established cheapies. Guest rooms are cramped, but OK for the cost, although the US$15 charged for air-conditioned guest rooms is not quite justified. The Capitol offers reasonably priced day trips to numerous destinations outside the city, and a decent backpacker restaurant is attached.

Diagonally across the road from the Capitol, the French-run **Dragon Guest House** (238 Street 107, tel. 012/239-066, US$6, with a/c US$12) offers slightly brighter though sometimes noisy guest rooms. Guests can relax in the nice balcony restaurant that has good traveler ambience. The menu is extensive and includes Khmer, Indian, and international favorites.

Also very nice is the **Spring Guest House** (24 Street 111, tel. 023/222-155, with fan US$9, with a/c US$13). The front looks like the entrance to a DIY shop, but the small and simple guest rooms are clean and bright. Long-term stays are welcome.

The **Bright Lotus Guest House 2** (76 Street 172, tel. 023/365-640, with fan US$7, with a/c US$14) is a clean budget hotel that

balconies of The Quay hotel

offers medium-size guest rooms with attached baths. The guesthouse offers bicycle and motorcycle rentals but has no restaurant.

US$15-25

A step up from the rock-bottom cheapies is the well-maintained **Angkor Bright Guest House** (84 Street 63, tel. 023/221-162, www.angkorbright.com, US$15-25). Large and simple guest rooms have wood paneling and air-conditioning; the bigger rooms have windows, and some have balconies.

US$25-50

The oddly named **Blue Tongue Café** (39 Street 174, tel. 023/224-639, www.bluetonguecafe.com, US$30-45) is on the corner of Street 51, right on the edge of one of the city's nightlife areas. You'll find boutique aesthetics at decent prices and a good restaurant to boot. This non-smoking hotel also has some environmentally friendly features such as hot water generated by solar energy and the use of recycled materials for construction.

Very attractive and comfortable modern, air-conditioned guest rooms with views over the pool can be found at the small **Billabong Hotel** (5 Street 158, tel. 023/223-703, www.thebillabonghotel.com, US$42), which has a swimming pool framed by co-conut palms, a great restaurant that serves a wide variety of Thai dishes, and a 24-hour poolside bar.

The new **Elite Boutique Hotel** (53 Street 63, tel. 023/211-566, www.eliteboutique-hotel.com, US$40), some 500 meters south of Central Market, offers simple but smart rooms with air-conditioning, fridges, bathtubs, and Wi-Fi. The restaurant serves Japanese and Chinese food.

US$50-100

Yet another fine 1960s Cambodian villa is home to the **Manor House** (21 Street 262, tel. 023/992-566, www.manorhousecambodia.com, US$42-62), a gay- and straight-friendly bed-and-breakfast place with a decent pool in a leafy private courtyard. Guest rooms are nice but not large; it's very quiet, and there's free Wi-Fi.

The **Diamond Hotel** (172-184 Monivong Blvd., tel. 023/217-221, http://diamondhotel.com.kh, US$55-75) is a good hotel for business travelers, offering large and clean standard mid-range guest rooms, some with balconies over Monivong Boulevard. A Khmer and Thai restaurant serves decent main courses (US$3). Breakfast is included in the room rates (US$5 for non-guests). There have been some renovations recently; pick one of the redecorated guest rooms.

US$100-200

The **Frangipani Fine Arts Hotel** (43 Street 178, tel. 023/223-320, www.fran-gipanihotel.com, US$100) is close to the School of Fine Arts, in a quiet side street away from the main strip leading to the National Museum. The bright, sparsely furnished rooms are kitted out in con-temporary design, with rattan furniture, sculptures, and other features created by

Cambodian artists. There's a good restaurant serving Cambodian and French cuisine. Breakfast is included in the room rates. Bicycles are free for guests.

SOUTH OF SIHANOUK BOULEVARD
Under US$15

One of the few real cheapies around Street 278, the friendly **Top Banana** (Street 51 and Street 278, tel. 012/885-572, www.topbanana.biz) is on the 2nd floor of a Khmer town house. The common area is relaxing, the rooftop bar is sociable, but the guest rooms are a bit dark and can be noisy if there's a party going on. It's US$10 for a box with a bed and a fan, US$16 for large, air-conditioned guest rooms. There's a restaurant offering traveler standards, and a travel service is attached.

US$15-25

If you don't mind staying directly opposite the Tuol Sleng Museum, the **Boddhi Tree Umma** (50 Street 113, tel. 012/565-509, www.boddhitree.com, US$18) is a good choice. Smart rooms decorated in an airy contemporary style are located in a well-restored traditional Khmer house, and the restaurant is not bad either, with plenty of healthy choices like salads and fruit juices. Service is prompt if not particularly friendly.

US$25-50

There are two good mid-range choices on Street 278. The **Anise Hotel** (2C Street 278, tel. 023/222-522, www.anisehotel.com.kh, US$42-55) is a simple but clean and stylish hotel with lots of traditional Khmer paintings on the walls and pleasant outdoor seating. The 20 air-conditioned guest rooms are large, spotless, and convenient. The larger rooms also feature safes and DVD players. The downstairs restaurant serves superior Asian food and international traveler fare.

Across the road, the **Amber Villa** (1A Street 57, tel. 023/216-303, www.amber-kh.com, US$36) is more traditionally Khmer in its choice of decor but is professionally run, offering air-conditioned rooms with safes, TVs and DVD players, and an Internet connection. Some guest rooms have kitchens. Breakfast, laundry, and newspapers are also included.

US$50-100

The intimate **Boddhi Tree Del Gusto** (43 Street 95, tel. 023/998-424, www.boddhitree. com, US$58) is located in a colonial villa with a shady forecourt under rose apple and mango trees and has just eight bright and airy air-conditioned guest rooms. There's a great café for meeting people downstairs.

US$100-200

One of Phnom Penh's top hotels and part of the international chain, the **InterContinental** (296 Mao Tse Tung Blvd., tel. 023/424-888, www.intercontinental.com, from US$190) has everything a business traveler or high-end tourist might desire. The InterContinental offers large, air-conditioned guest rooms and suites with modern amenities, a swimming pool, a nightclub, a gym, and conference facilities. Breakfast is included in the room rates, and there's a decent spa and sauna. Guest rooms are available from US$130, if you book online. Wi-Fi access costs a whopping US$25.

Food

Phnom Penh offers a vast culinary range, and new restaurants seem to open every week. Besides food served at markets, there are countless Khmer restaurants, some of them roadside stalls, others fully air-conditioned diners. Food from the region is also present, with Thai, Japanese, and Indian restaurants to choose from. Finally, the selection of international eateries in the capital is simply astounding. You won't have to go far for a pizza, a steak, pasta, or a good piece of cake. Most restaurants are a very good value by U.S. standards, with dishes usually ranging US$3-6.

WAT PHNOM AREA
International

Tell (13 Street 90, tel. 023/430-650, daily 11am-10:30pm) is Phnom Penh's most established German restaurant. Expect generous portions of international standards, especially German and Swiss dishes, served in a typically homey yet smart atmosphere. The *Eisbein mit sauerkraut* (grilled pork leg with sauerkraut) is popular. Main international entrées cost US$10-15, but there's also a large selection of Asian standards at more modest prices.

The excellent Italian restaurant **La Volpaia** (20-22 Street 13, tel. 023/992-739, lunch Mon.-Fri., lunch and dinner Sat.-Sun. until 10:30pm) is located on the beautiful post office square and serves great pizzas, pasta dishes, steaks, and other Italian specialties. The restaurant is smart, air-conditioned, and comfortable, and it's also possible to sit outside and watch the bustle on the square.

For some of the best French dining in town and a unique experience, head to the former Indochina Bank on the post office square, a handsome colonial-era building erected in 1900. The former bank has been lovingly restored and now houses **Van's Restaurant** (5 Street 102, tel. 023/722-067, www.vans-restaurant.com, daily 11:30am-2:30pm and 5pm-10:30pm), one of Phnom Penh's upscale eateries, with most items on the menu—including some excellent veal and seafood dishes—priced at US$15-30.

Khmer

The **Sophy Khut** (28 Street 104, tel. 023/991-578), a more sophisticated Khmer restaurant just off the post office square, serves a wide variety of tasty Khmer and Thai dishes, including excellent wing bean salad and various

Around the Riverfront

110
AMARA SPA
PONTOON
THE FROG AND PARROT
13
118
MEMPHIS BAR
DARA REANG SEY HOTEL
GRASSHOPPER ADVENTURES
PHNAH ST
INDOCHINE 2 HOTEL
SHE-E-PUNJAB
LEMONGRASS
U-CARE PHARMACY
136
THE RED FOX
THE CHIANG MAI RIVERSIDE
KANIKA CATAMARAN
CADILLAC BAR
144
KANDAL HOUSE
VELKOMMEN INN
LA CROISETTE
THE BLUE PUMPKIN
BOJANGLES
148
METRO CAFÉ
THE QUAY
ANJALI RESTAURANT AND BAR
BOUGAINVILLIER HOTEL
154
AMANJAYA
Tonlé Sap River
WAT OUNALOM
13
172
KABBAS
OPERA CAFÉ
BOHR'S BOOKS
HAPPY HERB PIZZA
2 COLORS
FRANGIPANI
CANTINA
MEKING ART
ROYAL PALACE HOTEL
U-CARE PHARMACY
ASASAX ART GALLERY
DIAMOND PALACE II HOTEL
THE RISING SUN
THE MANSION
BRIGHT LOTUS GUEST HOUSE
CAFÉ FRESCO/
FOREIGN CORRESPONDENTS' CLUB OF CAMBODIA
HAPPY PAINTINGS
ORANGE RIVER
SISOWATH QUAY
MOHAVTHEI
SOTHEAROS
216
0   100 yds
0   100 m
© AVALON TRAVEL

curries and stir-fries. Prices for entrées range US$4-12.

The **Bopha Phnom Penh Restaurant and Titanic Lounge** (Sisowath Quay) is everything it promises. Located next to the ferry dock for boats to Siem Reap, this huge multicuisine restaurant, in the shape of a ship, is very popular with Khmer. There's a long chrome bar inside and plenty of outdoor seating by the riverbank. Besides standard Khmer and international meals, vegetarians have a large choice, and there are also some pretty exotic main courses, such as stir-fried water buffalo with pumpkin. Prices range US$5-15. There's an *apsara* dance performance daily at 7pm.

AROUND THE RIVERFRONT
Asian

The Chiang Mai Riverside (227 Sisowath Quay, tel. 011/811-456, daily 10am-10pm) has been around for years and is located on the ground floor of a small shophouse. Customers can sit inside the air-conditioned restaurant or curbside. The menu is extensive and prices are moderate (from US$4). The food is pretty authentic and not too spicy, although you can always ask for additional heat. Vegetarians will be happy, and the restaurant runs a delivery service.

If you fancy something a bit more classy (and pricey, too), head to **The Duck** (49 Sothearos Blvd., tel. 089/823-704, Mon. 5pm-10pm, Tues.-Sun. 8am-10pm), an Asian fusion restaurant serving an interesting variety of dishes prepared with French cooking styles but crammed with Asian flavors. Try tofu with onion and chili jam (US$7.50) or the crisp-skin red snapper (US$11). And hey, there's not a single burger on the menu.

The very chic **Metro Hassakan** (Sisowath Quay and Street 148, tel. 023/222-275, daily 10am-11pm, entrées US$10-15) looks like a postmodern sushi bar but actually serves great salads, sandwiches, and strange original Asian snacks like grilled squid with lychee and chili jam, as well as great steaks. Mostly though, the Metro is justly famous for its eggs Benedict, allegedly the best in town. The Metro has takeout service and offers Internet access to customers.

Lemongrass (14 Street 130, tel. 012/996-707, daily 10am-10pm, entrées US$4-8) serves reliable Thai and Khmer standards, including a number of vegetarian dishes, great Thai dips, and salads, all in a relaxed, modern atmosphere just a few meters off the riverfront.

Right next door is the equally reliable but altogether different ★ **She-E-Punjab** (16 Street 130, tel. 023/992-901, daily 10am-11pm, entrées US$3-8). As the name suggests, the food is predominantly Punjabi, but many Indian favorites, from chicken tikka to lamb korma, are available. There are quite a few vegetarian meals on the menu.

Anjali Restaurant and Bar (273B Sisowath Quay, tel. 012/457-901, daily 7am-11:30pm) offers all manners of food in an attractive colonial building on the riverside, but it's really the Indian dishes that are worth checking out. Reasonably priced, entrées are around US$5 and up, and the chicken tikka masala is recommended. Portions are good sized, too.

A number of restaurants have opened along Street 240. Among them, the small and elegant **Frizz** (67 Street 240, tel. 023/220-953, www.frizz-restaurant.com, daily 10am-10pm, entrées US$4-8) serves Chhnang Phnom Pleung, or Cambodian Volcano Pot, which is a local version of a Korean-style barbecue, and a wide variety of good Khmer dishes, including several vegetarian courses that use local ingredients. Frizz will deliver daily 11am-9pm and also organizes cooking classes (www.cambodia-cooking-class.com, 1-day course US$23, half-day course US$15).

Very close to the river on a quiet backpacker strip, the **Kathmandu Kitchen** (13 Street 258, tel. 098/527-120, daily 7am-10pm) offers Nepali standards such as *momo* (a kind of ravioli, either steamed or deep fried, filled with either vegetables or meat) as well as a good variety of Indian dishes. There's both indoor and outdoor seating, and entrées are around US$6.

International

★ **Kandal House** (239 Sisowath Quay, tel. 023/986-203, daily 10am-midnight) is a friendly hole-in-the-wall eatery on the riverfront that seems to play mostly 1980s rock music, serves excellent freshly baked pizzas, and has a free Internet terminal for guests. Kandal House has indoor and sidewalk seating and serves a wide variety of cocktails.

Not bad and very low-key is the long-running **Bojangles** (269 Sisowath Quay, tel. 012/457-901, daily 7am-1am, entrées US$4-7), which has a wide variety of vegetarian dishes as well as a decent selection of salads—vegetarian or otherwise.

With its arty ambience (a large painting of Bridget Bardot graces one wall), great international dishes (around US$12), and Khmer standards (from US$6), ★ **La Croisette** (241 Sisowath Quay, at Street 144, tel. 023/220-554, daily 7am-midnight) is a more upscale option nearby and the perfect place for a sumptuous dinner. Roadside tables or smart indoor seating, eclectic music, free Wi-Fi access, and a good wine list round off this reliably excellent restaurant. Occasional low-key concerts take place here, too.

One of the best places to watch the hustle and bustle on Sisowath Quay is the Mexican joint ★ **Cantina** (347 Sisowath Quay, Sun.-Fri. 7pm-midnight, meals around US$10), run by Hurley, an eccentric but agreeable American who has been in Cambodia since the UNTAC days. The little bar-restaurant is only open in the evenings and serves a wide variety of Mexican dishes, cocktails, and beer. Customers usually gather after sunset when tables and chill music spill out onto the sidewalk. Cantina is also an exhibition space, and Hurley has managed to persuade the legendarily moody American photographer Al Rockoff (played by John Malkovich in *The Killing Fields*) to exhibit his finest work here. Stark and iconic black-and-white images of the fall of Phnom Penh have lost none of their harrowing effect, but the somber mood is tempered by excellent stills from Matt Dillon's film shoot *The City of Ghosts,* by equally renowned photographer Roland Neveu. Free advice is available from Hurley.

A couple of doors down the road, the long-established **Happy Herb Pizza** (345 Sisowath Quay, tel. 023/362-349, daily 7am-11pm) is nothing like your local Pizza Hut. Toppings include not just mushrooms, olives, and pineapple but also generous helpings of marijuana. Do you want it happy, very happy, or extremely happy? By the way, the weed has always been an integral part of Khmer cuisine, long before Cambodia discovered pizza.

A great vantage point to watch the sunset over the Tonlé Sap River is the ★ **Foreign Correspondents Club of Cambodia** (363 Sisowath Quay, tel. 023/724-014, www.fcccambodia.com, daily 7am-midnight), better known as the FCC. Established in 1993 and long famous as a hangout for journalists, film stars, expatriates, and travelers, the FCC is located on the 2nd floor of a beautifully restored colonial building and hosts regular photo exhibitions and occasional live-music events. Wood-fired pizzas are delicious, if pricey, but what you're really paying for is the excellent ambience.

As much a great hangout as a restaurant, Phnom Penh's most established American bar, the **Freebird Bar & Grill** (69 Street 240, tel. 023/224-712, Mon.-Fri. 7:30pm-11pm) is a good place to get a cold beer, meet people, and consume generous portions of excellent American and Mexican food in a gentle biker-style ambience. The Freebird Bar seems to have been teleported from the United States lock, stock, and barrel. Decor, music, food, free home delivery, and friendly service make it feel like home. The humongous Freebird Burger is US$7, while steaks are around US$10.

A number of cheap but decent eateries have recently opened on Street 172. The **Laughing Fatman** (43 Street 172, around US$5) offers pizzas, pasta, breakfast, and Khmer standards. You get a free beer with your pizza.

Across the road, the **Blue Dolphin Bar and Restaurant** (30 Street 172) is deservedly popular for its well-priced breakfasts and also serves pizza and pasta at budget prices. A bit more upscale, **La Dolce Vita** (36 Street 172) does wood-fired pizzas (US$5-12) as well as Khmer standards.

Also on Street 172, **Felix Bar** (8 Street 172, tel. 095/589-612) is a new French bistro with a smart menu of sandwiches and salads. The plat du jour comes with a free choice of beer or soft drink, though there's also a good selection of cocktails. On Friday, you can get a bottle of wine and all-you-can-enjoy *tartines* for US$25. Vive la France.

Just by the National Museum, **Opera Café** (Street 13, tel. 096/349-7242, daily 10am-midnight) is an atmospheric Italian joint that serves great pasta and, judging by the loud but cool decor, has artistic aspirations. One of the more laid-back places in the area, this small restaurant is a great place to escape the heat and hang out for a while between sights. Portions are a little small for the prices they charge (entrées from around US$6), but it's all about the vibe and the location.

One of the most exotic dining possibilities in Phnom Penh, **Tepui** at **Chinese House** (45 Sisowath Quay, tel. 023/991-514, www.chinesehouse.asia/, daily 5pm-midnight) offers Asian Fusion cooked by a Venezuelan chef in one of the most sumptuous venues the city has to offer. Chinese House is located in a French colonial building right by the river. Beautifully restored and home to an eclectic art collection, the venue offers a laid-back and slightly flashy bar downstairs and the Tepui restaurant on the 1st floor. The menu offers a lot of seafood, and the taste combinations are as outlandish as they are tempting—there's red tuna tartare with wasabi emulsion among the appetizers and baked paella negra (its very blackness due to octopus ink) as a main. With entrées US$25-30, Tepui is a great venue for that special occasion.

Khmer

The **Sinan Restaurant** (19 Street 172,

daily 7:30am-10pm, from US$2) is a really cheap hole-in-the-wall restaurant just down the road from the National Museum on Phnom Penh's budget hotel road, Street 172, with extremely friendly service, cheap beer, and decent Khmer and Western food. Loc Lak is US$2 and steaks cost US$1.50, so don't expect much, but the chicken salad is excellent.

Also on Street 172, **Turkish Delight** (61 Street 172, tel. 077/416-624, daily 5pm-midnight) offers great Middle Eastern cuisine, including the ubiquitous kebabs. Prices are a little higher than most of the backpacker joints on 172, but the vegetarian mezze is just US$9, probably feeds two (unless you're super starving), and includes spinach, feta salad, hummus, jajik, and eggplant. Lamb kebabs are US$7.

Right around the corner, the cozy **Kabbas Restaurant** (166 Street 13, daily 11am-9pm, entrées US$2-5) offers a good selection of Khmer and Thai dishes. Try the green mango salad with dry fish and shrimp, if you dare, or the special Khmer noodle salad with fresh shrimp, squid, and pork.

The **Kanika Catamaran** (tel. 012/848-802) is docked on the riverfront at Street 136 and offers high-tea river cruises (daily 4pm-6pm) and dinner (daily 5pm-9pm). Proceeds go to an educational NGO.

Street Cafés and Bakeries

Café Fresco (Ground Fl., FCC, tel. 023/217-041, daily 7am-9:30pm) is an excellent international delicatessen. Deli sandwiches with all imaginable toppings and great health juices battle for your stomach and wallet with freshly baked cakes, sold over the counter or enjoyed in a comfortable air-conditioned atmosphere. There's a second branch on the corner of Street 51 and Street 306; home delivery is also available.

Just around the corner is **The Rising Sun** (20 Street 178, tel. 012/970-719, daily 7am-11pm), a British-style pub and popular hangover cure that serves massive breakfasts all day. It has nice retro-pop decor, curbside seating, friendly service, and a wide variety of magazines and papers to read.

Already well established in Siem Reap, **The Blue Pumpkin** (245 Sisowath Quay, tel. 023/998-153, daily 6am-11pm) offers snacks, pastries, cakes, and great ice cream downstairs, with a futuristic upstairs setting that has free Wi-Fi, much like its sister branches in Siem Reap and the international airports.

AROUND CENTRAL MARKET
Asian

For a great variety of authentic Malay food—curries, seafood, soups—check out **D'Nyonya** (91 Street 126, tel. 023/690-2929, entrées US$3-5), on the north side of the Central Market. The restaurant will deliver food to your hotel for orders of US$5 or more.

The ★ **Pyongyang** (400 Monivong Blvd., tel. 012/565-311, entrées around US$15) is a truly unique dining experience. This restaurant is owned and run by the government of North Korea, a kind of advertisement for North Korean culture. The food, including kimchi (fermented cabbage), is great, but the main attraction is the cultural show on Saturday, put on by the all-female staff halfway through the evening. It's all very prim, proper, and communist, with dance routines, a violinist who unleashes a sonic inferno on diners, and the ubiquitous karaoke numbers. The staff, trained in China, all speak English and are happy to converse about their country, given that they are cultural ambassadors. The culture shows supposedly start around 8pm, but the timing can be erratic; call ahead for details. This restaurant's existence probably owes much to former King Sihanouk's friendship with North Korea's former leader Kim Jong-il, who died in 2011. There's a second branch in Siem Reap. Foreigners are welcome, and they even sell Coca-Cola.

The **Peking Canteen** (93 Street 136, daily 11am-10pm) is located on a small road between the Diamond Hotel and Central Market in a row of several small Chinese eateries. Unlike the others, the Peking Canteen has an English menu.

Khmer

Another good Khmer restaurant is the **Ebony Apsara Café** (42 Street 178, tel. 012/581-291, daily 11am-midnight), which touts itself as a late-night eatery and serves a wide variety of Khmer and Asian dishes. The *tom yum* soup is not bad (US$2.50).

The **Café Ratanakiri** (84 Street 63, tel. 023/221-162, daily 10am-10pm), downstairs in the Angkor Bright Guest House, is a pleasant buzzing restaurant, very popular with the office lunchtime crowd in the area, that serves Khmer delicacies including pig brain and black chicken. If you want to get off the beaten culinary track, this is not a bad place to start.

Street Cafés and Bakeries

For a great treat on a hot, sultry day, try the large selection of high-quality ice cream at **Bonbon** (38 Street 63), directly opposite the Sorya shopping mall. Cakes and fresh coffee are also served in this colorful little café.

SOUTH OF SIHANOUK BOULEVARD
Asian

The ★ **Banyan** (245 Street 51, tel. 012/850-065, daily 7am-10pm, entrées around US$10)

serves very good Thai standards in a relaxed setting—customers can choose whether they want to dine at a table or on cushions on the floor.

A bit remote but well worth a visit is the ★ **Man Han Lou Restaurant** (456 Monivong Blvd., tel. 023/721-966, daily 5pm-midnight) in the far south of the city. This bright and gaudy Chinese restaurant not only serves great food—try the excellent dim sum or seafood salads (around US$5 per plate)—but also brews its own beer in huge copper vats on the premises. To be precise, the Man Han Lou serves a blond beer, a red beer, and a green beer, which has seaweed in it.

For a great selection of both Khmer and regional dishes, head to **Mok Mony** (63 Street 294, tel. 093/696-799, daily 10am-10pm, entrées around US$8), run by a Malay-Canadian chef. The grilled betel leaf with marinated beef is especially recommended, and there's a fine selection of fresh juices.

Sumatra (35 Street 456, tel. 016/561-980, Mon.-Sat. 11am-8pm), as the name suggests, offers Indonesian cuisine. There's a wide variety of interesting dishes as well as familiar standards on offer, and the prices are great, too. Chicken satay with rice, vegetables, and a chili dip is US$4 while a bowl of tofu

dried fish and shrimp for sale at Central Market

soup, crammed with stewed cassava leaves in Indonesian spices with coconut milk, is just US$1.75. Many of the dishes are cooked in *balado,* a Sumatran sauce of tomato, chili, and garlic.

International

★ **Artillery Café** (Street 240, near Street 19, and 13B Street 278, tel. 078/985-530, Mon. 7:30am-5pm, Tues.-Sun. 7:30am-9pm, entrées US$5) is popular with the NGO crowd, and deservedly so. Fantastic, lovingly prepared, organic food includes some raw food and vegan choices and juices. Meat is also on the menu, and portions are decent. There's Wi-Fi too, and quite a lot of people while the afternoons away here working. The branch on Street 240 also hosts art events.

Khmer

The long-established ★ **Boat Noodle Restaurant** (8B Street 294, tel. 012/774-287, daily 7am-10pm, entrées US$5-10) is a few minutes away from the riverfront. This simple but atmospheric eatery, located in a traditional wooden house overgrown by vegetation, is worth a visit. All the Khmer standards as well as a decent list of Thai dishes are on the menu, and the dining experience is enriched by a group playing traditional Khmer music.

If you want to experience some of the best Cambodian cooking in the country, head for **Malis** (136 Norodom Blvd., tel. 023/221-022, www.malisrestaurant.com, daily 7am-midnight), a first-class Khmer restaurant in its own delightfully upscale compound on Norodom Boulevard. Guests sit among pools and vegetation and can choose from an eclectic menu of contemporary and traditional Khmer dishes. Since it's open all day, you could indulge in scallop dumplings (US$2.20) for breakfast, frogs legs with curry paste and palm wine (US$6.80) for lunch, and a baked goby fish with mango dips (US$10) for dinner. Naturally, there's an extensive wine list.

Next door to the Rock nightclub is the **Good Dream Restaurant** (Monivong Blvd., daily 6pm-midnight), a truly authentic and very popular Cambodian open-air eating experience. The Good Dream is moderately priced, with steaks served with a peppery lemon sauce (US$4).

Also recommended though a bit more pricey is **St. 63** (179 Street 63, tel. 015/647-062, entrées from US$3.50), which is open around the clock and offers a wide selection of Cambodian and international dishes. The Khmer dishes include soups, curries, and stir-fries, and the portions are generous. The Western dishes include salads, sandwiches, burgers, soups, cuts of beef, chicken, pork, pork ribs, pasta, and pizza. There's also a wide selection of fresh juices and some 29 cocktails on offer. The Khmer and pumpkin curry is a personal favorite. St. 63 gets very crowded in the evenings with a lively Khmer and foreign clientele.

For great Khmer seafood dishes, head to **Andart Rom** (Street 51, tel. 015/455-338, daily 11am-midnight), which serves standards such as fried shrimp with Kampot pepper as well as far more exotic fare like the eggs of the rather weird-looking horseshoe crab—a so-called living fossil—with mango salad. Portions are huge and easily justify the prices—entrées are US$8-12, in tune with the Cambodian tradition of ordering several platters and sharing them among friends or family.

Street Cafés and Bakeries

A branch of the delicatessen **Café Fresco** (Street 51 and Street 306, tel. 023/224-891, www.cafefresco.net, daily) offers deli sandwiches, fruit juices, and cakes—much like its sister operation at the FCC. You can choose between the rooftop terrace or indoors with air-conditioning. A delivery service is available. There's a second branch at 361 Sisowath Quay (daily 7am-9pm).

The small and very smart **Café Yejj** (170 Street 450, tel. 012/543-360) is an excellent getaway after cruising the hot and dusty aisles of the nearby Russian Market. On offer is a great selection of coffees along with pasta dishes and cakes.

Information and Services

VISITOR INFORMATION

Phnom Penh's **tourism office** keeps moving and appears to serve no tangible purpose. The best sources of information on the sights of the city are the widely distributed and free visitors guides published by **Canby** (www.canbypublications.com). There are also a number of small pocket guides published regularly, focusing on the city's vibrant nightlife as well as Phnom Penh's increasing dining and shopping possibilities. These publications live from the advertising revenue of the businesses they feature, so don't expect objective reviews, but as a source for sights and contacts, they are useful. Most hotels and restaurants stock copies.

LIBRARIES
The National Library

The **National Library** (Street 92, tel. 023/430-609, Mon.-Fri. 8am-11am and 2pm-5pm) is located in a stunning and well-restored 1924 French colonial building. During the Khmer Rouge years, members of the Pol Pot regime used the building as accommodations and destroyed many of the books. The library reopened in 1980 and now houses more than 100,000 titles in several languages. Special collections, including numerous palm-leaf manuscripts, which can be seen on microfilm, have been established in recent years.

The Buddhist Institute Library

Located in a magnificent group of buildings adjacent to Hun Sen Park and the Naga World Hotel, the Buddhist Institute, founded in 1930, houses a large **library** (tel. 023/212-046, daily 7:30am-11am and 2:30pm-5pm) that documents religious and other aspects of Cambodian culture. Also on the grounds is the Kampuja Surya Bookstore, which sells a wide variety of books on Buddhism. Since early 2014

there've been public protests against the adjacent Naga Casino, which is allegedly trying to acquire the institute property to expand its operations.

MONEY

Banks, usually with **ATMs** attached, can be found all over central Phnom Penh. Hours are usually Monday-Friday 8 am-3pm or 4pm and sometimes Saturday 11:30am-3pm or 4pm. All ATMs, including those at the airport, dispense U.S. dollars. Large-denomination dollar bills with tears will not be accepted by Cambodian businesses.

Credit cards (especially Visa, MasterCard, and JCB) are now widely accepted, and businesses usually charge a few percent commission on transactions. Traveler's checks are accepted at most banks, some hotels, and some money changers.

Money changers can be found all over the city, offering a marginally better rate for riel than the banks. Banks with foreign-exchange facilities include **CAB** (439 Monivong Blvd., tel. 023/220-000), **ACLEDA Bank** (61 Monivong Blvd., tel. 023/998-777), **ANZ Royal Bank** (20 Street 114, tel. 023/726-900), and **Canadia Bank** (265-269 Street 114, tel. 023/215-286).

HEALTH AND EMERGENCIES

If you become seriously ill or sustain injuries in a traffic accident, have yourself evacuated as quickly as possible to Bangkok or Singapore. For less serious emergencies, visit the international-standard **Royal Rattanak Hospital** (11 Street 592, tel. 023/991-000) or **International SOS** (161 Street 51, tel. 023/216-911 or 012/816-911, www.internationalsos.com). This clinic also has a dentist and can assist with evacuations. Also recommended for minor injuries is the **American Medical Center** (tel. 023/991-863), which has a doctor licensed in California operating out of the Cambodiana Hotel.

Note that ambulances may or may not show up if you have an accident, and that emergency numbers (tel. 119 from 023 phones or tel. 023/724-891) often go unanswered.

The main local hospital is **Calmette** (3 Monivong Blvd., tel. 023/426-948), but it's not at all recommended. Also avoid all other hospitals in the capital. Cash or credit-card payment is always expected prior to treatment.

Avoid buying antibiotics or other serious medications over the counter of small pharmacies, as many are fake. **U-Care Pharmacy** (Sothearos Blvd., 39 Sihanouk Blvd., 41-43 Norodom Blvd., 844 Kampuchea Krom Blvd., tel. 023/222-499) sells a wide selection of basic authentic medicines.

INTERNET ACCESS

Phnom Penh has scores of Internet cafés, from small hole-in-the-wall operators crammed with video game-playing schoolchildren to high-tech outfits around the riverfront where you can make international Internet phone calls and video calls and upload documents and pictures. All of them have pretty fast connections, as the days of dial-up are thankfully gone. Rates in the built-for-tourists places are around US$1 per hour. Many hotels, restaurants, and bars now also offer Wi-Fi access to customers.

POST OFFICE

Phnom Penh's main post office (daily 6:30am-9pm), located on its own square near Wat Phnom, a restored historical building from the French colonial era, is one of the best places to mail anything important. Make sure everything you send is franked properly.

TRAVEL AGENTS

Most hotels and guesthouses in Phnom Penh offer reliable travel services and can procure visas for neighboring countries. The few dollars extra you are likely to pay for boat, plane, or bus tickets and visas can save you lots of time and hassle. The **Capitol Guest House** (154A Street 182, tel. 023/217-627) is not a great place to stay, but it offers reliable and cheap trips around the Phnom Penh region and has its own regional bus service.

LAUNDRY

Virtually all hotels, from budget flophouses to first-class boutique hotels, offer laundry service.

Getting There and Around

GETTING THERE

Phnom Penh is one of two transportation hubs in Cambodia, Siem Reap being the other. Regular buses and taxis travel to virtually all destinations in Cambodia from the capital.

Air

From **Pochentong International Airport,** it's a 20-minute drive to downtown Phnom Penh, a trip that costs US$9 in a taxi, US$7 in a tuk-tuk, and US$2 with a *motodup* (motorcycle taxi). There are currently only two domestic air routes in operation: There are several flights each day between Phnom Penh and Siem Reap with **Siem Reap Airways** (65 Street 214, tel. 023/720-022, www.siemreapairways.com) and **Cambodian Angkor Air** (206 Norodom Blvd., tel. 023/666-6786, www.cambodiaangkorair.com), and Cambodian Angkor Air also flies between Siem Reap and Sihanoukville. Airports in the northeast are currently being redeveloped, and flights from Phnom Penh to other destinations may start up again in 2016.

AIRLINE OFFICES

Phnom Penh has the following airline offices:

- **Air Asia:** 179 Sisowath Quay, tel. 023/983-777, www.airasia.com

- **Bangkok Airways:** 61A Street 214, tel. 023/722-545, www.bangkokair.com
- **Cambodian Angkor Air:** 294 Mao Tse Tung Blvd., tel. 023/666-6786, www.cambodiaangkorair.com
- **China Southern Airlines:** 168 Monireth, tel. 023/424-588, www.csair.com
- **Dragon Air:** 168 Monireth Blvd., tel. 023/424-300, www.ce-air.com
- **Lao Airlines:** 111 Sihanouk Blvd., tel. 023/222-956, www.laoairlines.com
- **Malaysia Airlines:** 172-214 Monivong Blvd., tel. 023/218-923, www.malaysiaairlines.com"
- **Qatar Airways:** 135A/B296 Mao Tse Tung Blvd., tel. 023/424-012, www.qatarairways.com
- **Silk Air:** 219B, Himawari Hotel, tel. 023/426-808, www.silkair.net
- **Thai Airways:** 294 Mao Tse Tung Blvd., tel. 023/214-359, www.thaiair.com
- **Vietnam Airlines:** 41 Street 214, tel. 023/990-840, www.vietnamairlines.com

Train

For many years, the train system in Cambodia was dilapidated, the rolling stock was in terrible condition, speeds averaged 20 kilometers per hour, and a train ride was only an option if you had lots of time on your hands. Two routes operated: Phnom Penh-Battambang, which took more than 12 hours, and Phnom Penh-Kampot, 9 hours, and on to Sihanoukville, a leisurely 13 hours. A bus or taxi does the trips in less than half the time. The railroad system is currently being restored to pre-Khmer Rouge standards and, if all things go as planned, should be reopened sometime in 2015. An extension of the Battambang line will eventually go all the way to the Thai border at Poipet and connect with the Thai railroad system. In decades to come, if the planned extension of the Cambodian railroad system continues, it will be possible to catch a train all the way from Bangkok to Ho Chi Minh City via Phnom Penh. But for now, this remains only a plan.

Bus

Phnom Penh does not have central bus stations, and buses leave and arrive at different points in the city. **Phnom Penh Sorya Buses** (tel. 023/210-359) arrive and depart opposite the southwest corner of Phsar Thmey (Central Market) and offer services to Siem Reap, Sihanoukville, Kampot, Battambang, Kompong Cham, Tbeng Meanchey, Kratie, Stung Treng, Banlung, Sisophon, Poipet, and the Lao border. **Capitol Tour & Transport** (14AEo, Street 182, tel. 023/217-627) has buses going to Siem Reap and Sihanoukville. **Giant Ibis** (Street 106, tel. 023/999-333) runs buses to Siem Reap, Sihanoukville, Kampot, and Kep. Buses depart next to the Night Market, and there's a night bus service with sleeping bunks to Siem Reap at 11pm. Several other bus companies, most of them also leaving from around the Central Market area, offer similar services.

Most hotels and guesthouses can save you the hassle of booking your own ticket. Prices vary widely; fares to Siem Reap range US$3.50-10. Buses to regional destinations generally leave 7am-noon.

It is possible to travel directly from Phnom Penh to Bangkok and Ho Chi Minh City. Sorya Buses and Capitol Tours have a direct connection to Bangkok (daily 6:30am, US$15). You may have to change buses at the Thai border. Sorya Buses, Mekong Express, and a couple of other companies run buses to Ho Chi Minh City (daily 6:30am-2:30pm, US$15-18). Make sure you have a visa for Vietnam.

Boat

Due to improved road conditions, many boat services have been canceled in recent years, but it's still possible to reach Siem Reap via the Tonlé Sap Lake July-March. Ferries depart at 7:30am from the boat landing on Sisowath Quay near Street 104. Journeys take 4-6 hours and cost around US$30-35, significantly more than a bus ticket. If you're planning to sit on the roof, take strong sunblock. Most hotels and guesthouses can save you the hassle of booking your own ticket.

A far more luxurious alternative to Siem Reap is a three-day trip on a traditional wooden riverboat with **Compagnie Fluevial du Mekong** (tel. 012/240-859, www.cfmekong.com, from around US$400 per passenger, depending on season and cabin).

Taxi

Taxis ply many regional routes, either hired privately or shared taxis. Shared taxis cost about as much as buses but are extremely cramped, unless you buy yourself two seats. Shared taxis generally leave from around Phsar Thmey (Central Market). The fare to Siem Reap in a shared taxi is around US$10, to Battambang is 40,000 riel. In a private taxi, Siem Reap is around US$60, and Battambang is US$40-50. It's slightly faster and arguably more dangerous to travel by taxi than by bus. Rising fuel prices keep these fares in flux.

GETTING AROUND

Most sights are relatively close together in Phnom Penh, and much of the city can be explored on foot. Phnom Penh does not have a public bus system. Regular metered taxis were introduced in 2008 (insist on using the meter), and there are also on-call taxi services. Try **Global Taxi** (tel. 011/311-888 or 092/889-962) or **Choice Taxi** (tel. 023/880-023). If you want to get around in style, contact **Royal Cambodian Limousine Services** (tel. 023/218-808, www.royallimousine.com.kh). A taxi from the airport into town costs US$9.

If you have lots of time, grab a **cyclo** (bicycle taxi), 1,000-4,000 riel for short rides. The most common form of transportation in

Cyclos

A distinctive feature of Phnom Pen traffic are cyclos, bicycle-rickshaws that are steered, for the most part, by dried-up grinning old-timers who slowly move through the city streets on the lookout for a fare. Cyclos are not really suitable for long distances, but in the daytime they are great for short hops or sightseeing trips around the riverfront. Expect to pay 1,000-4,000 riel for a short distance, US$6 for a half-day fare, although you'll probably be sick of the traffic before your time is up. Agree on a fare before you embark. It's not recommended to use cyclos at night.

Phnom Penh is the trusty *motodup.* Drivers can be recognized by their baseball caps. Short rides cost the same as a cyclo; expect to pay about US$8-12 for a full day's rent. Alternatively, safer and slightly more expensive are the numerous **tuk-tuks** that ply the roads of the capital. These motorcycle-trailers seat 2-4 people and are more comfortable than a *motodup.* Short trips should be US$1-2; expect to pay US$15-20 for a full day's rental.

If you feel that you must brave the Phnom Penh traffic by yourself, plenty of shops rent motorcycles (100-250 cc), although the heavier bikes are hard to maneuver in city traffic. Only experienced riders should attempt to drive in Phnom Penh. Always wear a helmet, drive on the right side of the road, and keep in mind that medical facilities are lacking in Cambodia. Try **Angkor Motorcycles** (92 Street 51, tel. 012/722-098) for quality bikes or **Lucky Lucky** (413 Monivong Blvd., tel. 023/212-788) for bargains. Both businesses also offer visa services.

Vicinity of Phnom Penh

★ CHOEUNG EK KILLING FIELDS

វាលពិឃាតបឹងជើងឯក

Following the victory of the Khmer Rouge in 1975 and the construction of the S-21 torture center in Phnom Penh, prisoners—men, women, and children—were brought to this site of a former Chinese graveyard and executed. In order to save ammunition, the guards forced prisoners to kneel next to freshly dug graves, into which they were beaten with shovels, hammers, and wooden spikes before being quickly buried. An estimated 17,000 people were killed here.

In 1980, following the Vietnamese liberation of Cambodia, 129 mass graves were dug up. Some of the skulls and bones of the victims found here are on display in a mausoleum in the shape of a stupa, although many graves were left undisturbed. Visitors can walk among the opened overgrown pits near the mausoleum at **Choeung Ek** (daily, US$2). For a better understanding of what happened here, a guide can be hired at the ticket office; expect to pay US$5. In 2005, the city authorities signed the Killing Fields over to a Japanese company on a 30-year lease in order to promote the tourism potential of the site. The company is planning to build a visitors center and substantially increase entrance fees.

Choeung Ek lies 15 kilometers southwest of Phnom Penh; many *motodups* and tuk-tuk drivers know the way. Expect to pay around US$10 round-trip.

★ OUDONG

ឧដុង្គ

Oudong (daily, free) rises from the flat expanse of paddy fields north of Phnom Penh like a fairy-tale castle. A city here served as the Cambodian capital from the early 17th century until 1866, when the government moved, for the last time, to Phnom Penh. There's nothing left to indicate that this was once a population center, but several stupas, temples, and shrines cover three hills, from where the views across the surrounding paddy fields are spectacular.

The main stairway to the highest outcrop takes about 10 minutes to climb. Here, on a broad terrace, stand three large stupas. The first, painted in ocher, is called **Chet Dey Mak Proum** and contains the remains of King Monivong, who reigned in Phnom Penh 1927-1941. The middle stupa, **Tray Troeng,** contains the ashes of King Ang Duong, who reigned at Oudong from 1845-1859. The third stupa, **Damrei Sam Puan,** contains the ashes of Oudong's founder, King Sorypor, who reigned 1601-1618.

A number of other structures can be found around the hillsides, including the remnants of several temples, all of them blown up by the Khmer Rouge. Some new shrines have been built in recent years. At the base of the hills, picnic pavilions have been set up, and, especially on weekends, it gets really busy. The base of the hill is also the site of a killing field, which is commemorated with a stupa containing victims' skulls. The area was heavily bombed by U.S. and government forces after 1970, the temple was blown up by Khmer Rouge troops in 1977, and it was fought over fiercely by Khmer Rouge and invading Vietnamese troops in 1979. The second stairway leads past murals illustrating Khmer Rouge atrocities.

Not far from Oudong, **Prasat Nokor Vimean Sour** is a concrete replica of Angkor Wat, huge in proportion and playful in its interpretation of the nation's most important building.

Oudong is 40 kilometers northwest of Phnom Penh on Route 5. The hills are clearly visible on the left side of the main road, and there are several small roads leading through the rice fields to the monuments. It's best to rent a taxi (around US$15) to get here.

SILK ISLAND

កោះដាច់

Just 5 kilometers north of Phnom Penh, in the Mekong River, this oasis of calm is well worth a visit, even for those who are not particularly interested in silk, to get away from the capital for a while. Silk Island (Koh Dach) is actually two small islands. There are plenty of weavers here, spinning their silk on old bicycle wheels. You are likely to be approached by sellers when you arrive. There are a couple of temples worth looking at, and the scenery is sublime. Take some food and have a picnic by the banks of the Mekong.

To get there, grab a tuk-tuk (US$10) across the Japanese Bridge. After 4.3 kilometers on Route 6, turn off for the river and take a ferry. Alternatively, rent a boat near Wat Phnom and sail up the river in style. This is likely to set you back about US$20 an hour, and it takes an hour to get to the islands and an hour to get back, plus however long you spend on the islands. The cheapest way, of course, is to bicycle and grab the river ferry off Route 6.

TEMPLES OF TONLÉ BATI

ទន្លេបាទី

Tonlé Bati is probably best known for its lake, a popular picnic spot surrounded by small pavilions where locals relax, especially on weekends. On the road to the lake, two Angkor-era temples, **Ta Prohm** and **Yeay Peau** (daily, free), can be visited. Don't expect massive ruins as in Siem Reap, although Ta Prohm is quite impressive and kept spotlessly clean by a gang of rather rapacious old ladies out for your dollar.

Take a bus from Sorya Transport headed for Takeo along Route 2. At kilometer 35, get off and grab a *motodup* to the temples.

TEMPLE OF PHNOM CHISOR

ភ្នំជីស្ស

More impressive than Tonlé Bati is **Phnom Chisor** (daily, US$2), a mountaintop temple also near Takeo. This is a great place to go for

the stupendous views from the isolated hill as well as the well-preserved 11th-century temple; best of all, you will have it virtually to yourself as few visitors make it here. The climb to the top of the hill, 500 steps in all, will make you sweat, and the monkeys at the top will make you laugh.

Take a bus from Sorya Transport, headed for Takeo along Route 2. At the kilometer 52 road marker, a big sign will point you in the right direction.

PHNOM TAMAO WILDLIFE RESCUE CENTER

រមណីយដ្ឋាន និង សួនសត្វភ្នំតាម៉ៅ

The **Phnom Tamao Zoological Gardens and Wildlife Rescue Center** (daily, US$4) is really more of a safari park than a zoo. Not as cruel as some Asian zoos, tigers, leopards, and elephants are kept in large enclosures, but predatory birds sit in tiny cages. The animals on display here have been rescued from traffickers. A ruined 11th-century temple sits nearby on top of Phnom Tamao.

The zoo is 39 kilometers south of Phnom Penh on Route 2. Take a taxi (US$30) or hop on a Sorya Transport bus to Takeo, and tell the driver where you want to get off.

TEMPLE OF PHNOM DA

ភ្នំដា

Located near the dusty village of Angkor Borei, which has a small museum exhibiting Funan-era artifacts, the hilltop **Temple of Phnom Da** (free) offers great views, all the way to Vietnam. The temple itself hails from the 11th-century and is built of brick and sandstone. The area around the temple is strewn with garbage left by Cambodian visitors, but the climb is worth it for the views.

Take a Sorya Transport bus, headed for Takeo along Route 2. Get off at the kilometer 52 road marker, close to Phnom Chisor, and catch a *motodup* from there. In the rainy season, the temple can only be reached by boat from Takeo. It's probably best to have your own wheels to get here.

Background

The Landscape

GEOGRAPHY

Cambodia is a Southeast Asian country that borders on Thailand on the west and north-west, Laos on the north, and Vietnam on the east and southeast. The country's southern coast faces the Gulf of Thailand. Cambodia stretches over 181,035 square kilometers. Under French colonial rule it was part of Indochina, along with Laos and Vietnam, and the current borders were largely drawn up by the French. The country is divided into 21 provinces, which are in turn divided into districts.

The Tonlé Sap Basin covers two-thirds of Cambodia and lies at an altitude of 5-30 meters above sea level. This gigantic low-lying area, with Tonlé Sap Lake, Southeast Asia's largest body of freshwater, in its center and the Tonlé Sap and Mekong Rivers to the lake's east, is partially flooded during the rainy season, which generates the nutrient-rich soil that a large part of the population relies on for agriculture. The basin is hemmed in by the Dangrek Mountains to the north, the Cardamom Mountains to the west, the Elephant Mountains to the southeast, and the high plateaus of Mondulkiri and Ratanakiri to the east. Cambodia's coast is lined with beaches and mangrove forests, and numerous islands of varying sizes lie in the Gulf off the country's shores. Phnom Aural, in the Cardamom Mountains, is the country's highest peak at 1,813 meters.

CLIMATE

Cambodia lies between 10 and 15 degrees latitude in the northern hemisphere and is a tropical country. The rainy season, from May to October, is brought on by monsoons from the southwest. This period is also characterized by high humidity, especially in September and October. From November to March, the dry season raises temperatures as high as 40°C. April tends to be uncomfortably hot. The best time to visit Cambodia is from November to January, when temperatures and humidity are lowest.

In recent years, these seasonal patterns have been disrupted by climate change, posing serious challenges to farmers. In 2008, heavy rains engulfed much of the country until early December.

FLORA
Forest

Cambodia has two types of forest. Evergreen forests grow above 700 meters, and tropical forests grow below this elevation. Kirirom National Park, a strange exception to this distribution of flora, has pine forests. Many tree species long threatened elsewhere in Asia still grow in profusion in Cambodia. Generally, the distribution of tree species is similar to Indonesia and quite different from China. Until fairly recently, Cambodia was home to some of the largest and most undisturbed forest areas in Asia.

Grassland

Large tracts of Cambodia are covered by low-lying savanna-type grasslands. The soil in these areas is mostly poor, and the vegetation is almost desertlike.

FAUNA

Cambodia has varied wildlife and is home to many unique animals, including some very rare large mammals in the country's forests. But as rapid development is depleting the country's forest cover, and as animals

---

Previous: *apsaras*, Ta Prohm; water buffaloes, Siem Reap Province.

are endangered by poachers, many species are likely to face extinction over the next few years. Visitors almost never encounter the rarer species, and wildlife organizations do most of their surveys with infrared cameras that are left in the forest for weeks. The chance of encountering a wild elephant or a tiger in Cambodia is extremely rare. More common sights include monkeys, snakes, and birds.

Endangered species include the tigers and elephants as well as dolphins, gaur, clouded leopards, sun bears, numerous species of wildcats, pangolins, and the Siamese crocodile, thought to be extinct until some were spotted in the Cardamom Mountains a few years ago. For the rhino, once indigenous to Cambodia, it's already too late.

Mammals

Cambodia has a huge variety of mammals, most notable among them the Asian elephant and the tiger. Other wildcats such as panthers and leopards are also indigenous. Deep in Cambodia's forests, several bear species continue to survive. Wild deer, such as the banteng and gaur, have made headlines recently because they are, along with all other large mammals, being hunted close to extinction. A number of deer, including the mouse deer, and wild boar survive in Cambodia's forests. Many smaller mammal species also live in Cambodia—among them numerous types of monkeys, such as rare lemurs and lorises and the more common macaques and gibbons, along with a wide variety of rodents, from rice paddy rats and badgers to squirrels.

Marine mammals such as dugongs and whales in the Gulf of Thailand are becoming increasingly rare, and the Irrawaddy dolphin is fighting for survival with a quickly decreasing population in the upper reaches of the Cambodian stretch of the Mekong River.

Birds

More than 500 bird species are said to be native to Cambodia, including cormorants, cranes, numerous types of hornbills, egrets, herons, parrots, and pheasants. The greater adjutant, a huge stork with a wingspan of more than 2.5 meters, nests only in Assam and Cambodia. Predatory birds include the crested serpent eagle as well as several types of owls.

Reptiles

Opinions on just how many types of reptiles live in Cambodia vary, not least because so little research has been done in recent decades. Some of the country's wilderness areas are home to extremely rare turtles, lizards, crocodiles, and snakes, with some species only recently discovered. Reptiles are especially vulnerable to trafficking, and while illegal transportation of turtles and snakes is occasionally intercepted by wildlife NGOs or government agencies, these successes only catch a fraction of the animals smuggled out of the country.

Freshwater Life

More than 850 species of fish are said to live in Tonlé Sap Lake and the Mekong River, although only about 40 of those have any nutritional significance. Turtles and crocodiles, though no longer common, still survive in remote river areas, and the upper part of the Mekong River in Cambodia is home to two shrinking populations of Irrawaddy dolphins.

Sealife

Cambodia's coastline is dotted with coral-fringed reefs that are home to a huge variety of fish, including small sharks and rays, as well as dolphins and whales. Occasionally, whale shark sightings are reported.

ENVIRONMENTAL ISSUES

With Cambodia's economy booming, environmental considerations take a backseat for policy makers in Phnom Penh. The extraordinarily rapid depletion of natural resources does not benefit ordinary Cambodians and widens the gap between a tiny self-enriching elite and the vast majority of the population. While NGOs try to counter some of this expansion, as often as not the effect of foreign donor money can be described as corrosive, enabling the allegedly cash-strapped government to pursue exploitative environmental policies with impunity.

Logging and Land Grabs

Cambodia is facing severe environmental degradation, not least because of continued widespread illegal logging. Land-grabbing is a serious issue, and in past years, the Cambodian government has sold significant parts of the country, including islands, beaches, and forest areas, to foreign investors. Other large tracts of land have been grabbed from local people by Khmer businesspeople with political influence in order to cultivate monocultures such as rubber and cashew trees. The locals, who usually do not have titles to the land, are simply removed, if necessary by force. Land-grabbing has been the biggest people-displacement factor in Cambodia since the days of forced relocation under the Khmer Rouge. Some foreign observers estimate that more than 50 percent of the country has been leased or sold to foreigners since the turn of the millennium. Phnom Penh is particularly affected.

Monocultures

Until the global economic downturn that began in 2008, Cambodia's economic growth hovered at 10 percent per year, a result of international investment and the country's cash crop expansion program. To achieve high productivity, crops have to be planted on giant monoculture plantations. Monocultures require external input to sustain themselves and to produce high yields. The resulting loss of nutritious soil through erosion is extremely high. Soil mulching—the introduction of other plant species into plantations to enrich the soil—is considered to be an obstacle to monoculture management; hence plantation floors are cleared of other species.

Dams

Numerous dams have been constructed in the Tonlé Sap watershed area and on the upper reaches of the Mekong River. This causes the fragmentation of floodplain habitats. While mega-dam projects are widely recognized to have a detrimental effect on biodiversity and on people, China is damming the Mekong further.

Overfishing

Large-scale fishing, the expansion of the fishing industry, and fishing with destructive gear have severely affected fish stocks in Tonlé Sap Lake. Attempts by the Cambodian government to reduce the catch of small fish have not been successful. Illegal fishing is widely practiced, and the abundance of fish continues to decline sharply in the lake.

History

There is no group of people in Southeast Asia that remains so connected to—if not burdened by—their history as the Cambodians. The descendants of the master builders of Angkor almost destroyed themselves in a vicious communist revolution. Both momentous periods—the regional supremacy of the Khmer Empire between 800 and 1400 and the almost four years of terror under the Khmer Rouge between 1975 and 1979—continue to hold a powerful sway over the nation's psyche, society, and politics and keep attracting scores of international observers, academics, and writers.

THE FIRST KHMER (4200–500 BC)

The origins of the Khmer are uncertain. Prehistoric finds from around Cambodia suggest that people lived in caves in the region as far back as 4200 BC, if not much longer. Pottery dated back to this time is very similar to pottery produced in Cambodia today, and historians make much of this fact—some things in Cambodia have not changed for more than 6,000 years. It is possible that even then, Cambodians lived in simple wooden houses on stilts, planted rice, and caught fish. What is certain is that people lived in small village communities and that big changes came along with an influx of people from what is today India around the beginning of the Common Era.

FUNAN (500 BC-AD 550)

The Indians brought with them a written language (Sanskrit), a religion (Hinduism), new ways of looking at the world, ideas about social hierarchies, the concept of the god-king, architecture, politics, and astronomy as well as a name—Kamboja. There has been some debate about where this name comes from—research suggests that the Kambojas were an Indo-Iranian tribe that slowly migrated from today's Afghanistan into India and Sri Lanka, eventually set sail for Southeast Asia, and founded a Kamboja colony on the Mekong River, probably in today's southern Vietnam, which at the time was populated by Khmer.

An origin myth tells a different story, also with Indian connections. A Brahmin named Kaundinya sailed a ship to the Far East and encountered the princess daughter of a local ruler who tried to attack him. Kaundinya used his magical bow to shoot an arrow into the princess's boat, and she, perhaps in fear, agreed to marry him. To be able to give his daughter a dowry, the so-called dragon or *naga* king drank the water that covered his land, built the couple a new capital, and called it Kamboja. The name does not appear in Cambodian inscriptions until the 9th century AD. Prior to that, though, the story was recorded by Chinese traders who were active in the region.

Unfortunately, there are no contemporary descriptions of the era available to us today. But several archaeological sites in today's eastern Cambodia (including Angkor Borei near Takeo) and Vietnam's Mekong Delta point to the establishment of a first kingdom, or at least a group of allied city-states from the 1st century AD onward, although the origins of this entity could be much farther back. The Chinese called it Funan, and the Khmer called it Bnam. Since World War II, Roman, Chinese, and Indian goods have been found at digs, pointing to maritime trade. It is assumed that the kingdom's influence stretched all the way into what is now Laos, Thailand, Burma, and even the Malay Peninsula. Kamboja seemed to be a halfway point of trade between India and China and was perhaps the first Southeast Asian empire.

CHENLA (AD 550-802)

The Chenla Empire started as a dependent of Funan in the middle of the 6th century AD and quickly absorbed the earlier empire, perhaps because of disruption of traditional trade routes between Europe and China following the collapse of the Roman Empire. The Chenla Empire was less seafaring than its predecessor. Its capital, Isanapura, was located near Kompong Thom and included the temples of Sambor Prei Kuk, which give an impression of how relatively powerful this early Khmer Empire might have been. Some scholars have pointed out that Chenla may well have been more of a shifting set of alliances of local chieftains than anything resembling a centralized state.

By the late 7th century AD, Chenla was divided into a northern and southern half based in southern Laos and the Mekong Delta before breaking into smaller states in the early 8th century AD. These weakened states were continually invaded by Javan kings during the 8th and early 9th centuries, which pushed the remaining local chieftains northwest of Tonlé Sap Lake into the region that later became Angkor.

ANGKOR (AD 802-1431)

Jayavarman II had grown up at the Javan courts (or had been kept hostage there). He returned to Kamboja and conquered as well as united several Chenla courts in AD 790, thus establishing his authority as king and kick-starting a 600-year period during which Angkor was the world's biggest and most powerful empire. Eventually he founded a city, Hariharalaya, in the area near Roluos, 15 kilometers from Siem Reap, and declared himself a god-king in 802. Hariharalaya was a long way from the sea and at the northwestern end of Tonlé Sap Lake, a strategically advantageous location given that the greatest danger to the Khmer king came from enemy navies. This move enabled Jayavarman II to declare independence from Java.

But rather than rest on his laurels, the god-king, or *devaraja,* decided to continue uniting parts of what is today Cambodia under his authority, and he fought numerous wars against his enemies until his death in AD 850. His son Jayavarman III consolidated his father's authority, and in AD 877, Indravarman I became the first god-king to build significant structures in the Angkor region, such as the Preah Ko and Bakong temples. His son, Yasovarman I, built the adjacent Lolei temple and founded a new capital called Yasodharapura, which settled around the sacred mountain temple of Phnom Bakeng. Yasodharapura was the first Angkor capital.

Yasovarman I also built the first massive reservoir, so important for the Khmer Empire's growing wealth and stability. Now called the Eastern Baray, this artificial lake was 7.5 kilometers long and 1.8 kilometers wide, and its waters are estimated to have irrigated more than 8,000 hectares of farmland. The hilltop temple of Preah Vihear on the Cambodian-Thai border is also attributed to Yasovarman I. For a while, though, Yasodharapura was abandoned, and the capital was moved to Koh Ker, some 80 kilometers northeast.

Jayavarman IV, who seems to have come from a different part of the royal family, ruled at Koh Ker AD 921-942 and was the first Khmer king to introduce sandstone in his temple architecture. The most remarkable result is the massive pyramid-shaped temple of Prasat Thom at Koh Ker.

The capital returned to Angkor in 944 under Rajendravarman II, who promptly built the Eastern Mebon and began construction of Banteay Srei while extending the Angkor Empire into Thailand, Laos, and even southern China. Rajendravarman II was the first Khmer god-king to sack the kingdom of Champa to the east. He was succeeded by his 10-year-old son Jayavarman V. Surprisingly, the young man managed to remain in charge

battle scene in a bas-relief at Angkor Wat

for more than 30 years. He built a new city called Jayendranagari, and the temples of Banteay Srei and Ta Keo were constructed during his reign. Poets, philosophers, and artists found a home at his court, but following his death in 1000, the empire subsided into turmoil for a decade.

Then Suryavarman I took over for 40 years and extended his realm's borders all the way to Lopburi in Thailand. He also began construction on the Western Baray, an even larger reservoir that measured 8 kilometers by 2.2 kilometers and was designed to expand the king's economic power. Following the death of Suryavarman I in 1050, chaos ensued once more, until Suryavarman II took over in 1113. One of the greatest of Angkor's rulers, he reigned for 37 years and had Angkor Wat, a temple dedicated to Vishnu, constructed in that time. He extended his troops' reach to the borders of Bagan (Burma) and farther into the Malay Peninsula. He died around 1150.

Shortly after, the Cham and Khmer had a huge naval battle in which the Khmer Empire was defeated and declared a vassal state of Champa. Jayavarman VII, the last great king of the Khmer, a follower of Mahayana Buddhism and a military leader, retook Angkor from the Cham and ascended to the throne in 1181. He continued to fight the Cham for 22 years, until that eastern empire's defeat in 1203. More importantly, he built Angkor Thom, the Khmer Empire's most magnificent city—and the one we are left with today. In its center, the Bayon, a massive Buddhist temple, was not only dominated by the famous stone towers of the bodhisattva but also featured detailed murals of ordinary Cambodian life during his rule. Jayavarman VII also laid out a grid of high roads that connected all the outlying provincial capitals of the Khmer Empire and built more than 100 hospitals. The overgrown forest temple of Ta Prohm was constructed under his reign. With its last true god-king, the Khmer Empire had reached its peak.

Following Jayavarman VII's death, Angkor gradually lost power as Champa to the east and the kingdom of Sukothai to the west began to assert themselves. In the middle of the 12th century, Jayavarman VIII came to power. A strong believer in Hinduism, this king had thousands of Buddha statues destroyed and paid tribute to Kublai Khan out of fear of China to the north. Jayavarman VIII was eventually removed by his son-in-law Srindravarman, who was an adherent of Theravada Buddhism. His reign is remarkable in that it was recorded by the Chinese diplomat Chou Ta-Kuan, who described not only the temples of Angkor but also the daily life of its people—thus giving us the only eyewitness account of life in the Khmer Empire.

Knowledge of what happened in the following decades and centuries is sketchy. Perhaps Theravada Buddhism undermined the authority of the *devaraja,* the god-king. Perhaps the empire's infrastructure was neglected as the king could no longer muster thousands of slaves for his massive projects. Perhaps the neglect affected the rice harvests and caused floods and droughts. Another explanation points to the logging of trees in the Kulen hills to make space for fields to accommodate a quickly growing population. The subsequent erosion may have silted up the sophisticated network of canals and irrigation channels around Angkor and paralyzed its agriculture and trade. To the west, the Siamese kingdom of Ayutthaya conquered Sukothai to its north and then attacked Angkor several times, finally conquering and plundering the Khmer capital in 1431.

CAMBODIA IN LIMBO (1432-1863)

It's unlikely that Angkor was abandoned altogether at any time from the Siamese invasion of 1431 until the first French explorers came across the ruins in 1860—even then, Angkor Wat was active, and more than 1,000 monks lived around the temple. Unfortunately, hardly any inscriptions were carved into stone between the middle of the 14th century and the beginning of the 16th century, and the only references to Cambodia during

The Kings and Their Temples

The most successful rulers of Angkor built temples and cities to support them. The following list illustrates who built what, giving an overview of the development of temple construction during the Khmer Empire.

JAYAVARMAN II

· **Reign:** AD 802-850

· **Capital:** Hariharalaya, Mhanddrabarapeata

· **Temples constructed:** Phnom Kulen

INDRAVARMAN I

· **Reign:** AD 877-889

· **Capital:** Hariharalaya

· **Temples constructed:** Bakong, Preah Ko

YASOVARMAN I

· **Reign:** AD 889-910

· **Capital:** Hariharalaya, Yasodharapura

· **Temples constructed:** Phnom Bakheng, Lolei, Phnom Krom, Eastern Baray, Preah Vihear

JAYAVARMAN IV

· **Reign:** AD 921-942

· **Capital:** Koh Ker

· **Temples constructed:** Koh Ker

RAJENDRAVARMAN II

· **Reign:** AD 944-968

· **Capital:** Yasodharapura

this period can be found in Chinese and Thai chronicles.

Research hints at the possibility that Angkor, apart from being sacked by its enemies and having overreached itself, was no longer economically viable, as it was too far from the sea, where all the lucrative trade was happening. Several new capitals were built at the confluence of the Mekong and Tonlé Sap Rivers. From here, Khmer rulers could control the trade on Tonlé Sap Lake as well as the flow of goods on the Mekong River, down from Laos and up from the Mekong Delta. But moving the capital farther east did not end the strife with Siam, and while Cambodia enjoyed periods of stability and wealth because of increasing trade in the region, the country was also encroached on by Vietnam to the east.

King Ang Chan, who ruled what was left of the Khmer Empire 1516-1566, established a capital at Loveck. For the first time, significant numbers of Westerners—adventurers,

- **Temples constructed:** Preah Rup, Eastern Mebon

JAYAVARMAN V

- **Reign:** AD 968-1001
- **Capital:** Yasodharapura
- **Temples constructed:** Banteay Srei, Ta Keo

SURYAVARMAN I

- **Reign:** AD 1010-1050
- **Capital:** Yasodharapura
- **Temples constructed:** Banteay Srei, Kbal Spean, Western Baray, Preah Vihear

UDAYADITYAVARMAN II

- **Reign:** AD 1050-1066
- **Capital:** Yasodharapura
- **Temples constructed:** Western Mebon, Baphuon

SURYAVARMAN II

- **Reign:** AD 1113-1150
- **Capital:** Angkor Wat
- **Temples constructed:** Angkor Wat, Beng Mealea, Banteay Samre, Wat Athvea

JAYAVARMAN VII

- **Reign:** AD 1181-1218
- **Capital:** Angkor Thom
- **Temples constructed:** Angkor Thom, Ta Prohm, Neak Pean, Banteay Chhmar, Preah Khan, Bayon

mercenaries, and traders—visited Cambodia. Toward the end of the 16th century, Chinese, Indonesian, Japanese, Malay, Portuguese, Spanish, Arabs, and a few British and Dutch settlers made their home in the capital. In 1593, the Siamese attacked Loveck and left a governor in the city. The Khmer were now ruled by foreigners.

Soon the Vietnamese controlled the Mekong Delta, and the Khmer kings no longer had effective access to the sea. Today's widespread distrust of the Vietnamese may have originated in this period. During the 17th and 18th centuries, Cambodia's neighbors were preoccupied with their own conflicts. In the late 18th and early 19th centuries, Cambodia tried to play off its larger neighbors and lost parts of its territory as a consequence. Vietnam expanded its territory to its present borders by the late 18th century, while the Siamese annexed Battambang, Sisophon, and Siem Reap Provinces in 1794. For a while,

Cambodia was controlled by both neighboring states.

THE FRENCH IN CAMBODIA (1863-1953)

The French arrived in Southeast Asia in the late 1850s and decided that Cambodia would make an ideal buffer zone between their new colony of Cochinchina and Siam, which lay within the sphere of influence of Britain, France's main colonial competitor. King Norodom, who'd been on a very wobbly throne since 1860, saw a chance to free Cambodia from the dominance of both the Siamese and the Vietnamese, and allowed Cambodia to become a French protectorate in 1863.

In 1884 the French forced the weak king to accept increased French authority, and by 1887, French Indochina, including all of today's Vietnam and Cambodia, had been formed. King Norodom died in 1904 and was replaced by the more pliable Sisowath. In effect, Cambodia was run by the French Resident-General, who was appointed from Paris. The bureaucracy around the Resident-General, the men who now ruled Cambodia, was largely run by Vietnamese, whom the French thought more capable than the Khmer, a situation that bred further resentment against the Vietnamese.

Economically, the French brought only modest advancements to Cambodia. The colonizers built some roads and a couple of railroad lines. Rubber, corn, and rice were cultivated for export. Besides that, the French collected a lot of taxes, more than anywhere else in Indochina. In 1907, Siam was pressured to return Battambang, Sisophon, and Siem Reap Provinces to Cambodia, and Angkor once again became part of Cambodian (although occupied Cambodian) soil.

The French did little to educate the Khmer, which gave Vietnamese and Chinese business-people the opportunity to run the banking and trade system.

Resistance to the French became a moot point when the Japanese entered Cambodia in 1941 and ordered the French Vichy government to continue administering Cambodia. That same year, King Monivong died, and the throne was handed to Norodom Sihanouk, the great-grandson of King Norodom, thought to be too young to be of any danger. In March 1945, Cambodia, at the behest of the Japanese, declared independence, and remained so for seven months, until Allied troops regained control of the country. After the war, the French were determined to recover Indochina, but by then, effective rebel groups such as the Khmer Issarak and the Viet Minh had formed. Under increasing pressure, the French allowed elections in 1946 and 1947. But the king largely ignored the democratic movement in his country. Instead, he dissolved parliament, suspended the constitution, and became prime minister in 1952.

INDEPENDENCE UNDER SIHANOUK (1953-1970)

In 1953, after some wrangling between Sihanouk and the French, Cambodia was granted full independence. In some ways, Cambodia, though under the sometimes watchful and autocratic eye of its former king, bloomed in its newfound independence. But discontent over repressive actions against political opponents and the increasing American presence in the region—despite the proclamations at the Geneva Conference in 1954 that Cambodia would be a neutral country—made for a short Cambodian honeymoon.

In 1955, King Sihanouk abdicated in order to become even more directly involved in politics, and founded a party that preached loyalty to the monarchy and to the Buddhist religion, which implied that social inequalities in Cambodia were due to karma rather than the struggle of people and ideologies. He then rigged and overwhelmingly won elections, soon driving most of his opposition underground while he gallivanted around the country shooting feature films, designing hotels, and indulging in earthly pleasures. And while Cambodia was one of the richest countries in the region during his long reign (1954-1970), the nation was slowly crumbling.

Sihanouk distrusted the Americans and Thais, and let the Viet Cong, who were fighting the South Vietnamese and Americans in South Vietnam, establish bases in northeastern Cambodia, which the United States soon bombed, allegedly with Sihanouk's tacit agreement.

A small Paris-educated left, among them Saloth Sar, slowly became more influential. Sihanouk called them the Khmer Rouge and invited some of them, including Khieu Samphan, later head of state, to join his government. Nevertheless, through the 1960s, leftists were persecuted, detained, and killed by Sihanouk's security police. But while Sihanouk alienated the left, he could not make peace with the right either. He nationalized banking, insurance companies, and a trade organization in order to eliminate the influence of foreigners, especially Chinese and Vietnamese, which led to widespread corruption and cronyism.

Now both sides of the political divide as well as large sections of the population were becoming fed up with the former king. The National Assembly elections in 1966 swung the country to the right under the leadership of General Lon Nol. In 1967, following the nationalization of rice exports, farmers protested violently in Samlot, near Battambang, and Sihanouk had 10,000 of them killed. The god-king's world was caving in. By 1968 he also had a small but growing communist armed resistance on his hands; by 1970 the Khmer Rouge controlled about one-fifth of the country. Meanwhile, the United States, searching for Viet Cong bases in Cambodia, continued to carpet bomb the northeastern part of the country, killing thousands of civilians. Sihanouk chose to ignore many of these developments and busied himself with his feature-film projects, often using Angkor as a movie backdrop.

CAMBODIA UNDER GENERAL LON NOL (1970-1975)

In March 1970, after Prime Minister Lon Nol had signed a declaration supporting a vote against the prince, the National Assembly voted in a new, insignificant chief of state while Lon Nol remained prime minister. The Khmer Republic was born. Sihanouk, in China at the time and suddenly deposed, perhaps with the help of the CIA, made a spectacular political somersault and allied himself with the Vietnamese and Cambodian communists, whom his army had been fighting just a month before. Lon Nol promptly had thousands of Vietnamese civilians killed. As the United States and the South Vietnamese were running armed incursions into Cambodia, the communists pushed deeper into Cambodian territory. And with renewed U.S. military aid, corruption in the armed forces was so rampant that the Cambodian army was soon an ineffective fighting force.

By the end of 1972, the Khmer Republic was in control of little more than Phnom Penh and a few provincial capitals. But the Lon Nol government lasted another four years, thanks to a brutal bombing campaign by the United States, which, in the first half of 1973, dropped more than 100,000 tons of ordnance onto Cambodia—authorized by President Nixon and Henry Kissinger, his National Security Advisor.

But it was all to no avail. The Cambodian communists, the Khmer Rouge, simply hardened under the bombardment, killed their erstwhile North Vietnamese sponsors, and began to turn those parts of the countryside into collectives. By early 1975 the rebels controlled the river supply routes into Phnom Penh, which had swollen with two million refugees fleeing the bombing, which is said to have claimed 500,000 lives.

THE TERROR OF THE KHMER ROUGE (1975-1979)

On April 17, 1975, Khmer Rouge troops, many of them as young as 15, poured into Phnom Penh. The initial joy about the end of the war evaporated quickly. The victors had not come to celebrate but to launch the radical revolution that became Democratic Kampuchea. In the weeks that followed, all borders were closed, and money, education, Buddhism, private property, and freedom of expression and movement were abolished. The inhabitants of Phnom Penh and all other cities were herded into the countryside to work. Thousands perished immediately. The communists had made it their priority to increase the country's rice output for export, which was in turn to finance industrialization.

Angkar, the revolutionary organization made up of members of the communist party, also banned family life and individual expression, right down to clothing. In the new communist utopia, everyone would be the same. For some time, no one even knew who the leaders of the revolution were. Outside observers were told that Sihanouk, who had aligned himself with the communists following his ouster, was still in charge. Those who had been driven from the cities were labeled "new people" and were put to work growing rice. Initially, some "new people" were elated—for the first time in years, the country was at peace and there was enough to eat in most areas. The "base people," rural Cambodians, on the other hand, had tasted authority for the first time, freed from the shackles of the monarchy and Buddhism. The young Khmer Rouge warriors, at the forefront of the communist movement, were all "base people." After victory over the hated Vietnamese and Americans, they drove the revolution forward with increasingly vicious zeal.

Perhaps 100,000 people who were part of the establishment of the Khmer Republic, which included teachers, monks, police officers, engineers, and many others, were killed. But it was the radical policies of Angkar—above all overworking the population and not willing or able to distribute enough food—that killed more than one million Cambodians, perhaps one in seven people, between 1975 and 1979.

In 1976, Sihanouk was placed under house arrest, and Comrade Pol Pot, a.k.a. Saloth Sar, was announced as prime minister. In early 1976, a National Assembly was elected. "New people" were not allowed to vote, and

the assembly met only once, to pass a constitution. The new government announced a four-year plan to triple the rice yield per hectare, regardless of soil conditions. Other crops were to be grown for export. The Cambodians were expected to work long days year-round to meet the revolutionary goals. Nevertheless, by 1976, rice was in short supply, and the population began to starve. More severe famines followed in 1977 and 1978.

In the meantime, Pol Pot had become paranoid about opposing forces within his own government and began a cycle of internal purges that would sweep away thousands in the coming years. Many of his former allies ended up at S-21 Tuol Sleng in Phnom Penh, a former school turned interrogation center, where some 17,000 people were tortured and subsequently taken away to be executed. Other such centers operated around the country.

While Cambodia was now almost totally isolated, the Chinese supplied the government with military equipment in order to foment the traditional antagonism of the Khmer toward the Vietnamese, who were backed by the Soviets and distrusted by the Chinese. Pol Pot, like Lon Nol and Sihanouk before him, would have liked to absorb part of the Mekong Delta—Kampuchea Krom—into Democratic Kampuchea. Goaded by his Chinese sponsors, he soon ran brutal incursions into Vietnam, indiscriminately killing thousands of civilians.

In response, Vietnamese troops invaded Cambodia on Christmas Day 1978 and, on January 7, 1979, entered Phnom Penh, ending the Khmer Rouge reign of terror. At the time, the capital had fewer than 50,000 inhabitants. But Cambodia's horrors were far from over.

VIETNAMESE LIBERATION AND OCCUPATION (1979-1991)

The country the Vietnamese encountered was on its knees, dotted with mass graves and starving people. Yet thousands of

Cambodians, while relieved that the Khmer Rouge had fallen, had no intention of living under the authority of their traditional enemies, the Vietnamese, and fled west into Thailand.

The Vietnamese installed a regime in Phnom Penh and renamed the country the People's Republic of Kampuchea. In the wake of the Khmer Rouge fall, widespread famine occurred. While the occupiers did their best to feed a helpless, traumatized, and antagonistic population, the United States and China made sure that only limited amounts of help reached the Cambodian people. In response to Vietnam's invasion and liberation of Cambodia, China, with the support of the United States, attacked Vietnam in February 1979, but failed to force a change in Vietnamese foreign policy.

The Vietnamese soon had even bigger problems on their hands. In the Cambodian provinces, three different resistance forces had formed—the Khmer Rouge; FUNCINPEC, a royalist grouping under Sihanouk's son Prince Ranariddh; and the right-wing KPNLAF. These groups initially fought independently against the Vietnamese, but they formed a coalition in 1982, which was recognized as Cambodia's legitimate government by the United Nations. Thailand also sided with the United States and China, allowing the various anti-Vietnamese factions to arm in numerous refugee camps along Cambodia's border. The Khmer Rouge troops, supplied with money and new weapons, quickly re-formed into an effective guerilla force. Not only had the United States and China rewarded one of the 20th century's most heinous regimes, but the superpowers also condemned the Cambodian people to 18 more years of suffering. Many provinces fell under the control of one rebel faction or another, while the new government in Phnom Penh was made up of Khmer Rouge who had defected to Vietnam prior to the fall, among them Heng Samrin, Chea Sim, and Hun Sen.

The civil war continued unabated until 1989, when the Vietnamese left. In October 1991, the four warring factions signed a peace deal in Paris and formed a unity government under Prince Sihanouk, who returned to Cambodia in 1991. The United States and China withdrew their support of the rebel movements, marking the beginning of the downfall of the Khmer Rouge.

UNTAC AND THE 1993 ELECTION (1992-1993)

The Paris agreements made possible the formation of the United Nations Transitional Authority in Cambodia (UNTAC), which poured more than 20,000 personnel into the country with the aim of disarming the various factions and organizing free and fair elections. But the most expensive United Nations action ever, at US$2 billion, proved to be a story of mismanagement and incompetence, with tragic consequences for Cambodia.

The Khmer Rouge refused to disarm, barred the United Nations from entering the territories under its occupation, and massacred Vietnamese civilians as well as U.N. soldiers and Cambodian civilians. Consequently, the other factions also refused to disarm. Yet despite the Khmer Rouge's threats to execute voters, elections for a National Assembly took place on May 22, 1993.

Approximately 90 percent of Cambodia's registered voters turned out, a clear signal for peace. FUNCINPEC won 45 percent of the vote, while the CPP, the Vietnamese-installed ruling government, garnered just 38 percent. The CPP refused to accept the election results, and Sihanouk stepped in, made himself king once more, and announced the CPP's Hun Sen and his son, FUNCINPEC's Prince Ranariddh, as joint prime ministers. The U.N. did nothing to counter the fact that the will of the people had been betrayed in the country's first-ever democratic election in more than 20 years. The legacy of that decision haunts Cambodia to this day.

Hun Sen soon outmaneuvered the prince and set about intimidating opponents while embarking on a nationwide program of building schools. Young, brash, and ruthless, the war hero, who had lost an eye in the battle for Phnom Penh, was digging in.

END OF THE CIVIL WAR (1993-1997)

Meanwhile, the Khmer Rouge, encamped near the Thai border in Pailin, was growing rich from gemstone and logging deals with the Thai military. They boycotted the elections and continued in their attempts to destabilize the country while fishing for a slice of power. In 1994, Khmer Rouge fighters attacked a train in southeastern Cambodia and killed a number of tourists and Cambodians. In 1996, Ieng Sary, head of one of the main Khmer Rouge factions, moved his troops over to the government side. With Ieng Sary and Pailin gone over, Pol Pot and his remaining troops clung to the small enclave of Anlong Veng in the far northwest of the country.

In the meantime, Sam Rainsy, a FUNCINPEC minister fired for his attacks on government corruption, started his own party, the Sam Rainsy Party (SRP). With all this political maneuvering and sporadic fighting, nothing much was done for the Cambodian people, and by the mid-1990s the countryside still languished in abject poverty.

A FRAGILE PEACE (1997-2008)

In 1997, a grenade attack on a Sam Rainsy gathering in Phnom Penh killed numerous activists, and rumors of a coup swirled around the capital. Soon after, Hun Sen seized control of the government during two days of bloody fighting. Prince Ranariddh and Sam Rainsy left the country. In 1998, new elections were contested by all parties, except the Khmer Rouge, and Hun Sen's CPP extended its stranglehold on power. The other parties refused to accept election results, but a power-sharing deal between the CPP and FUNCINPEC was eventually worked out, while Sam Rainsy went to the opposition.

The fortunes of the Khmer Rouge continued to decline during the late 1990s, but echoes of their reign of terror continued to reverberate around the world. In 1997, Pol Pot was put on trial by his erstwhile comrades, was sentenced to house arrest, and died in April 1998, possibly poisoned with the help of the Thais and the United States, thereby escaping justice. Shortly after, the last Khmer Rouge leaders, among them Khieu Samphan and Nuon Chea, defected to the government. The Khmer Rouge had ceased to exist as a military force.

In 1999, Cambodia joined ASEAN. In 2002, local elections were largely peaceful, as were national polls in 2003. The CPP extended its power base in the countryside, while Sam Rainsy made gains among urbanites, especially the young, not least for his speeches against the Vietnamese. FUNCINPEC, involved in ever more infighting and corruption, lost its second-party status. Hun Sen, now virtually without effective opposition, had consolidated his power, and Cambodia had become one of the most corrupt states in the world. Crucially though, Cambodia, however battered and dysfunctional, was at peace.

In 2004, King Sihanouk abdicated for the last time, and his son Sihamoni ascended the throne. The 2008 election, fought against a bitter and politically motivated conflict with Thailand over the temple of Preah Vihear, brought Hun Sen's CPP an overwhelming majority.

SELLING THE NATION (2008-PRESENT)

A decade after the cessation of serious armed conflict, Cambodia was doing well: Tourists were visiting the country in record numbers, the economy was booming, and investment was strong. But there was a dark side, which has come to dominate the life of ordinary people. Government corruption has become so prevalent that large portions of Cambodia's land have been sold to foreign investors, resulting in the biggest displacement of Cambodians since the Khmer Rouge years. In 2009, some 150,000 Cambodians faced eviction from their homes. In all, some 770,000 Cambodians have been affected by land grabs.

Former king Norodom Sihanouk died in October 2012, bringing to an end the illustrious era of Cambodia's last god-king. The 2013 election was disputed by the opposition, and it took more than a year and some under-the-table horse trading to establish a new government in 2014. But the corruption continues unabated. That same year, stories emerged of soldiers being forced to evict their own families from their land. Despite logging and land laws, influential business tycoons and elements of the military continue to deplete the country's resources. Intimidation of the media is common, political opponents are frequently assassinated, and foreign NGOs reporting on abuses have been shown the door.

Also in 2014, a U.N.-backed war crimes tribunal sentenced Khieu Samphan, the regime's 83-year-old former head of state, and Nuon Chea, its 88-year-old chief ideologue, to life in prison on war crimes charges.

Some observers have noted that the culture of impunity that has befallen the country is supported by Western nations and China with generous financial aid packages as well as countless NGOs engaged in self-serving scams. For a report on just how much the aid industry contributes to suffering and autocracy in Cambodia, read *New York Times* reporter Joe Brinkley's book *Cambodia's Curse* (2011).

Cambodia appears to be sliding into ever more authoritarian repression, seemingly unable to join the larger world. The country continues to languish in a semi-isolated limbo, which rests on the compliance of an impoverished people.

Government and Economy

GOVERNMENT
Organization
Cambodia is a multiparty democracy under a constitutional monarch. Since 2004 the head of state has been King Norodom Sihamoni. The Cambodian people go to the ballot every five years and elect a National Assembly of 123 members. The government is formed by the winning parties. The 2008 general election, won resoundingly by Hun Sen's CPP, fell short of international standards. In the general election of 2013, the CPP received 48.79 percent of the votes and earned 68 seats, while the opposition CNRP party won 55 seats with 44.45 percent of the vote. The vote was contested by the CNRP and criticized by international bodies, and it took more than a year to finalize Cambodia's current government. Hun Sen, a former Khmer Rouge soldier and the prime minister since 1985, continues to rule the country with an iron fist.

The 58-member-strong Cambodian senate is dominated by CPP nominees, along with nominees of the other two main parties as well as a couple of the king's nominees and two parliamentarian nominees. Chea Sim, also a former Khmer Rouge, is the current senate president. Heng Samrin, also a former Khmer Rouge, is the president of the National Assembly.

Political Parties
Cambodia's political life is dominated by three parties. The CPP (Cambodian People's Party) is currently Cambodia's strongest party and evolved out of the PRPK, the People's Revolutionary Party of Kampuchea, installed in 1979 by the Vietnamese. The FUNCINPEC Party was founded by Sihanouk as a rebel movement against the Vietnamese. Due to corruption, the party had significant losses in the 2008 elections and has since been doomed to obscurity. The SRP (Sam Rainsy Party) is Cambodia's only other parliamentary political force worth mentioning. Led by former FUNCINPEC finance minister Sam Rainsy, the party has made significant gains in recent elections on a platform of

anticorruption and anti-Vietnamese xenophobia. In 2012, the Sam Rainsy Party and the Human Rights Party merged to form the Cambodian National Rescue Party (CNRP). In recent elections, a gaggle of other parties put up candidates, but none of them have any impact on the political scene.

The Military

Cambodia's current military force, the Royal Cambodian Armed Forces (RCAF), was founded in 1993, following the establishment of a democratically elected government. Throughout the 1990s, the RCAF absorbed soldiers from the other civil war factions. In 2000, it began to demobilize some of its soldiers to reflect Cambodia's peacetime conditions. The military is divided into army, navy, air force, and military police and operates under the jurisdiction of the Ministry of Defense. Cambodia's monarch is the supreme commander of the RCAF, while the prime minister is the commander in chief.

Judicial System

Cambodia has lower courts, an appeals court, and a supreme court as well as a military court. The 1993 constitution guarantees an independent judiciary, although this remains largely an aspiration, with few judges properly trained and many of them clearly in the pockets of influential politicians. The courts are further weakened by police corruption, substandard police procedures, and a brutal prison system. Justice remains elusive for Cambodians.

Slightly different, though no less troubling circumstances, apply to the Extraordinary Chambers in the Courts of Cambodia for the Prosecution of Crimes Committed during the Period of Democratic Kampuchea (Extraordinary Chambers or ECCC), the international court set up by the United Nations to deal with the remaining leaders of the Khmer Rouge, which became seriously compromised by corruption among its judges and pressure from the Cambodian government and has only managed three convictions in seven years of deliberations.

Corruption

According to an international survey on corruption perception in 2011 by Transparency International (www.transparency.org), Cambodia was number 164 out of 182 surveyed nations, following Myanmar at 180 as the most corrupt Southeast Asian nation. This translates into land-grabbing, illegal logging,

collecting firewood in front of a political advertisement, Siem Reap Province

a compromised judiciary and police force, and a culture of impunity that reigns as much on the streets of the capital as it does in the provinces. Cambodians know from long and bitter experience that in order to get anything done, someone will have to be paid.

ECONOMY

Since the end of the political wrangling in Phnom Penh in the late 1990s, Cambodia's economy has grown rapidly. Yet according to World Bank data, annual per capita income in 2013 was US$1,008, and the country remains one of the poorest in the region. Due to massive wealth disparity, this means that people in the countryside remain extremely poor, with thousands in need of food aid despite the fact that Cambodia grows sufficient rice to feed itself. Some of the urban population benefits from the massive recent economic gains, but at least 20 percent of Cambodians live below the poverty line, while another 20 percent hover just above it. Today, foreign investment outstrips (official) foreign aid, and prior to the global financial crisis, the Cambodian economy was growing at around 10 percent. But with continuing resource depletion on a massive scale, the vast majority of the population

mired in poverty, and global economic influence on the country, continued growth, for which a modicum of stability is required, is somewhat uncertain. Rice, fish, wood, and clothing are Cambodia's major exports. The kingdom is a member of the World Trade Organization (WTO).

Agriculture

According to 2004 figures, 73 percent of Cambodians are farmers. Most rural households are engaged in agriculture or fishing, sometimes both. Besides rice, the main crops are rubber, corn, vegetables, tapioca, and cashews. About 85 percent of agricultural land is used to grow rice.

The Garment Industry

Cambodia's garment industry almost went under in 2005, when a WTO agreement on clothing expired, which forced Cambodia to compete directly with countries that pay even lower wages to its workers, such as China and India. Amazingly, the industry has rebounded and accounts for some 70 percent of Cambodia's exports today. More than 500,000 people are employed in the garment industry, though the future of this trade remains uncertain due to international

street scene in front of the Royal Palace, Phnom Penh, home to King Norodom Sihamoni

competition. In 2014, garment workers demonstrated for a better minimum wage. Some were shot by police, partly at the behest of the Korean Embassy. Many of the country's garment factories are owned by South Korean companies.

Tourism

Tourism has grown rapidly since 1999. With two international airports open (and another two planned), some four million tourists visited the country in 2013, most of them to see the ruins of Angkor. By far the largest numbers of foreign visitors, other than from neighboring countries, come from China, Korea, and Japan, followed by the United States (185,000 Americans visited Cambodia in 2013). As infrastructure improves and more sites of interest to tourists become accessible, it is hoped that the industry will diversify away from the major Angkor ruins and promote other attractions around the country in order to distribute income from tourism more widely.

People and Culture

DEMOGRAPHICS

When the Khmer Rouge took power in 1975, Cambodia's population stood at around 7.2 million. An estimated 1-2 million people died between 1975 and 1978. In 1981 the population was around 6.3 million. According to a 2011 estimate, the population hovers just below 15 million, with a median age of 24 years and a population growth rate of just 1.8 percent. Infant mortality is 97 per 1,000, and life expectancy is 63 years, four years higher on average for women than it is for men. The literacy rate is about 74 percent. Cambodia is a multiethnic society with a majority of ethnic Khmer (about 90 percent). The remaining populations are Vietnamese (5 percent), Chinese (5 percent), Cham, and indigenous peoples. Given the large ethnic Khmer majority, Cambodia is one of Southeast Asia's most ethnically homogenous countries.

ETHNIC GROUPS

The Khmer

The Khmer, much like the Thais next door, typically appear ready to smile and be helpful, and they are in constant search of harmonious relations. This tolerance finds its limits in the notion of "face," common to many Southeast Asian cultures. Nothing worries a Khmer more than loss of face—that is, to somehow look bad in front of other people, especially friends or foreigners. This has wide-ranging consequences in everyday contact with Cambodians. If you ask for directions and the person you are asking does not know where to send you, he or she will avoid giving the impression of being uninformed and is more likely to send you in any direction that springs to mind.

Also extremely important is the Khmer's position in society, defined by status (wealth), gender, and age. Visitors will notice that farmers often appear to be subservient when in contact with educated or wealthy Khmer, or even foreigners. That's because the ancient hierarchical codes of Cambodian society define everyone's relation to everyone else. Every Khmer respects the authority vested by power or money in other Khmer that he or she may encounter. Old people are rarely questioned or criticized, and political power is rarely openly challenged by ordinary people.

The Vietnamese

The relationship between the Khmer and their neighbors to the east is difficult. In Cambodia's long-gone, semi-mythical past, wars between the Angkor Empire and the Cham, who came from Vietnam, were frequent. In the 19th and early 20th centuries, the French brought lots of Vietnamese into Cambodia to help with skilled tasks like accounting and administration, responsibilities that the colonial power did not trust to the Khmer. In the 1970s, both the right-wing general Lon Nol and later the hardline communist Khmer Rouge murdered large numbers of Vietnamese. Throughout Pol Pot's reign, Khmer Rouge troops invaded Vietnamese villages and killed civilians. When the Vietnamese invaded Cambodia in 1979 to stop these brutal incursions, and brought an end to the reign of terror the Khmer Rouge had unleashed, the historical resentment barely wavered. Opposition leader Sam Rainsy has made a career out of verbally attacking the Vietnamese. Most Vietnamese in Cambodia today work in fishing (the floating villages on the Tonlé Sap Lake are largely populated by Vietnamese who returned in the 1980s) or in construction.

The Chinese

The Chinese have been living in Cambodia for some 700 years, and while they retain a distinct culture and way of life, many have intermarried with Khmer and speak Khmer. Prior to 1975, the Chinese dominated business and trade and usually belonged to the upper echelons of society, as they do in other Southeast Asian nations. During the Khmer Rouge era, the Chinese either left or were killed. Today, an estimated one million people in Cambodia are said to be Chinese-Khmer. In a country entirely drained of its intellectual resources, the Chinese community fulfills a vital function in helping to power the reemerging economy. Go to a car showroom or a computer shop in Phnom Penh today, and chances are that the owner will be Chinese or Chinese-Khmer.

The Cham

The Cham once ruled most of southern Vietnam, but following the dominance of the Vietnamese in the region, many Cham fled to Cambodia from the 15th century on. In the 17th and 18th centuries, large parts of the community converted to Islam. During the Khmer Rouge years, Pol Pot's communists killed many Cham and burned down their mosques. Today, the Cham, thought to number less than 500,000, generally live in small village communities along the Mekong River and to the south of Phnom Penh.

The Khmer Loeu (Chunchiet)

In Cambodia, indigenous minorities are often called Khmer Loeu, which means "upland Khmer," and therefore are referred to as "hill tribes" or "highlanders." The hill tribes of the northeast are called *chunchiet* by the Khmer, a term the minorities reject. In French, they are called *montagnards*. Most of the indigenous peoples live in the four northeastern provinces—Kratie, Mondulkiri, Ratanakiri, and Stung Treng. Most other provinces are also inhabited by some indigenous peoples.

Due to the lack of population studies, it is difficult to quantify the total number of ethnic groups in Cambodia. The 1998 National Population Census identified 17 indigenous groups based on their languages, but there could be more. Recent assessments showed that around 160,000 Cambodians are from indigenous groups, accounting for 1.5 percent of the total population. While speaking distinct languages and following their own religious practices, the indigenous peoples of Cambodia have much in common. Most importantly, they depend almost entirely on their natural environment for their livelihoods, having formed a close symbiosis with the land they inhabit. During the Khmer Rouge years, most were forcibly resettled into communes, just like ethnic Khmer, and were forbidden to practice their animist rituals and their traditional lifestyles.

Today, most ethnic Khmer regard the Khmer Loeu as backward, and land grabs in the minorities' village areas are common. Western missionaries pose another serious threat to their unique cultures. Some ecotourism projects run by NGOs work with the minorities, if only to stop them from using the slash-and-burn agriculture they have practiced for generations. The aim is to save Cambodia's dwindling forest reserves, but as one Voluntary Service Overseas staffer in Ratanakiri put it, that policy may just pave the way for professional loggers with government backing to move in anyway and cut down the trees.

FESTIVALS AND CULTURAL EVENTS
Chinese New Year

Primarily celebrated by the Chinese and Vietnamese communities in Cambodia, Chinese New Year, or Tet, takes place over a week in **January** or **early February.** Many shops are closed at this time. The holidays are traditionally spent attending lavish family reunions and dinners.

Choul Chnam (Khmer New Year)

Khmer New Year is one of the most important festivals for Cambodians. The three-day event, in **April,** celebrates the beginning of the Buddhist faith. At this time, a new Buddhist deity, or *Tevoda,* is welcomed with offerings of incense, food, and glasses of water, which people leave outside the doors of their homes. On the first couple of days of the festival, people visit their local temple and bring food offerings to the monks. Young people dance and take the opportunity to get to know the opposite sex a little better. On the third day, Buddha statues are washed and the water is collected for a ritual wash. In practice, though, this usually ends as a massive water fight inside the pagodas. What's more, the battle-style water-throwing that takes place in neighboring Thailand is catching on in Cambodia too. In recent years, the government has had to ban high-powered water guns, a somewhat ironic move in a country that, until recently, was armed to the teeth. During Khmer New Year, be prepared to share Angkor with thousands of celebrating Cambodians, who travel from all over the country to picnic and celebrate among the ruins.

Viskha Puja (Buddha Day)

The Buddha's birth, enlightenment, and death are celebrated on a full moon day in **May.** Local people visit their pagodas, offer food to the monks, and in the evening, meditate and pray in the temples.

Chrat Preah Angal (Royal Plowing Ceremony)

The Royal Plowing Ceremony is a somewhat archaic event that takes place at the beginning of the planting season in **May.** The empty space in front of the National Museum is plowed, more or less symbolically, by several oxen. Then, eight royal oxen are each offered seven bowls of food, including rice, corn, green beans, grass, sesame, water, and wine, to predict the future of the farming season. Those offerings preferred by the oxen are said to be especially suitable for planting in the coming year. If the oxen eat grass, then the coming season is likely to be terrible. If one of the oxen goes for the wine, the kingdom is said to be in trouble. The tradition, which is hundreds of years old but was discontinued between 1970 and 1994, is followed closely by all Khmer, the majority of whom are farmers.

Bonn Pchum Ben (Ancestor Worship Festival)

The festival of the dead takes place in **September** or **October** and lasts for two weeks. During this time, it's believed that the souls of the dead are looking for their relatives and are likely to be disappointed if they don't find offerings in seven temples around the capital. In order to appease the dead, people will bring food to the temples, which is blessed and later eaten by the monks. It is said that the dead pick this time for the monks, who traditionally have problems finding enough food during the rainy season. The final day of Bonn Pchum Ben is the most important, when people gather at the temples and pray with the monks for the well-being of the souls of the dead.

Bonn Om Tuk (Water Festival)

At the end of the rainy season, as the water levels in the Mekong River subside, the Tonlé

Sap River reverses its direction and drains Tonlé Sap Lake back into the Mekong. Bonn Om Tuk, a three-day event, celebrates the changing direction of the river around the full moon with boat races in front of the Royal Palace. Tens of thousands of people attend. It's not certain what the origins of the festival are. More than 200 boats from all over the country race in front of the royal family, perhaps in reference to ancient naval battles between the Khmer and the Cham on Tonlé Sap Lake.

The boats, around 25 meters long and decked out with garlands, are rowed by 20-30 men and women. The riverfront takes on a fantastic carnival atmosphere and is crowded with hawkers and their customers. After dark, a boat procession circulates on the river, accompanied by fireworks. Bands set up on small stages and blast music at the passing crowds. Each of the 10 boats in the procession carries a board with a brightly lit image: The first represents the colors of the king, the second those of parliament, and the third shows a map of Cambodia. The remaining boats represent various ministries. The same program repeats itself each day. On the third day of the festival, the king makes a brief appearance in front of the Royal Palace. The best views of this spectacle can be enjoyed from the first floor of the Foreign Correspondents Club of Cambodia (FCC). Alternatively, you can wander through the happy crowds along Sisowath Quay, bearing in mind that there are pickpockets afoot.

During the three-day holiday, Phnom Penh is extremely crowded, and hotels are often fully booked. Buses from outside the capital may take longer than usual and might even get stuck on the outskirts of town. The first few blocks off the riverfront are closed to traffic.

In 2010, about 350 people were stampeded to death on a swaying new bridge after police failed to regulate the massive crowds visiting the city during the festival. To date, no one has been held responsible for Cambodia's most serious peacetime disaster. The festival was suspended for several years, and boat races only resumed in 2014.

CLOTHING

According to Chou Ta-Kuan, a Chinese diplomat who visited the imperial city of Angkor Thom in August 1296, both Cambodian men and women wore only a strip of cloth around the waist. This included not just ordinary people but also the wives of the king. This changed with the arrival of the French and the introduction of Christian ideas of modesty. The minorities in the northeast had their own textile traditions, but these were largely lost during the Khmer Rouge years, when everyone in the country wore the same clothes—black pajamas.

The main traditional garment for farmers and workers, the *sampot,* a wraparound rectangular piece of cloth similar to a sarong, is for the most part now just worn in the privacy of the home to relax after work. High-society Khmer wear a more sophisticated version of the same garment, the *sampot chang kben,* which is twisted and pulled between the legs, then tucked into a cloth belt at the back. Cambodian men and women of all backgrounds wear this piece of clothing for special occasions, such as wedding parties. Besides these traditional cotton garments, finer silk versions are also produced, especially by the Cham.

Traditional dress in Cambodia is slowly going out of fashion, especially in urban areas and among the younger generation. Blouses, shirts, and jackets now complement the *sampot* as upper garments. The ever-present *krama,* the cotton head scarf worn by almost everyone a decade ago, is becoming a rare sight in Phnom Penh, though not in the countryside. Young Cambodians wear jeans and T-shirts.

THE POSITION OF WOMEN IN CAMBODIA

Traditionally, in Cambodia the man is the head of the family, and the woman is expected to be a loyal wife. Decades of civil war and

The *Krama*: Cambodia's All-Purpose Scarf

The cotton *krama* is one of the most common objects in Cambodia, worn by virtually every adult in the countryside. The checkered scarf comes in many colors and sizes, and Cambodians find seemingly endless uses for it. It is used as shade and dust protection, a hammock or carry-bag for infants, a container, and a towel, and farmers even tie them around their legs to help them climb trees. Some mothers sew *krama* together to make dolls for their children. During the Khmer Rouge years, the Khmer were forced to wear a red checkered *krama*. Nowadays, young urbanites have begun to shy away from wearing the scarves, and many *krama* offered to tourists are woven from mixed synthetic threads. A small *krama* should cost around 4,000 riel (US$1); the bigger the size, the bigger the price. Don't be shy to bargain.

insecurity have further weakened the position of women, with high incidences of violence against women within the family recorded. The flourishing sex industry also demeans the status of women.

On the other hand, within the family circle, women take part in important decisions—such as education, or the choice of a husband or wife for their children—and they often manage to mediate in family conflicts that might otherwise be resolved with violence.

Women take part in public life, and a small number of women have managed to establish themselves as entrepreneurs, actors, and politicians, a development that will hopefully continue. But the disparate literacy rates for men and women tell the story: In 2009, literacy stood at 87 percent—88 percent of men could read and write, while 85.1 percent of women could claim the same privilege.

LANGUAGE

Khmer, or Cambodian, is spoken by the population of Cambodia and is the country's official language. The older languages of Sanskrit and Pali have a significant influence on Khmer due to the foreign influences of Hinduism and Buddhism. Khmer has its own script, and several dialects are spoken around the country and beyond its borders. Notable local dialect variations include Phnom Penh; Battambang; Khmer Surin, the Khmer spoken by some people in northeast Thailand; and Khmer Krom, the Khmer spoken by some people in the Mekong Delta.

The dialects are close enough to be mutually intelligible.

RELIGION

Early Khmer empires were generally Hindu, although a few early kings were Buddhists. Since the 13th century, Buddhism has been at the heart of Cambodian cultural life and identity. Non-Buddhists include Muslims, recently converted Christians, and a smattering of indigenous people adhering to animism.

Buddhism

Buddhism has been present in Cambodia for almost 2,000 years, probably as long as Hinduism. Initially, different Buddhist currents existed under the early Khmer Hindu empires. During the early Funan kingdom, Buddhism was already marginally present and tolerated. King Jayavarman II (AD 802-850), an early king of the Angkor Empire, was a Hindu but was very tolerant of Mahayana Buddhism. Gradually, the Khmer Empire shifted away from Hinduism. Jayavarman VII (AD 1181-1218), one of the most powerful kings of the Angkor era, was a devout Mahayana Buddhist who attempted to achieve enlightenment by working to save his people. This monarch moved away from the god-king concept consistent with Hindu thinking. Instead of supporting a vast Brahmanic clergy, he founded the *sangha*, an assembly of monks, and established libraries and public works.

Jayavarman VII sent his son to Sri Lanka to study Theravada Buddhism, and in the

13th century the Angkor Empire adopted Theravada Buddhism as a new state religion. It has been the dominant faith ever since, except during a brief resurgence of Hinduism following Jayavarman VII's death and, more recently, during the Khmer Rouge years. The goal of Theravada Buddhism is enlightenment, reaching nirvana, and the end of all suffering. This goal is achieved by leading a life free of desire in the hope for a higher level of reincarnation the next time around.

Religion has always been used in politics in Cambodia. During the 17th-19th centuries, Thai influence over the Cambodian monarchy extended into the Cambodian *sangha* (national Buddhist council), which in 1855 split into two factions: the Dhammayuttika Nikaya (Thammayut sect), which was connected to Thailand, followed strict discipline, and was supported by the monarchy; and the Maha Nikaya, to which most of today's monks in Cambodia belong.

Following independence from France in 1953, King Sihanouk managed to impress the idea of institutionalized inequality on his people by aligning himself with Buddhism and Hinduism. One was born a king or a peasant, the reasons for which lay in a past life, the monarch argued, supported by the Buddhist clergy. The Khmer Rouge tried to destroy Buddhism, and during their reign of terror between 1975 and 1979, thousands of monks were killed and most of the country's temples were destroyed. The teaching of Buddhism was interrupted for several years, and scholars fled or were executed.

Following the fall of the Khmer Rouge, the Vietnamese attempted to create one *sangha*. In 1981, a monk who had gone into exile to Vietnam during the Khmer Rouge years was officially ordained by the government as the new *sangharaja* of Cambodia. As soon as the Vietnamese had left, the ruling CPP aligned itself with the *sangha*, declaring Buddhism Cambodia's state religion, but in 1991 King Sihanouk appointed new *sangharajas* for both Buddhist factions. Within the *sangha*, further divisions exist, primarily between traditionalists and modernists. Members of the traditionalist wing value repetition of Khmer and Pali passages to accrue merit. This stems partly from the fact that the traditionalists reject study of Buddhist philosophy, because they don't understand the texts.

To this day, prominent members of the Maha Nikaya, especially the *boran* grouping, an ultraconservative movement of monks, promotes government policies and even calls for the arrest of monks who are not prepared to toe the government line. Modernists, on the other hand, are keen to use their influence in daily Cambodian life to effect social change. Finally, the so-called Young Monks Movement is in favor of openly facing down the government over corruption. Members of the Dhammayuttika Nikaya tend to stay out of politics, following a more literal interpretation of Buddhist scriptures and valuing discipline and study over political engagement.

More than 90 percent of today's Cambodians are Buddhist. New temples continue to be constructed all over the countryside, and irrespective of its political links, Buddhism can provide much-needed social cohesion in a country where no one trusts anyone outside the family, a consequence of decades of war. On the other hand, the traditional Buddhist tendency to accept one's misfortune as something caused in a previous life continues to affect Cambodians.

In recent years, countless politically active monks have been beaten and arrested by security forces.

THE WAT

A *wat,* a Buddhist monastery (this defines the entire compound, not just the prayer hall), is the religious and social center of every community in Cambodia. Local people flock here on holidays to make merit and donate food to the monks in the hope of shortening their cycle of rebirths and reaching nirvana. Normally, between 5 and 100 monks reside in a *wat,* which generally consists of a prayer hall, a sanctuary, accommodations for monks and sometimes nuns, a kitchen, a bell tower, and a pond. The sanctuary contains a shrine with Buddha statues and is used only by the monks. Large ceremonies involving the local community take place in the prayer hall. Stupas containing the ashes of monks and local residents, or Buddhist relics, are usually dotted around the *wat* or just outside its compound. Most *wats* have a gate, somewhat removed from the compound and often found at the turnoff of a temple road from a main road.

Many *wats* were destroyed during the Khmer Rouge years or used as stables and warehouses. Plenty of money has been raised since to rebuild monasteries, and nowadays even historic *wats,* some almost 100 years old and constructed of wood, are being knocked down to make way for new structures, invariably made of concrete.

THE LIFE OF A MONK

Monks are very much part of daily life in Cambodia, and every young Cambodian male is expected to join the monastery for a year or less. In times of economic hardship, a family might receive its only food from the local *wat* because one of their children serves as a novice there. Most novices do not become fully fledged monks (*bikkhu*). Novices can be as

young as 7, but to become a *bikkhu*, they have to be at least 20.

The lives of monks are governed by Buddhist law. All Buddhists are supposed to follow five basic precepts: not to lie, not to kill, not to steal, not to engage in sexual misconduct, and not to consume intoxicants. Everyone living in a *wat* must follow a further five precepts: not to eat after noon, not to consume entertainment (such as watching TV or going to a party), not to use personal adornments, not to sleep in a comfortable bed, and not to have contact with money. Furthermore, all monks are supposed to be celibate. *Bikkhu* have to follow 227 rules on top of the 10 precepts. Monks are also not supposed to be involved in politics or appear in court. Some of these rules have been updated or are simply ignored. Monks are allowed to vote in Cambodia, though this is opposed by senior conservative members of the *sangha*.

Women are not ordained at all, but older women, especially widows, often shave their heads, join the monastery, and become nuns.

Islam

Most of the Muslim minority (less than 1 percent of the population) living in Cambodia have ancestors that arrived sometime in the

prayer hall in a *wat* next to Lolei, Roluos Group

15th century, after the defeat of the Cham by the Khmer and the end of the Cham Empire. Large Cham Muslim communities can be found along the Mekong around Kompong Cham, as well as south of Phnom Penh on the road to Kampot. The Cham maintain some of their pre-Muslim animist beliefs, and in contrast to other Muslims, only go to prayer once a week.

Hinduism

Hinduism was the dominant religion in Cambodia for more than 1,000 years, until the 13th century, when it was gradually replaced by Buddhism. Subsequent Hindu empires in Cambodia followed either Shiva or Vishnu, or a combination of both deities. While there's no Hindu community in Cambodia today, many elements of Hinduism survive in daily religious life—statues of the elephant god Ganesh are still common, for example.

Christianity

Christianity didn't make significant inroads in early Cambodia, and the few churches that did exist prior to the Khmer Rouge were destroyed by the communists. In the 1980s, many Cambodians, coerced by Christian relief operations, converted to Christianity in the refugee camps along the Thai border. Many of these people returned to Buddhism as soon as they had reestablished their lives in Cambodia.

More recently, Christian groups, especially missionary outfits, have come back to Cambodia and are engaged in persuading or forcing, depending on the observer's point of view, the minority groups in the northeast away from their animist beliefs. This has contributed to the Khmer Loeu losing their roots and becoming more marginalized than they already were. Typically, missionaries approach the most destitute elements of the population and help them out of trouble—in return for converting. The Cambodian government sees the minorities as a problem rather than an asset, and missionary organizations take heart from this.

Animism

Animism, the worship of nature and natural spirits, lies at the center of the belief systems of Cambodia's minorities. Animism is fast becoming rare in Cambodia as missionaries make more and more inroads into traditional societies.

Superstition

Superstitions are an integral part of daily life in Cambodia. This has much to do with the fact that, until very recently, information exchange in Cambodian society was based on oral beliefs. Country life in Asia is cut off from the rest of the world by lack of mobility and education at the best of times, but Cambodia's catastrophic recent past has not only kept many folk beliefs and superstitions alive, but it has also created an atmosphere where change is unwelcome. Hence, outmoded beliefs manage to accrue plenty of mileage.

When King Sihanouk passed away in 2012, many Cambodians believed they saw his face in the moon. In Phnom Penh, one could even buy postcards of this phenomenon.

The Arts

ARCHITECTURE
Temple Art and Architecture

The temples of the Angkor Empire and its predecessors are all we have left of a culture that dominated Southeast Asia for centuries. Cambodian temple ruins date from about AD 500-1220. At the time they were built, the temples were surrounded by infrastructure that supported thousands of people, be they temple staff, soldiers, farmers, slaves, or other subjects. Most Cambodians lived in wooden buildings then, much like today, and naturally there is nothing left of those. Thus it is the religious structures that tell us about the cultural and political development of the Khmer empires.

PRE-ANGKORIAN (AD 500-800)

Early Cambodian temple architecture was heavily influenced by architectural ideas and techniques from India. As the early Khmer kings were Hindus, and the state religion of the Angkor Empires prior to the 11th century was Hinduism (although Buddhism was tolerated), every aspect of temple building was defined by the Hindu world view. Central to this view was the cult of the god-king, who saw his creations as a miniature map of the universe over which he reigned. Architectural elements that can be traced back to India include the symmetry of temple layouts, the temple ponds or moats symbolizing the cosmic ocean, and the central tower (*prasat*). But the Angkor architects soon began to interpret these influences from the west, and architectural ideas from Java and China changed the temples over time.

Some of Angkor's major monuments, including Angkor Wat, are temple mountains: earthly representations of Mount Meru, home of the Hindu pantheon. Temple mountains are shrines built on a multilevel base. Initially, at Bakong, for example, just one tower would stand on the base. But by the 10th century, five towers, one in the center of the temple mountain's platform and the others at the four corners, had become the established norm.

But not all major Khmer temples follow this design. Ta Prohm was a flat temple compound. Concentric walls surrounded the sanctuary, symbolizing the mountain chains surrounding Mount Meru. In between these walls, enclosures were lined by roofed galleries. In order to step from one enclosure into another, you had to pass through a *gopura*, an entrance hall, often mounted by towers. *Gopuras* were often flanked by stone guards and decorated with impressively carved lintels (crossbeams above doorways). Above the lintels, triangular pediments also featured carvings. On some door frames to the *gopuras*, Sanskrit writing was carved into the sandstone. Blind windows and doors were also common elements. As most temples opened to the east, blind doors were introduced at the remaining sides to maintain symmetry. Blind windows were used to decorate blank walls. At the heart of every temple lay the sanctuary, a small hall buried underneath the central tower (*prasat*). The temple foundations were often built from laterite, clay that hardened when exposed to the sun, but this material was usually hidden from view, as laterite is not suitable for carving. Other temple structures included libraries (although these may have served as shrines rather than as repositories for scriptures or manuscripts) and the *barays*, massive reservoirs built for irrigation purposes and possibly also religious reasons.

The earliest substantial temple ruins in Cambodia date back to the early-7th-century Chenla Empire, a precursor to Angkor. Its capital, Isanapura, can still be visited today, at Sambor Prei Kuk in Kompong Thom Province. These temples were built from brick with carvings usually added onto stucco on top of the brick, although some brick carvings can also be found. Early Khmer temples often feature a linga, a phallic representation of Shiva, in their sanctuaries. Some of the largest linga can be found at Koh Ker.

ANGKORIAN (AD 800-1220)

At the beginning of the 9th century, Jayavarman II was the first Khmer king to build a capital to the northwest of Tonlé Sap Lake at Hariharalaya (the Roluos group of temples). Subsequent kings added temple structures such as the Bakong temple mountain, dedicated to Shiva; Preah Ko, with its red brick towers and finely carved lintels; and Lolei (also at Roluos), a temple with four brick towers and fine carvings of Indra, the sun god.

From the 10th century on, the Khmer increasingly used sandstone. At first, because the stone had to be laboriously extracted from the Kulen Mountains, only small parts of the temples were made of sandstone. But as the empire grew in wealth, sandstone became increasingly popular. Ta Keo, built in the 10th century, was the first temple built almost entirely of sandstone.

During Jayavarman VII's reign in the 13th century, new building elements were added. *Dharamshalas* (rest houses for pilgrims), spread along the Angkorian highways across the kingdom. Next to some later temples, such as Ta Prohm, a hall of dancers, decorated with dancing *apsaras*, was erected. The exact function for these buildings is not known, although they may indeed have served as dance halls.

Many temples are decorated with bas-reliefs: figures or scenes that stick out from the background, carved into stone walls or lintels. Fine examples of bas-reliefs can be seen at the 10th-century temple of Banteay Srei, but the greatest masterpiece is the outer gallery of Angkor Wat, which features some 12,000 square meters of continuous narrative depicting mythological scenes as well as historic battles. The outer walls of the Bayon, on the other hand, are covered in bas-reliefs depicting the life of ordinary Khmer going about their daily chores, giving visitors a unique insight into how humans fit into all this architectural grandeur.

Impressive too are the stairs leading up to the temple towers, which often have an ascent of up to 70 degrees. This rather impractical design may have served a visual purpose, with the small base of the tower making the entire structure look more heaven-bound.

Incredible carvings lend Angkor its unique otherworldly character just as much as its monumental proportions do, and some motifs return again and again to engage the visitor. *Apsaras*, heavenly nymphs cast in stone, originate in the *Mahabharata* and lend the temple ruins a very sensuous ambience. Stories in the Hindu myth tell of how the gods used these celestial dancers to seduce demons, heroes, and holy men. *Devatas* are female deities similar to *apsaras*, although they never dance. *Dvarapalas* are temple guards, sometimes carrying a stick, carved near the entrance doors to the shrines. *Nagas*, mythical multiheaded snakes, are prominent in Khmer mythology. They can often be found as part of lintels or as freestanding sculptures, sometimes shielding Buddha in meditation. Some larger temples have causeways flanked by balustrades shaped as *nagas*. Often these *nagas* are held by gods and demons, symbolizing the churning of the ocean and the fight between the two parties for *amrita*, the nectar of immortality, a central story in Hindu mythology. *Garudas* are half-man, half-bird creatures that serve as transportation for Vishnu. *Garudas* can be found as part of lintels or as part of *naga* heads. Sometimes they appear to be the enemies of the mythical snakes; at other times the two are part of the same harmonious sculpture.

French Urban Architecture (1870-1952)

The French left a wealth of interesting if mostly crumbling architecture behind. The absolute highlight is the Bokor Palace on the southeast coast, which is unfortunately being developed into a new casino complex. Phnom Penh still has a fair legacy of French buildings. The beautiful art deco Central Market

(Phsar Thmey), built in the 1920s and 1930s, was restored in 2009. Sadly, many French buildings have been knocked down to be replaced by chrome and glass monstrosities. In the provinces, almost every small town has a few blocks of French town houses still standing, and restoration is under way for some of these buildings. Especially attractive are the colonial remnants of Kampot, Battambang, Kratie, and Chhlong, as well as the now fully restored area around the Old Market in Siem Reap.

Urban Architecture Under King Sihanouk (1953-1970)

After the departure of the French, King Sihanouk personally got involved in how his newly independent kingdom was to look. The king actively promoted a new building style, the so-called New Khmer Architecture, largely the brainchild of architect Vann Molyvann. Traces of this movement, which sought to combine traditional Khmer and modern aesthetics, can still be seen around the Cambodian capital and in some provincial towns.

Rural Architecture

Most Cambodians live as they have always lived. The typical family home is constructed on high stilts, which keeps animals out of the living space, protects from flooding, and offers shade and storage space underneath the home. The higher the stilts, the wealthier the owner is likely to be. A narrow stairway leads to the first floor, which is usually fronted by a veranda. The first floor might be divided into a couple of living spaces, one for the parents to sleep in, another one for the children and possible guests. Everyone sleeps on thin mats. A kitchen is usually separated from this large room. Bathroom and toilet, if they exist, can be found in a concrete or wood outhouse somewhere behind the main building. Most houses in the country are surrounded by a small garden. Sometimes there's also a small pond. Despite the fact that the buildings are simple, they are clean and comfortable and

offer a higher standard of living than the overcrowded tenement blocks in Phnom Penh.

MUSIC

The typical Khmer orchestra is called *phleng pinpeat* and usually performs in temples on public holidays or during special religious ceremonies. The main instruments used are gongs, flutes, a type of xylophone, violins, and horns, often made from animal horn. For the Western listener, this music may sound a bit arbitrary and off-key. Songs appear to meander without a particular structure.

Played outside the temple, traditional Khmer music often features sentimental lyrics about love and farewells, and about the simple life of the farmer. The Khmer Rouge picked up on these folk traditions and subverted them for propaganda purposes. Since the 1990s, some of these music traditions have been revived, especially at temple fairs. In the 1950s, the French introduced jazz to Phnom Penh's nightclubs, and classic dances such as the waltz and the tango also became popular among the Cambodian elite. In the 1960s, rock music, first imported, then homegrown, also made some inroads; several tapes that have surfaced in recent years attest to a pretty wild music scene.

Today's pop music is divided into sentimental ballads, harking back to the 1960s, or rock music and techno introduced from Thailand and loosely translated into Khmer. Most popular is karaoke. Even small country towns and villages will have several karaoke bars in which local men, with or without the help of the resident taxi girls, will engage in drunken musical performances late into the night. A basic karaoke bar has a TV, a stereo system, a DVD player, and a microphone— quite an investment, although this is recouped quickly as men, young and old, compulsively perform heartbreaking melodies for their friends, for the hostesses, and for themselves.

In recent years, some mixed Khmer-Western bands have emerged in the country, including The Cambodian Space Project. The Phnom Penh-based music collective Dub

The New Beat of Cambodia

Travelers are rightly worried about contracting dengue fever in the remoter parts of tropical countries, especially in the rainy season, but there's one variety worth catching up with—the musical kind. In 2001, two brothers from Los Angeles, Ethan and Zac Holtzman, formed a band called **Dengue Fever** after Ethan had visited Cambodia. In Los Angeles, they looked for and found a Cambodian singer, Chhom Nimol, a karaoke star who'd moved to the United States to make money for her family back home and was performing regularly in Little Phnom Penh in Long Beach, California. The band put out their first album in 2003, an eclectic mix of Cambodian pop tunes from the 1960s as well as some original songs. In 2005, the band first visited Cambodia and went down like a storm. A documentary feature about the trip, titled *Sleepwalking through the Mekong,* was released shortly after. Since then, the band has released several more albums, most recently on Peter Gabriel's Real World label, and returned to Cambodia for a string of performances in 2011.

Dengue Fever is highly entertaining, but they have also performed a great service to Cambodian music. In the 1960s, Cambodian bands had a pretty original take on rock and roll. The bands sang in Khmer, and the sounds they produced had a raw, real quality, usually unheard of so far away from the United States or Britain. Most of the musicians of that era were killed by Pol Pot's Khmer Rouge. Dengue Fever rediscovered the song material that had fallen into obscurity and reintroduced Cambodians, as well as the rest of the world, to a sound that was almost wiped out in the genocide.

More recently, the Cambodia-based band **The Cambodian Space Project** (CSP), led by the enigmatic singer Srey Thy, has been touring the Khmer rock sound around the world. Less slick than Dengue Fever, but with a keener eye on Cambodia's musical history, the band has been involved in theater and films and is trying to break out of the traditional rock band mold. The Cambodian Space Project: Not Easy Rock 'N Roll, a BBC and ABC Australia-produced feature documentary by Marc Eberle, charts the band's history and looks back at the birth and demise of Cambodia's rock music at the hands of the Khmer Rouge. For more information on Cambodian rock music, check out www.denguefevermusic.com, and find out about current CSP performances and projects on Facebook.

Addiction tours its hip-hop reggae sound internationally and frequently brings the house down in the country's bigger music venues.

DANCE

Cambodia has quite a dance culture, with three distinct types of dances. Best known is the royal ballet (*apsara*), considered the classic dance of Cambodia. Once upon a time, this dance was performed purely for the enjoyment of the royal family, but in recent years it has become very much a tourist attraction. Also popular, though increasingly fading, is the lively folk dance, far less restrained and artificial than the *apsara* dance and popular in the countryside. Dances revolve around themes that farmers can relate to, such as the beginning of the rains, the harvest, or even a fruit. These dances go back to the region's pre-Buddhist times and have their roots in animism. Finally, there's *ram vong,* a dance that is designed purely for enjoyment. Any Khmer festival, celebration, or even an evening in a nightclub will feature this dance. Dancers move single file in a circle against the clock and turn their hands back and forth, inspired by simple *apsara* dance movements, in time to the music.

THEATER

The royal theater is based on the *Reamker,* the Khmer version of the *Ramayana,* a 2,000-year-old Hindu epic. The story of how Rama frees his wife, Sita, with the help of Hanuman, god of the monkeys, from the evil clutches of Ravana is performed by masked dancers.

The Greatest Movie Set in the World

Cambodia has long been used as a movie location. Foreign documentaries were shot around the country as early as the 1920s. In the 1950s Khmer filmmakers began to shoot their own features, and by the 1960s a small but vibrant film industry had established itself and turned out some 300 popular movies until the Khmer Rouge takeover.

The first big-budget foreign film made in Cambodia is an excellent adaptation of Joseph Conrad's *Lord Jim* (1965), partly shot around Angkor and starring Peter O'Toole.

King Norodom Sihanouk, then a prince, was also an ardent filmmaker, and in the 1960s he wrote, produced, and directed numerous romantic melodramas in which he often took the lead role. Some of his films can be found in the video shops around Phnom Penh and are still shown regularly on Cambodian TV.

Following their takeover in 1975, the Khmer Rouge destroyed Cambodia's film industry. The communists did produce some propaganda films, however. The best known foreign movie about life under the Khmer Rouge is *The Killing Fields* by Roland Joffe, shot in Thailand in 1984. This brilliant movie follows the true story of journalist Dith Pran on his journey through the Cambodian genocide.

Since the end of the civil war, Cambodian and foreign filmmakers have slowly begun to rediscover the country for cinema. Cambodian director Rithy Panh's interesting 1994 movie *The Rice People* deals with the aftermath of the Khmer Rouge reign and was the first Cambodian film ever submitted for an Oscar. Panh is the director of Bophana, Cambodia's audiovisual center, which aims to preserve Cambodia's film, photographic, and audio history. Less serious, but seriously successful, are locally made low-budget horror films.

Angelina Jolie, a.k.a. Lara Croft, rediscovered the country for the international cinema with *Tomb Raider*, an action flick based on a computer game that was shot around Angkor. Jolie loved the country so much that she adopted a Cambodian child, a boy called Maddox, and is involved in various NGO projects. Wong Kar-Wai's 2001 *In the Mood For Love* was partly shot in Angkor, and the 2003 French production *Two Brothers* by Jean-Jacques Annaud, a film about two tigers set during the French colonial period, followed shortly after. *The Gate,* based on the memoirs of François Bizot in Khmer Rouge captivity, a French-Belgian-Cambodian production, was released in 2014.

The most interesting recent foreign film about Cambodia is perhaps Matt Dillon's *City of Ghosts.* Shot independently in 2002, the plot, which follows a young American man (Dillon) looking for his crooked boss and possible father (James Caan) in Southeast Asia, is forgettable, but the performances of the ensemble cast, featuring Gérard Depardieu, Stellan Skarsgård, and excellent Cambodian newcomer Kem Sereyvuth, against the mesmerizing backdrop of a beaten, raw country trying to get back on its feet, is remarkable. Dillon goes for local color all the way and comes up with a dark and brooding tale that perfectly portrays a moment in Cambodia's painful rebirth. The Khmer rock-and-roll soundtrack is great too.

Theater in the Western sense has barely made any inroads in Cambodia, although the first rock opera, called *Where Elephants Weep*, was launched in late 2008 to be televised; it immediately ran afoul of the Supreme Council of Buddhist Monks and had to be modified. The Phare Circus in Battambang and more recently in Siem Reap produces the country's most dynamic and beguiling performances, mixing traditional story and dance elements with modern narratives.

LITERATURE

Cambodian folk literature is a rich seam of stories with both entertainment and educational value that is traditionally handed down from generation to generation. Fairy tales, fables, ghost stories, and stories illustrating aspects of Cambodian history, usually with a great bloodthirsty hero who kills thousands of enemies in great battles, are common. Most of this literature is designed to teach common people that they must accept

Phnom Penh cinema advertising a local horror flick

as backdrops. Many of the actors and directors involved in the golden age of Cambodian cinema were killed by the Khmer Rouge, and many of the films were lost.

In the 1980s, after the Vietnamese had expelled the Khmer Rouge from government, foreign films with socialist messages became the vogue, but no Cambodian film industry was reestablished. Only at the end of the 1980s did some production companies start business again, but most of these local efforts were hampered by the emergence of VCRs and the consequent closure of the few cinemas open at the time.

In the 1990s, the film industry made a comeback, first with a deluge of cheap karaoke videos, then slowly with cheap horror flicks. Rithy Panh, who had escaped the Khmer Rouge, trained to be a filmmaker in France and has since made several internationally acclaimed features and documentaries dealing with Cambodia's recent tragic past, inspiring several other local filmmakers to produce interesting documentaries and feature films. His most recent documentary feature, *The Missing Picture* (2013), is an autobiographical account of the Khmer Rouge period using clay figures to tell its story. The film won the Un Certain Regard section at the Cannes Film Festival and was nominated for an Oscar. Panh is also the founder of the much lauded Bophana cultural film center in Phnom Penh. The documentary *Enemies of the People* (2009) by Thet Sambath, co-directed by Robert Lemkin, is a great investigative piece of journalism in which the Khmer director manages to win the trust of and interview Nuon Chea, Brother Number 2 in the Khmer Rouge regime. Widespread DVD piracy is seen as a major reason why the local film industry has not developed faster in recent years.

the prevailing power structures. During the Sihanouk and Lon Nol years, a handful of Cambodian writers produced novels, short stories, and political nonfiction. Not much of a literary scene has managed to reestablish itself in Cambodia, though cartoons are hugely popular.

CINEMA

The first films made by Cambodians for Cambodians were silent movies shot in the 1950s. In the 1960s, more than 300 movies were made in Cambodia, and cinemas opened in the capital and some smaller towns. Today, the 1960s are considered the golden age of Cambodian cinema. King Sihanouk, a cinema enthusiast, made a string of feature films in the late 1960s, often using the Angkor temples

Essentials

Getting There

AIR

Cambodia currently has two international airports, one in Phnom Penh, the other in Siem Reap. It is expected that Sihanoukville Airport will also eventually receive international flights. While Cambodia is no international hub, connections have improved dramatically in recent years and, with ever-increasing visitor numbers, should continue to do so.

For now, the majority of foreign travelers arrive in Siem Reap, which, besides frequent flights to Bangkok, has international connections to Beijing, Cheng Du, Guangzhou, Kunming, Shanghai, and Hong Kong in China; Singapore; Ho Chi Minh City and Hanoi in Vietnam; Vientiane in Laos; Seoul in Korea, Doha in Qatar, and Taipei in Taiwan. Both airports are quite small but modern, and arrival and departure procedures are smooth and professional. Snacks and drinks are available. Unlike at land borders, travelers are not hit for bribes at the airports. Monument Books has branches in the departure lounges in Phnom Penh and Siem Reap. Numerous other shops have also set up in the international airport terminals, including artist Stéphane Delaprée's Happy Painting.

Arriving by Air

Getting your visa and clearing customs is little more than a formality in Cambodia (unless you are on a blacklist). An official taxi from Siem Reap Airport to your hotel costs US$7 and takes around 20 minutes. A *motodup* (motorcycle taxi) will do it for US$2, a tuk-tuk for US$5. A taxi from Phnom Penh International Airport into town costs US$9 and takes about 30 minutes; a *motodup* will do it for US$2, a tuk-tuk for US$7. As a rule,

hotels are happy to pick up guests from either airport free of charge or for a nominal fee, but you must arrange this with your hotel in advance.

Departing by Air

Departure taxes are no longer collected before you get on your flight. They are now included in the ticket price.

OVERLAND

Cambodia shares land borders with Thailand, Laos, and Vietnam. A number of international border crossings, where Cambodian visas are issued on the spot, connect the kingdom to its neighbors. Some of these land crossings are frequently used by foreigners, while others are so remote that they hardly see any international traffic. Cambodia's international borders are generally open 6am-8pm. You need a visa for Laos or Vietnam to cross the land borders into these countries. If you enter Thailand from Cambodia overland, without having previously applied for a tourist visa, you get a 30-day entry stamp. If you arrive by plane from Cambodia, you also get 30 days. These 30-day entry stamps can currently be extended by another 30 days at any immigration office in Thailand for 1,900 baht (US$58).

In order to enter Cambodia and get a visa, you need a passport photograph, hard to come by at the remote crossings. Cambodian immigration officers are engaged in a number of scams to force foreign visitors to pay more for their visas than they should. Entering from Thailand, especially via Poipet or Koh Kong, you may be forced to pay 1,200 baht (US$36), instead of the official rate of US$30. Arriving from Laos, extra fees are also often demanded. Leaving Cambodia via Poipet on busy days, immigration officers may suggest foreign travelers pay a 200 baht (US$6) VIP fee to jump ahead of the Khmer travelers.

Some guidebooks encourage their readers to confront officers. Remember that at the border crossings, the officials you are dealing with are the local—and only—authority. Threatening them or getting noisy is likely to be counterproductive. Get your Cambodian visa in advance if you want to avoid the problem altogether. Never try to cross into Cambodia without a visa or at an unauthorized crossing. Besides the fact that this is against the laws of the country you are leaving and the one you are entering, sections of Cambodia's border are heavily mined.

Border Crossings with Thailand

Cambodia and Thailand currently have six international border crossings. Cambodian visas are issued at all of these crossings. There's one exception: Crossing from Thailand at Preah Vihear, when this is possible, does not entitle visitors to travel farther into Cambodia, as the hilltop temple is not an international border crossing. There is no requirement to change foreign currency at any border. The Cambodian E-Visa is only accepted at the Poipet/Aranyaphratet Thai border and the Moc Bai/Bavet Vietnam border crossing.

There are direct buses from Bangkok to Siem Reap and vice versa, though travelers have to cross the border on foot and sort out their visas themselves. Prices are around US$25-30 (750 Thai baht). In Bangkok, buses leave from Morochit Station. Tickets can be purchased at the station. In Siem Reap, tickets can be purchased from travel agents, and passengers are usually picked up at their guesthouse. Buses leave, in both directions, 7am-9am.

POIPET/ARANYAPHRATET

ប៉ោយប៉ែត

The most popular overland route into Cambodia is the border crossing at **Poipet** (**Aranyaphratet** on the Thai side). It is possible to make the 465-kilometer run between Bangkok and Siem Reap in a day.

But be forewarned: While through-tickets from Khao San Road in Bangkok cost just 400-800 baht, they are often a scam. Travelers are cheated in a number of ways. Usually, onward transportation on the Cambodian side is so slow that travelers arrive in Siem Reap very late and are forced into a hotel that pays commission to the transportation company that brought them. Those who try to change hotels might get into an ugly argument. Sometimes travelers have been taken through other, far more remote border crossings where they were hit by additional scams.

The safest and quickest way is to do the journey independently. On the Thai side of the border, which can be reached from Bangkok by train, bus, or minibus, things are pretty straightforward. There are ATMs and shops at the border, and Aranyaphratet has reasonable accommodations and a half-decent hospital. From town it is six kilometers to the border, best traveled in a tuk-tuk. Across the border in Cambodia, it is best to leave Poipet as quickly as possible. Note that buses leave Poipet in the morning until 8am. The best way to avoid any hassles is to stay in Aranyaphratet overnight and then connect to a morning bus out of Poipet. If you arrive in Poipet during the day, get in a shared taxi or hire a taxi to get out of town. Otherwise you might find yourself at the mercy of hordes of touts eager for your money. Do not stay in Poipet overnight unless you absolutely have to; if you do, the casinos located in the no-man's-land between the immigration posts are the best bet.

To get out by bus, head for the bus station, 1.5 kilometers from the border along Route 5, and then turn right. Don't get roped into the free shuttle service to the bus station, as it will take you to a "Tourist Lounge" where tickets to onward destinations are sold at inflated prices. Instead, try to book your own bus ticket with one of the bus company offices at the station. Note that buses go around the southern shore of Tonlé Sap Lake. Routes

5 and 6 from the border to Siem Reap are in good condition nowadays and are a quick three-hour drive.

KOH KONG/HAT LEK
កោះកុង

After Poipet, the **Hat Lek** border crossing near **Koh Kong** is the most popular overland route from Thailand into Cambodia. Frequent minibuses from Trat, the last Thai town of note before the Hat Lek border crossing, take 90 minutes and cost 120 baht. There's nothing much to see in Hat Lek except for a small market along the road. Coming from Thailand, a motorcycle taxi from the border to Koh Kong will set you back 100 baht, a tuk-tuk 150 baht, and a private taxi 250-300 baht. A daily bus to Phnom Penh (US$13) run by Virak Buntham Express Travel (tel. 012/322-302) leaves Koh Kong at 8am. There is no direct connection to Siem Reap.

PHSAR PROM/BAN PAKARD
ផ្សារ ព្រហ្ម

The closest border to Pailin is becoming a more convenient spot to cross into Cambodia as the roads around Pailin are improving. A *motodup* from Pailin to the border post, some 20 kilometers out of town, costs US$5. A taxi from Battambang costs US$40. On the Thai side, minibuses take two hours to Chanthaburi and cost 100 baht. From Chanthaburi, frequent buses leave for Bangkok, four hours away.

To get to this border from Bangkok, head for the Eastern Bus Terminal at Ekkamai and board one of the frequent buses for Chanthaburi. Travel time is about four hours. In Chanthaburi, regular minibuses (100 baht) make the run to the border in under two hours.

DAUN LEM/BAN LAEM
ដូនលែម

Located north of the Pailin border crossing, this is a remote international border where Cambodian tourist visas should be available for US$20, although this is at the discretion of the immigration officers on duty. Crossing into Thailand and getting a 30-day entry stamp should not be a problem for most nationalities. There are some casinos on the Cambodian side, hence the crossing's international status. The village on the Cambodian side is called **Daun Lem**, on the Thai side **Ban Laem.** The border is open daily 7am-8pm. There is onward travel available on the Thai side; don't count on that on the Cambodian side.

ANLONG VENG/CHONG SA-NGAM
អន្លង់វែង/ចុងសាងាម

The closest border crossing to **Anlong Veng** is at **Chong Sa-Ngam,** eight kilometers from Pol Pot's grave and just three kilometers from Ta Mok's forest hideaway. The border is open to foreigners coming from either side. On the Thai side, the nearest village is Khu San in Si Saket Province, from where there are direct buses to Bangkok and elsewhere in Thailand. The village has a bank with an ATM as well as simple guesthouses. The border is open daily 7am-8pm.

To get to the Chong Sa-Ngam border, try to hitch a ride with Cambodian traders from Anlong Veng who cross the border in the morning; otherwise you might be in for a long walk on the Thai side. There is no regular transportation from Siem Reap to this border crossing, though there's a once-a-day bus service along the tarmac road from Siem Reap to Anlong Veng. Buses leave at 7:30am and take around two hours.

From Bangkok, the quickest way to this remote and rather inconvenient border crossing (unless you plan to see the Khmer temples of Issan on the way) is a flight to the regional hub of Ubon Ratchasima. From this small city, you can get a regular bus to Khu San in Si Saket Province, the closest village to the border. Alternatively, there's a regular bus from Bangkok's Eastern Bus Terminal to Si Saket town (8 hours), from where you can catch several daily local buses to the border. Also, in the morning, plenty of *songthaews* (converted pickup trucks with benches in the back) on their way from Si Saket to the border markets can give you a lift.

Note that since the border spat over the Preah Vihear temple, the Thai military has set up a number of roadblocks in this area, although foreigners are never stopped.

O'SMACH/CHONG JOM

អូរស្មាច់

You can also cross the border at **O'Smach** (**Chong Jom** on the Thai side), farther west, although this crossing is farther from Anlong Veng, there's no public transportation on the Cambodian side, and the road is not as good. To get to O'Smach, grab a regular bus from the Thai town of Surin (100 baht), which takes around 90 minutes to the border. From the O'Smach border to Siem Reap is a 125-kilometer ride via Samrong, possible only in a shared taxi (4 hours, about US$8) or in an expensive private taxi.

Border Crossing with Laos

In order to enter Laos, travelers have to have a valid Lao visa in their passports. It is now possible to get a visa on arrival when crossing from Cambodia into Laos. U.S. citizens pay US$41 for a 30-day visa. Coming into Cambodia from Laos, tourist visas are issued on the spot for US$20, business visas for US$25, although immigration officials often demand extra fees at this crossing.

DOM KRALOR/VOENG KAM

ដំក្រឡ

Onward travel from Stung Treng to the Laotian border and beyond is a little bit confusing but easy enough. From Stung Treng, you have two possibilities to get to the border. The easiest way is to travel by road (Route 7), which has recently been upgraded. The border at **Dom Kralor** is about 55 kilometers from Stung Treng, and minibuses (US$5) now ply this route irregularly. Phnom Penh Sorya runs three daily buses from Phnom Penh to Stung Treng (7 hours). The same bus company also runs one bus all the way to the Lao border and

onward to Pakse, which leaves Phnom Penh at 6:45am.

Once at the border (open 7am-5pm, tourist visas to Laos are available, rates vary depending on nationality and the level of greed of the immigration officers), you might have to walk between the two border posts, a distance of two kilometers. Also note that there is no regular onward transportation on the Laotian side, although through-tickets can be booked in Stung Treng.

Coming from Laos into Cambodia is straightforward; Cambodian tourist and business visas are now issued at both border crossings. Note that Cambodian immigration officials regularly extort extra fees for stamping you in or issuing visas. If you have time, resist these corrupt attempts to make extra cash, but be prepared for aggressive border guards. Stay calm.

Border Crossings with Vietnam

Coming from Vietnam, Cambodian visas are available on arrival at all the border crossings detailed here. E-visas are only accepted at the Moc Bai/Bavet crossing. Make sure you have a passport photo for the Cambodian authorities. Going into Vietnam, you must have a visa issued by a Vietnamese consulate.

O'YADAW/LE TANH

អូរយ៉ាដាវ

Opened in 2008, this small border crossing 75 kilometers east of Banlung in Ratanakiri is hard to reach. There is no regular direct transportation on the Cambodian side of the border, and a taxi ride from Banlung costs around US$50. The border on the Vietnamese side is called **Le Tanh.** In Pleiku, the nearest city on the Vietnamese side, some 80 kilometers from the border, head for the central market, where you might be able to find a yellow local bus or minibus going to Duc Co for about 50,000 dong. In Duc Co, you will have to find a *motodup* to take you to the border at Le Tanh for around another 50,000 dong. It's possible to get from Pleiku to the border in about two hours.

Phnom Penh Sorya has one daily bus going to Banlung from Phnom Penh (13 hours), which leaves at 7:30am.

TRAPAENG THLONG/XA MUT
ត្រពាំងថ្លង់

The border crossing (7am-5pm) at **Trapaeng Thlong** (Xa Mut on the Vietnamese side) is off Route 7, a few kilometers before the town of Memot. The turnoff from Route 7 to the right (coming from Kompong Cham) is clearly signposted. There are many buses from Phnom Penh to Kompong Cham (2 hours, US$5). There is no regular transportation on either side of the border to this crossing, which is rarely used by foreigners.

TRAPAENG SRE/LOC NINH
ត្រពាំងស្រែ

In 2008, the border at **Trapaeng Sre** (**Loc Ninh** on the Vietnamese side, 7am-5pm) opened near Route 7, some 40 kilometers south of Snuol. There are many buses from Phnom Penh to Kompong Cham (2 hours, US$5). There is no regular transportation from Kompong Cham to this border crossing.

From Snuol, you can get a *motodup* for US$4 all the way across the border to Loc Ninh, from where regular buses leave for Ho Chi Minh City (50,000 dong). From the Vietnamese side, buses leave Ho Chi Minh City from Mien Dong Bus Station and take about four hours to Loc Ninh, from where it's a short motorbike ride to the border. Coming from Vietnam into Cambodia, there are not many transport options to Snuol. Grab a *motodup* if you can find one.

BAVET/MOC BAI
បាវិត

Daily buses from Sorya Transport and minibuses from Capitol Guest House in Phnom Penh and Neak Krohhorm Bus Company travel along Route 1 east of Phnom Penh, across the border and all the way to Ho Chi Minh City. Tickets are US$10-12. This is the

fastest overland connection between Phnom Penh and Ho Chi Minh City—the trip should not take more than six hours, including formalities at the border. Guesthouses and travel agents in Ho Chi Minh City, especially on Pham Ngu Lao Road, offer frequent buses and similar ticket prices to Phnom Penh. This is the only border crossing where Cambodian e-visas are accepted.

KAAM SAMNOR/VINH XUONG
ក្បមសំណ

To reach this popular border crossing from Phnom Penh, you have two options. Capitol Guest House in Phnom Penh and Neak Krohhorm Bus Company offer combined boat and bus tickets (US$21-24). A more luxurious alternative is a speed boat trip with Blue Cruiser (www.bluecruiser.com). Their trips (US$55 from Phnom Penh and US$44 from Chau Doc, not including visa fees) take just 4.5 hours and leave Phnom Penh daily at1:30pm or Chau Doc at 7:30am. If you want to travel independently, grab a shared taxi at the Central Market to Neak Loeung, on the banks of the Mekong River, and then board a ferry down to the village of **Kaam Samnor.** It's a short ride with a *motodup* to the Vietnamese immigration post, and from there another few kilometers in a minibus to Chau Doc, from where there are regular buses to Ho Chi Minh City (US$3). From Ho Chi Minh City, grab a bus to Chau Doc (6 hours), from where minibuses (1 hour, US$3) head to Vinh Xuong.

PHNOM DEN/TINH BIEN
ភ្នំដិន

This border crossing (open 6am-6pm) in Takeo Province can be reached in a shared taxi (around US$10) from Phnom Penh; ask around the Central Market. Alternatively, take a bus to Takeo and then proceed from there by shared taxi (US$3), private taxi (US$30), or with a motodup (US$10). On the Vietnamese side, there's transportation to Chau Doc, 10 kilometers away, from where onward travel to Ho Chi Minh City is available. From Ho Chi

Minh City, catch a bus to Chau Doc (6 hours, US$3). From there, it's a 40-minute ride to the border with a *motodup*.

The *motodups* on the Vietnamese side engage in a couple of other scams, such as taking passengers to a private bus stop rather than the public terminal in Chau Doc. Don't pay anything until you get to your destination. In general, there's little to be done about the transportation scams at this border crossing. The border is usually open daily 6am-6pm.

PREK CHAK/XA XIA

ព្រែកចាក

The ride to the border takes about an hour from Kep and leads through picturesque countryside. Two roads lead to the border crossing of **Prek Chak (Xa Xia** on the Vietnamese side). One follows the coastline from Kep, while another, better road goes via Kompong Trach. There are direct buses from Phnom Penh (5 hours, US$18), Sihanoukville (5 hours, US$18), Kampot (2 hours, US$10), and Kep (90 minutes, US$8). A *motodup* from Kampot costs about US$10, a little less from Kep. A taxi should be around US$25.

On the Vietnamese side, the nearest town to the border is Ha Tien, from where a *motodup* will charge around US$3 to get to Xa Xia, a trip of about 10 kilometers. Ha Tien is in the Mekong Delta, and it's possible to take a twice-daily ferry (230,000 dong) from here to the tourist island of Phu Qoc.

Getting Around

AIR

Generally speaking, travel in Cambodia is adventurous but not as crazy and dangerous as just a few years ago. Planes are the easiest way to get around, but domestic air routes are limited. At the time of writing, the only regular flights, several times daily, are from Phnom Penh to Siem Reap and back with Siem Reap Airways and Cambodia Angkor Air, and from the coastal resort of Sihanoukville to Siem Reap and Phnom Penh, also with Cambodia Angkor Air. There are unsurfaced airstrips in a number of smaller towns, but none of these have any commercial flights at present.

TRAIN

Cambodia's railroad system is in bad shape but picked up investment from Japan in 2008. Plans were drawn up to have the railroad system back to pre-Khmer Rouge standards by 2015, but with many delays in the restoration process, it may well take longer.

In the 1990s, train travel was extremely dangerous; passengers in the front car, in front of the engine, traveled for free because there was a real risk that the train could hit a mine placed on the tracks. Since 2009, all train travel has ceased. In years to come, the tracks will be restored between Phnom Penh and Battambang and between Phnom Penh and Sihanoukville via Kampot. The tracks will also be extended all the way to the Thai border at Poipet, where it should be possible to connect to the Thai rail network.

The only other passenger trains currently operating in Cambodia are the illegal but delightful Bamboo Trains, homemade handcars that ferry passengers along short lengths of track in areas where roads are still in bad condition. Something of a tourist attraction near Battambang, the Bamboo Trains also exist around Pursat.

BOAT

A few years ago, river traffic on the Mekong was frequent, and it was possible to catch a ferry all the way from Phnom Penh to Stung Treng, at least during and after the rainy season when water levels were adequate. With improving road conditions, many of the regular routes have closed down; Cambodians prefer to go by bus.

Notable exceptions are the daily ferries from Phnom Penh to Siem Reap (November–March only) and from Siem Reap to Battambang. Neither ride should be considered safe by Western standards. It's not unheard of for a boat to run out of gas halfway through the journey or for luggage to be dumped overboard and lost. When the buses started plying the same route, the boat operator raised his prices, perhaps not the best business strategy. The trip from Siem Reap to Battambang is the more spectacular of the two. In Siem Reap, a number of boat excursions across Tonlé Sap Lake can be arranged.

BUS AND TAXI

The regional **bus** system in Cambodia is steadily growing, with more and more companies competing for passengers. Every provincial capital and some smaller towns are now reachable on regular buses, although some routes, especially in the northeastern provinces of Ratanakiri and Mondulkiri, may not operate during the rainy season.

Most buses have air-conditioning as well as a TV set, which blasts karaoke or action thrillers at passengers, often at top volume and with maximum distortion. Some buses have toilets, and all stop every few hours at roadside restaurants with basic facilities. Thankfully, none of the journey times are epic. A bus trip from Phnom Penh to Siem Reap takes five hours. Bus travel can be slow, but it is also cheap and safe, and you'll share your journey with local people.

A faster and somewhat more risky and uncomfortable alternative is the increasing traffic of regular **shared taxis** or **minibuses.** Shared taxis tend to be either Toyota Camrys or pickup trucks. Minibuses and shared taxis leave when they are full, and to have even a little comfort, you need to book two seats for yourself. The front seat next to the driver counts as two seats and is probably the most comfortable option.

You can also book an entire **taxi** for yourself, which can be especially worthwhile if you can get a group of 4-5 people together. A major advantage is that you can tell the driver to stop off anywhere en route. A private taxi from Phnom Penh to Siem Reap costs around US$60. In remote areas where roads are bad, renting a private taxi is more expensive.

TUK-TUK, *MOTODUP,* AND CYCLO

While there are metered taxis on the streets of Phnom Penh now, most visitors get around by more basic means. In Phnom Penh, a few **cyclos** (man-powered cycling rickshaws) continue to ply their trade around the riverside area. The cheapest way to get around Cambodian town centers is probably via *motodup* (motorcycle taxi)—they take up to two passengers. Short journeys in Siem Reap or Phnom Penh should cost 1,000-4,000 riel. Safer and more comfortable are the countless **tuk-tuks** that are found all over the country. Basically a motorbike with an attached trailer large enough to seat four passengers comfortably, these vehicles are slow but provide a modicum of security in the country's chaotic traffic. Short journeys are about US$1, across town it's US$2. Most tourists who visit the Angkor temples choose tuk-tuks as their preferred mode of transport. The day rate around Angkor is around US$15. Travelers should always agree on the price of any journey or vehicle hire in advance to avoid later misunderstandings.

RENTAL CAR OR MOTORCYCLE

It's quite straightforward to rent a **car,** with or without a private driver. Most people opt for the driver, thus reducing their own responsibility and increasing their safety, as a Cambodian driver is more familiar with the local driving culture and should, at least in theory, be better equipped to keep the vehicle safe. This might not always be obvious when you are being thrown around the backseat doing 80 kilometers per hour across a sea of potholes with smoke-belching trucks bearing down on you. The difference in price between driving and being driven is marginal.

A car around Phnom Penh, Angkor, or Battambang is likely to cost US$25-40, including gas. Gas is not cheap in Cambodia, at about US$1 per liter, and fluctuations in gas prices influence rates. For longer drives between major cities, prices vary. Even small towns have gas stations, though plenty of private operators sell gas from small stalls by the roadside, often storing the fuel in soft-drink bottles. Note that this gas is often low quality and should be used only in an emergency.

One of the best ways to explore the more remote areas and temples of Cambodia is by **motorcycle,** preferably on a 250-cc dirt bike. Motorcycles can be rented in most towns where there's tourism. Small 100-cc Chinese or Thai mopeds cost US$5-8 per day, less if you rent for longer than a week. Most 250-cc dirt bikes can be rented for US$15-25, depending on where you rent them, how long you rent them, and what condition they are in. Dirt bikes can be rented in Phnom Penh, Sihanoukville, Battambang, and Banlung. Check the bikes as best as you can, since some are in appalling condition. Tourists are not allowed to drive around the Angkor temples, and consequently, motorcycles cannot be rented in Siem Reap.

There are real advantages to exploring the provinces and remote temple sites at length with a guide and bikes from an experienced dirt-bike tour company. **Red Raid** (www.motorcycletourscambodia.com) is highly recommended, and **Dancing Roads** (www.dancingroads.com) and **Hidden Cambodia** (www.hiddencambodia.com) are equally competent. These excellent outfits have offices in Siem Reap and Phnom Penh and offer guides, route suggestions, and some degree of safety backup, coupled with local knowledge, which reduces driving risks dramatically. Red Raid, which has been operating on Cambodia's trails since 2001, has guides that speak English, German, or French and offers helicopter rescue in case of a serious accident. Prices aren't cheap (the larger the group, the lower the price), so count on at least US$150 per day for a motorcycle, fuel, a guide—and

backup, which you will be glad for if your bike's frame collapses on a muddy path 200 kilometers from the nearest road.

Driver's License

When renting a motorcycle or car, a driver's license is rarely demanded. Rental agents prefer to retain the driver's passport (make sure you carry a photocopy with you at all times if your passport stays with the rental agency). In case of an accident, having an International Driving Permit could be helpful.

Insurance

Renting a vehicle in Cambodia does not mean you are insured to drive it. If you damage the vehicle, the shop will demand cash compensation as per the rental agreement. The same applies if the vehicle is stolen. In case of an accident involving another vehicle or people, foreign drivers are liable to pay whatever damages are demanded. The local police are likely to side with the Cambodian party. In case of personal injury, personal travel insurance should cover possibly horrendous medical costs. If you rent a vehicle with a driver, that vehicle is usually insured, and the driver or rental agent bears all responsibilities.

TOUR COMPANIES AND TRAVEL AGENTS

Just a few years ago, large parts of Cambodia were inaccessible to all but the most hardy travelers, but in-country travel agents as well as international operators now offer tours that go well beyond the ruins of Angkor. Cambodia is a country where visitors will hugely benefit from personal encounters they might have with the Khmer people, and travel nowadays is generally straightforward to most points of interest. Nevertheless, there are exceptions, and going with a group and a guide does have distinct benefits.

Whether you want a tailor-made historical tour of the Angkor temples or a trek into the wilds of Ratanakiri, it's all possible and need not hurt your wallet if you don't expect five-star service, which in any case is hard to come by outside Phnom Penh and Siem Reap. On the other hand, if you'd like to see the temples in style, there's barely a limit to how much you can spend. Some local operators work closely with the local community, which is involved in the tour programs, making the trip a more personable experience. Finally, for adventure seekers, several motorcycle touring companies offer visitors some really off-the-beaten-path trips to forest temples and remote villages on challenging roads.

Cambodia Travel Specialists in the United States

- **Abercrombie and Kent** (U.S. tel. 800/323-7308, www.abercrombiekent.com) offers luxury tours around Cambodia, usually in conjunction with a visit to Thailand or Vietnam.

- **Asiatranspacific** (U.S. tel. 800/642-2742, www.asiatranspacific.com) organizes a range of interesting high-end tours around Southeast Asia. The company's Angkor program includes a sumptuous dinner inside a temple ruin and a meeting with a representative of the World Monument Fund.

- **Wilderness Travel** (U.S. tel. 800/368-2794, www.wildernesstravel.com) also offers touring in style at slightly lower prices, including a 13-day temple package that takes in some remote locations around the country. Other Southeast Asia tours on this company's itineraries include Angkor.

Tour Operators in Asia

- **AboutAsia** (tel. 092/121-059, U.S. tel. 914/595-6949, www.aboutasiatravel.com) has an office in the United States but is based in Cambodia and runs tour packages around the temples and the country that involve the local community.

- **Green Elephant Travel** (tel. 063/965-776, www.greenelephantravel.com) is based in Siem Reap and operates a variety of tours with an emphasis on a reduced carbon footprint. While some tours are almost entirely walking and cycling, others are just as comfortable as a standard tour but keep an eye on preserving the environment. Tours range from mid-range to high-end prices, depending on the desired level of comfort.

- **Asian Trails** (Cambodia tel. 023/216-555, www.asiantrails.info), a tour operator from Thailand, offers a wide range of 2-10-day trips around Cambodia at competitive mid-range prices.

- **Exotissimo** (Cambodia tel. 063/964-323, www.cambodia.exotissimo.com), a Vietnam-based operator, offers interesting high-standard camping tours around some of the more remote temples.

- **Angkor T.K. Travel & Tours** (117 Street 6, Siem Reap, tel. 063/963-320, www.angkortk.com) runs competent single- and multiday tours around the Angkor temples at competitive prices.

- **The World of Cambodia** (11 River Side St., Siem Reap, tel. 063/963-637, www. angkor-cambodia.org) offers small group tours for mid- and high-budget travelers, including hotels and guides, to the Angkor ruins as well as destinations around Phnom Penh.

- **Khmer Angkor Tour Guides Association (KATGA)** (No. 311, Group 9, Phom Mondol 1, Khum Svaydangkum, tel. 063/964-347, www.khmerangkortourguide.com) is the organization for official tour guides based in Siem Reap. The guides are trained by the Ministry of Tourism and the APSARA Authority.

Adventure and Motorcycle Travel in Cambodia

- **Red Raid** (bmerklen@camnet.com.kh, www.motorcycletourscambodia.com) has a varied program of dirt-bike tours around the remoter parts of Cambodia as well as cross-border tours into Laos and southern China.

- **Dancing Roads** (tel. 012/753-008, www. dancingroads.com) offers a wide variety of dirt-bike tours around the temples, the northeast, the coast, and the Cardamom Mountains as well as two-week bicycle tours to remote parts of the country.

- **Hidden Cambodia** (tel. 012/655-201, www.hiddencambodia.com) also offers dirt-bike tours as well as Angkor packages, sustainable ecotourism trips, and humanitarian tours into the countryside to aid village development.

- **Grasshopper Adventures** (29 Street 130, Phnom Penh; Street 26, Siem Reap, tel. 012/462-165, www.grasshopperadventures. com) offers excellent cycling tours around the capital, the Angkor temples, and the villages around Siem Reap.

Visas and Officialdom

VISA REQUIREMENTS

Foreign visitors, including Americans, require a visa to enter Cambodia. At international airports and all land border crossings mentioned in this guide, tourist visas (US$30) as well as business visas (US$35) are issued on the spot. Those who are considering working, investing, or setting up a business in Cambodia should apply for a business visa. Tourist visas are valid for a month and are single-entry. It's possible to get an online e-visa (http://evisa. mfaic.gov.kh, US$37), which is also valid for one month but is not extendable. Regular tourist visas, whether issued by a Cambodian embassy abroad or at the border, can only be extended once, for one more month, for US$35. Business visas can be extended several times. A one-year extension is around US$200.

Immigration and government officials from Cambodia, Thailand, Laos, and Vietnam are involved in discussions on whether to issue joint tourist visas for visitors who want to travel among these countries. At the time of writing, no decision had been reached.

CUSTOMS

There does not seem to be a legal limit as to how many **cigarettes** or how much **alcohol** one might carry in one's luggage, but visitors should note that both cigarettes and spirits are far cheaper in Cambodia than in any duty-free shop. Needless to say, illicit drugs, weapons, and explosives of any kind must not be imported. Pets may be imported if the owners have applied for an **International Veterinary Certificate.** For more information, check www.pettravel.com/immigration/ cambodia.cfm. Finally, it is strictly illegal to export **antiques** from Cambodia. Offenders will be prosecuted.

FOREIGN EMBASSIES IN CAMBODIA

Numerous countries have embassies in Phnom Penh. Those that don't probably have an embassy in Bangkok.

The **U.S. Embassy** (1 Street 96, tel. 023/728-000, http://cambodia.usembassy. gov) is located in a new, fortified building near Wat Phnom and contains Phnom Penh's only McDonald's. The embassy is open for U.S. citizen services (Mon.-Thurs. 1pm-4pm). The Consular Section is closed for both U.S. and Cambodian holidays and is closed to the public on Friday. However, the American Citizen Services unit will assist U.S. citizens with emergencies 24-7; there's no special emergency number.

There is a **British Embassy** (27-29 Street 75, tel. 023/427-124, http://ukincambodia. fco.gov.uk/en, Mon.-Thurs. 8:15am-noon and 3pm-4:45pm, Fri. 8:15am-1:15pm) and an **Australian Embassy** (16B National Assembly St., tel. 023/213-470, www.cambodia.embassy.gov.au).

Since almost being destroyed by a government-sponsored mob in 2003, the **Thai Embassy** (tel. 023/726-306 or 023/726-310, www.thaiembassy.org/phnompenh/)

Cambodian Embassies and Consulates Abroad

- **Australia:** 5 Canterbury Crescent, Deakin, ACT, tel. 02/6273-1259, camemb.aus@mfa.gov.kh

- **Canada:** Consulate of Cambodia, 903-168 Chadwick Court, North Vancouver, BC, tel. 604/980-1718, dglo@shaw.ca

- **Japan:** 8-6-9 Akasaka, Minato-Ku, Tokyo, tel. 03/5412-8521, camhc.hok@mfa.gov.kh

- **Laos:** Thadeua Road, KM2, Vientiane, tel. 02/131-4950, camemb.lao@mfa.gov.kh

- **Singapore:** 400 Orchard Road, #10-03/04 Orchard Towers, tel. 6341-9785, camemb.sg@mfa.gov.kh

- **Thailand, Embassy of Cambodia:** 518/4 Prach Uthit Road (Soi Ramkamhaeng 39), Bangkok, tel. 02/254-6630, camemb.tha@mfa.gov.kh

- **Thailand, Royal Consulate General of Cambodia:** No. 666, Sowanasone Road Tambun Thakasem, Ampheu Meung Sa Kaew, tel. 037/21-734, consulsk@cscoms.com

- **United Kingdom:** 64 Brondesbury Park, Willesden Green, London, tel. 020/8451-7850, camemb.eng@mfa.gov.kh

- **United States, Embassy of Cambodia:** 4530 16th St. NW, Washington DC, tel. 202/726-7742, camemb.usa@mfa.gov.kh

- **United States, Royal Honorary Consulate of Cambodia: Long Beach, CA** (3448 E. Anaheim Street, Long Beach, CA, tel. 562/494-3000, cambodian.hcg.ca@gmail.com); **New York City** (327 East 58th Street, tel. 212/336-0777, camemb.un@mfa.gov.kh); **Lowell, MA** (93 Chelmsford Street, tel. 978/408-1760, camhc.low@mfa.gov.kh); **Philadelphia** (5734 North 5th Street, tel. 267/592-7344, camhc.phila@mfa.gov.kh); **Seattle** (1818 Westlake Avenue North, Suite 315, tel. 206/217-0830, camemb.sea@mfa.gov.kh

- **Vietnam, Embassy of Cambodia:** 71A,Tran Hung Dao St., Hanoi, tel. 04/942-4789, camemb.vnm@mfa.gov.kh

- **Vietnam, Royal Consulate General of Cambodia:** No. 41, Phung Khac Khoan, Ho Chi Minh City, tel. 08/829-2751, camcg.hcm@mfa.gov.kh

relocated to 196 Preah Norodom Boulevard. The **Vietnamese Embassy** (436 Monivong Blvd., tel. 023/726-274, www.vietnam-embassy-cambodia.org/en/) is joined by Vietnamese consulates in Sihanoukville and Battambang.

Other embassies in Cambodia include **China** (156 Mao Tse Tung Blvd., tel. 023/810-928), **France** (1 Monivong Blvd., tel. 023/430-020), **Germany** (76-78 Street 214, tel. 023/216-193), **India** (5 Street 466, tel. 023/210-912), **Japan** (194 Norodom Blvd., tel. 023/217-161), **Laos** (15-17 Mao Tse Tung Blvd., tel. 023/997-931), **Malaysia** (5 Street 242, tel. 023/216-177), **Myanmar** (181 Norodom Blvd., tel. 023/223-761), **The Philippines** (33 Street 294, tel. 023/222-303), and **Singapore** (129 Norodom Blvd., tel. 023/221-875).

Accommodations and Food

ACCOMMODATIONS

A wide range of good-value accommodations await visitors in Cambodia's main towns and tourist spots. Siem Reap has more than 8,000 beds, from US$5 for a cell in a backpacker flophouse up to several thousand dollars for a chance to wallow in five-star luxury for a night. In the mid-range bracket, this town near the Angkor temples also offers great places to stay, from modern boutique guesthouses to smart hotels with a whiff of colonial nostalgia.

Phnom Penh also offers a wealth of different sleeping options, and a number of stylish upscale hotels have recently opened in the capital. Sihanoukville welcomes visitors with quality beach accommodations. In neighboring Kampot and Kep, old villas and town houses have been refurbished and turned into mid-range and upscale hotels. In Banlung in Ratanakiri and Sen Monorom in Mondulkiri, remote towns in the northeastern part of the country, a number of attractive eco-lodges have opened in the last few years.

Elsewhere around the country, in the smaller provincial capitals, good-value Khmer hotels, usually with clean and quite simple air-conditioned guest rooms, can be had for under US$15.

FOOD AND DRINK

For many first-time visitors, the essence of Cambodian food might not be obvious, or if it is, the thought of partaking in typical Cambodian cuisine might not appear to be an altogether attractive option. After all, Cambodia's staple diet consists of *prahoc,* a strong-smelling fermented fish paste, and rice.

Rice (*bai*) is the most important food in the country, and more than 2,000 species once grew in Cambodia. There's hardly a dish that does not contain rice, including noodles made from rice, desserts, cakes, and alcoholic beverages, and no Khmer meal is complete without boiled rice. Also central to Khmer cooking is **fish,** from lakes, rivers, and the Gulf of Thailand. Fish is smoked, fried, boiled, grilled, fermented, or served in soup. Perhaps even more important, especially for the country's poor, who can't afford fish or meat, is *prahoc,* which serves as a condiment to every Cambodian meal. But there's plenty of variety to be discovered beyond *prahoc,* which the uninitiated should perhaps first try in a restaurant before indulging in the market variety. Soups and fried dishes with fish, meat, and vegetables are an integral part of Cambodia's staple food, and **fruit** is amazingly abundant and varied. Chou Ta-Kuan, a Chinese diplomat who spent almost a year in Angkor during the late 13th century, reported the consumption of vegetables like mustard greens, cucumbers, squashes, leeks, eggplants, and onions, and fruit such as watermelons, oranges, lychees, pomegranates, lotus roots, and bananas. All are still common in Cambodia today.

Cambodia's cuisine is not unlike that of its two larger neighbors, Thailand and Vietnam, and many dishes available in those countries are also Cambodian standards, although local flavors vary. The Cambodians are not nearly as obsessed with chili as the Thais and aim for milder, more rounded flavors infused with herbs, pepper, and sugar. Tamarind is used in soups and sauces, and turmeric, ginger, lemongrass, kaffir lime, and galangal are integral building blocks of many Khmer dishes. *Kroeng,* a typical Khmer sauce, contains cardamom, cinnamon, nutmeg, cloves, and star anise as well as the aforementioned ingredients. As recently as a decade ago, Cambodians cooked a great deal with marijuana, until Western pressure removed the evil weed from market stalls.

The closer you get to the border with Thailand, the more Thai dishes appear on local menus, and the same goes for the country's border with Vietnam. In a larger international context, Cambodia lies, geographically and culturally, between India and China, and this is reflected in its kitchen—think curry (with coconut milk) and spring rolls, both integral dishes to any local menu, done in Cambodian style, of course. The French presence in the country has also left its culinary legacy: No other Southeast Asian nation consumes as much bread, mostly the traditional French baguette, sold fresh in the morning on busy street corners. Sandwiches filled with pickled vegetables and pâté are served from roadside stalls.

At home, families usually sit in a circle on a mat on the floor to eat. Cambodians eat mostly with chopsticks. For breakfast, noodle soup with vegetables and meat is a favorite. In the countryside, there's little else to eat in the morning. For lunch and dinner, most Cambodians try to eat at home. A usual meal consists of boiled rice along with soup (*samlor*), *prahoc,* and fried fish or meat as well as unripe papaya or mango.

Street stalls usually set up in Cambodian towns in the afternoon, often around the market or by a bridge, serving a variety of fried dishes, sandwiches, sugarcane juice, and some very sweet fruit desserts. Small-town restaurants usually have no menu and display the available precooked meals in large pots. Just point at the desired dish and it will be served with rice.

Typical widely available standards include:

- *Amok trey:* Fish cooked in coconut milk, wrapped in banana leaves, and steamed, one of the most popular dishes in Cambodia.

- *Bai cha:* Rice fried in soy sauce, generally with garlic, pork, and herbs, although ingredients vary widely.

- *Bok I'hong:* A papaya salad with a lime sauce base and baby tomatoes, string beans, peanuts, dried fish, fermented crabs, and chili, similar but not as fierce as Thailand's *somtam.*

- *Kuytheaw:* Beef noodle soup.

- *Loc lac:* Cubes of stir-fried beef with onions, served with rice on salad, cucumbers, and tomatoes seasoned with lime sauce or black pepper. Sometimes includes a fried egg on top.

- *Somlar kari:* Red coconut chicken soup with sweet potatoes and bamboo shoots.

- *Somlar machu yuon:* Tamarind-based soup with fish or meat and pineapple, tomatoes, and onions.

In recent years, thanks to tourism, a wide variety of international cuisine, sometimes awful, sometimes splendid, has become available in Phnom Penh and Siem Reap. Sometimes it's even found in some provincial capitals, but on the whole, once you are in the provinces, you are likely to have to stick to Cambodian staples. Also note that international food is significantly more expensive than the local fare.

Fruit

Cambodia is a great place to sample a wide variety of tropical fruits, some familiar to Western visitors, others inviting discovery. What follows is a list of the most commonly available varieties.

- **Avocado**—*avocaa* (May-Aug.): The avocado can be round, oblong, pear-shaped, or bottle-shaped and has yellowish-green to dark-green skin. The skin is shiny or thick and leathery. The fruit has a large seed, which constitutes half its weight.

- **Banana**—*jeik* (year-round): Many varieties of banana grow in Cambodia. Bananas are usually seedless and can be short and fat or long and slim.

- **Cashew**—*svai jantee* (Mar.-June): Eaten fresh, candied, or stewed and has a sweet and astringent taste. The cashew nut is the actual fruit.

- **Coconut**—*dawng* (year-round): While the young green coconut fruit is cut open for its clear and nutritious juice, the milk of the ripe coconut is used as a cooking ingredient.

Prahoc: Cambodia's National Dish

jars of *prahoc,* a fermented fish paste

Every chef familiar with fish will tell you that there can't be Cambodian cuisine without *prahoc,* the fermented fish paste that is a Cambodian staple. The pungent dish (enter any market in the country and you will encounter its fine odor soon enough) is part of the national psyche, and even Prime Minister Hun Sen prides himself on being able to make an excellent *prahoc.* In a reference to a political opponent, Hun Sen once said that a Khmer who does not know how to make *prahoc* will never lead the country.

More importantly, for millions of Cambodians, it is their only source of protein. *Prahoc* is the Khmer name of the freshwater fish that is used for the paste, which is eaten with rice and vegetables but is served with pretty much all other food as well. If you are scared of the common market variety, try *prahoc* in one of Phnom Penh's upscale restaurants like Malis or Romdeng. The five-star *prahoc* on offer at these eateries is made from fresh fish and lacks the ferocious smell.

- **Custard apple**—*dtiep bpai* (June-Sept.): About the size of a baseball, greenish with a powdery surface, and sweet. The flesh is white and comes apart in segments; each segment contains black seeds.

- **Dragon fruit**—*srawgahneeak* (year-round): Has shiny reddish to pink skin with greenish scales. The flesh is often white, sometimes reddish, and has small black seeds mixed in its texture. Tastes not unlike a pear.

- **Durian**—*toorayn* (Apr.-June): A huge fruit with a hard, green to yellow, spiky rind and a very distinctive and strong smell that many foreigners find hard to take. If you can get past the odor, the durian is deliciously sweet and extremely high in fat.

- **Guava**—*dtraw bai* (year-round): Can be round or pear-shaped. Size is variable, from that of a lime to a grapefruit. Its flesh is soft and white or pink, with a lot of small seeds. It is usually consumed fresh and has a sweet taste.

- **Jackfruit**—*knao* (year-round): Huge and green with yellow flesh, it looks a bit similar to the durian but lacks the pungent smell.

- **Lime**—*plai kro ch'mah* (year-round): A small fruit with smooth green or yellow skin. The juice is used for drinks and as food flavoring.

- **Longan**—*mien* (Aug.-Sept.): A small round fruit, about the size of a grape, with a thin, brown leathery shell and a blackish stone. The flesh is juicy and white and sweet in taste.

- **Lotus seeds**—*chook* (year-round): Grows in green pods that look like a showerhead. Each pod contains many oval seeds that have smooth green skin. To eat, peel the skin away. The youngest seeds have the sweetest taste.

- **Lychee**—*guhlean* (Apr.-June): About the size of a plum, heart-shaped with bright-red to purplish leathery skin. The flesh is milky white with a sweet taste and has a reddish to brown stone.

- **Mango**—*suh-ai* (year-round): There are many types of mango, eaten both raw and ripe; the raw mango is green to dark green, according to variety, and can be sour. A ripe mango is usually yellow and has a sweet taste.

- **Mangosteen**—*mawkuht* (Aug.-Nov.): A smooth berry, dark purple when ripe. The flesh is white and divided into several segments. It has a pleasantly sweet taste.

- **Orange**—*plai kroidt poosat* (Nov.-Feb.): Oranges in Cambodia generally have green skin and taste a bit sour.

- **Papaya**—*la-hong* (year-round): A fleshy fruit with thin, smooth skin. The skin turns from green to yellow or orange while ripening. It has a sweet taste, and its aroma can be overwhelming when very ripe. Papaya is an excellent laxative.

- **Pineapple**—*manawa* (year-round): The Cambodian pineapple is deliciously juicy, a perfect combination of sweet and sour.

- **Pomegranate**—*dtoteum* (year-round): About the size of a tennis ball, with smooth yellow or reddish skin. The fruit contains several segments, and each has many gemstone-like seeds that are sweet in taste.

- **Pomelo**—*kroitlaung* (year-round): A larger version of the grapefruit, though less juicy and less bitter.

- **Rambutan**—*sao mao* (May-Sept.): About the size of a plum, ellipsoid, purplish-red, and covered in dense hair. The flesh is white and juicy and contains white seeds. It has a sweet taste.

- **Santol**—*kom peeng riech* (June-Aug.): About the size of a tennis ball with yellow-brownish color and a thick rind. It has several large seeds covered by white pulp, which is sweet to slightly acidic. Usually it is eaten fresh by peeling the rind off, cutting the fruit into small pieces, and dipping it

dragon fruit

into a mixture of salt, sugar, and chili powder. Pickled *santol* is also popular. It has a laxative effect.

- **Sapodilla**—*leumuht* (Aug.-Sept.): Also called *chiku*, it has a thin brown rind and black seeds. The soft brown flesh has a sweet taste.

- **Soursop**—*dtiep barang* (year-round): Has green leathery skin and soft, curved spines. Its flesh is whitish and juicy with hard black seeds. It has a sweet and sour taste and makes a good ingredient for a milk shake.

- **Star fruit**—*speu* (year-round): Shiny yellow-green when ripe, with five pronounced ribs. It has a sweet citrus flavor and is eaten fresh, in salads, or pulped into a drink.

- **Sugarcane**—*aumpo* (year-round): A perennial crop, the cane is eaten fresh by peeling off its hard skin. Cut yourself a piece and chew it, but spit out the fiber. More convenient is the freshly squeezed juice, available from mobile stalls.

- **Tamarind**—*ompeul khoua* (year-round): Has brown skin and grows in straight or curved pods. The mature pods have brown flesh and black seeds. Used as a cooking ingredient to flavor soups and as a snack.

- **Watermelon**—*aolak* (year-round): Has smooth greenish to dark skin and is round or oval in shape. The juicy flesh is usually red and sometimes yellow, peppered with small, flat brown seeds. It has a sweet refreshing taste.

Nonalcoholic Drinks

In small-town restaurants, very weak cold or hot tea is usually served with the food. If a village has a shop, it's likely to sell Western soft drinks and small bottles of drinking water. Roadside stalls often sell juices, especially sugarcane juice. If you have a sensitive stomach, avoid the ice.

In tourist restaurants, fruit shakes and juices are usually on the menu, although it's worth asking if the juices are canned or fresh. Cambodian coffee is strong and bitter and is often drunk with sweet condensed canned milk. Coffee is also served with ice.

Alcoholic Drinks

The two most popular beers are Angkor and Anchor, available in cans and bottles and usually drunk with ice. Again, be careful with the ice in the beer, especially in the provinces. Popular foreign beers include Beer Lao, Tiger, and Heineken. Traditional Khmer restaurants are populated by armies of beer girls in skimpy uniforms who encourage customers to drink the brand they represent.

Local liqueurs are usually made from rice and tend to be great facilitators of terrific hangovers if consumed in any volume. Shops in Phnom Penh and Siem Reap sell a wide variety of foreign-made spirits and wines.

Travel Tips

WHAT TO TAKE

It's hot and sticky in Cambodia, so it's perhaps tempting to walk around in shorts or a bikini. Keep in mind, though, that Cambodia is **conservative** and locals are genuinely offended and embarrassed by foreigners letting it all hang out. **Light cotton clothing** is best. An **umbrella** comes in handy in the rainy season. Bring an **adapter plug** and a **current converter.** If you plan to spend prolonged periods in remote areas, invest in a **mosquito net.**

TRAVELERS WITH DISABILITIES

Cambodia is not easy for travelers with disabilities, despite the fact that a significant segment of the population has to cope with disabilities caused by land mines and unexploded ordnance. No matter where you go in Cambodia, pavement tends to be potholed; sidewalks are cracked, uneven, and crumbling; and special facilities, such as ramps for wheelchair users, are virtually nonexistent. Notable exceptions are the two international airports and a few luxury hotels.

Unfortunately, the temples of Angkor are a real challenge for travelers with disabilities. Virtually every temple visit requires some climbing—although the central tower of Angkor Wat has been closed off to visitors because the crumbling steps leading to the top are so steep and worn away that even the able-bodied risk breaking their limbs.

On the plus side, ground-level guest rooms are available in many Cambodian hotels, and if you need help, it's cheap to hire someone to help you get around. In some temples, such as Ta Prohm and Beng Mealea, ramps have been built to make access somewhat easier. Check travel blogs and forums for other visitors' experiences before you set off.

TRAVELING WITH CHILDREN

Traveling through Cambodia with kids can be an extremely rewarding experience.

Cambodians love children, and foreign kids are likely to be quickly integrated into any social gathering. If you travel with infants, Siem Reap and Phnom Penh provide enough infrastructure and services not to have to worry, although this is not the case away from these main centers. Keep in mind that medical services remain limited, and make sure your child drinks enough, does not get sunburned, and does not eat objects off the sidewalk.

Beyond the health issues, the chaotic traffic, especially in Phnom Penh, is an issue for children old enough to walk around by themselves. The same goes for the countryside, as children, even teenagers, are unlikely to understand the dangers of land mines.

WOMEN TRAVELING ALONE

Women travelers must always be careful in Cambodia and should not travel to remote areas alone or walk around in quiet city areas after dark, even in areas frequented by foreigners. Violence against Cambodian women is rampant, and several foreign women have been attacked and raped in recent years. Drive-by snatchings of handbags have also increased significantly in Phnom Penh in recent years.

GAY AND LESBIAN TRAVELERS

Cambodia is a gay-friendly country. That's not to say that homosexuality is celebrated in this conservative Buddhist nation, but with former King Sihanouk commenting positively about gay rights, gay and lesbian visitors are generally welcome. Phnom Penh and Siem Reap have several gay hangouts.

Whether you're gay or straight, public displays of affection might be offensive to some.

VOLUNTEER OPPORTUNITIES

Following decades of conflict, Cambodia is still an extremely poor country. There are a

Photography in Cambodia

Cambodia is a very photogenic country: spectacular temples that change personality with the shifting light of day, colonial architecture, river and lake vistas, forests and white sand beaches, and, most importantly, the country's enigmatic and friendly people. Here are a few basic tips on how to get the best shots on your travels.

Light: As in all countries close to the equator, early morning, between sunrise and 9am, and in the afternoon 4pm-sunset, the so-called golden hours, are the best times to take pictures outside. Note that the light varies considerably from season to season. The Cambodian landscape generally looks best during and after the rainy season, June-December, before the plants wilt and dust covers everything. Some really dramatic light can be caught during the rains. The Angkor ruins look very otherworldly on storm-laden days in the summer.

People: For the most part, Cambodian people are happy to be photographed, although it is always polite to ask. Photography in temples is usually also not a problem, but it is advisable to ask before photographing monks. There are notable exceptions to this liberal attitude: Photography of police and the military as well as of military installations should be avoided. The Kompong Loeu, the indigenous people of Ratanakiri and Mondulkiri, don't like to be photographed at all and may simply run away as soon as you pull your camera out. In some minority villages, the influx of tourists has led to demands for money. Photographers have to decide for themselves whether this is a good way to get a holiday snap.

Dust: The main enemy of camera gear in Cambodia, apart from heat and rain, is the dust. Especially in the northeast during the dry season, the fine red dust that swirls around anywhere there's a road has a way of entering cameras and dirtying sensors, even if the lens is never separated from the body. Even fixed-lens cameras are not immune from this. Always make sure photography gear is well wrapped in plastic before setting off on a motorcycle trip.

Equipment: Cameras and camera accessories are not particularly cheap in Cambodia, and visitors who intend to buy a camera during their trip around Asia would be better off doing so in Singapore, Malaysia, or Thailand. That said, i-Qlick (146 Sihanouk Blvd., tel. 023/996-638, www.i-qlick.com) is an authorized Canon shop in Phnom Penh that can undertake basic repairs of Canon models. Nikon also has a rep in Cambodia (HGB at #30, Russian Blvd., Sangkat Phsar Depo III, tel. 023/988-067).

Memory cards and film are available in Phnom Penh, Siem Reap, and, to a lesser degree, in Sihanoukville. Some smaller towns may have photo shops that sell cheap compact cameras, film, and occasionally some memory cards.

Having your pictures developed is not a problem in Phnom Penh, whether you use a digital or film camera. Be aware, though, that it's unlikely a shop in Cambodia will handle your negatives with particular care. If you want to be certain no scratches appear on your film, have them developed when you get home.

Safety: Finally, always make sure your camera is securely stored when you take a walk in the busy streets of the capital. Fly-by robberies, typically two kids on a motorcycle zipping past and grabbing whatever you have over your shoulder, are not common, but they do occur more and more often. The risk increases if you take your camera out at night.

---

plethora of aid projects in the country, some definitely more beneficial and philanthropic than others, many downright criminal and exploitative. Make no mistake: Development and aid are businesses, and the steady flow of foreign aid is what keeps Prime Minister Hun Sen in power and denies Cambodian citizens political emancipation. That said, there are some worthwhile projects. Orphanages, schools, and environmental protection top the lists.

The **Cooperation Committee for Cambodia** (tel. 023/214-152, www.ccc-cambodia.org) is an umbrella organization for local and international nongovernmental organizations (NGOs) operating in Cambodia.

The committee's website features a handy map of the country indicating what projects are currently running in which areas of the country, with project descriptions and website links.

You can also check the following programs, organizations, and charities for aid projects in Cambodia.

- The **U.S. Peace Corps** (www.peacecorps. gov) has been sending volunteers to countries around the globe since 1961, when this U.S. government program was founded by President John F. Kennedy. Its current acting director is former U.S. president Jimmy Carter. The Peace Corps has been active in Cambodia since 2006 and is currently involved in teacher training. Tours usually last two years and are preceded by language and project-specific training.

- **GoAbroad** (U.S. tel. 720/570-1702, www. goabroad.com) is an organization based in the United States that connects young people with jobs and volunteer opportunities abroad. They publish a long list of teaching and care opportunities in Cambodia.

- **HealthCareVolunteer** (www.health-carevolunteer.com) is the world's largest listing of health-related volunteer opportunities around the world. This U.S.-based charity offers volunteer placements for skilled health professionals in a dental clinic and a private medical clinic in Cambodia.

- **Voluntary Service Overseas** (VSO, www.vso.org.uk), a UK-based charity, sends skilled volunteers to participate in aid projects around the world, including many placements in Cambodia. Candidates are expected to stay with their projects at least 1-2 years.

- **Globalteer** (www.globalteer.org) is another UK-based nonprofit charity that places volunteers for shorter periods into aid programs around the world, including interesting and rewarding projects in Cambodia.

ECOTOURISM

Cambodia is trying to diversify its tourism industry in order to lure visitors away from the overcrowded temples. Eco-friendly tourism is the new, much-talked-about future of travel in Cambodia—or is it? Whether private or NGO initiatives, ecotourism projects are all the rage in Southeast Asia at the moment, and while many projects actively contribute to more sustainable tourism practices and protection of the environment, some merely aspire to such lofty goals, while a few simply use the catchword to draw in business.

Ecotourism is dependent on Cambodia's rapidly shrinking natural wealth and beauty, and there's a danger that areas pioneered by ecotour operators will soon be gobbled up by loggers, plantation owners, or other investors. Most importantly, if ecotourism is to work, projects must be run within local communities. Without direct participation by and benefit for ordinary Cambodians, ecotourism merely exploits natural resources without giving anything back, a typical precursor of mass tourism. Visitors interested in ecotourism should be careful to check who benefits from their money. Numerous homestay options and eco-friendly tourism projects are mentioned in this guide.

CONDUCT AND CUSTOMS

Reasonably smart appearance and a smile go a long way in Cambodia. Remember that the kingdom is very conservative, and given its recent tragic history, it is not enamored by cultural challenges or rapid social change. So the way you look is very important. Beachwear should only be worn on a beach designated for tourism. When entering active temples, make sure that your clothing is respectful and that your upper arms and legs are always covered.

Visitors—particularly women—should not touch Buddhist monks. If you are a woman and want to pass something to a monk, do it through a third, male person, or place the object on the floor in front of the monk so he can pick it up. Conversing with monks, or posing for photographs with monks, is absolutely no problem for either sex. Also, if you enter a temple's prayer hall or a private home, be sure to remove your shoes, and don't point the soles of your feet toward a Buddha statue or a person. Couples showing affection in public are looked at with disdain.

When dealing with officials, patience and politeness will eventually get results. Getting impatient, noisy, or patronizing toward anyone, but especially police officers and immigration officials, has the opposite effect.

Finally, if you eat with chopsticks, lay them vertically across your bowl when you have finished eating. Leaving them stuck in the bowl is associated with incense burning for the dead.

RESTROOMS

Toilets in Cambodia are not always as sophisticated or hygienic as you might be used to back home. Cheaper guesthouses sometimes have squat toilets. Because the sewer system in Cambodia is rudimentary, many guesthouses ask guests to deposit their paper in buckets or baskets next to the toilet, rather than flushing it. Toilet paper as well as soap are readily available in convenience stores. Public restrooms are few and far between, though the public toilets around the temples in the Angkor Archaeological Park are clean and well maintained. Public restrooms may lack toilet paper and soap, so visitors may want to carry a small supply of toilet paper and hand sanitizer. When trekking in forest or remote countryside, visitors should not step off the beaten paths to relieve themselves, as there's a danger of stepping on a land mine.

Health and Safety

BEFORE YOU GO
Resources

Numerous specialty travel health guides have been published in recent years. Whether it's worth lugging one of these around in your luggage depends on your priorities and where you intend to go. *Staying Healthy in Asia, Africa and Latin America,* by Dirk G. Schroeder (Avalon Travel Publishing, 2000) is an excellent guide to problems and diseases you might encounter in the tropics and is small enough to fit in your backpack. For up-to-date information, take a look at the Cambodia page of the U.S. Centers for Disease Control and Prevention (CDC, http://wwwnc.cdc.gov/travel/destinations/cambodia.htm).

Vaccinations

It is essential that your **tetanus** and **diphtheria** shots are up to date. It is generally recommended to get immunized against **typhoid, tuberculosis,** and possibly **hepatitis A** as well. For visitors who intend to spend prolonged periods in remote areas, **rabies** shots and a vaccination against **Japanese encephalitis** might be appropriate. Those who are likely to have blood contact with locals or travelers should consider taking a course of **hepatitis B** vaccinations.

During the rainy season, **malaria** is prevalent in border areas and remote forest locations. It's best to visit your doctor eight weeks before departure, as some vaccinations require several shots over a period of time. Get an International Certificate of Vaccination (Yellow Card) on which all inoculations should be recorded. The Cambodian authorities require visitors to have **yellow fever** vaccinations if they arrive from a potentially affected area such as parts of Africa and South America.

Travel Insurance

I strongly recommend that travelers purchase good travel insurance covering the entire length of stay in Cambodia. Health facilities are at best rudimentary, except for a couple of hospitals in Siem Reap and Phnom Penh, which are prohibitively expensive.

STAYING HEALTHY

Cambodia poses more health challenges than other Southeast Asian countries. Food hygiene is so-so, and medical facilities are limited. Travel can be arduous and exhausting, and the heat can have more severe consequences than travelers might realize at first. Always stay hydrated, especially when climbing the temples of Angkor for hours on end. It's best to carry a supply of oral rehydration powders, available in different flavors in the United States, to counteract dehydration, diarrhea, sunstroke, infections, and hangovers.

Wash your hands every time before you eat, and avoid eating raw, unpeeled food in cheap local restaurants. Western food, including salads, is mostly safe to eat because it's served only in tourist areas. Also be careful with shellfish. If you are a long way from the coast, or if it's not quite fresh, don't eat it. Keep the flies out of your food and drink; they can be persistent. Never drink the tap water, and brush your teeth with bottled water, which is available virtually everywhere. Ice cubes seem safe in the bigger cities, but anyone who's spent a little time traveling around the country will have seen the extremely unhygienic ice trucks delivering large blocks of frozen water covered in sawdust to provincial restaurants.

Cambodia is a tropical country, and visitors will notice that the Khmer go to extreme lengths to avoid the sun. People who work outdoors are generally covered from head to toe. Visitors are unlikely to follow local routine, nor will they stay indoors 10am-3pm, and should therefore wear long sleeves and pants (which, in any case, the conservative Khmer will appreciate), along with a hat and strong sunscreen. The effects of the sun are especially powerful on long trips through the temples. Traveling on the roofs of river ferries and train carriages can also lead to serious burns. Treat sunburn with aloe vera cream and avoid repeated burns.

DISEASES AND COMMON AILMENTS
Fungal Infections

By far the most common infections visitors to Cambodia suffer from are fungal infections, brought on by high temperatures and humidity. Common types include athlete's foot, which occurs between the toes, fingers, and in the groin area, as well as ringworm, which occurs all over the body. To avoid fungal infections, wear loose cotton clothes and wash frequently. Dry thoroughly after taking a shower, and, as the locals do, use talcum powder. If you do develop an infection, apply antifungal cream regularly.

Diarrhea and Dysentery

The second most common ailment travelers suffer from when in Cambodia is diarrhea, although incidents are nowhere near as common as when traveling on the Indian subcontinent. If you do get diarrhea, drink plenty of water, eat very plain food (such as boiled rice), and use oral rehydration salts. Avoid stomach blockers (such as Imodium), which will merely clog your insides and not get rid of the bug that's causing your discomfort.

If you develop a fever or find blood in your stool, go to a doctor for a stool test. This can be an impossible undertaking in the remoter parts of Cambodia, so if you do not get better, travel to Phnom Penh or Siem Reap as quickly as possible and seek treatment there. Diarrhea symptoms could also point to a case of amoebic or bacillary dysentery, which require professional diagnosis and treatment either with drugs that clean your intestines or with antibiotics. Most travelers to Cambodia never experience diarrhea, never mind dysentery, and pass their time here with a perfectly normal stomach.

Malaria

Malaria, transmitted by mosquitoes that carry the disease, is a serious problem in Cambodia, and several thousand Khmer succumb to the parasitical disease every year, with thousands more infected. In the border regions of Cambodia and Thailand, malaria is almost entirely resistant to most prophylaxis because thousands of refugees living in camps in the area were dosed with preventive medications in the 1980s and 1990s. Malaria is also present in the northeastern provinces of Mondulkiri and Ratanakiri as well as in Kompong Cham and around Pursat, although there it is not as resistant to drugs. Around Tonlé Sap Lake, in Siem Reap, and in Sihanoukville, malaria is rare, and it is virtually unheard of in Phnom Penh.

Doctors prescribe different prophylaxis, so make sure you get the right one for Cambodia if you choose to take preventative steps. Note that immunity is not 100 percent certain if you do take medication, and malaria contracted despite the use of prophylaxis is very hard to treat. Prevention and common sense are still the best ways to avoid contracting the disease. Most importantly, do not get bitten at dusk or at night, when malaria-carrying mosquitoes are most active. If you think you have contracted malaria, consult a doctor immediately. Symptoms include fever, diarrhea, stomach cramps, and aching joints. Untreated malaria can be fatal.

Dengue Fever

Dengue fever, once also called "bone-breaking fever" by the British in India, is transmitted around the clock by mosquitoes. There's no medication to counteract its crippling effects, so those who are infected need to drink as much water and oral rehydration salts as possible and get plenty of rest. Even though there's no treatment for most strains, get a blood test if you suspect you have dengue fever, as there's a fatal variety that does need to be treated.

In Cambodia, dengue fever is especially prevalent in Phnom Penh as well as in Battambang and Kratie, and is more rarely found around remote temples such as Preah Vihear and Koh Ker. It is also rare but present in parts of Ratanakiri and Mondulkiri. Symptoms are usually severe and include high fever, nausea and vomiting, muscle pains, and skin rashes. Avoid taking aspirin to counteract the disease's effects. Full recovery may take several weeks.

HIV/AIDS

Contact with blood and bodily fluids can lead to contracting the human immunodeficiency virus (HIV), which can lead to acquired immune deficiency syndrome (AIDS), which is fatal. Besides sexual contact, dirty needles can also lead to transmission of the virus, so be careful with acupuncture and tattoo needles, and avoid intravenous drug use. If you need an injection in a Cambodian hospital, ask for a fresh, wrapped syringe.

Complete abstinence is the safest way to avoid contracting HIV or other sexually transmitted diseases (STDs), but this is not an option for everyone. Always use a condom, whether you have sexual contact with Cambodians or other travelers. Condoms are widely available in Cambodia, and locals usually know them as "Number 1," the most popular brand in the country. Condoms produced in the United States are likely to be of higher quality than Cambodian ones.

BITES AND STINGS
Mosquitoes

A whole world of insects and reptiles seems to be out there just to make locals and visitors alike miserable. Mosquitoes are at the top of the list of annoying creatures and are responsible for spreading malaria, dengue fever, and Japanese encephalitis. They are most prevalent during or after the rainy season, when much of the country is flooded. Mosquitoes breed in ponds and rice fields. It's best not to get bitten at all, so stay indoors during the hour before dusk, when they are most active; wear long sleeves, trousers, and socks after dark; and use an effective repellent. If your room is not mosquito free, as is often the case in wooden houses, sleep under a net. Some guesthouses provide nets in their rooms. If you sleep in the forest, always use a net. Mosquito coils, widely available in Cambodia, do not kill the insects, but keep them at bay. Try not to sleep inhaling the smoke from the coil. If you have no other option, turn the fan in your room on full speed to keep them off your skin.

Other Insect Bites

When walking in the forest, be aware that ticks may fall onto your skin from branches. Use a pair of tweezers to remove these nasty creatures by carefully pulling them out by the head. Scorpions and spiders, including tarantulas, are common in Cambodia. The scorpions tend to be of the large black variety, and their sting is not fatal, hardly more serious than a wasp sting. Spiders bite humans only very rarely.

Leeches

Leeches are very common on moist forest floors and are often not detected by trekkers until their shoes have filled up with their own blood. To prevent leeches from climbing into your shoes, soak your socks in tobacco prior to setting off. If you find leeches on your body, use a cigarette lighter or salt to get them off your skin. If you pull them off, the wound may become infected.

Snake Bites

Cambodia is home to a number of poisonous snakes. Always wear shoes and long trousers when walking through grassland and forest. If you get bitten, do not attempt to suck out the poison or cut the wound. Keep still, and if possible, have yourself transported to a hospital (that means Phnom Penh or Siem Reap), although there are few if any antivenins available in Cambodia. If the snake that bit you is dead, take it with you for identification.

Rabies

Some doctors suggest getting a rabies vaccine if you are planning to spend a long time in rural areas or caves, but for most travelers that's not necessary. If you get bitten by an animal, wash the wound with soap and water, and iodine if available, and go to a hospital as quickly as possible. The danger of contracting rabies is substantially reduced by cleaning the wound immediately. If the animal is dead, take it with you.

MEDICAL FACILITIES

Medical facilities of international standards were virtually unheard of in Cambodia as recently as 2007. Since then, the **Royal Angkor International Hospital** (24-hour tel. 063/761-888, 012/235-888, 063/399-111, www.royalangkorhospital.com) in Siem Reap has been treating those with wads of cash or travel insurance.

Accident victims in Phnom Penh are often taken to Calmette Hospital, which lacks basic hygiene and equipment, while its staff suffer from a serious lack of work ethics. Avoid this hospital if you can and head to the new **Royal Rattanak Hospital** (11 Street 592, tel. 023/991-000, www.royalrattanakhospital.com) instead. Make sure you have travel insurance; this place is prohibitively expensive. Otherwise, the best place to go might be **International SOS** (161 Street 51, tel. 023/216-911 or 012/816-911, www.internationalsos.com), which can treat less critical injuries and ailments and help with evacuation procedures in serious cases. Provincial hospitals and other hospitals in the capital, as well as private clinics and dentists, are best avoided. In an emergency in the provinces, contact a nearby NGO and ask for advice.

Fake Medicines

There are reports of Cambodian clinics and pharmacies prescribing and selling phony pharmaceuticals. The consequences of taking pirated medicines can be serious, so don't purchase anything from small hole-in-the-wall outlets and doctors. In Phnom Penh and Siem Reap, the branches of the U-Care pharmacy (daily 8am-9pm) are reliable.

EVACUATION SERVICES

In Phnom Penh, **International SOS** (tel. 023/216-911 or 012/816-911, www.internationalsos.com) can arrange for a plane to pick you up and take you to Singapore or Bangkok for emergency medical treatment. In Siem Reap, the Royal Angkor International Hospital can help with similar arrangements. Make sure

The Land of Land Mines

The war in Cambodia ended almost 20 years ago, but its deadly legacy continues to harm Cambodian people—in fact, the war lives on underground. Thousands of land mines and unexploded ordnance (UXO) lie buried in Cambodia's fertile soil. The U.S. attacks against North Vietnam on Cambodian soil in the 1960s, the Khmer Rouge government in the 1970s, and the Vietnamese army and the Cambodian army in the 1980s and 1990s have all contributed to Cambodia's accumulation of land mines and buried bombs, and they have made the kingdom the most heavily mined country on the planet. The result is a human tragedy of epic proportions: Cambodia has one of the world's highest proportions of land-mine victims, with one in every 275 people maimed by a mine or by UXO.

NGOs and government agencies have been working on mine clearance for many years. The Cambodian Mine Action Center (CMAC) is the biggest organization, with more than 2,300 staff. The Hazardous Areas Life Support Organization (HALO Trust) has 1,200 staff. The Mines Advisory Group (MAG) trains Cambodians in mine clearance and also carries out demining. The Royal Cambodian Armed Forces conduct demining in support of government priorities, such as the development of infrastructure. All these groups are gathered under the Cambodian Mine Action and Victim Assistance Authority (CMAA), which has been set up to regulate and coordinate mine action throughout the country.

Cambodia ratified the International Mine Ban Treaty in 1999 and aimed to be mine impact-free by 2012, although this lofty goal was not achieved. Demining work in Cambodia relies almost entirely on international funding. On January 19, 2007, seven CMAC's deminers died, and the NGO's work drew concerns among donors when an investigation into the incident was blocked by CMAC and higher authorities. This has raised the question of the competency of the deminers and the transparency of the Cambodian government.

Despite these problems, the situation is improving, with a steady decline in casualty figures, from 875 in 2005 to 186 in 2012. Regardless of whether an area has been demined or not, the risks never disappear completely. It is quite common for long-buried UXO to rise to the surface during the rainy season, making areas that had already been demined unsafe once more.

Never leave well-trodden paths, always listen to the advice of local people, and don't go trekking into the wilderness by yourself.

you have travel insurance to cover a medevac, which can cost up to US$20,000.

SAFETY

Generally, Cambodia is a pretty safe country for travelers. The riskiest aspect of Cambodian life affecting visitors is no doubt the traffic. Ordinary Cambodians want no harm to come to foreign visitors. While some civilians still own guns, armed robbery is relatively rare, although it's wise not to walk around late at night, especially in the capital. Take a taxi instead, and always keep your belongings close. Bag snatchers on motorcycles have become very common, especially in Phnom Penh.

If possible, check your passport and valuables into the hotel safe, but don't be too paranoid about hotel theft. While theft does take place in mid-range establishments, especially in Phnom Penh, it is rare. If you do have everything stolen in a hotel and it looks like an inside job, get in touch with your embassy if the police prove to be unhelpful; the embassy might, in some cases, be able to mediate.

No doubt, Cambodia as a whole and Phnom Penh in particular offer many opportunities to engage in nefarious behavior. Before you embark on an activity you would not consider at home, remind yourself that looking for the company of thieves in an impoverished, at times desperate, country carries incalculable risks. Visitors who indulge in drugs, prostitution, or any other illegal activity in Cambodia are on their own and will need to rely on their own wits to get out of potential difficulties.

Traffic

Cambodia offers some of the most dangerous driving conditions in Southeast Asia. With the construction of new roads and rising incomes, the number of vehicles has increased dramatically in the past decade. The local driving style is haphazard, and accidents, often fatal, are shockingly frequent. Cambodia has no effective driver's license system in place. Many cars driving around the country have no plates and are not insured. People die on Cambodia's roads every day, and the average Cambodian who has crashed a motorcycle or car on a highway will not be picked up by an ambulance. At best, they end up in a provincial hospital, where there are virtually no facilities. If the injuries are severe, the accident victim almost always dies. The same goes for foreigners who don't have travel insurance. Those who do have insurance will want to be airlifted to Singapore or Bangkok in case of a serious accident. Several visitors die in traffic accidents every year.

Until a few years ago, Phnom Penh was one of the most traffic-free cities in Asia. Now traffic jams in the early mornings and early evenings block the main arteries, and the city's traffic problem will soon be comparable to those of Bangkok or Ho Chi Minh City. During the water festival, traffic in the capital is brought to a virtual standstill.

In Cambodia, people drive on the right side of the road. Road conditions vary wildly, and some major highways might be in great shape one year and in appalling condition the next. Driving at night is not recommended; plenty of nighttime traffic in the countryside doesn't use any kind of lighting, while most drivers on the roads of Phnom Penh in the small hours appear to be drunk.

All this is not to say that you should not drive in Cambodia. I've logged thousands of kilometers around the country, on both motorcycles and in cars. Drive responsibly, wear a helmet when on a motorcycle, and yield to traffic.

Police

Cambodian police are underpaid—regular street cops earn as little as US$25 per month—and have a reputation for corruption. Make sure you follow traffic rules; otherwise you might be asked to pay anything from a few dollars to outrageous demands of US$50 for a minor infraction at one of the numerous informal roadblocks the authorities have set up, primarily in Phnom Penh. In case of a robbery, the police are likely to be of little help, and do not, as a rule, investigate or fill out the necessary insurance forms unless they are induced to do so. There is a tourist police office (tel. 012/942-484) in Phnom Penh.

Drugs

Recreational drugs are illegal in Cambodia. That includes marijuana, despite the fact that the plant is traditionally used in Cambodian cooking and is available more or less openly in Phnom Penh. Marijuana's availability may have more to do with the general culture of impunity than with a policy of tolerance, and travelers are occasionally arrested for flaunting that impunity or for becoming involved in big deals. While it may be possible to pay to get out of a tight spot, there is no guarantee of this—and Cambodian prisons have a reputation as fearsome places best avoided. If you do indulge, be very discreet. Several pizza outlets in the capital offer so-called "happy" pizzas, topped with marijuana. Strictly speaking, this is illegal, but they are sold openly.

Most other drugs seem to have reached Phnom Penh. Opium from Laos (none grows in Cambodia) and cheap amphetamines from Thailand are sometimes offered to visitors on Phnom Penh's riverfront. Given that you don't know what you're getting, and that 1,000 eyes will watch your every move, succumbing to temptation could be a really bad idea. The Siem Reap that visitors experience is virtually drug-free, although marijuana is occasionally offered to young visitors around Pub Street in the evening.

Prostitution

Most visitors will notice that Cambodia's nightlife has a dark edge. Prostitution, though illegal, is nothing new to Cambodia and very much part of ordinary life in towns across the country. Countless local brothels cater to Cambodian men, and many young women have few if any other employment opportunities that pay a living wage. With the arrival of highly paid U.N. personnel in the early 1990s, the sex business got a serious boost and expanded rapidly. Today, it's everywhere. Check into a mid-range guesthouse or hotel and you might be offered a massage of dubious intent at the reception desk. Go to any number of bars in the capital and you will be accosted by armies of cash-strapped hostesses, usually called taxi girls, eager to be taken home. Several bars also employ male sex workers. The economic and social circumstances are no different for these male escorts as they are for the taxi girls.

Many of Cambodia's sex workers are migrants, legal or otherwise, from Vietnam. Tens of thousands of girls and young women are pressed into the sex business, and pedophilia has become an increasing problem in recent years, not just among Cambodians; foreigners also search for underage sex in Cambodia.

As long as sex with minors is practiced by Cambodians, as long as the police regularly turn a blind eye to people with cash or clout, and as long as young girls and sometimes boys can barely survive on the money their parents make planting rice, the problem is unlikely to go away.

Thanks to NGO and government initiatives, the openness with which sex criminals broke the law a few years ago has gone. Many of the cruelest manifestations of the business have shifted into a murky underground scene, invisible to casual visitors, but they have not disappeared. If you have any information on the sexual exploitation of children, call the national help hotline (tel. 023/997-919).

Demonstrations and Elections

Cambodia's political life is often tumultuous and sometimes violent. Demonstrators may clash with security forces, and political acts of violence, such as assassinations of vocal social critics and political candidates, are unfortunately far too common, especially around election time. For foreign visitors, there's no reason to become involved in the twists and turns of Cambodian politics, and it's best to stay away from large political gatherings.

Information and Services

VISITOR INFORMATION

Cambodia's tourism offices are not well equipped to deal with requests for information, and staff rarely speak English. In many guesthouses, smaller hotels, and eco-lodges around the country, staff can be quite well informed about the local area. There are no Cambodian tourism offices abroad.

For up-to-date listings, the so-called Canby guides (www.canbypublications.com), which cover Siem Reap, Phnom Penh, and Sihanoukville, are of some use. In Siem Reap and Phnom Penh, Pocket Cambodia Guides offer tips on dining, sleeping, and partying.

For hotels, currency rates, weather, and

some cultural info, visit www.tourismcambodia.com.

MAPS

Reliable provincial maps can be bought in bookstores and at the Central Market in Phnom Penh. The German Embassy in Phnom Penh has published a good Cambodian road atlas in Khmer and English, which is free and can be found in some hotels. The petroleum company Total has published a similar atlas, in French and English, with some travel information included. Try to find it at Monument Books in Phnom Penh. Free tourism maps are available from hotels in Siem Reap, Phnom Penh, and Battambang.

MONEY

Cambodia's official currency is the **riel,** but **U.S. dollars** and, in the western part of the country, **Thai baht** are also widely used. Tourists who use only dollars tend to pay a bit more than those who try to conduct at least simple transactions, such as bills in guesthouses and restaurants, in riel. In the countryside, dollars will be accepted, but local people generally stick to the riel. There are no coins in Cambodia, and the riel comes in 100, 200, 500, 1,000, 2,000, 5,000, 10,000, 20,000, 50,000 and 100,000 bills. In touristed areas, prices on menus and expensive souvenirs tend to be in dollars. This guide quotes prices as they are quoted in the country.

Your change in any transaction could be in riel or U.S. dollars, or even Thai baht. Change smaller than US$1 will invariably be in riel.

ATMs always dispense U.S. dollars, generally can be accessed with **Visa** and **MasterCard,** and can now be found in all the major cities. In provincial capitals, bank machines are only likely to accept Visa cards. ANZ Bank has the largest number of ATMs, but in the provinces, only ACLEDA Bank offers international banking services and ATMs.

Changing money in tourist centers and provincial banks is also generally not a problem, especially if you change euros. Banks will give you U.S. dollars in exchange. If you want to stock up on riel, head for a money changer; their stalls are usually located around market areas. Don't expect better rates than the official exchange rate, though. Traveler's checks can be changed in banks in major cities and provincial capitals as long as they are in U.S. dollars or euros. Expect to pay 2 percent commission.

Major **credit cards** are becoming more accepted at hotels and restaurants as well as at some upmarket shops and all airlines operating in Cambodia. Be careful, though, as there's often a 5 percent charge to the customer. It's also possible to get cash advances on major credit cards in Phnom Penh, Siem Reap, and the provincial capitals, though sometimes only Visa cards are accepted. Major hotels in Siem Reap and Phnom Penh also offer cash advances, but besides the 5 percent or so surcharge, the exchange rate is also not as competitive as at the banks.

Tipping may not be common in Cambodia, but it is welcome in restaurants and hotels, as the staff earn very little. **Bargaining** is part of virtually every monetary transaction in the street or at the local

tourist information office, Sambor Prei Kuk

market. Bargain for taxi, tuk-tuk, and *moto-dup* fares, but keep it all in proportion: Saving 1,000 riel, which you will hardly notice spending, means depriving a Cambodian of a significant part of his daily income.

COMMUNICATIONS AND MEDIA
Internet Access

Internet cafés are widespread in Cambodia, and even smaller towns usually have one or two. In Phnom Penh and Siem Reap, Internet access is often provided in bars and restaurants, and most hotels now offer in-room Wi-Fi. Compared to the United States, Internet speed is slow in Cambodia. Since power outages are relatively common, you should frequently save important documents while you're working. The more sophisticated Internet cafés will have USB ports on their computers as well as printing and CD-burning facilities and Internet phone software. Calling abroad is cheapest via the Internet. Rates range 300-1,300 riel, depending on the country you call. It is cheapest to call the United States and European countries, while calls to neighboring countries such as Thailand can be more expensive.

Telephones
CELL PHONES

Because of Cambodia's abominable infrastructure, cell phones have been the preferred choice of communication for years. Tall glass boxes, covered with stickers of phone prefixes, are the equivalent of a phone booth in the West. Behind the glass box, a local person with a bag full of phones (one for each prefix) will hand you the one that corresponds to the number you want to ring. Rates are very reasonable, around 300-500 riel per minute. This is cheaper than using a landline if you want to make a regional call.

Since 2009, foreigners have been able to buy SIM cards, which can be replenished with prepaid cards available everywhere in Cambodia. SIM cards cost around US$1, and pay as you go cards can be bought in many shops. Roaming charges for international mobiles are hefty in Cambodia.

PUBLIC TELEPHONES

The years of civil war destroyed Cambodia's telephone infrastructure, but it is slowly being rebuilt. Local calls are cheap, while regional calls are better made on a local mobile. Big cities and towns are all on a national grid now and have their own local codes. Nevertheless, many hotel numbers in this guide are for mobile phones. There are few public phone booths in Cambodia, but those that do exist can be used for international calls, providing you have a MPTC or Camintel phone card (available at hotels, post offices, and some shops for US$5-50). Using an Internet phone in an Internet café is cheaper, quicker, and more convenient.

TV, Radio, and Film

A couple of decades ago, the country's media barely existed. Cambodian television and radio have come into their own in recent years, and besides the rather staid and controlled government channels, several private channels bombard the population with a mixture of game shows, soap operas upholding traditional stereotypes, karaoke clips, and news that is shaped by whoever owns the station. Press freedom in Cambodia is limited, assassinations of local journalists are not unheard of, and the flow of real information from the mass media to the people is poor.

Contemporary Cambodian movies tend to be cheap romances or gruesome no-budget horror flicks. There are notable exceptions from a new generation of Cambodian filmmakers such as Rithy Panh, with his movie *The Rice People.*

Radio Love FM (97.5 MHz) is the country's only English-language radio station and plays Western pop music. **Radio Australia** (101.5 MHz), **BBC World Service Radio FM** (100 MHz), and the Voice of America broadcast in and around Phnom Penh and Siem Reap. Several television channels feature news in English. All other broadcasting is in

Khmer, although satellite TV (including UBC from Thailand) is widely available.

The English-Language Press

The *Cambodia Daily* (www.cambodia-daily.com) and the *Phnom Penh Post* are the two most important English-language newspapers published in Cambodia. The *Daily* carries international news culled from mainstream American and European papers and does some fine local reporting. The *Phnom Penh Post* used to be a critical, courageous, and well-informed biweekly publication, but it went daily in 2008, losing some of its bite in the process.

Asia Life (www.asialifehcmc.com) is a free monthly listings publication with visitor-friendly articles. The monthly *South Eastern Globe* (www.se-globe.com), published since 2006, is Cambodia's most professionally produced and critical newsmagazine. With substantial features, great photography, and its finger on Cambodia's pulse, it is a good introduction to what's going on in the country and the region. *The Advisor,* a weekly, is the new kid on the block—loud, trashy, and brash with good entertainment listings and occasionally brilliant reports on Cambodian culture.

Mail

Both Siem Reap and Phnom Penh have large **post offices** (www.cambodiapost.com.kh/), though they're not always reliable. When sending postcards or letters, be sure to see them franked after you have attached your stamps. Avoid sending anything from small, local post offices. Sending heavy souvenirs is also not necessarily reliable via the Cambodian post office system. **DHL** (15A Sivatha Blvd., Siem Reap, tel. 063/964-949) is the best option for parcels. Small parcels tend to be quite expensive to send (up to US$100 a kilogram), while heavy loads are much cheaper—from US$10 per kilogram. Postcards are available in many tourist-oriented outlets and vary hugely in quality and price, from US$0.10 to US$1.50.

WEIGHTS AND MEASURES

Cambodia uses the metric system. Electricity is 220 volts, 50 hertz; power cuts are common in the provinces and not unheard of in the capital. Siem Reap seems to have the most reliable power supply. Electrical sockets are of the two-prong variety, either with flat pins, as in the United States, or with round pins, as in Europe and neighboring Thailand.

Resources

Glossary

anastylosis: archaeological technique to reconstruct monuments by the dismantling and subsequent rebuilding of a structure

apsara: heavenly nymph, often depicted on Khmer temple walls

asura: demon

baht: Thai currency

barang: Western foreigner

baray: ancient water reservoir

bodhisattva: a person or being who uses his or her wisdom to help others toward enlightenment

boeung: lake

Brahma: important Hindu deity, creator of the world

Cham: refers to two groups of people: the people who lived in Champa, an empire that spread across today's central and south Vietnam between the 2nd and 15th centuries; and today's Cham, a Muslim minority in Cambodia

chedi: a cone-shaped edifice under which Buddhist relics or the ashes of a Buddhist teacher are buried

chunchiet: Khmer term for Cambodia's indigenous minorities

cyclo: bicycle-powered rickshaw

deva: god

devaraja: god-king

devata: female guardian spirit

dharamshala: rest house for pilgrims

Ganesh: popular Hindu deity with an elephant head; son of Shiva; remover of obstacles

garuda: mythical half-man, half-bird figure

gopura: pavilion; entrance hall in Hindu temples

Kampuchea: the name Cambodians call their country

Khmer: an ethnic Cambodian; the Cambodian language

Khmer Issarak: Cambodian nationalist rebel movement of the 1940s

Khmer Krom: ethnic Khmer living in Vietnam's Mekong Delta

Khmer Loeu: Cambodia's indigenous minorities

Khmer Rouge: term coined by King Sihanouk for Cambodia's communist movement that seized power in 1975 and engaged in a cruel four-year socialist experiment, costing the lives of millions of Cambodians

kimchi: fermented cabbage; a standard Korean dish

kouprey: possibly extinct Cambodian jungle ox

krama: Cambodia's traditional all-purpose scarf

Krishna: one of the most popular gods in the Hindu pantheon, seen by some Hindus as an avatar of Vishnu, by others as a Supreme Being; he is depicted as god-child, lover, or Supreme Being

Lakshmi: Hindu goddess of wealth and prosperity; consort of Vishnu; married Rama under the name Sita

linga (or lingam): phallic symbol

lintel: a carved sandstone block above doorways into temples

Mahayana: a branch of Buddhism; also called Great Vehicle

mahout: elephant handler

montagnard: French term for Indochina's indigenous minorities *motodup:* motorcycle taxi driver

Mount Meru: in Hindu mythology, home of Shiva

naga: mythical snake, often featured in Khmer architecture

nagara: Sanskrit for "capital"; Angkor is supposedly a mutation of this word

norry: unofficial handcar used by local people on some of Cambodia's railroad tracks

Pali: Indian language and part origin of the Khmer language

payapee: the Irrawaddy dolphin

phnom: hill or mountain

pho: Vietnamese noodle soup

phsar: market

prahoc: fermented fish paste, the staple source of protein for most Cambodians

prasat: temple or palace hall; general word for "temple"

preah: sacred

Rama: incarnation of Vishnu and hero of the *Ramayana* and the *Reamker*

Ravana: demon of the *Ramayana* and the *Reamker*

Reamker: Khmer version of the *Ramayana,* an epic Hindu poem

riel: Cambodia's currency

sampot: traditional piece of cloth that is wrapped around the waist (sarong)

sangha: assembly of monks

sangharaja: head of assembly of monks

Sanskrit: Indian language and part origin of the Khmer language

Shiva: Hinduism's most important deity; creator and destroyer of the universe

stung: river

stupa: a cone-shaped edifice under which Buddhist relics or the ashes of a Buddhist teacher are buried

temple mountain: architectural design that represents the mythological Mount Meru, home to the Hindu pantheon

thali: Indian meal of several types of vegetables, fish or meat, yogurt, chapati, and rice

-varman: suffix attached to the names of Khmer rulers, meaning "protected by"

vihear: main building of a Buddhist pagoda

Vishnu: important Hindu deity; protector of the world

wat: Thai word designating a contemporary Cambodian Buddhist temple complex

yoni: female fertility symbol and the counterpart to the linga

yuon: derogatory word the Khmer use for the Vietnamese

ABBREVIATIONS

APSARA: Authority for the Protection and Management of Angkor and the Region of Siem Reap

ASEAN: Association of Southeast Asian Nations

CIA: U.S. Central Intelligence Agency

CNRP: Cambodian National Rescue Party

CPP: Cambodian People's Party

DK: Democratic Kampuchea, the Khmer Rouge incarnation of the country

EFEO: École Française d'Extrême-Orient

FUNCINPEC: Front Uni National pour un Cambodge Indépendant, Neutre, Pacifique, et Coopératif, "National United Front for an Independent, Neutral, Peaceful, and Cooperative Cambodia," Cambodia's royalist political party

KGB: Soviet-era Russian secret service

KPNLAF: right-wing rebel force aligned with the Khmer Rouge and FUNCINPEC to fight the liberation of Cambodia by the Vietnamese

KR: Khmer Rouge

NGO: nongovernmental organization

NVA/NLF: The North Vietnamese Army/National Front for the Liberation of South Vietnam

PRPK: People's Revolutionary Party of Kampuchea

RCAF: Royal Cambodian Armed Forces

SRP: Sam Rainsy Party

UNESCO: United Nations Educational, Scientific, and Cultural Organization

UNTAC: United Nations Transitional Authority in Cambodia

Khmer Phrasebook

PRONUNCIATION GUIDE

Khmer, unlike Lao, Thai, and Vietnamese, is not a tonal language, which means that a word has one meaning that does not change with slight changes in pronunciation. Khmer grammar is simple; sentences follow a subject, verb, object structure, and nouns do not change with singular and plural. Nevertheless, speaking Khmer is not easy as there are some sounds that cannot easily be replicated by English speakers. What follows are approximations.

Vowels

No one knows how many vowels there are in Khmer, as the language has not been properly studied by local scholars. The precise number of vowels therefore varies from dialect to dialect. For the purposes of this phrasebook, commonly used vowel sounds are described here.

a   as in "cat"
ah as in "father"
ai as in "sky"
ao as in "cow"
au as in "bond"
aw as in "draw"
ay as in "play"
e   as in "bet"
ea as in "yeah"
ee as in "tea"
eh as in "tell"
eu as "u" in "burden"
ew as in "few"
i   as in "bit"
o   as in "toe"
oa as in "toe" but the vowel is cut short
oo as in "zoo"
oy as in "toy"
u   as in "fun"
uh as "u" in "album"

Consonants

Khmer consonants often occur in clusters that are hard for nonnative speakers to pronounce. Some of the very common (but, for the West-ern ear, not exactly definable) consonants are listed here.

bp no such sound in English; in between "b" and "p"
ch as in "child"
dt no such sound in English; in between "d" and "t"
g as in "go"
j as in "June"
k as in "king"
ng as in "ring"
ny as in "union"
ph as in "plain"
r as in "red" but with a hard rolling sound
th as in "tell"
wr as in "red"

Stress

Most Khmer words have one or two syllables, and the stress usually falls on the second syllable. Longer words tend to be modern and often refer to science or arts. Such words borrow from Sanskrit, Pali, and French.

BASIC AND COURTEOUS EXPRESSIONS

Hello. (formal) *juhm reeab sooa.*
Hello. *soo'as dai.*
Good morning. (used rarely) *a'roon soo'as dai.*
Good evening. (used rarely) *prolop soo'as dai.*
Good night. (used rarely) *reea trai soo'as dai.*
Good night. (I'm going to bed) *k'ngnyom dto dtaic.*
How are you? *soksabai?*
Very well, thank you. *k'ngnyom soksabai jeea-dteh.*
OK; good. *k'ngnyom meun aidteh.*
Not OK; bad. *k'ngnyom meun soksabai dteh.*
So-so. *k'ngnyom tawm madah dteh.*
And you? *joa ngea win?*

Please. *somehdtah.*
Thank you. *awkuhn.*
Thank you very much. *awkuhn chahran.*
You're very kind. *ngea geu chet bahn na.*
You're welcome. *man aidteh.*
Goodbye. *lee-a haoee.*
See you later. *dchooab kneer pail graoee.*
yes *dcha* (female speaker), *baht* (male speaker)
no *ahdtay*
I don't know. *k'ngnyom adt dang.*
Just a moment, please. *Som mehdah jahm mooee playt.*
Excuse me/Sorry. *somdtuh.*
My name is . . . *k'ngnyom chmooa . . .*
What is your name? *dtaeu ngea chmooa ai?*
Pleased to meet you. *wridt reeay.*
Do you speak English? *tah ngea niyai anglais?*
Is there anyone here who speaks English? *meean ngea nah niyai anglais no dteeni?*
I don't speak Khmer. *k'ngnyom meun niyai peeyai-sah khmer.*
Please speak slowly. *som niyai yuhdt yuhdt.*
I understand. *k'ngnyom yuhl.*
I don't understand. *k'ngnyom adt yuhl.*
No problem. *aut bannye hah.*
How do you say . . . in English? *dtah . . . hao dtah meud jeea peeyai-sah anglais?*
Would you like . . . *dtah ngeea jawng . . .*
Let's go to . . . *dtaw ngoam kngeea dto . . .*

TERMS OF ADDRESS

I *k'ngnyom*
you (formal) *ngea*
you (informal) *ain/hain*
you (plural) *ngea dtaeng aw kngeea*
he/him *kuhadt*
she/her *kuhadt* (older), *ngeeang* (younger)
we/us *yeung/puhyeung*
they/them *puhkai*
Mr., sir *looc*
Mrs., ma'am *looc srey*
Miss, young woman *ganyah*

husband *p'dtai*
wife *prawpuhn*
friend *meutpe*
sweetheart *ouhnsamlann* (female), *bawngsamlann* (male)
boyfriend *meut praw*
girlfriend *meut srei*
son *gawn praws*
daughter *gawn srei*
brother *bawng praw* (older), *ba-own praw* (younger)
sister *bawng srei* (older), *ba-own* (younger)
father *aeu puhk*
mother *madai*
grandfather *dtah*
grandmother *yai*

TRANSPORTATION

Where is . . . ? *gawn lain nah . . . ?*
How far is it to . . . ? *jangnai baun nah dto . . . ?*
from . . . to . . . *bpee . . . dto . . .*
Where (Which) is the way to . . . ? *ploeu nah dto . . . ?*
the bus station *jomm nawd ruhtyunnkrong*
the bus stop *gnai lahnkrong chuk*
Where is this bus going? *dtah lahn krong nee dto nah?*
the taxi stand *jomm nawd lahn taxi*
the train station *sattanee ruhtpleum*
the boat *dtoo*
the dock *dto salang*
the airport *prawleean yuhnhoa*
I'd like to buy a ticket to . . . *k'ngnyom jomm dteng samboat . . .*
first/second class *muh/kraoee*
round-trip *dto mao*
reservation *kao*
baggage *aiwann*
Stop here, please. *som chuhb naeu dteeni.*
the entrance *plao jol*
the exit *plao chen*
the ticket office *gonlain dtinn sambot*
near *jet/kbai* (depends on context)
far *chnai*

to/toward *toeu gann*
by/through *chlong gadt*
from *bpee*
the right *s'damm*
the left *chueng*
straight ahead *dteu dtrong*
in front *bee muk*
beside *jet/kbai*
behind *kahng groaee*
the corner *gachrung*
the stoplight *pleung stop*
a turn *baud*
right here *dtrong dknai nee*
somewhere around here *meudtaum kbai nee*
road *plao*
street *plao*
highway *plao jiat*
kilometer *kilomedt*
bridge *speeann*
toll *loi kongtrau*
address *assaiyatahn*
north *kahngjeung*
south *kahngt'bong*
east *kahnggaot*
west *kahnglait*

ACCOMMODATIONS

hotel *santahgeea*
Is there a room available? *mien bantuhk tuhmnay?*
May I see it? *k'ngnyom saum meul banh dteh?*
What is the rate? *daumlai bannmmah?*
Is there something cheaper? *Mien ahseing taochieng ni?*
single room *bauntuhk samrahp maunuh menea*
double room *bauntuhk samrahp maunuh bpee nea*
double bed *krea kaying bpee nea*
twin beds *krea pbee*
with private bath *mien bahntuhkteuk*
hot water *teuk k'dao*
shower *teuk p'gah chuhk*
towels *gaun saing*
soap *saboo*

toilet paper *kreua dah juhd moat* (literally "tissue")
blanket *pooee*
sheets *gomrah bpook*
air-conditioned *mahsinn drawjea*
fan *gong hah*
key *sao*
manager *neakruhbkrong*

FOOD

I'm hungry. *k'ngnyom klienn bai.*
I'm thirsty. *k'ngnyom srai teuk.*
breakfast *ahhah beilbpreuk*
lunch *ahhah tngnai dtrong*
dinner *ahhah beileungnee-ek*
snack *jamngai ngahmleing*
menu *maunui*
order *g'mong*
the check *kat loi*
glass *kao*
fork *saum*
knife *gahmbut*
spoon *slahpreea*
napkin *kreua dah juhd moat* (literally "tissue")
soft drink *peasechia*
coffee *kahfai*
tea *dtai*
drinking water *teuk pak*
bottled carbonated water *teuk soda*
bottled uncarbonated water *teuk saut*
beer *s'rahbeer*
wine *s'rah*
milk *teukdawgo*
juice *teukplaicheu*
sugar *skaw*
salt *ahmball*
eggs *bpong dteea*
bread *nuhmbpang*
chili *mateh*
rice *bai*
soup *suhp*
fruit *plai cheu*
vegetables *baunlai*
fish *dtray*
shellfish *keptaepkluonaeng*
shrimp *baunggeea*
meat (without) *(komm dea) sait*

chicken *sait mauan*
pork *sait chruh*
beef *sait go*
fried *chah*
grilled *ang*
roasted *ang*
barbecue *ang*
spicy *hall*
not spicy *adt hall*

SHOPPING

money *loi*
bank *tauneeageea*
money-exchange bureau *gariyahlai dopra*
What is the exchange rate? (How many riel for one dollar?) *muhi dollah p'do bahn baunnmahn loi riel?*
How much is the commission? *Bahn kaumissong baunmahn?*
Do you accept credit cards? *dta k'ngnyom ahg prao credit card?*
How much does it cost? *daumlai bannmahn?*
What is your final price? *dtai baunn neung?*
expensive *t'lai*
cheap *tao*
more *teym dtiedt*
less *teakchieng ngeh* (specific for food, money)
a little *baun teak*
too much *chrahn bpeik*

HEALTH

Help me, please. *sommehdtah juhee k'ngnyom paung.*
I am ill. *k'ngnyom cheu.*
Call a doctor. *dooresap hao doctor.*
Take me to . . . *yau k'ngnyom dto . . .*
hospital *muhndtee pead*
drugstore *fahrmacee*
pain *cheu*
fever *krung k'dao*
headache *cheu k'bahl*
stomachache *cheu bpuh*
burn *rawleek*
cramp *lemool krawpeu*

nausea *mien ahram tahcheu*
vomiting *k'aood*
diarrhea *ree aht*
medicine *t'namm peadt*
antibiotic *t'namm p'sa*
pill; tablet *gruhap t'namm*
aspirin *aspirin*
bandage *baung ruhm raubuh*
sanitary napkins *samlay a-namai*
birth control pills *t'namm buhnyeea kaumnaodt*
condoms *sraom a-namai/condom*
toothbrush *chra*
toothpaste *t'namm-dogh-t'meung*
dental floss *ksai samahdt anchahn-t'meung*
dentist *pead t'meung*
toothache *cheu t'meung*

POST OFFICE AND COMMUNICATIONS

long-distance telephone *dtoolasap graheu prawteh* (literally "overseas call")
I would like to call . . . *k'ngnyom chaung dtoolasap . . .*
credit card *credit card*
post office *praysannee*
letter *saumbaut*
stamp *teamp*
postcard *bahn praysannee*
air mail *air mail*
package *geanjawb*
box *lang*
string *k'sai*
tape *scot*

AT THE BORDER

border *bruhmdain*
customs *goi*
immigration *police antao prawes*
inspection *chaik*
passport *passpaw-likatchlongdain*
profession *muhkrawbaw*
single *naolee-uh*
married *reapgah*
divorced *leanglea*
widowed *mehmai* (female), *bpuhmai* (male)

insurance *teeaneer-rapraung*
title *neeam k'puhng bpuh*
driver's license *banbahlbaw*

AT THE GAS STATION

gas station *sattani chiadtsang*
gasoline *sang*
full *peunn*
tire *saumbawgang*
air *bom k'chahl*
water *teuk*
oil (change) *p'dau prayn mahssin*
My . . . doesn't work. . . . *rawbau
k'ngnyom kodt.*
battery *ahkuhi*
radiator *tuhng dteuk*
alternator *deenamo*
generator *mahssin pleun*
tow truck *lahn samdao*
repair shop *gaunlain chuha-chaul*
auto parts store *gaunlain luh gruhang
lahn*

NUMBERS

0 *son*
1 *muhi*
2 *bpee*
3 *bai*
4 *buhan*
5 *pram*
6 *pram muhi*
7 *pram bpee*
8 *pram bai*
9 *pram buhan*
10 *daup*
11 *daup muhi*
12 *daup bpee*
13 *daup bai*
14 *daup buhan*
15 *daup pram*
16 *daup pram muhi*
17 *daup pram bpee*
18 *daup pram bai*
19 *daup pram buhan*
20 *maupay*
21 *maupay muhi*
30 *sahmsap*
40 *saisap*
50 *hasap*
60 *hoksap*
70 *jetsap*
80 *peadsap*
90 *gaosap*
100 *muhroi*
101 *muhroi muhi*
200 *bpee roi*
500 *pram roi*
1,000 *muhi-puh-aun*
10,000 *muhi meun*
100,000 *muhi sayn*
1,000,000 *muhi leean*
one-half *gaunnla*
one-third *muhi peeabai*
one-fourth *muhi peeabuhan*

TIME

What time is it? *maong baunmahn
haoee?*
It's one o'clock. *maong muhi guht.*
It's three in the afternoon. *maong bai
rawseel.*
It's four in the morning. *maong buhan
preuk.*
six-thirty *maong pram muhi gaunla*
a quarter till eleven *kwa dta pram
maong dta muhi*
a quarter past five *maong pram leu dta
pram ngeeadtee*
noon *tangngai dtrong*
midnight *ahtriadt*
one minute *muhi neeadtee*
one hour *muhi maong*

DAYS, MONTHS, AND SEASONS

Monday *tangngai jan*
Tuesday *tangngai aungkeea*
Wednesday *tangngai puht*
Thursday *tangngai prawhaw*
Friday *tangngai sauk*
Saturday *tangngai sao*
Sunday *tangngai ahteut*
January *kai meagreah*
February *kai guhmpeak*
March *kai mineea*
April *kai mehsah*

May *kai uhsapeea*
June *kai mi-tauknah*
July *kai gakadah*
August *kai saihah*
September *kai ganya*
October *kai tauklah*
November *kai t'chikah*
December *kai t'noo*
dry season *kai reang*
hot season *kai k'daol*
rainy season *kai pleeang*

today *t'ngai ni*
tomorrow *t'ngai s'aik*
yesterday *masseu muhan*
now *ailaoni*
day *t'ngnai*
week *sabpadah*
month *kai*
year *chnam*
after *bauntoabp*
before *muhn*

Khmer Names

The Khmer language, *aksar Khmer,* has one of the longest alphabets in the world (35 consonants, 15 independent vowels, and 16 dependent vowels; the latter appear only in combination with a consonant) and is thought to have developed from Indian scripts. The first Khmer inscription dates from the 6th century.

SIEM REAP

Siem Reap	សៀមរាប
Wat Bo	វត្តបូព៌
Wat Damnak	វត្តដំណាក់
Wat Athvea	វត្តអធ្វា
Wat Thmei	វត្តថ្មី
Phnom Krom	ភ្នំក្រោម
Chong Khneas	ជុងឃ្នាស
Prek Toal	ព្រែកទួល
Kompong Phluk	កំពង់ភ្លុក
Kompong Kleang	កំពង់ខ្លាំង

ANGKOR

Angkor	អង្គរ
Angkor Wat	អង្គរវត្ត
Angkor Thom	អង្គរធំ
The Bayon	បាយ័ន

The Baphuon	បាពួន
The Phimeanakas	ភិមានអាកាស
Phnom Bakheng	វត្តភ្នំខែង
Baksei Chamkrong	បក្សីចាំក្រុង
Thomanon	ធម្មនុន
Chaosay Tevoda	ចៅសាយទេវតា
Ta Keo	តាកែវ
Ta Prohm	តាព្រហ្ម
Banteay Kdei	បន្ទាយក្ដី
Prasat Kravan	ប្រាសាទក្រវាន់
Pre Rup	ប្រែរូប
Eastern Mebon	មេបុណ្យខាងកើត
Neak Pean	នាគព័ន្ធ
Ta Som	តាសោម
Preah Khan	ព្រះខ័ន
The Western Baray and Western Mebon	បារាយខាងលិច និង មេបុណ្យខាងលិច
The Roluos Group of Temples	ប្រាសាទរលួស
The Bakong	បាគង
Banteay Samre	បន្ទាយសំរែ
Banteay Srei	បន្ទាយស្រី
Kbal Spean	ក្បាលស្ពាន
Beng Mealea	បឹងមាឡា

EXCURSIONS
Banteay Chhmar

Banteay Chhmar	បន្ទាយឆ្មារ
Banteay Top	បន្ទាយទ័ព
Sisophon	ស៊ីសុផុន

Sambor Prei Kuk

Sambor Prei Kuk	សម្បូរព្រៃគុហ៍
Phnom Santuk	ភ្នំសន្ទុក
Kompong Thom	កំពង់ធំ
Wat Kompong	វត្តកំពង់

Preah Khan, Koh Ker, and Preah Vihear

Preah Khan	ព្រះខ័ន
Koh Ker	កោះកែរ
Preah Vihear	ព្រះវិហារ
Tbeng Meanchey	ត្បែងមានជ័យ

Battambang

Battambang	បាត់ដំបង
Battambang Museum	សារមន្ទីរបាត់ដំបង
The Bamboo Train	ឡូរី
Phare Ponleu Selpak	ស្ថិតពន្លឺសិល្បៈ
Wat Ek Phnom	វត្តឯកភ្នំ
Wat Samrong	វត្តសំរោង
Wat Banan	វត្តបាណន់
Wat Phnom Sampeau	វត្តភ្នំសំពៅ
Kamping Poy Reservoir	កំពីងពួយ
Pailin	ប៉ៃលិន

PHNOM PENH

Phnom Penh	ភ្នំពេញ
Boeng Kak	បឹងកក់
Wat Phnom	វត្តភ្នំ

The Royal Palace and Silver Pagoda Complex	ព្រះបរមរាជវាំង វាំង និង វត្តព្រះកែវមរកត
The National Museum	សារមន្ទីរជាតិ
Wat Botum	វត្តបុទម្ពវរារាម
Wat Ounalom	វត្តឧណ្ណាលោម
The Cambodia Vietnam Monument	ស្មូរមិត្តភាពកម្ពុជាវៀតណាម
The Olympic Stadium	ពហុកីឡ្ឋានជាតិ
The Independence Monument	វិមានឯករាជ្យ
Wat Moha Montrei	វត្តមហាមន្ត្រី
S-21 Tuol Sleng Museum	ស-២១ សារមន្ទីរគុកទួលស្វែង
Wat Lanka	វត្តលង្កា
Bophana	បុប្ផាណា
Phsar Thmey (Central Market)	ផ្សារធំថ្មី
Phsar Toul Tom Poung (Russian Market)	ផ្សារទួលទំពូង
Phsar Chas (Old Market)	ផ្សារចាស់
Phsar Orussey (Orussey Market)	ផ្សារអូរុស្ស៊ី
Choeung Ek Killing Fields	វាលពិឃាតបឹងជើងឯក
Oudong	ឧដុង្គ
Silk Island (Koh Dach)	កោះដាច់
Tonlé Bati	ទន្លេបាទី
Phnom Chisor	ភ្នំជីសូរ
Phnom Tamau Zoological Gardens and Wildlife Rescue Center	រមណីយដ្ឋាន និង សួនសត្វភ្នំតាម៉ៅ
Temple of Phnom Da	ភ្នំដា

BORDER CROSSINGS
Thailand

Poipet	ប៉ោយប៉ែត

Koh Kong	កោះកុង
Phsar Prom	ផ្សារ ព្រហ្ម
Daun Lem	ដូនលែម
Anlong Veng	អន្លង់វែង
Chong Sa-Ngam	ចុងសាងាម
O'Smach	អូរស្មាច់

Laos

Dom Kralor	ដុំក្រឡរ

Vietnam

O'Yadaw	អូរយ៉ាដាវ
Trapaeng Thlong	ត្រពាំងថ្លុង
Trapaeng Sre	ត្រពាំងស្រែ
Bavet	បាវិត
Kaam Samnor	កុមសំណ
Phnom Den	ភ្នំឌិន
Prek Chak	ព្រែកចាក

Suggested Reading

Cambodia, along with Vietnam, is the most extensively written about country in Southeast Asia, and new titles on the country's history, most of them by foreign authors, are published every year. Many of the titles mentioned here, whether fiction or nonfiction, can be bought as pirate copies in Phnom Penh.

FICTION

Ryman, Geoff. *The King's Last Song.* Easthampton, MA: Small Beer Press, 2008. Uneven but entertaining historical novel juxtaposing scenes from the Angkor court with a crime story from the UNTAC years.

The Reamker. Phnom Penh: Reyum Publishing, 1999. The Khmer version of the *Ramayana,* a famous Hindu epic.

Vater, Tom. *The Cambodian Book of the Dead.* Hong Kong: Exhibit A Books, 2013. Detective Maier travels to Cambodia to find the heir to a Hamburg coffee empire, a search that leads through the country's communist revolution to a Nazi war criminal who reigns over an ancient Khmer temple.

HISTORY AND POLITICS

Becker, Elisabeth. *When the War Is Over.* New York: Simon & Schuster, 1986. Exhaustive telling of the Khmer Rouge revolution from the French colonial era to the death of Pol Pot in 1998 by a *Washington Post* journalist who managed to enter Cambodia during the Khmer Rouge years.

Brinkley, Joe. *Cambodia's Curse: The Modern History of a Troubled Land.* New York: PublicAffairs, 2011. Flawed but nevertheless punchy indictment of foreign donor nations and NGOs instrumental in supporting Cambodia's autocratic rulers.

Cain, Kenneth, Heidi Postlewait, and Andrew Thomson. *Emergency Sex.* London: Ebury Press, 2004. Both hilarious and dispiriting account of three United Nations workers trying to come to grips with postwar societies in Cambodia, Rwanda, Somalia, and Haiti.

Chandler, David. *A History of Cambodia.* Boulder, CO: Westview Press, 2007. Excellent history of Cambodia from its pre-Angkorian origins to its modern period.

Chandler, David. *Voices from S-21: Terror and History in Pol Pot's Secret Prison.* CA: University of California Press, 2000. A study of the archives of Tuol Sleng S-21, the Khmer Rouge's interrogation camp in Phnom Penh, where some 17,000 people were tortured.

Chou Ta-Kuan. *The Customs of Cambodia.* Chiang Mai, Thailand: Silkworm Books, 2007. Chou wrote the only surviving account of the Angkor Empire after visiting Cambodia in 1296. The text usually available in Cambodia was translated from Chinese into French in 1902, and sometime later from French into English. A new direct translation from Chinese into English by linguist Peter Harris, correcting mistakes from earlier editions, was published in 2007.

Coates, Karen. *Cambodia Now.* Jefferson, NC: MacFarland & Company, 2005. Captivating analysis of the legacy of the Khmer Rouge terror and how Cambodia deals with its dark past today.

Dunlop, Nick. *The Lost Executioner.* London: Bloomsbury Publishing, 2005. An incredible and personal account by an Irish photojournalist of his search and eventual finding of Comrade Duch, the commandant of the S-21 torture camp in Phnom Penh. Duch was responsible for more than 20,000 deaths during the Khmer Rouge years. *The Lost Executioner* asks serious questions about why it is taking so long for Khmer Rouge leaders to be brought to justice and contemplates the role of the media in conflict situations.

Lieb, Kraig, and Tom Vater. *Cambodia: Journey through the Land of the Khmer.* Monte Rio, CA: Purple Moon Publications, 2014. Sumptuous coffee-table book with emphasis on Angkor temples.

Neveu, Roland. *The Fall of Phnom Penh.* Bangkok: Asia Horizons Books, 2007. Stunning photographic account by a French photojournalist of the fall of Phnom Penh to the Khmer Rouge in 1975.

Osbourne, Milton. *Sihanouk—Prince of Light, Prince of Darkness.* Chiang Mai, Thailand: Silkworm Books, 1994. Critical biography of Cambodia's enigmatic former king.

Shawcross, William. *Sideshow: Kissinger, Nixon and the Destruction of Cambodia.* New York: Pocket Books, 1979. Account of how Cambodia was manipulated and destroyed by the superpower policymakers and the Khmer Rouge.

Short, Philip. *Pol Pot: The History of a Nightmare.* London: John Murray Publishers, 2005. Solidly researched and engagingly written biography of Brother Number 1.

Strangio, Sebastian. *Hun Sen's Cambodia.* Yale University Press and Silkworm Books, 2014. The first authoritative biography of Cambodia's current ruler.

Vickery, Michael. *Cambodia 1975–1982.* Bangkok: White Lotus, 2001. Authoritative, landmark report by one of the leading scholars of Cambodian history, much maligned by revisionist writers, is somewhat dated, but still provides an interesting and unique perspective on the Khmer Rouge period and its causes.

PERSONAL ACCOUNTS OF THE KHMER ROUGE YEARS

The survivor account has almost become a genre in itself as more and more refugees who fled to France or the United States put pen to paper to recall the horrors Cambodia went through in the 1970s. The strength of these books is their subjectivity: The Cambodian tragedy is retold in very personal terms, offering an alternative perspective to academic analysis of the period.

Bizot, Francois. *The Gate.* New York: Vintage, 2004. Gripping telling of the French author's experience of being incarcerated by the Khmer Rouge.

Nath, Vann. *A Cambodian Prison Portrait.* Bangkok: White Lotus, 1998. A firsthand account of the infamous S-21 torture facility by the painter Vann Nath, one of the prison's seven survivors. Nath's harrowing images of Khmer Rouge torture practices are displayed at S-21, the Tuol Sleng Genocide Museum in Phnom Penh. Nath died in 2011 of kidney failure. Despite Nath being a national treasure, the Cambodian government refused to support the ailing painter in his last years.

Ung, Luong. *First They Killed My Father.* New York: HarperCollins, 2001. Ung's account of life as a five-year-old under the Khmer Rouge is based on the author's journey through Cambodia's horrors, from work camp to work camp, and finally escape to Vietnam.

TRAVELOGUES

Livingston, Carol. *Gecko Tails: A Journey Through Cambodia.* London: Trafalgar Square, 1997. The first travelogue about Cambodia to be published in 30 years, this informative book chronicles the journeys and stories of a foreign correspondent in Cambodia in the early 1990s.

Pym, Christopher. *Mistapim in Cambodia.* London: Hodder & Stoughton, 1960. Quaint travelogue that offers insights into Cambodia prior to the country's 30 years of conflict.

ARCHAEOLOGY

Dagens, Bruno. *Angkor, Heart of an Asian Empire.* London: Thames & Hudson, 1995. Small companion guide to the temples of Angkor with excellent illustrations and information on the Angkor Empire, its subsequent rediscoveries, and the fate of the ruins in the 20th century.

Freeman, Michael, and Claude Jacques. *Ancient Angkor.* Bangkok: River Books, 1999,

extended edition 2003. Fantastic companion guide to the Angkor temples, packed with color photographs and ground plans. For all those who like their temple guides picture-heavy.

Mouhot, Henri. *Travels in Siam, Cambodia, Laos, and Annam.* Bangkok: White Lotus, 1864, reprint 2000. Mouhot, a natural-history researcher, rediscovered the ruins of Angkor in the Cambodian forest.

Rooney, Dawn F. *Angkor.* Hong Kong: Odyssey Publications, 2001. Brilliant illustrated introduction to the temples of Angkor.

NATURE AND FIELD GUIDES

Francis, Charles. *A Guide to the Mammals of Southeast Asia.* Princeton, NJ: Princeton University Press, 2008. A complete, illustrated, and up-to-date guide to the mammals of mainland Southeast Asia.

Robson, Craig. *Birds of South-East Asia.* London: New Holland Publishers, 2005. With 1,250 native bird species covered in 142 color plates, this paperback edition is a handy title to have with you while exploring Cambodia's wilderness regions.

HEALTH AND PRACTICAL INFORMATION

Jacobson, Matt. *Ultimate Cambodia.* Phnom Penh: Coastal Books, 2008. A great guide for motorcycle enthusiasts.

Schroeder, Dirk. *Staying Healthy in Asia, Africa, and Latin America.* Berkeley, CA: Avalon Travel Publishing, 2000. An excellent resource that fits into your pocket for easy reference.

Internet Resources

Cambodian culture tips
http://andybrouwer.blogspot.com
A great website on life in Cambodia from the point of view of an expatriate professional. Long-running institution by American blogger Andy Brouwer.

Cambodia travel tips
www.movetocambodia.com
Learning Khmer? Want to know about movies shot in Cambodia? The latest film festival? A great blog loaded with news relevant to ex-pats and interested travelers to the kingdom.

Cambodian culture by a Cambodian
http://blueladyblog.com /
www.kounila.com
Two blogs by young and feisty Khmer Kounila Keo about education, politics, lifestyle, press freedom, culture, and social issues in Cambodia.

Cambodia listings
www.canbypublications.com
Companion website to Cambodia's best free listings guide.

Cambodia restaurant and hotel listings
www.cambodiapocketguide.com
Companion website to pocket guides published in Phnom Penh and Siem Reap.

Hotels and tours
www.visit-mekong.com/cambodia
Hotel booking website, useful for Phnom Penh and Siem Reap.

The official site for tourism in Cambodia
www.tourismcambodia.com
Government website with facts about the country, destination highlights, travel contacts, maps, and events calendars.

Recent Cambodian history in articles and photos
www.mekong.net/cambodia
Oral histories, photographs, and articles about Cambodia and Cambodians abroad.

Documentation Center of Cambodia
www.dccam.org
Since its inception in 1994, the Documentation Center of Cambodia (DC-Cam) has been at the forefront of documenting the myriad crimes and atrocities of the Khmer Rouge era. The website contains survivors' stories, extensive archives, and material on the Khmer Rouge Tribunal.

Khmer arts and culture
www.khmerculture.net
Friends of Khmer Culture is an organization involved in Cambodian heritage.

Natural resource exploitation in Cambodia
http://www.globalwitness. org/campaigns/corruption/ oil-gas-and-mining/cambodia
Global Witness exposes the corrupt exploitation of natural resources and international trade systems to drive campaigns that end impunity, resource-linked conflict, and human rights and environmental abuses. The organization was thrown out of Cambodia for reporting on illegal logging.

The Mekong River
www.mrcmekong.org
The Mekong River Commission provides information on one of Asia's largest rivers.

Cambodia discussion groups
www.cambodia.org
Information on Cambodia and its people as well as news, discussion groups, and Khmer fonts.

Cambodia information
www.khmer440.com
News and information on Cambodia; archive of anything that's published on Cambodia.

Transitions Abroad
www.transitionsabroad.com
Information on working, studying, and volunteering abroad.

Working in Cambodia
www.expatexchange.com
Practical advice for people contemplating a move to Cambodia.

Index

L

M

N

UV

WXYZ

List of Maps

Photo Credits